CO-PRODUCTION IN YOUTH JUSTICE

Co-production in Youth Justice offers both theoretical contributions and empirical evidence to shed light on the extent and nature of participatory and engaging practices within the field of youth justice.

Examining co-production initiatives from different youth justice systems, this book demonstrates how co-production connects with lived experience, trauma-informed practice, creative research methods, and child-friendly practices. It illustrates new ways of viewing and working with children and young people in conflict with the law, including the extent to which they can influence youth justice systems. It also offers new insight into under-researched areas, such as creative co-production with Black and Mixed heritage children, and child-friendly forms of co-production within the context of Violence Reduction Partnerships.

Co-production in Youth Justice is an important new resource for students and scholars within criminology and criminal justice, as well as professionals working within youth justice services, relevant charities, and inspectorates.

Sean Creaney is a Criminologist and Senior Lecturer in Criminal Justice, School of Law and Criminal Justice at Edge Hill University. Sean is a member of the Transdisciplinary Research for Youth Justice (TRYJustice) network. He recently co-edited *Knowledge and Skills Partnerships in Youth Justice* which looks at the role of knowledge in enhancing youth justice practice.

Samantha Burns is currently a senior research associate in Youth Justice at Manchester Metropolitan University. Samantha is also co-chair of the National Association for Youth Justice, an academic advisor at Peer Power Youth, and co-director of the Child-Centred Youth Justice network.

"This book is a really important resource, demonstrating how ideas of participation and co-creation can be brought to life in work with young people, and especially with those who are marginalised or made the subject of intrusive justice interventions. This is a powerful call to anyone involved in youth justice, and the wider domain of practice associated with it, to recognise the necessity of building partnerships and alliances with young people, so that they can take the lead in shaping their own future. Giving them a stake in decision-making, and choice in determining outcomes lies at the heart of this collection, and it is inspiring to see so many examples of positive action to achieve these ends explored and demonstrated here. This book deserves to become established as a benchmark for good practice."

Roger Smith, *Emeritus Professor of Social Work at Durham University*

"In 1999, the Youth Justice Board introduced a brand new, trailblazing assessment tool – *Asset* – which was designed as a means of gathering information to provide youth justice practitioners with a clear indication of the types of intervention necessary to help a young person lead a law-abiding life. Firmly embedded within the *Asset* documentation package was an innovative, child-friendly self-assessment tool entitled '*What Do YOU Think?*' to be completed by the young person. This form intended to give young people an explicit opportunity to state their views; ensure that the assessment took their views into account; highlight issues that they were worried about; and to facilitate a comparison between the practitioner's assessment and the young person's own perspective. Ultimately, the form attempted to engineer a process of engaging with the young person, to assist in developing a relationship with them, helping them to see that practitioners are genuinely interested in their views. However, what the *Asset* omitted to include was any sense of eliciting ideas of collaborative endeavours between the young people and their supervising practitioners or any attempts to co-construct tailored intervention practices.

Asset was superseded some 18 years later by the remodelled, dynamic and iterative process of assessment entitled *AssetPlus*. This document thoughtfully contains a young person's self-assessment section which provides greater opportunity for them to reflect on their offence, focus on their perception of the consequences of their offending and an emphasis on future aspirations and identifying steps needed to achieve them. Here, we moved a step closer to granting young people agency by alluding to the possibility that they may input their own ideas concerning improving their life chances. Notwithstanding, the overarching narrative surrounding *Assetplus* is its specific focus on the use of practitioners' professional judgement to achieve the best outcomes for young people, thus stifling young people's voices in terms of their expressive involvement in decision-making over their future.

Creaney and Burns' groundbreaking text has achieved the remarkable pioneering feat of bridging this gap. Their absolute focus on the inclusion of young people as equal partners in the generation of positive youth justice practices has taken us closer still to the contemporary emphasis on 'Child First' principles. In this book, the authors and their contributors explain lucidly the benefits of co-constructed praxes and demonstrate unequivocably how the co-production of participatory rights-based approaches can be achieved. Remaining true to their stance on this concept, the authors and contributors have welcomed and included young people's voices and narratives concerning their lived experiences of co-production in action, hence actively un-silencing their voices. One can only hope that the authors' forward-thinking concepts and ideas are embraced by the Youth Justice Board, helping to positively re-shape and re-frame the next iteration of the *AssetPlus* document."

Dr Vicky Palmer, *Senior Lecturer in Youth Justice, Nottingham Trent University*

"This collection offers a timely and much-needed contribution to the youth justice field, bringing conceptual clarity to what co-production is, why it matters and how it can be meaningfully embedded in practice. Spanning theory, policy and lived experience, the editors bring together an impressive breadth of work that confronts – rather than glosses over – the tensions, limitations and contradictions inherent in attempting participatory approaches within systems historically driven by risk, surveillance and punishment.

My perspective on this book is shaped by years of modern slavery casework and research with children subjected to criminal exploitation. Too often, youth justice processes are imposed on children with little regard for their agency, expertise or the rational decisions they make in the context of adversity. Many of the young people I work with demonstrate remarkable capabilities – including entrepreneurial and leadership skills – that are ignored or penalised rather than recognised and developed. This book echoes what I see repeatedly in practice: children's decisions often make sense when viewed through the lens of their lived realities, and co-production provides a structured, principled way of working with rather than on them.

What distinguishes this collection is its honest engagement with power. Across chapters exploring race, structural inequality, secure environments, trauma, risk panels and creative methodologies, the book centres the voices and experiences of children while scrutinising the organisational, cultural and political barriers that restrict participation. It offers practical illustrations of how professionals can share power safely and ethically, even in involuntary or high-risk contexts, and shows the potential of co-production to reshape relationships, build trust and strengthen procedural justice.

This will be an essential resource for students, researchers, practitioners, policymakers and anyone committed to developing evidence-informed, child-centred systems. By positioning children as experts in their own lives and by challenging entrenched assumptions about capability, risk and 'unchildlike' behaviour, the book provides a compelling foundation for rethinking how youth justice can be delivered. It is a rigorous, innovative and deeply important contribution to transforming practice with some of the most marginalised children in society."

Dr Grace Robinson,
Director, Black Box Research and Consultancy Ltd

CO-PRODUCTION IN YOUTH JUSTICE

Edited by Sean Creaney and Samantha Burns

Routledge
Taylor & Francis Group
LONDON AND NEW YORK

Designed cover image: Getty Images

First published 2026
by Routledge
4 Park Square, Milton Park, Abingdon, Oxon OX14 4RN

and by Routledge
605 Third Avenue, New York, NY 10158

Routledge is an imprint of the Taylor & Francis Group, an Informa business

British Library Cataloguing-in-Publication Data
A catalogue record for this book is available from the British Library

ISBN: 978-1-032-99225-9 (hbk)
ISBN: 978-1-032-99223-5 (pbk)
ISBN: 978-1-003-60299-6 (ebk)

DOI: 10.4324/9781003602996

Typeset in Sabon
by Newgen Publishing UK

CONTENTS

Lists of illustrations *x*
List of contributors *xi*
Acknowledgements *xxi*

Introducing co-production in youth justice 1
Sean Creaney and Samantha Burns

PART I
Theory and principles: contextualising the unique challenges of co-production **13**

1 Unravelling the conceptual ambiguity of co-production for transformation 15
Samantha Burns

2 Co-production in youth justice: power-sharing, procedural justice, and reflexive critical pragmatism 37
Shelley Turner

3 Challenges in capturing the authentic voice of the 'unchildlike child' 51
Samantha Walker, Rebecca Oswald, and Sarah Soppitt

4 Co-production and harm reduction: collaborating *with* children assessed as 'high risk' 68
Sean Creaney and Samantha Burns

5 Co-production or exploitation?: mind the exploitation trap! 82
Kierra Myles

PART II
Values and policy implications: co-production approaches and evidence-informed policymaking 97

6 Children's right to participate in youth justice research: opportunities and challenges in Irish youth justice 99
Louise Forde

7 Co-producing a Child First policy framework for the West Yorkshire Violence Reduction Partnership 119
Georgia Watkinson

8 Opportunities for progressing trauma-informed youth justice case management through co-production principles 134
Catia Malvaso, Andrew Day, and Lorna Robinson

9 Using creative arts approaches for co-production in youth justice 151
Laura Caulfield and Dean Wilkinson

10 Black space making: co-creating hope for Black and Mixed heritage boys in and outside the Criminal Justice System 166
John Wainwright

11 Interdisciplinary methodological innovations for enhancing co-production with professionals and children in secure settings 184
Stefan Kleipoedszus, Caroline Andow, Raymond Arthur, Rachel Dunn, and Nicola Wake

PART III
Lived experiences of practice: children and young people's voices within narratives of co-production 213

12 Youth justice lived experience as carceral capital in the co-production of peer support programmes in prisons 215
Sarah Nixon

13 'I would want to see young people working in here, that's what I want to see…': How peer support opportunities in youth justice services can support a Child First, trauma-informed, and reparative model of practice for youth justice 231
Naomi Thompson and Morgan Spacey

14 Drawing on lived experience in a youth justice context 248
David Porteous and Anthony Goodman

15 'You learn to rebel by being locked up': children's experience of restriction, control and agency in the secure estate 266
Romana Farooq, Katie Burgess, and Hannah Smith

16 Co-production as social justice: a reflection on creative consultations with young adults and young people 287
Sarah Page, Dana Jundi, Nicky Twemlow, Emma Head, and Zsofia Majer

Conclusion: co-production as the vehicle? The journey to transform justice with children and young people 304
Samantha Burns and Sean Creaney

Index 319

ILLUSTRATIONS

Figures

11.1 Diamond9 198
11.2 Example showing data collected with adults 199
11.3 Stakeholder Diamond9 200
15.1 Thematic map 271

Tables

8.1 Focus group topics and example questions 139
8.2 Description of children and young people who participated in the study 139
8.3 Opportunities for strengthening case management practice based on the views and ideas of children and young people 144
9.1 A checklist for developing creative approaches to youth justice 159
15.1 Demographics of the children 270
15.2 Definition of themes 272
C.1 Transformative co-production in youth justice 313

Box

7.1 Engagement should be engaging – ten steps for successful engagement 124

CONTRIBUTORS

Caroline Andow is Senior Lecturer in Criminology at Bournemouth University. Her research focuses on improving experiences and outcomes for young people in secure residential childcare. Dr Andow uses a range of methodological approaches to engage participants in research.

Raymond Arthur is Professor of Law at Northumbria who specialises in researching children's right to self-determination in justice settings and developing a broader understanding of the experiences of troubled and vulnerable young people. This inter-disciplinary research embraces innovative methodologies to shape and advance the research of children's rights and family justice in novel child-centric ways which empower young people by giving a voice to their experiences. He has previously worked at Teesside University, the Open University, the University of Birmingham, and the University of Limerick.

Katie Burgess is currently a Trainee Clinical Psychologist at Newcastle University. Katie has experience across a range of settings, in both the United Kingdom and New Zealand, however finds working with children and young people, and those with a learning disability most rewarding. Katie is particularly interested in research that gives a voice to the needs of children and young people living in hardship.

Samantha Burns is currently a senior research associate in Youth Justice at Manchester Metropolitan University. Samantha is also co-chair of the National Association for Youth Justice, an advisory board member at Peer Power Youth, and co-director of the Child-Centred Youth Justice network.

Laura Caulfield, PhD, is Dean of Research Culture and Postgraduate Research at the University of Wolverhampton, United Kingdom. Laura is a psychologist whose research focuses on the impact of interventions in criminal justice, with a particular interest in the role of the arts. Laura's work has influenced the practice of arts programmes in the criminal justice system and has developed new methodological approaches in seeking to evidence the impact of the arts. She was involved in the design of the National Criminal Justice Arts Alliance Evidence Library, a repository for key research and evaluation documents on the impact of arts-based projects, programmes, and interventions within the criminal justice system. She has published two recent books with Routledge: *Criminological Skills and Research for Beginners*, 3rd Edition (Caulfield & Hill, 2025); *Arts in Criminal Justice and Corrections: International Perspectives on Methods, Journeys, and Challenges* (Gardner & Caulfield, 2024).

Sean Creaney is a Criminologist and Senior Lecturer in Criminal Justice, School of Law and Criminal Justice at Edge Hill University. Sean is a member of the Transdisciplinary Research for Youth Justice (TRYJustice) network. He recently co-edited *Knowledge and Skills Partnerships in Youth Justice* which looks at the role of knowledge in enhancing youth justice practice.

Andrew Day (University of Melbourne; Flinders University; Swinburne University [Australia] and the University of Waikato [Aotearoa New Zealand]) is an academic who has research interests in areas of rehabilitation, violent offending, and youth justice. A clinical and forensic psychologist by training, Andrew is currently working on projects related to the topics of trauma-informed correctional care, case management in youth justice, assisting desistance in prisons, and preventing institutional violence. He is a co-founder of the Magnolia Project, a not-for-profit community group that aspires to promote a more compassionate criminal justice system. Andrew is widely published in the fields of forensic psychology and criminal justice; recent books include *Social Work: In the Shadow of the Law*, 6th Edition (with Simon Rice, Linda Briskman, and Sacha Jamieson, Federation Press) and *Preventing Prison Violence: An Ecological Perspective* (with Armon Tamatea and David Cooke, Routledge).

Rachel Dunn is a Reader and Course Director at Leeds Law School, Leeds Beckett University. She specialises in areas relating to vulnerable beings, including young people in secure residential homes and animal law. Rachel utilises several methods in her research, including visual methods.

Romana Farooq is a Consultant Clinical Psychologist in Tier 4 Inpatient CAMHS and a Specialist Alternative to Hospital Service for children and young people. She is also Academic Director on the Newcastle Doctorate in Clinical Psychology Programme. She was awarded the British Psychological Society Early Career Award for outstanding contributions to Clinical Psychology in respect of her work with children and young people subject to sexual exploitation. Romana specialises in working with children, young people, and their families who are subject to human rights violations, child exploitation, trafficking, modern-day slavery, forced criminality, gangs, and harmful sexual behaviour. Romana has been involved in shaping, developing, and delivering services for children and young people subject to sexual exploitation, sexual violence, or displaying harmful sexual behaviour. Romana has also worked in a range of locked and secure settings such as the Children and Young People's Secure Estate as well as Forensic CAMHS. She has developed a keen interest and passion for working with diverse communities and has spent over 10 years working with grassroots communities, marginalised groups, and disenfranchised youth. She also provides organisational consultancy, development, and change in respect of working with complex systems, focusing on co-production and co-design.

Louise Forde is Senior Lecturer in Law at Brunel University of London. Louise holds a PhD in Law from University College Cork, awarded in 2018, for research entitled '"Welfare" and "justice" in Irish youth justice: A children's rights analysis of diverse approaches to youth justice'. She has researched and published extensively on international children's rights law and youth justice, and is particularly interested in participatory research with children, and in the implementation of international children's rights principles in the development of domestic law and policy. She has been published in *Youth Justice: An International Journal*, the *International Journal of Children's Rights*, and *Criminology and Criminal Justice*, among others. She is Managing Editor and a member of the Editorial Board of *Youth Justice: An International Journal.*

Anthony Goodman is Professor of Community Justice at Middlesex University and is a former probation officer. His most recent research is on the work of a London borough to limit youth violence in a high-crime area and has highlighted the importance of collaboration between the statutory and voluntary sectors. He has also evaluated two projects on diversion of young offenders from custody; and working with domestic abusers and victim-survivors in minoritised communities.

Emma Head is a sociologist at Keele University, United Kingdom. Her research is grounded in the sociology of the family, with particular interests in motherhood, children and young people, and everyday relationships of care. Dr Head completed her PhD in Sociology at the University of Bristol in

2005. She was subsequently awarded an ESRC postdoctoral fellowship at the University of Leeds. Her recent research includes collaborative work with the YMCA and two projects addressing contemporary challenges facing families and children: one exploring the barriers to social inclusion for children with sensory needs, and another investigating how digital technologies are reshaping parental involvement in primary school education.

Dana Jundi formally worked for the University of Staffordshire and is now an independent researcher and community engagement specialist. She has experience in participatory music initiatives and other outreach and engagement activities, particularly with students, communities affected by forced migration and, more recently, underrepresented groups within Stoke-on-Trent. Her work focuses on creative approaches to evaluation, participatory research and co-production. She is particularly interested in how inclusive methods can support people with lived experience to share their expertise and influence change. She aims to create practical, inclusive ways for people to contribute to conversations and decisions that affect them.

Stefan Kleipoedszus is Associate Head of School for the School of Health and Care at Bournemouth University (BU), where he has held academic leadership roles since 2015. He qualified as a Social Pedagogue at Leuphana University in Lüneburg, Germany, and has since built a career that spans research, frontline social work, and senior management in statutory children's services. Before joining BU, Stefan worked as a researcher at the Thomas Coram Research Unit (University of London), a social worker in child protection teams in the southwest of England, a team manager, and eventually a principal social worker. His wide-ranging professional experience informs his teaching and research. Stefan's research interests focus on social work decision-making, children's residential care, online safety for children, and the integration of social pedagogy into practice in England. He has also conducted studies on the reintegration of women released from prison and the prevention of juvenile delinquency. He completed his PhD at the Centre for Seldom Heard Voices: Marginalisation and Societal Integration at Bournemouth University, examining decision-making in social work. Currently, he is involved in research on secure children's homes and is evaluating an intervention that supports parents and children affected by domestic abuse. He has expertise in both qualitative and quantitative research methods and is proficient in data analysis tools including NVivo, Atlas.ti, SPSS, MATLAB, and the R programming language, particularly for text mining and machine learning.

Zsofia Majer holds a Master's degree in Social and Political Psychology with distinction, as well as a BA (Hons) in Politics with International Relations. Her academic background is grounded in critical, applied research with a focus on young people's experiences, agency, and social change. Throughout her academic journey, Zsofia has participated in several multi-agency qualitative research projects, including partnerships with Green Football Weekend and Newcastle-under-Lyme Council. These initiatives enabled her to collaborate with non-academic partners to explore sustainability, youth engagement, and local policy through participatory methods. Her work in these projects deepened her understanding of collaborative research practices and the importance of cross-sector engagement in producing meaningful, actionable insights. She transferred these skills into her role as a research assistant for a city-wide Youth Consultation, where she helped develop youth-friendly materials, coordinated large-scale workshops, and facilitated engagement with diverse groups of young people. This work bridged academic research and real-world application, strengthening her ability to design inclusive, impactful consultations. Zsofia now applies her research, engagement, and organisational expertise in her role as a Personal Development Coach at YMCA North Staffs, where she supports young people in building resilience, accessing opportunities, and shaping their own futures.

Catia Malvaso is an Associate Professor in the School of Psychology and Co-Director of BetterStart Health and Development Research in the School of Public Health at the University of Adelaide. Catia leads a programme of research on understanding pathways between the child protection, youth, and adult criminal justice systems, with the overarching goal of identifying prevention and early investment opportunities to improve outcomes for children, families, and communities.

Kierra Myles is a Mentor Team Leader based in Jersey Channel Islands. Kierra is a compassion and empathy led practitioner; she has been working with children in conflict with the law and care experienced people for the last five and a half years. Kierra delivers keynote talks and enjoys developing and delivering workshops. Kierra has a degree in youth justice; she is now studying for her PhD with the University of Bedfordshire.

Sarah Nixon is a Senior Lecturer in Criminology at the University of Winchester. She lectures on prisons/penology, desistance, youth crime/deviance and sport and crime. Prior to education, she worked as a prison officer at HMP Leicester for 6 years (2003–2009). She completed her PhD in 2019 at De Montfort University in applied criminology, exploring peer support and desistance. Her research identified the strengths of peer support programmes to support not only the desistance process but also challenges to operationalising peer support programmes in both prison and community settings. Her other research interests include writing around being a gay female prison officer (in an adult category 'B' prison) and personal experiences of suicide/self-harm in prison using an autoethnographic perspective. She has recently published a book with Dr Darren Woodward (2025) around role exit in prison officers (returning to civvy street), exploring attrition rates and complex role exit and transitional processes. She has a chapter in *Pracademics in Criminal Justice* (2025), which aligns with her pedagogical approach and practice values of bringing lived experience into the domain of teaching criminology and criminal justice. Future plans include contributing to contemporary publications to understand the dynamic processes of 'becoming' a prison officer and also a book chapter on carceral geographies, drawing upon personal lived experience of carceral settings and how these spaces are navigated. Another future publication involves a comparative narrative around 'being gay on the inside', working collaboratively with a current serving life sentenced prisoner – a staff and prisoner comparison around discrimination from both sides around LGBTQ+ identities. This will offer a unique dimension to understanding identity and navigation through predominantly heteronormative prison policies and practices in England and Wales.

Rebecca Oswald is an Assistant Professor in Criminology and Sociology in the Department of Social Sciences at Northumbria University. Rebecca's research interests lie in the areas of youth crime, youth justice, desistance from offending and Work Integration Social Enterprise and their role in supporting criminalised individuals to desist from crime. Her research is currently focused on exploring the changing picture of serious youth violence in the North East of England and the interventions and best practices that can support young people impacted by violence and child criminal exploitation. Rebecca, together with colleagues at Northumbria University, is a co-founder of the 'Safer Children Network North East', a knowledge exchange platform for academics and practitioners to support young people impacted by violence, harm, and exploitation.

Sarah Page is Associate Professor in Social Justice and Social Learning at the University of Staffordshire and teaches on criminology, sociology, and mentoring courses. She is part of the leadership team for the Research Centre for Crime Justice and Security and mostly engages in research that aims to address health and social inequalities, along with poverty issues and crime. Such topics lend themselves to participatory action research. Prior to working for the University, Sarah worked in a strategic management role for a Health Action Zone, helping partnerships to work more effectively together to tackle inequalities and to better engage community members in strategic decision-making at project and partnership board level. She continues to be engaged in strategic partnership work, specifically pertaining to drug and alcohol partnership boards and the HMPPS-led strategic partnership for reducing gambling-related harms in Wales. Sarah has practitioner experience of working in the criminal justice system within youth offending services and probation in a therapeutic capacity addressing addiction issues.

David Porteous is an Honorary Associate Professor in Criminology at Middlesex University. His work has mostly focused on youth justice policy and practice. His most recent research, in conjunction with Prof. Anthony Goodman, examines the contribution which young people with lived experience of the youth justice system can make to work with children currently in the system. David is Co-Editor (with Dr Timi Osidipe) of the *Safer Communities* journal.

Lorna Robinson is a lived experience leader and advocate who works to reshape how we design services and understand social issues. Drawing on her lived experience, she works to centre the voices of those most affected by the systems meant to support them. Lorna is the South Australian Coordinator (Children and Young People) at the Justice Reform Initiative and the Lived Experience and Project Coordinator at the Australian Alliance to End Homelessness, where she leads the Systems Navigator project, co-designing a lived experience-informed approach to supporting young people exiting the OOHC and youth justice systems. As an independent consultant, she supports government and community organisations to work in partnership with people with lived experience through co-design, facilitation, training, and systems reform.

Hannah Smith is a trainee forensic psychologist currently in the final stages of completing a Doctorate in Forensic Psychology (DForenPsy) at the University of Nottingham. She specialises in working therapeutically with individuals with personality difficulties who have experienced trauma as part of the Offender Personality Disorder Pathway. She also has experience working with children in secure forensic settings. Her research interests relate to the care and supervision of children in conflict with the law, both in the community and in secure settings. Her thesis is on the topic of first-time entrants to the youth justice system and aims to explore how children can be better supported by, and ultimately diverted from, the youth justice system. She is passionate about giving children a voice within research in this field.

Sarah Soppitt is a Criminologist in the Department of Social Sciences at Northumbria University. Her work focuses on youth justice, policing, and intervention strategies that support pathways away from offending. She has a particular interest in public criminology, aiming to make academic research accessible and relevant to practitioners, policymakers, and communities. With over 20 years of experience in criminal justice research and evaluation, Sarah's work has explored the role of early intervention and partnership approaches in supporting young people. She is involved in collaborative projects with a range of organisations, including local authorities and voluntary sector services, and values working closely with those who have direct experience of the justice system. Her research contributes to ongoing conversations about how to improve outcomes for individuals and communities affected by crime and social disadvantage. Through teaching, research, and engagement activities, she is committed to supporting more informed and reflective approaches to justice.

Morgan Spacey was a researcher in the Department of Social, Therapeutic and Community Studies (STaCS) at Goldsmiths University of London from 2020 to 2024. His research focuses on issues of oppression and exclusion experienced by young people and communities, particularly in their access to and engagement with institutions such as education and youth justice services. His recent studies span hate crime experienced by Roma and Traveller Communities, access to higher education for care leavers, and young people's experiences of the youth justice system. His recent publications include articles on youth justice in the *British Journal of Community Justice* and *Safer Communities*.

Naomi Thompson is a Reader in Youth and Community Work in the Department of Social, Therapeutic and Community Studies (STaCS) at Goldsmiths University of London. She is a sociologist of youth and inclusion. Her research explores issues of inclusion and exclusion for young people and communities across a range of intersectional identities including faith, race, and gender. She is interested in people's engagement with services and institutions. Her recent publications explore the secular culture of youth work training, community work with migrant and refugee women, and young people's engagement with youth justice services.

Shelley Turner is Executive Director of a state-wide, forensic mental health hospital in Victoria, Australia, and holds honorary academic appointments in the Department of Social Work at Monash University and at Swinburne University's Centre for Forensic Behavioural Science. She has extensive clinical leadership, management, teaching, and research experience, with expertise in youth justice and forensic social work. Shelley has a particular interest in lived experience and models for ethical and effective practice with involuntary service users. She has co-authored a book on co-production and criminal justice and is published in peer-reviewed journals and international textbooks.

Nicky Twemlow is a passionate and driven community leader, dedicating her time to championing young people and creative communities though her role as Director of Communities & Partnerships at YMCA North Staffordshire. She has secured significant investment into the city to enrich the lives of children and young people, working hard to ensure that children and young people are involved in all aspects of delivery, including championing co-design initiatives and youth-led consultation. Nicky is also the co-founder and Chair of Made in Stoke, the philanthropic network for the city, and she co-founded Stoke Creates, the Cultural Compact for Stoke-on-Trent and North Staffordshire.

John Wainwright has several years' experience working with children, young people, and their families in the care and youth justice system. His research interest is in (anti)-racism, ethnicity, youth justice, children and young people in the care system, and adoption. He is Co-Director of the Global Race Centre for Equality (GRACE) Research Centre at the University of Lancashire.

Nicola Wake is Equality, Diversity and Inclusion Director for Northumbria University Law Department, and Honorary Subject Sections Secretary for the Society of Legal Scholars. Professor Wake's research focuses on vulnerability within the criminal justice system, including young people in the secure estate.

Samantha Walker is Assistant Professor of Criminology and Sociology in the Department of Social Sciences at Northumbria University. Her research explores both interpersonal and structural forms of violence, with a particular interest in how violence is experienced and understood by individuals and communities. Her recent work centres on youth-related violence, including child-to-parent/carer violence and abuse and serious youth violence. She is currently involved in a series of collaborative projects examining trends in serious youth violence in the North East of England, with a focus on identifying effective interventions and support mechanisms for young people affected by violence and child criminal exploitation. Samantha is also a co-founder of the Safer Children Network North East, a collaborative initiative at Northumbria University aimed at promoting knowledge exchange between academics and practitioners to improve outcomes for children and young people exposed to harm, violence, and exploitation.

Georgia Watkinson is a Research and Evaluation Specialist at the West Yorkshire Violence Reduction Partnership, responsible for leading their Child First workstream. Within this role Georgia strives to create opportunities for children across West Yorkshire, allowing them to influence decision-making and have their voices heard on key issues that impact their lives. Within this, Georgia has a particular interest in incorporating creative and innovative approaches to capturing and sharing children's experiences and ensuring these are shared with decision-makers on a local and national scale. Prior to this role, Georgia completed her undergraduate degree at Liverpool John Moores University in Forensic Psychology and Criminal Justice where she developed an interest in youth justice policy, specifically around the implementation of Child First. Georgia's interest in Child First in policy and practice has developed in her career, having recently been published in the *British Journal of Community Justice* with an article focused on youth justice practitioners' perspectives of Child First practice. The recommendations from this research are informing the future direction of Georgia's work within the Violence Reduction Partnership. Her chapter outlines recent experiences in co-producing professional guidance with children and the impact they have been able to make as a result.

Dean Wilkinson is a chartered psychologist, chartered coaching psychologist and a Senior Lecturer in the Department of Psychology at Edge Hill University, United Kingdom. Dean has more than 15 years' experience of evaluation and research work exploring issues, interventions, and preventative approaches across the Criminal Justice System. His work has explored alternative programmes in prisons and community, including working directly with the youth justice service. He has published on the usefulness of arts-based prison activities with specific groups of individuals in prison, leading to a focus on the criminogenic needs of the older prison population (aged 50+ in prison). During the COVID-19 pandemic, Dean brought together a team to explore, using creative methodologies, the responses, experiences and needs of staff and young people in the youth justice service. This work informed the post-COVID recovery plan of the service. Dean's current work explores violence reduction and prevention efforts in community, health, and education settings.

ACKNOWLEDGEMENTS

The editors would like to take this opportunity to thank Morwenna Scott and Ananya Singh who both work at Routledge, Taylor & Francis (Informa), for providing extensive support and guidance throughout the whole process. The editors are grateful to all the chapter authors for contributing to this collection and for providing insightful perspectives into the meaning, value, and presence of co-production across the youth justice system.

INTRODUCING CO-PRODUCTION IN YOUTH JUSTICE

Sean Creaney and Samantha Burns

Introduction

Co-production has the potential to transform how youth justice operates, yet its implementation is fraught with tensions, particularly when children are the service users within systems that are traditionally hierarchical, risk-averse and adult-led. This book explores the extent to which co-production can exist meaningfully within youth justice systems and what it could look like in research and practice. Co-production has been utilised both as a concept and as an invitation to reconstruct relationships between professionals and service users. It seeks to redistribute power through more equal partnerships in order to improve children's lives, enhance service provision, and shift institutional cultures of knowing and doing justice with children (see Johns et al. 2022; see also Burns et al. 2024). Put simply, co-production is a concept that aims to bring together service users (children and young people) and adult professionals into various aspects of governance, management, and service delivery processes to make 'better use of each other's assets, resources and contributions' (Bovaird and Loeffler 2013:4). Acknowledging and valuing children's and young people's skills and expertise within youth justice may lead to the development of more responsive and effective service provision to nurture mutually agreed outcomes and have the potential to offer wider social benefits.

As a form of participation in a public service context, co-production with children and young people has developed with varied success across health, education, social care, youth work, and community development (Brady 2020; Checkoway et al. 2005; Milbourne 2009; Tisdall 2017), reflecting a growing interest in recognising children and young people's capability to make decisions about their own lives, and thinking differently about how children

DOI: 10.4324/9781003602996-1

and young people participate in the services they receive. Furthermore, the impetus for progressing co-production can be associated with the children's rights agenda, especially the need to ensure professional responses account for the participatory rights of children (Yin 2024). While the rights of children include being able to comment on issues that affect them, co-production can enhance children's participation rights and bring them to the forefront of youth justice practice. As co-production in criminal justice has gained traction in the criminological sphere (Weaver et al. 2019; Johns et al. 2022), this book aims to examine the extent to which the voices and experiences of children and young people are at the forefront within wider debates and developments around co-production across criminal justice. The book does this by exploring in what ways could co-production be considered a vehicle for public service reform, shifting how adults and institutions respond to children.

This book, the first of its kind in the youth justice field, examines the extent to which co-production principles can be meaningfully developed and implemented within youth justice systems, what this might look like in research and practice, and whether the concept can catalyse systemic and cultural transformation. This introductory chapter sets the scene and provides a context for forthcoming chapters around the theory and practice of co-production, examining enablers and barriers across practice with children and young people in conflict with the law.

The struggle for co-production in youth justice

Youth justice as a system has been much slower to embrace co-production, partly due to a punishment discourse and risk-averse cultures. There is a recognition that agencies and services within the criminal justice system must navigate the salient issue of redistributing power and shifting institutional cultures against the backdrop of 'justice', which functions through structures built on logics and rationales of punishment, surveillance, risk, and control (McCulloch 2016; Johns et al. 2022). This issue is intensified when considering the specificity of children and young people as service users with specific rights and needs traditionally defined by adults. A further challenge in attempting to co-produce practice within involuntary interventions or mandated contexts is that risk and need assessment processes tend to be adult-driven, leaving children with limited opportunity to question or contest practitioner interpretations (Creaney and Burns 2024). Indeed, it is a process which has historically tended to privilege professional judgements as opposed to children's own wishes (Smith and Paddock 2025; Creaney and Burns 2025). Those who are working, researching, and studying the concept of co-production are faced with the persistent question: can co-production meaningfully exist in a youth justice context, and under what conditions? This book seeks to explore this question by synthesising a growing but underdeveloped body of work, capturing key developments of co-production theory and practice, aiming to inform researchers, policymakers, practitioners, and students.

Youth justice is a particular public service context that has historically neglected children's voices, assets, and contributions, prioritising professional expertise, authority, and adult-centric processes (Burns and Creaney 2023; Case et al. 2020; Creaney 2020). These tensions in adult–child relations within the constraints of a justice system highlight contradictions that require deeper critical attention. In 2023, these tensions encountered greater visibility during our guest editorship of the *Safer Communities* journal special edition on the theory and practice of co-production and co-creation in youth justice (Creaney, Burns and Day 2023a, 2023b). We received a high volume of articles reflecting a diversity of views, with interconnected terms such as co-production, collaboration, participation, consultation, and co-creation. Together, these illustrate the field's commitment to involving children in decision-making processes to varying extents. This book intends to clarify and distinguish these concepts while evidencing innovative, child-centred, and creative youth justice practice which has been developing across various contexts. By enabling a deeper understanding of the values and principles of co-production within youth justice, we hope it can influence and innovate forms of practice with children at the heart of the youth justice system.

The book raises several issues around the extent and nature of young people's involvement in practices of co-production, with children playing an equal role in decision-making processes, which can be perceived to be at odds with the key functions of a justice system. This is especially relevant when there is a contradictory emphasis on responsibilisation and surveillance (Goldson and Muncie 2015). Functions of a justice system apply stigmatising labels to children and young people as 'risky' or at 'high risk' of involvement in further criminality or harmful behaviours and mandate them to comply with requirements as part of court-ordered work or sentence children to penal custody (Creaney, Burns and Day 2023a, 2023b; Kemshall 2008; Goldson and Muncie 2015). This functioning maintains power imbalances and hinders the efficacy of shared decision-making and may even engage children in processes that are (re)traumatising, causing more harm despite the rhetoric of trauma-informed services.

Children can also be instructed by professionals in positions of authority to comply with adult-centric processes and meet behavioural expectations, which may harbour a sense of distrust, limiting opportunities for relationship building between children and practitioners. These issues raise important questions about the feasibility of co-production in a justice context with children and the compatibility of co-production within justice settings due to power inequalities and systemic barriers (Smithson and Jones 2021; McCulloch 2016). This book also offers a critical lens through which to further understand what co-production means in youth justice contexts for public service reform, particularly in relation to the conceptualisation of childhood, crime, and justice, how children's contribution is valued, and to what extent their participation has the potential to inspire systemic and cultural transformation across youth justice policy and practice.

Overview of this collection

Against the backdrop of power inequalities and systemic barriers in youth justice such as risk-averse organisational cultures and limited opportunities for meaningful participation, there have been tangible efforts to implement different ways of working with justice-involved children, generating a greater focus on their preferences, appreciating their strengths as opposed to a deficit-based approach that pathologise them or focus solely on their offending behaviour. This edited collection presents cutting-edge scholarship and research into the meaning, value, and presence of co-production within youth justice settings, with attempts at developing different forms of co-production to enhance service provision and maximise positive outcomes for children and wider society. One example has been to involve peers in the development of interventions with mentors or advisors, which utilises lived experience of the criminal justice system to share unique insights and help overcome personal and social barriers (Creaney et al. 2024). However, tensions have been recognised with power issues around monitoring behaviours of mentors and navigating trauma (Day et al. 2023). It is important to note that the development of valuing lived experience has sometimes been separated from initial theoretical ideals of co-production, and like most criminal justice research, most theory has been developed with adults in mind, being applied to children with limited critique. Notions of desistance, trauma-informed approaches, lived experience, and peer mentoring may all have a place in understanding the meaning, value, and presence of co-production within youth justice systems and processes, but there is a need to further examine the implications of how frameworks of practice and philosophies can enhance children's involvement in the design, delivery, and implementation of services and interventions, which could support the value of co-production in the youth justice context.

Despite challenges, co-production has persisted and even evolved, with new practices and perspectives emerging across youth justice systems. Rather than relying on adult-dominated methods of engagement, this book draws on a growing evidence base suggesting that the ability for children and young people to meaningfully participate in youth justice processes is contingent on child-friendly and creative methods of engagement. Creative methods and artistic approaches can be useful mechanisms to enable children to express themselves and voice their needs in a way most suited to them, rather than adult-dominated ways of engagement. However, what scope is there to work in a creative way with children in the confines of a rigid bureaucratic adult-dominated system that is reluctant to transform ways of working with children and young people? Chapters in this book intend to consider the methodological implications of working in a co-produced way with children in both research and practice. By consolidating theory and practice, this book aims to provide an understanding of how co-production is interpreted and applied into youth justice systems and processes, including what tangible efforts are made to redistribute power between institutions, professionals, and children, and what co-production means at interpersonal and institutional levels. Overall, this book invites readers to engage critically with the notion of co-production in youth justice, to rethink the role of children in shaping the justice systems that serve them, and to ask not only how co-production can be done as a different way of doing public services but also how it might transform justice with and for children in conflict with the law.

Structure of the book

This book includes 16 chapters which cover theoretical and empirical contributions of co-production in the contexts of youth justice systems. The book is structured into three parts.

Part I: Theory and principles: contextualising the unique challenges of co-production
Chapter 1: Unravelling the conceptual ambiguity of co-production for transformation. ***Samantha Burns***
Samantha Burns unravels the conceptual ambiguity of co-production. The chapter provides a synthesis of literature on co-production and children's participation to develop an understanding of the contextual challenges and to formulate a framework to assist understandings of what co-production could mean in a youth justice context. It will summarise the origins and evolution of co-production theory more broadly, unpacking key debates and principles, including how co-production can be valuable when working with children and young people for both individual and system transformation.

Chapter 2: Co-production in youth justice: power-sharing, procedural justice, and reflexive critical pragmatism. ***Shelley Turner***
As Shelley Turner notes, co-production is increasingly cited in youth justice discourse, policy, and practice as a key principle for person-centred practice. The author states that it is essentially an approach to working together that involves power-sharing between those who use and those who administer services to achieve an equal partnership for equal benefit. Turner notes that co-production has its roots in citizen and consumer rights movements and, at its pinnacle, is touted as a transformative process that can upend traditional power structures and reconstruct what and how knowledge is produced. Turner goes on to note that, in criminal legal contexts, where 'consumers' or service users are involuntary or mandated clients, is it realistic to imagine them as genuine decision-makers or equal partners with the people explicitly holding power over them? More so in youth justice, is it realistic to imagine such power-sharing between adults, who are paid to administer the system,

and children and young people, who are mandated to be part of it? This chapter is a critical reflection on these questions, exploring the benefits and challenges of co-production and participatory approaches in youth justice. It draws on a review of the literature about co-production and youth justice and learnings from the author's practice and research aimed at 'giving voice' to justice-involved children and young people.

Chapter 3: Challenges in capturing the authentic voice of the 'unchildlike child'. ***Samantha Walker, Rebecca Oswald, and Sarah Soppitt***
This chapter, by Samantha Walker, Rebecca Oswald, and Sarah Soppitt, reflects critically on the challenges in capturing the authentic voice of the 'unchildlike child'. As the authors note, while there is increased recognition that children engaged in serious violence are often victims of child criminal exploitation (CCE) and abuse, children and young people involved in serious criminal activities, including violence, personify the 'unchildlike child'. The authors outline the importance of understanding the wider socio-historical, cultural, and local contexts in which violence arises and exists; the complexities of capturing the 'authentic voice' of these 'unchildlike' children to inform co-production approaches to youth justice; and implications for the adoption of 'Child First' rhetoric in policy and practice.

Chapter 4: Co-production and harm reduction: collaborating with children assessed as 'high risk'. ***Sean Creaney and Samantha Burns***
This chapter focuses on the tensions that can exist between risk management, rights-based discourses, and commitments to embed children's voices into practice. While a fundamental aspect of youth justice work involves risk management and harm reduction, this can present difficulties when striving to cement co-production principles into practice and achieve equal power among children and professionals. Youth Justice Service 'high-risk' management panels are a multi-agency coordinated approach to monitor and address concerns related to behaviour, harm, safety, and well-being. They remain wedded to mechanisms of control and surveillance, which creates challenges in terms of enhancing co-production principles in practice. This chapter explores the extent to which practitioners collaborate with children identified as 'high-risk'. It evaluates the benefits and challenges of a co-productive approach as a legitimate or possible endeavour, with children assessed as 'high risk'. This chapter makes the case for a co-productive approach to working with children assessed as 'high risk'. This approach is potentially more inclusive than existing methods which tend to exclude or marginalise their voices.

Chapter 5: Co-production with children in youth justice services: mind the exploitation trap! ***Kierra Myles***
This chapter by Kierra Myles focuses on the importance of trauma-informed collaboration and the development of a pro-social identity with children in

conflict with the law. This chapter explores the use and value of activity-based, relationship-building methods such as sport, arts, or peer mentoring. As the author argues, including children within decision-making processes and empowering them to recognise their strengths and abilities can help to nurture pro-social identities.

Part II: Values and policy implications: co-production approaches and evidence-informed policymaking

Chapter 6: Children's right to participate in youth justice research: opportunities and challenges in Irish youth justice. ***Louise Forde***

This chapter by Louise Forde considers, from a children's rights perspective, how children in conflict with the law can be supported to make their voices heard and how the lived experiences of children can contribute to understandings of how children's rights within the youth justice system can be better realised, drawing on examples from research with young people in the Irish youth justice system. The chapter draws on the experiences of the author in conducting research with children in the Irish youth justice system, based on the Lundy model of child participation. As Forde notes, while the chapter will spotlight the benefits and opportunities inherent in ensuring children's voices are at the centre of youth justice research, it will also reflect on some of the practical challenges and barriers to conducting this type of research and consider some means for further enhancing research with children in this area.

Chapter 7: Co-producing a Child First Policy Framework for the West Yorkshire Violence Reduction Partnership. ***Georgia Watkinson***

This chapter by Georgia Watkinson explores the early process of implementing a Child First approach within West Yorkshire, considering the barriers encountered and, significantly, the steps taken to overcome them. It begins with an exploration of the ambition for Child First in West Yorkshire, which was initially focused on the Violence Reduction Partnership before quickly developing into the ambition for a co-ordinated, whole-system Child First approach across the region. The chapter outlines the approaches used to capture the voices of children, how this was adapted to fit the various needs of the children involved, and how their words were translated into a framework aimed at multi-agency professionals at all levels of services.

Chapter 8: Opportunities for progressing trauma-informed youth justice case management through co-production principles. ***Catia G. Malvaso, Andrew Day, and Lorna Robinson***

This chapter by Catia Malvaso, Andrew Day, and Lorna Robinson presents an example of involving and engaging children and young people under youth justice supervision in a research project designed to identify opportunities for strengthening youth justice case management activities through increased alignment with trauma-informed principles. Within the chapter, the authors describe how they drew upon the insights of children and young people under youth justice supervision to shape recommendations to assist the development of a trauma-informed approach to case management to guide service delivery.

Chapter 9: Using creative arts approaches for co-production in youth justice. ***Laura Caulfield and Dean Wilkinson***
This chapter by Laura Caulfield and Dean Wilkinson explores how the arts provide an important tool by which engagement and participatory approaches can be pioneered and implemented. This ethos is in keeping with the move towards a contemporary 'Child First' approach, leading to legitimate and authentic services for children and young people across youth justice settings. This chapter aims to discuss the evidence of the impact of arts-based approaches to co-production in youth justice. The chapter includes examples from the experiences of the authors working with three youth justice teams in England through research and evaluation, service design, and redesign. The chapter highlights the benefits and challenges of implementing arts-based approaches in youth justice.

Chapter 10: Black space making – co-creating hope for Black and Mixed heritage boys in and outside the Criminal Justice System. ***John Wainwright***
This chapter by John Wainwright explores how creative co-production with Black and Mixed heritage children can provide opportunities to reimagine and create a different world, a better world. As the author notes, the co-creation will privilege the (counter) voices of Black and Mixed heritage children and explore with them how to develop ways of moving away from offending through their lens. As Wainwright notes, their stories, challenges, and aspirations need to be heard and placed at the centre of any transformational plans for change in their lives. This chapter acknowledges their experience of racism, of Othering, of everyday threats of violence from peers and adults, and of harassment by the police. The chapter also acknowledges the individuality and intersectionality of their identities and aspirations.

Chapter 11: Interdisciplinary methodological innovations for enhancing co-production with professionals and children in secure settings. ***Stefan Kleipoedszus, Caroline Andow, Raymond Arthur, Rachel Dunn, and Nicola Wake***

The aim of the chapter by Stefan Kleipoedszus et al. is to illustrate the importance and practice of using innovative methodological approaches to engage with adult stakeholders of secure care, which can then be adapted to enable co-creation with children. As the authors note, this chapter prompts consideration about what co-production means in youth justice and child welfare settings, which includes involving and empowering professionals in the research process to improve collaboration with children through a range of creative methodologies. The chapter demonstrates why the methods adopted were ideal for the research and how they successfully fostered the co-production of data.

Part III: Lived experiences of practice: children and young people's voices within narratives of co-production

Chapter 12: Youth justice lived experience as carceral capital in the co-production of peer support programmes in prisons. ***Sarah Nixon***
This chapter by Sarah Nixon explores how integral carceral knowledge is in helping to shape and develop co-production of services in carceral settings. As the author notes, carceral capital is framed as an asset to draw upon, identifying those with first-hand knowledge and lived experience of navigating criminal justice services (see Brierley and Best 2025). Nixon explores how transmission of lived experiences (through drawing upon carceral capital) helps prison/professional staff bridge gaps in their knowledge and bridge gaps with those new to youth/criminal justice services, thus providing a voice for service users from those who have been there.

Chapter 13: 'I would want to see young people working in here, that's what I want to see…' How peer support opportunities in youth justice services can support a Child First, trauma-informed, and reparative model of practice for youth justice. ***Naomi Thompson and Morgan Spacey***
This chapter by Naomi Thompson and Morgan Spacey explores how peer support opportunities can contribute to a combined Child First, trauma-informed, and restorative approach for youth justice. The authors draw on qualitative data gathered with young people and parents/caregivers in a London youth justice service to evaluate the effectiveness of its model of practice. As Naomi Thompson and Morgan Spacey note, those who had completed their time with the youth justice service saw themselves as relatable role models with the insight and skills to support others and, in some cases, expressed a strong desire to develop long-term careers in supporting young people. As the authors note, peer support opportunities could offer a form of reparative practice that is Child First and trauma-informed. This would benefit both the young people being supported and those offering support, building a co-produced approach that is directly informed by the expressed needs and desires of the young people.

Chapter 14: Drawing on lived experience in a youth justice context. ***David Porteous and Anthony Goodman***
This chapter by David Porteous and Anthony Goodman outlines the promise of embedding a particular form of co-production within a Youth Justice

Team, where former child offenders, with lived experiences, are employed to act as mentors and supporters to children on court orders or licence. The authors outline how the project operates, providing support that can extend beyond statutory provision and, crucially, creating opportunities for children to develop confidence in engaging with authority figures they have often experienced as exercising power over them.

Chapter 15: 'You learn to rebel by being locked up': children's experience of restriction, control and agency in the secure estate. ***Romana Farooq, Katie Burgess, and Hannah Smith***

This chapter by Romana Farooq, Katie Burgess, and Hannah Smith highlights the benefits, challenges, and complexities associated with using participatory and narrative research methodologies within restrictive settings such as the Children and Young People's Secure Estate. As the authors note, the findings and the learning from implementing a participatory research methodology in the Children and Young People's Secure Estate may inform developments in other youth justice settings and beyond. The authors present analysis of interview data and outline key themes: expectations of secure settings, scrutiny, institutional transformation, powerlessness, and resistance. The findings in this study offer a comprehensive understanding of what 'least restrictive practice' should look like, informed by children's voices and lived experience, including how a whole-system change is required in line with the Secure Stairs Framework for Integrated Care.

Chapter 16: Co-production as social justice: a reflection on creative consultations with young adults and young people. ***Sarah Page, Dana Jundi, Nicky Twemlow, Emma Head, and Zsofia Majer***

This chapter by Sarah Page et al. outlines learning from the co-produced 'City Level Future Visioning Project', which gathered young people's views and aspirations on the future of the city of Stoke-on-Trent and the wider Staffordshire area. Co-production occurred between young people, university students, a voluntary sector organisation, and academics to co-design suitable conversational and creative data collection tools with ongoing collaborative data collection and analysis. The authors discuss the ethics of working with young people and the use of a co-produced pilot consultation to inform a wider research project with aspiration of influencing Citywide strategic plans, to give children and young people hope for their futures.

Conclusion: co-production as the vehicle? The journey to transform justice with children and young people. **Samantha Burns and Sean Creaney**

The chapters within this collection explore, dissect, and critically reflect upon co-production in youth justice from a range of theoretical, practical, and methodological perspectives. What emerges clearly is that co-production, while still a contested and evolving concept, holds the potential to reshape the contours of youth justice. This conclusion chapter invites the reader to reconsider who holds knowledge, who gets to decide, and how justice systems can be made more participatory, equitable, and responsive to children's lived realities, offering reflexive questions for undertaking co-production for system transformation.

Concluding thoughts

Uncertainty remains regarding to what extent youth justice can utilise and value co-production. Therefore, to have any prospect of becoming embedded within organisational structures and influencing service delivery, there is a need for clarity into what it is, including how the principles are defined and can be applied with children and young people in conflict with the law. Drawing upon theoretical insights and using examples from empirical studies, this book aims to critically showcase the diverse ways in which co-production principles are being developed and used in practice.

References

Brady, L-M. (2020). Introduction: Embedding young people's participation into healthcare. In Brady, L-M. (ed.). *Embedding Young People's Participation in Health Services: New Approaches*. Cambridge: Policy Press, 1–30.

Brierley, A. and Best, D. (2025). Desistance habitus: Strategically Using experience in practice. *Incarceration: An International Journal of Imprisonment, Detention and Coercive Confinement*, 6. https://doi.org/10.1177/26326663241310603 (Original work published 2025)

Bovaird, T. and Loeffler, E. (2013). The role of co-production for better health and wellbeing. In Loeffler, E., Power, G., Bovaird, T. and Hine-Hughes, F. (eds.). *Co-production of Health and Wellbeing in Scotland*. Birmingham: Governance International.

Burns, S. and Creaney, S. (2023). Embracing children's voices: Transforming youth justice practice through co-production and child first participation. In Case, S. and Hazel, N. (eds.). *Child First: Developing a New Youth Justice System*. London: Palgrave Macmillan.

Burns, S., Creaney, S., Hampson, K. and Case, S. (2024). Child First: Seeing children as the solution, not the problem. *CYCJ*. www.cycj.org.uk/resource/info-sheet-110/

Case, S., Creaney, S., Coleman, N., Haines, K., Little, R. and Worrall, V. (2020). Trusting children to enhance youth justice policy: The importance and value of children's voices. *Youth Voice Journal*. 2020 (Special Issue), 25–40.

Checkoway, B., Allison, T. and Montoya, C. (2005). Youth participation in public policy at the municipal level. *Children and Youth Services Review*, 27(10), 1149–1162.

Creaney, S. (2020). "Game playing" and "docility": Youth justice in question. *Safer Communities*, 19(3), 103–118. https://doi.org/10.1108/SC-01-2020-0002

Creaney, S. and Burns, S. (2024). Freedom from symbolic violence? Facilitators and barriers to participatory practices in youth justice. *Youth Justice*, 24(1), 31–52. https://doi.org/10.1177/14732254231156844

Creaney, S. and Burns, S. (2025). The Achilles heel of Child First: High-risk panels in youth justice service policy and practice. *Probation Journal.* Online First. 1–21. https://doi.org/10.1177/02645505251353719

Creaney, S., Burns, S. and Day, A.-M. (2023a). Guest editorial. *Safer Communities*, 22(2): 73–77. https://doi.org/10.1108/SC-04-2023-053

Creaney, S., Burns, S. and Day, A.-M. (2023b). Guest editorial. *Safer Communities*, 22(3): 149–155. https://doi.org/10.1108/SC-07-2023-054

Creaney, S., Burns, S., Douglas, A., Brierley, A. and Falconer, C. (2024). Desistance through participatory practice: Involving children in decision-making processes in youth justice. In Wigzell, A., Paterson-Young, C. and Bateman, T. (eds.). *Desistance and Children.* Bristol, UK: Policy Press. https://doi.org/10.51952/9781447369127.ch011 [Accessed 04 June 2024]

Day, A., Malvaso, C., Butcher, L., O'Connor, J. and McLachlan, K. (2023). Co-producing trauma-informed youth justice in Australia?. *Safer Communities*, 22(2), 106–120.

Goldson, B. and Muncie, J. (2015). *Youth Crime & Justice*, 2nd edition. London: Sage.

Johns, D., Flynn, C., Hall, M., Spivakovsky, C. and Turner, S. (2022). *Co-Production & Criminal Justice.* Abingdon: Routledge.

Kemshall, H. (2008) Risks, rights and justice: Understanding and responding to youth risk. *Youth Justice*, 8, 21–37.

McCulloch, T. (2016). Co-producing justice sanctions? Citizen perspectives. *Criminology & Criminal Justice*, 16(4), 431–451. https://doi.org/10.1177/1748895816639730 (Original work published 2016)

Milbourne, L. (2009). Valuing difference or securing compliance? Working to involve young people in community settings. *Children & Society*, 23(5), 347–363.

Smith, H. and Paddock, E. (2025). Does AssetPlus facilitate effective assessment of children within the youth justice system?: A critical evaluation. *Probation Journal.* Online First. 1–20. https://doi.org/10.1177/02645505241300687

Smithson, H. and Jones, A. (2021). Co-creating youth justice practice with young people: Tackling power dynamics and enabling transformative action. *Children and Society*, 35(3), 348–362.

Tisdall, E. K. M. (2017). Conceptualising children and young people's participation: Examining vulnerability, social accountability and co-production. *The International Journal of Human Rights*, 21(1), 59–75.

Weaver, B., Lightowler, C. and Moodie, K. (2019). Inclusive justice: Coproducing change; a practical guide to service user involvement in community justice. Glasgow: University of Strathclyde. https://pureportal.strath.ac.uk/en/publications/inclusive-justice-co-producing-change-a-practical-guide-to-servic/

Yin, M. (2024). Ascribed agency, denied influence: How adult narratives shape and constrain the right of children in the justice system to be heard. *The International Journal of Children's Rights*, 32(4), 998–1026.

PART I

Theory and principles

Contextualising the unique challenges of co-production

1

UNRAVELLING THE CONCEPTUAL AMBIGUITY OF CO-PRODUCTION FOR TRANSFORMATION

Samantha Burns

Introduction

What do we mean when we talk about co-production and youth justice? The concept of *co-production* has become a feature of public service reform over the last two decades, especially in relation to developments in youth participation and children's rights. Yet it is also still a profoundly ambiguous idea, often conflated with terms such as *participation*, *collaboration*, *engagement*, *co-design*, and *co-creation*. While all these practices suggest varying forms and ideals of service user involvement, this chapter acknowledges that, to some degree, all these concepts encompass a similar aspiration towards *power-sharing*, *reciprocity*, and *equal partnerships* between professionals and children (Burns 2023). Rather than being done *to* or *for* them, children are invited to act *with* and *by* professionals in shaping decisions, policies, and interventions. Co-production can, therefore, be used as a term to define children's and young people's participation, a form of democratic engagement in a public service delivery context to acknowledge children's individual rights (Burns 2020). Co-production, a term describing a shared, equitable decision-making process through equal partnerships, has the potential to become a transformative process since it can allow for a greater understanding of how relationships between children and adult professionals shift and how co-production transforms the role of adults and organisations (Johns et al. 2022, Burns 2023). There are also claims that co-production may go beyond individualised outcomes and support a shift in wider institutional, cultural, and social outcomes (Tisdall 2017).

There are multiple benefits to adopting co-production principles and practice, though it has been accused of being the next democratic buzzword alongside

DOI: 10.4324/9781003602996-3

participation (Voorberg et al. 2015). The concept has arguably been diluted into more tokenistic practices which ignore power dynamics, partnerships, and wider social transformation. These practices are influenced by specific social, cultural, and political challenges of working collaboratively with children and young people. Furthermore, co-production is underdeveloped in criminal justice systems (Johns et al. 2022, Loeffer and Bovaird 2021) relative to other public services. Therefore, this has implications for how far it is understood and adopted in a youth justice context. For instance, in the English context, in 2013, the Social Care Institute for Excellence (SCIE 2022) first published a co-production framework for working with children and young people. Then, in 2016, the Youth Justice Board (YJB) published its participation strategy, and in 2021, published guidance on participation and co-creation for youth justice services alongside its Child First policy framework, incorporating collaboration as a key principle.

Meanwhile, conceptual challenges remain in the field of youth justice with limited use of co-production (Hampson et al. 2024). This means that while co-production appears to be a buzzword for service user involvement across the public sector, it has been seldom used exclusively across youth justice systems as an explicit concept. Yet, principles of co-production can also be seen under the guise of other terminology, leading to conceptual ambiguity. This conceptual ambiguity may be contributing to policies and practices that fall short of the transformative potential co-production can offer.

This chapter provides a synthesis of literature on co-production and children's participation to develop an understanding of the contextual challenges of co-production in youth justice. It summarises the origins and evolution of co-production theory more broadly, unpacking key debates and principles which consider how the concept of co-production incorporates varying typologies of public sector involvement and whether this can be useful when working with children and young people in partnerships for both individual and system transformation and why co-production is needed in youth justice.

By the end of this chapter, the three key takeaways are as follows:

- The ambiguous nature of co-production and the potential for transformation
- The values of co-production in public services are needed when working with children and young people
- Why co-production is an important concept in a youth justice context

Origins of co-production

Historically, there has been a growth in societies across the world claiming for increased democracy, insisting that citizens play a more significant role in governing processes (Brigstoke 2013). Arnstein (1969) contributed to the critique of modern liberal democracy and citizen participation in the 1960s when evaluating citizen and public service professionals' collaborative work. The research contended that citizen participation must incorporate *power sharing* between government officials and citizens so processes of participation are meaningful and hold governing institutions accountable (Arnstein 1969). Arnstein (1969: 3) claimed '*to participate is to have power*' and instilled the idea of '*partnerships*', which arguably is the first step on the ladder to formulate 'true' participation and empowerment.

Ostrom et al. (1978) then first coined the term co-production in American community policing, highlighting the necessity of *interdependent relationships* between police and the community for effective crime prevention. Since then, co-production became a popular term during the early 2000s, with research development (Bovaird 2007), UK Government reports (Horne and Shirley 2009), and third-sector organisations (Boyle and Harris 2009) emphasising a specific approach between a broad range of public services and stakeholders, leading to the 'democratisation of public and personal decision making'. Service users increasingly became recognised as co-producers and problem solvers, emphasising the governance notion of citizen-driven services (Bovaird 2007). Boyle and Harris (2009) argue that co-production offers a different vision for public services built on the principles of reciprocity and mutuality, whereby service users become effective agents of change, highlighting the shift from service users as passive recipients to active participants in the service they receive.

The concept of co-production has emerged from multiple theoretical traditions within public administration and service reform (Bovaird 2007, Osborne and Strokosh 2013). While some scholars position co-production as an inherent feature of public service delivery, others view it as a transformative approach capable of redistributing power between professionals and service users. This distinction is important because it shapes how co-production is understood, implemented, and evaluated in practice. In attempting to bring together the two theoretical positions of co-production, Osborne and Strokosh (2013) developed three modes: consumer co-production, participative co-production, and enhanced co-production. Enhanced co-production meant participation is present at both the operational and strategic levels, with the aims of challenging and transforming current paradigms of service delivery, sometimes often described as '*co-creation*', to innovate public service design and delivery (Fox 2024). There has been a rapid evolution of co-production across multiple disciplines and sectors, with an abundance of models to guide thinking and practice (Boyle and Harris 2009). In the United Kingdom, The Care Act 2014 was one of the first pieces of UK legislation to include the concept of coproduction in its statutory guidance. SCIE (2022) asserts that organisations must change at every level – from senior management to frontline staff – if they want to achieve meaningful participation, which should be part of their daily practice and not just an 'add-on'.

Despite the varying modes of co-production and pursuit to transform public service paradigms, one of the core principles is recognising people's existing capabilities and challenging a hierarchy of knowledge creation by valuing service users as '*experts by experience*' (Creaney et al. 2024). This means co-production has been positioned to challenge power structures of knowledge by questioning what constitutes evidence and whose evidence is valuable in public services (Weaver et al. 2019, Johns et al. 2022). As part of this challenge to a hierarchy of knowledge through recognising skills and capabilities of service users, both trust and reciprocal relationships are required, to develop core collaborative governance mechanisms. This is where the importance of power and partnerships lies in co-production as a form of participation in public service contexts.

Conceptual ambiguity of co-production

Co-production can be simply viewed as a specific type of active participation in a public service context (Burns 2023), addressing power dynamics through partnership working to reform services and empower service users as a route for active citizenship and democratic governance. It is important to note that considerations of different forms of co-production have been acknowledged, with enhanced co-production arguably contributing to the transformation of individual, interpersonal, and institutional levels. Yet co-production remains a contested concept with a range of definitions and interpretations which have developed quite intensely over the last two decades (Bransden and Honingh 2018). Meanwhile, co-production also appears to be in conceptual competition with a range of other terms such as participation, engagement, and collaboration. How do these concepts differ? In some cases, participation has been considered to mean being involved in processes like attending meetings, whereas engagement involves forming positive relationships and feeling committed to the process, fostering genuine relational engagement in practice (Case and Browning 2021). Furthermore, collaboration has been utilised as an overarching term encompassing participation, engagement, and social inclusion (Hampson et al. 2024). Therefore, conceptual ambiguity for understanding co-production remains and requires further unpacking.

Unpacking co-production further highlights that it even has varied meanings across different public sectors. For instance, the SCIE (2022) argues that participation is not enough to gain power, and co-production critiques participation as consultative and merely 'taking part in something', whereas co-production is about joint decision-making throughout the whole process of service implementation. However, in public health, some scholars view co-production as the focus on implementation of a previously agreed solution (strategy) to a previously agreed problem and how to allocate resources and assets within these constraints to achieve better outcomes (Vargas et al. 2022). This latter concept framing appears less empowering relative to the first. As such, debates remain on seeking to define co-production and the extent it can be transformative for service users, professionals, organisations, and wider society. This may be dependent on whether co-production is part of a core process of an organisation or a 'complementary' part of service delivery (Bransden and Honingh 2018).

Co-production as a concept has also been dissected and reformulated as an umbrella concept encompassing a wide range of service management and delivery activities (Bovaird and Loffler 2012), or as a conceptual springboard for more innovative terms such as co-creation and co-innovation (Osborne et al. 2018, Fleming and Osborne 2019). This has meant a narrowing of the co-production definition, separating the strategic and operational levels of public service management and delivery. Co-production is used as a term to imply citizen contribution to the implementation of their services (Osborne et al. 2018); co-creation implies that citizens exercise agency to define their own goals in order to meet the needs they themselves judge to be important (Torfing et al. 2019).

Nonetheless, co-production focuses on the interaction between service users and service providers and has advanced thinking of public service management and delivery in a way that enables steps up the participation ladder (Arnstein 1969). There have been attempts to move away from consultation (voice without power) towards co-production (power-sharing and transformation); even if forms of co-production are only limited to service implementation, the transformation of power is key to understanding the difference. Yet where power sharing beyond interactions between service user and service provider is considered, co-production may still rely on co-creation for a more holistic understanding of transformation. It can be determined that co-production continues to be an ambiguous concept in public policy despite its maturation over previous decades (Bransden and Honingh 2018, Loeffler and Bovaird 2019).

There is also the critical importance of ensuring the social, political, economic, and cultural context is understood for embedding co-production into public services. Loeffler (2016) states it is crucial to assess co-production projects case by case to understand the complex social issues and specific local knowledge fully. Therefore, the success of co-production initiatives may not mean that this concept is successfully applied in all public service institutions and sometimes considered to be the most 'passive' form of collaboration relative to co-design and co-creation (Vargas et al. 2022). Therefore, wider conditions need to be conducive for principles of co-production to be embedded and practised in a way that offers individual, relational, and institutional empowerment for both service users and professionals involved and sufficiently considers the wider context of how power is shared, balanced, or transformed. Without addressing the wider context, the way co-production can be diluted into compliance and regulation needs to be understood.

Co-production, regulation, and power

The duality of co-production and regulation

While co-production is promoted as a departure from passive interventions, by promoting active citizenship and developing more equitable relationships through service delivery, this might imply that co-production also departs from forms of regulation that have been viewed through public service delivery. However, it has been argued that a more sophisticated understanding of the relationship between co-production and regulation is needed (Innes et al. 2019) to ensure that the principles of co-production as a democratic and empowering process can be realised. Sometimes, coercion or consultation will be masked as co-production, providing ambiguity of genuine partnerships, power sharing, and reciprocity. For instance, Creaney et al. (2024) describe how tokenistic practices in youth justice services in the United Kingdom can reduce children's contributions to procedural box-ticking exercises that maintain professional authority rather than redistribute it. Similarly, Innes et al.'s (2019) research discovered how co-production was being harnessed to enable more effective parental regulation of young people's potentially risky behaviour. McCulloch's (2016) work alludes to co-production being described as more 'bullshit bingo'. Meanwhile, in an Asian context, research demonstrated how social workers were displaying co-production as a dual-faced tool: it can create opportunities for transformation while also reproducing regulation and domination at the same time (Burns 2020). This duality is particularly acute in statutory settings like youth justice, where children's involvement is often mandated by criminal justice legislative frameworks and/or mediated by safeguarding processes and risk-based rationalities, inhibiting genuine power sharing.

Regulation via co-production as the solution?

However, the varying perspectives of co-production lend themselves to a debate regarding the dual-faced approach of co-production. Osborne et al. (2018) argue that service users do not have a choice whether co-production happens regardless of the public service. As a service user, the moment the user receives the service, they become a co-producer. It occurs regardless of whether the public service encounter is coercive or not. Yet this might result in co-production losing its ability to create a paradigm shift in public service reform and offer transformation in how services are designed and delivered.

Although even when regulation occurs through co-production, there is still a level of interdependency between service users and professionals at the operational level required, which demonstrates the co-existence of regulation and co-production. The criminal justice context provides the starkest example of this. McCulloch (2015) shares research on co-production from the perspective of people with lived justice sanctions. Focused on individual forms of co-production, that is, co-production focused on individual outcomes, the findings describe significant and transformative co-production experiences that occurred alongside criminal justice sanctions (McCulloch 2015), despite it being overly focused on individual behaviour change as a form of regulation. Likewise, within some of the case studies of co-production in criminal justice settings from Johns et al. (2022) in Australian contexts, the positive and progressive nature of co-production is highlighted.

Co-production and regulation relationship is complex

Ultimately research has uncovered that the relationship between regulation and co-production is delicate and nuanced. Scholars have explained in relation to both social interactions and the relationships between agency and structure and can provide some complementary explanations of co-production through regulation as the connection to understand power relations and structures. Considering the work of Bourdieu, when power inequalities persist, co-production can be viewed as 'symbolic violence', a form of domination that is often misrecognised by both service providers and service users (Bourdieu 1977, Hastings and Matthews 2015). Meanwhile, Foucault's (1977) work on governmentality could consider co-production as another creation of self-governing through the promotion of active citizenship and partnership working (Bessant 2003). Ultimately, when co-production is analysed through wider social and political contexts, it is undoubtedly complex to understand the transformative extent of its core principles. It is also more challenging to consider how co-production is achieved when there are multiple services involved competing for different outcomes (i.e. social work, police, health), as is often the case for children and young people in the youth justice system. Not only is there a need to look at power relations and forms of regulation, but there must also be a critical lens on the interconnectedness of the interactions at a service delivery level with wider institutional and structural power to determine the extent of how co-production can be transformative.

Often discussed less is that co-production is both celebrated and still seen as challenging due to the enhanced form of co-production that aims to move beyond the existing framework of hierarchal approaches to public service delivery, which intends to improve the efficiency and/or effectiveness of current arrangements and challenge the overall design (Osborne and Strokosh 2013). This could be considered a riskier approach, as it requires operational capacity and political willingness (Sorrentino et al. 2018). Political and professional willingness may be lacking inside public service organisations to move to more transformative notions of 'enhanced' co-production, particularly where it is seen as losing control. When co-production processes have occurred, they have been reported as being frequently diverse, intricate, and delicate, imbued with considerable complexity, particularly in time limitations related to building trusting and sustained relationships (Innes et al. 2019, Sorrentino et al. 2018), resource limitations and bureaucratic processes (Creaney and Burns 2024), and perceived risk of harm in the context of criminal justice (Johns et al. 2022, McCulloch 2016). It is within this space where practices will occur under the label of co-production but may only be consultation, or co-production becomes a 'piecemeal strategy' (Bovaird et al. 2019). This is where co-production is reduced to narrow interventions to address complex social problems and continues to ignore the causes of that problem, resulting in a more insidious form of regulation.

Co-production and its relationship with power and regulation indicate that co-production is a concept which requires a critical and reflexive lens to ensure that the barriers to co-production are understood. This results in the principles of equal partnerships, power sharing, reciprocity, and interdependency as ideals that are not guaranteed, especially when thinking about public service responses to crime and criminalisation that explicitly uncover the co-existence between regulation and co-production (Johns et al. 2022). This consideration compounds with the unique ethical and social justice considerations for working with children and young people, and particularly those children who end up in conflict with criminal law. This chapter now turns to the importance of co-production with children and young people.

Importance of co-production with children and young people

Co-production as a conceptual framework has advanced thinking in how services can respond to children, promoting more participatory ways of working across a range of settings in children's services (Tisdall 2017, Brady 2020, Slay and Penny 2014). The rise in co-production with children matters because it is central to the United Nations Convention on the Rights of the Child (UNCRC) and in particular, Article 12: *the right to be heard in matters affecting them*. (Arthur 2015, Lundy 2007) which is a fundamental starting point for children's participation in public services. Research has incorporated the promotion of children's voice and influence across a range of settings to make sure children's participation can be sustained and not tokenistic (Lundy 2007). Children's rights and their active citizenship have advanced discussions on the importance of recognising children's needs and taking account of their knowledge and experiences. Globally, there is a greater recognition that children have agency and can contribute to aspects of their lives. This challenges a traditional developmental perspective of children viewed as incompetent and as a process of becoming or 'adults in the making' (Wyn and White 1997). Meanwhile, sociological research has emphasised childhood and youth through lived experiences embedded within particular social, economic, and political structures (Thomson et al. 2002). The sociological paradigm recognises how children and young people are active beings with specific knowledge, perspectives, and valuable life experiences to contribute (Montgomery and Tatlow-Golden 2018). Therefore, a being-becoming dichotomy exists for children, which makes their role as active citizens more fragile relative to adults, recognising a clear intergenerational power imbalance, resulting in a greater importance to implement co-production to address this power imbalance.

The participation–protection paradox

Adults are powerful actors who determine the social construction of children and young people within systems of law, policy, and culture and socio-political events (Brown 2015, Hendrick 2015). Therefore, despite the recognition of the importance of children's human rights, this can be somewhat diluted through the (adult-dominated) public administration field discussing co-production. Therefore, it is important to approach co-production with children and young people through an interdisciplinary lens. By engaging with childhood and youth studies, law, sociology, and criminology disciplines, it is possible to explore the connection between children's lived experiences and their social and biological development in the social contexts of their lives. This interdisciplinary approach can situate governance and public management co-production theory through wider contextual understandings of childhood, social order, governance, and political responses (Muncie 2005). While there is an abundance of models of participation which exist for understanding the myriad ways children and young people develop agency and influence decision-making processes which affect their lives (see Dolaty et al. 2022, Karsten 2013), systems and processes have been dominated by the 'adult gaze' (Cheney 2023), which creates tensions of harnessing children's voice and agency in welfare and criminal justice settings. The UNCRC, while promoting children's right to be heard (Article 12), also promotes children's 'best interests' (Article 3). Farini and Scollan (2024) argue that children's best interests are predominantly defined by adults. The possibility to make autonomous choices is confined by adults' decision-making, positioning adults superior to children and responsible for children's needs (Thomas 2012). Children's agency may be promoted, but within limits imposed by adults' decision-making agendas (Cheney 2023). When applying this into a public service delivery context, how can co-production be successful in children's services when navigating the paradoxes of children's human rights? Answering this question in detail is beyond the remit of this chapter, but this topic is explored within this edited collection. At the very least, consideration must be given regarding the construction of childhood, developmental stages, and human rights and how this unfolds in public service practice for children in specific political contexts, particularly those who are subject to a range of adult-imposed interventions.

When is co-production considered transformative with children and young people?

The concept of 'co-production' has proliferated throughout various public services for children and young people, with reports of successful case studies where collaborative and relational ways of working with children and young people have been successful (Tisdall 2013). This is because co-production utilises children's knowledge, skills, talents, and energy as resources to incorporate them into the design and delivery of services (Tisdall 2017). Co-production seemingly advocates a deeper form of engagement and therefore can be more challenging for services (Tisdall 2013). Examples of this are found through Youth Commissions which have been set up on various topics, which sought deep engagement in the processes and understanding of issues defined by young people. Arguably, this was an intense process for adults and children, policymakers, practitioners, and service users, who worked collaboratively to increase the influence of children and young people informing policy by giving children and young people a leading, initial role to investigate issues through peer research and make recommendations (Tisdall 2013, Burns 2019). Co-production can also be a form of 'co-learning', where professionals can facilitate critical dialogue and awareness, building skills, and critical consciousness in partnership with children and young people (Tisdall 2017). This example of youth commissions, although only one form of co-production, can offer potential to challenge and transform public service provision (Osborne and Strokosh 2013, Slay and Penny 2014). This is mostly through adults proactively supporting children's and young people's participation in advisory and supporting roles. Therefore, it may be transformative in terms of challenging assumptions about children and young people's capacity to create impact.

Although, as indicated earlier, co-production has multiple meanings and interpretations. Co-production approaches are often viewed through one-off projects and the individual outcomes and benefits they provide to children and young people. Co-production can be considered transformative for the children and young people involved through its contribution to children's personal empowerment and development by building agency, confidence, and skills. While this is important, there is often a tendency to fall into a narrow, individualistic view of children and young people's participation, despite co-production principles aiming to promote greater social value (Tisdall 2013). The criticism comes from the notion that children are merely included in existing adult-centric institutions, offering individual rights to access services and facilities (Milbourne 2009). Subsequently, co-production within public management cannot be viewed as transformative relative to other forms of children's participation outside of the public service context. For instance, engagement in protests as a form of citizenship participation (Tisdall 2013) may be more conflictual and address deeper issues of structural inequalities.

Thinking beyond children's individual citizenship rights, Lundy's (2007) model of participation exemplifies how crucial it is to reflect on the influence children's participation has in a public service context. Tisdall's (2013, 2017) work on participation and co-production also argues that transformation comes through multiple levels:

- Transformation for individuals and relationships with adults
- Transformation as an outcome of activities (i.e. collective decision-making in service planning and delivery)
- Broader social transformation (a combination of the previous two).

Elsewhere, I have argued that the transformative potential of co-production needs to consider how reciprocal partnership working between adult professionals and children requires adults to move beyond outdated assumptions of children and young people as incompetent 'adults in the making' (Burns 2020). Therefore, by considering Osborne and Strokosh's notion of 'enhanced co-production' to challenge and transform paradigms of service delivery, this can only be considered when there is:

- Transformation of adults (their repositioning as reciprocal co-constructors of knowledge (Percy-Smith 2012))
- Transformation of institutional culture (collective attitudinal shifts connected to the transformation of adults)

For co-production to be transformative, adults must reposition themselves as reciprocal co-constructors of knowledge; then young people's knowledge is also valued, and they are viewed as capable co-producers (Burns 2019, 2020). However, previous research has uncovered attitudes towards children and young people being lazy, self-absorbed, immoral, and irresponsible relative to adults (Bessant 2003). There can be a dominance of preconceived attitudes and beliefs about young people's knowledge and capability and deservingness of citizenship rights, which can constrain co-production from being transformative. Therefore, if transformative outcomes from co-production occur, this does have the potential to challenge the 'status quo' beyond the confines of the public service context (Milbourne 2009, Bourdieu 1977). Two key concepts of interdependency and capability are briefly explored in this chapter to understand the requirements for the transformative nature of co-production with children and young people.

Dependency to interdependency

Children are viewed as dependent on adults for 'normal' development (Lee 2001), which risks denying children's and young people's agency, and therefore denying certain modes of co-production. On the other hand, viewing children as capable social actors can overemphasise the agency of young people by viewing them as autonomous and independent beings (Prout 2005). Children and young people *are dependent* upon adults to *facilitate* their participation in public services. In some cases, children's participation will be mandatory through statutory obligations. Academics and commentators have argued for an ontological turn in childhood studies and a more relational approach between children and adults (Montgomery and Tatlow-Golden 2018, Warming 2012). This relational approach can situate co-production through interdependency between adults and young people. This means recognising how adults are also dependent upon children for co-production to occur, whereby adults can reposition themselves as 'co-constructors of knowledge' (Percy-Smith 2012) for transformation to occur. Warming's (2012: 30) theoretical discussion of adults' facilitation of participation and citizenship can support the critical importance of the role of adults in co-production with children and young people by defining adult facilitation as '*counteracting the social constructions and power relations that impede and inhibit the recognition of children and young peoples' participation*'. This definition can be drawn upon to enhance co-production as a type of participation in public service contexts, which promotes transformative action. Although, for the counteraction of social contrcutions and power relations to occur, this relies on adults to *become aware* of the specific social constructions and power relations that deny young people's co-production for transformation. This can be challenging when relations and practices between adults and young people are co-constructed by both groups reciprocally, and roles can constantly change. Moreover, professionals have structured dispositions to think, feel, and act in determined ways, guiding their attitudes, values, knowledge, and beliefs (Bourdieu 1977). Children and adults remain interdependent for co-production to occur, but attention needs to remain on adults to critically recognise their integral role in the process of co-production being transformative.

Overcoming intergenerational hierarchies of knowledge

For 'interdependency' to support partnerships for transformative participation, adults reposition themselves as co-constructors of knowledge with young people. Nevertheless, this also requires adults to regard young people's knowledge as 'valid'. This emphasises co-production as 'multiple ways of knowing' (Brigstoke 2013). However, public services created adult professional expertise (Lee 2001) and, as previously discussed, act in children's best interests. Therefore, adults' expertise in public service professional roles has historically created 'hierarchies of knowledge' between themselves and the young people in receipt of welfare services. Percy-Smith (2012) shares that it is wrong to assume that adults who facilitate 'youth participation' are supportive of participation for transformation. 'Co-production' may fail to address how adult professionals' 'expert' knowledge can maintain power over young people, despite children being considered active citizens in the co-production relationship. The problem of an 'adult knows best' mentality can be more contentious when children display behavioural or intellectual difficulties, who find it hard to express agency (Forde 2018) or otherwise express agency and become labelled as risky or criminalised. Yet as co-production advocates, children bring lived expertise into public services, which can enrich service management and provision, ensure relevance, and challenge deficit-based assumptions. Recognising children as 'knowers' also reconstructs their role, knowledge, and capabilities; it also reconfigures a reciprocal professional–child dynamic, a key principle of co-production. Larkins et al. (2023) advocate a capability approach as a method for acknowledging children as both beings and becomings, living in contexts of injustice; this can help to promote discussions on the underlying cultural, economic, and political processes affecting children's experiences. Essentially, what this means is that there are approaches which can help to realise the potential for relational and social transformation through co-production, which is most important for addressing the problem of children's relative powerlessness in an adult-dominated society.

Can co-production counteract social injustice?

Children and young people are increasingly aware of social injustice matters. Percy Smith and Thomas (2023) argue that it is no longer possible to claim children are 'too young' to engage in democratic processes when they are increasingly aware of their own agency and collectively demand that their role as active citizens be welcomed by adult leaders. It is important to note that there are embedded intergenerational inequalities alongside social, cultural, and political influences, which all play out through the institutional contexts of public service provision. Therefore, the core principles of co-production, such as power sharing, reciprocity, and equal partnerships, come under scrutiny when understanding the social and political dynamics of children and young people in society. Co-production is also a contested concept in work with children and young people, as since children have historically been absent from formal democratic governance processes, there has been a parallel understanding of children's participation as self-initiated action in everyday spaces (Percy-Smith and Thomas 2023). Therefore, summarising aspects of transformative co-production includes an understanding of the connectivity of children's lived experiences through space and time, beyond the institutional confines of public service provision, to understand how power inequalities and social injustice impact their lives and how it can be addressed through public service reform. This could consider co-production as a mechanism of social justice, as long as it does not become reduced or isolated to the institutional context of the public service.

However, co-production within an institutional context may not be able to connect with the wider cultural and socio-political contexts beyond public services. For instance, co-production within public services is unlikely to resolve children experiencing forms of racism or poverty, unless co-production is viewed as a process for challenging institutional and system cultures while counteracting neoliberal, austerity-driven social policies (Gray and Smith 2024). Another problem which occurs is related to children being excluded from co-production activities, undermining the effectiveness and legitimacy of co-production. Equally, co-production may be tied to new forms of regulation over children and young people, specifically linked to formal targeted responses to 'risky' or 'at-risk' young people (Cullen and Bradford 2018) or mechanisms of governance using co-production to legitimise increased monitoring of vulnerable or deviant young people in paternalistic service provision (Fergusson 2016). There is a need to establish co-production as transformative by addressing the paradoxical nature of children's individual rights, balancing safety and protection, reconstructing the roles and relationships between adults and children in public service context settings, and raising awareness of the specific social constructions and power relations with the heterogeneity of children and young people, to resist co-production becoming a narrow or tokenistic form of participation which may contribute to social exclusion rather than social justice. This chapter now discusses the importance of addressing the challenges of transformative co-production within youth justice systems.

Why we need co-production in youth justice

Children and young people in the youth justice system are the most vulnerable and socially excluded group in society (Muncie 2014). Co-production may be able to challenge the exclusionary, adult-centric, and rights-limiting responses within youth justice systems, offering a framework for innovation and legitimacy. However, youth justice is a particularly *power-laden, involuntary, and risk-oriented system* (Burns 2020, Hampson et al. 2024), often critiqued for being overly focused on regimes of punishment throughout system contact (Bateman 2023). The youth justice system has been described as harmful for children due to its decontextualised individualisation, criminalisation, and dematerialisation of children's needs (Gray and Smith 2024). Paradoxically, for those children and young people who become involved in the youth justice system, it requires co-production to be viewed as an innovative approach to transform the role of adults and organisations related to wider social, cultural, and political contexts to ensure that the principled ideals of co-production become a reality. To grapple with the unique tensions of co-production in criminal justice systems, Johns et al. (2022: 16) ask:

> *How realistic is it to imagine criminal justice service users as... decision makers or equal partners in the production of criminal justice knowledge with services and professionals who hold power over them, and by whom they are (potentially) coerced, contained and punished?*

This is a poignant question but difficult to answer when evidence is suggestive that youth justice professionals can be more inclined to execute restrictive risk management strategies, fuelled by concern that some children present a risk of harm to others (Creaney and Burns 2025, Day 2023). While research into the application of co-production in youth justice is scarce, in England Peer Power, a youth-led social justice charity, was commissioned by the Youth Justice Board to explore co-production in multi-agency youth justice services (Peer Power Youth 2021). It introduced a *Participation Continuum* that runs from coercion, informing, and consultation, through engagement and co-design, to co-production. This continuum is non-linear and fluid, stressing that practices must be responsive to context, but it also makes explicit that co-production represents a qualitatively different level of influence: one where children act as co-creators with real power over decisions. Yet at the same time, note how co-production, co-creation, and participation were used interchangeably, which demonstrates that conceptual ambiguity may be prominent within youth justice practice. The project also allowed young people to co-produce five core principles for meaningful co-production: *relating and connecting* (trust and trauma-aware relationships); *power and inclusion* (acknowledging and redressing imbalances, providing paid roles); *strengths and positivity* (focusing on assets rather than deficits); *resources* (committing budgets and incentives to support involvement); and *rights and readiness* (ensuring practitioners are trained and supported to work in equal partnership) (Peer Power Youth 2021). These principles align closely with rights-based accounts of children's participation and with the 'Child First' policy framework promoted by the Youth Justice Board for England and Wales (YJB 2021). Importantly, the report exposes a common misconception, that many services believe they are co-producing when, in fact, their practices remain at the level of consultation or engagement, which is not problematic *per se*, based on the aforementioned challenges of youth justice systems overly focused on children's punishment and risk management, but is useful to acknowledge and reflect on opportunities for deeper engagement that co-production might offer.

Elsewhere, cutting-edge research from Smithson et al. (2020), through their co-produced 'Participatory Youth Practice' framework with children in youth justice across Greater Manchester in England, demonstrating the possibilities of 'doing' co-production with transformative intentions. This project was the first to co-create a set of participation principles with justice-involved children in England for practitioners to use in their day-to-day practice. However, Smithson and Jones (2021) document the difficult navigation of power dynamics through the research project, demonstrating the unique challenges of co-production within a youth justice context. Overall, these two studies provide examples to demonstrate that co-production with children in these settings requires an understanding that specific principles are needed but that there are multiple overlapping principles being promoted in different spaces within youth justice, and a coherent conceptual framework might be needed to ensure consistency across practice. Moreover, these projects demonstrate that there will be a range of degrees of children's voice and influence (see Johns et al. 2022 and chapters in this edited book). However, the temporal nature of children engaged within youth justice settings means that there are also concerns that co-production can only be successful within individualistic approaches or becomes restricted to interventions or short-term projects, lacking sustainability for transformation to occur within service culture and systems change.

Nevertheless, due to specific harms experienced by children in criminal justice processes, it is useful to adopt an interdisciplinary approach, for instance, drawing upon disciplines such as criminology, sociology, and youth studies to improve definitions of co-production for public service reform with children and young people in the youth justice system. As well as engaging with the relative experiences of children as a social group, there is a need to further contextualise the interactions between service provisions throughout stages of the youth justice system to understand the nature of interdependency and reciprocity with a range of criminal justice organisations, being mindful of 'fields of domination', which can impede wider transformative effects of co-production across youth justice settings. Co-production may not be a holistic solution for transformative effects in youth justice (issues around the specificity of youth justice settings will be explored in more detail in Chapter 2). Though it is worth being mindful of Carlen's (2008) argument that if justice practices are to be empowering rather than discriminatory and harmful, then this needs to involve collective responsibility. Perhaps then, co-production as a mechanism for public sector reform can only go so far unless it emerges as part of a commitment to social justice, expanding boundaries of transformation beyond the institutional context of public services within youth justice systems. There is a need to remain critical about the relationship between co-production as a concept and ensure it is not reformulated or rebranded as regimes of compliance and punishment.

Conclusion

Co-production has become widely used as a form of democratic participation in public services with children and young people, but its meaning can be confused or merged with concepts of collaboration, participation, engagement, or consultation, which involve varied levels of power and influence for children. This conceptual ambiguity can lead to uncertainty in practice and risks the term being used without any real shift in decision-making processes and service reform. By engaging with co-production literature, it can be viewed as improving services with the potential to offer transformative outcomes. When children are treated as capable and knowledgeable experts in their own lives, and their insights shape policies, programmes, and relationships, co-production can help shift service cultures and support young people to build confidence, agency, and positive identities. It can also transform professional practice, resulting in transformative shifts in the role of adults, who become 'co-constructors of knowledge', facilitating and fostering empathy, partnership, and relational working, rather than compliance and control.

However, co-production has a fragile relationship with regulation, and in the youth justice context, resolving this ambiguity is especially important due to punishment and risk management processes that contribute to the coercion and containment of children and young people, often undermining their human rights. Children who encounter the youth justice system often have the least say in decisions that shape their lives. Clear definitions of co-production may enable support for public service professionals in youth justice to see the difference between inviting children to give opinions and genuinely sharing influence and control, and then act on this through their shifting roles and reflexive approach. There are also considerations as to what extent social justice can be realised through co-production within the public service context. Understanding justice involved children's relationship to wider oppressive social and political structures and counteracting harmful social constructions through co-production activities may provide opportunities for transformation to happen beyond the confines of the youth justice system. However, any conceptual ambiguity of co-production in youth justice must be challenged to avoid it becoming another rebranding of compliance and punishment.

References

Arnstein SR (1969) A lLadder of citizen participation. *Journal of the American Institute of Planners* 35(4): 216–224.

Arthur R (2015) Recognising children's citizenship in the youth justice system. *Journal of Social Welfare and Family Law* 37(1): 21–37.

Barnes M, Newman J, and Sullivan H (2007) *Power, Participation and Political Renewal.* Bristol: Policy Press.

Bateman T (2023) Challenging punitive youth justice. In: Case S and Hazel N (eds), *Child First: Developing a New Youth Justice System.* Cham: Palgrave Macmillan, pp. 25–49.

Bessant J (2003) Youth participation: A new mode of government. *Policy Studies* 24(2–3): 87–100.

Brandsen T and Honingh M (2018) Definitions of co-production and co-creation. In: Brandsen T, Steen T, and Verschuere B (eds), *Co-Production and co-Creation: Engaging Citizens in Public Services.* London: Routledge, pp. 9–17.

Bourdieu P (1977) *Outline of a Theory of Practice. Outline of a Theory of Practice.* Cambridge: Cambridge University Press.

Bovaird T (2007) Beyond engagement and participation: User and community coproduction of public services. *Public Administration Review* 67(5): 846–860.

Bovaird T and Loeffler E (2012) From engagement to co-production. *Voluntas* 23(4): 1119–1138.

Boyle D and Harris M (2009) *The Challenge of Co-Production.* London: NESTA.

Brady L-M (2020) *Embedding Young People's Participation in Health Services.* Bristol: Policy Press.

Brigstoke J (2013) Democracy and the reinvention of authoritytle. In: Noorani T, Blencowe C, and Brigstoke J (eds), *Reflections on Authority, Democracy, and the Struggle for Common Life.* Lewes: ARN Press, pp. 7–13.

Brown K (2015) *Vulnerability and Young People: Care and Social Control in Policy and Practice.* Bristol: Policy Press.

Burns S (2019) Young people as co-producers in policing across England. An evaluation of the 'Youth commission' on police and crime. *Children and Society* 33(4): 347–362.

Burns S (2020) Exploring transformative participation constraints in practices of co-production with social workers and young people in Hong Kong. PhD thesis. City University of Hong Kong.

Burns S (2023) Exploring partnerships with justice-involved children in Hong Kong: The role of social workers and barriers towards transformation. *Safer Communities* 22(2): 133–148. https://doi.org/10.1108/SC-09-2022-0042

Carlen P (2008) Imaginary penalities and risk crazed governments. In: Carlen P (ed), *Imaginary Penalities.* Devon: Willan Publishing, pp. 1–25.

Case S and Browning A (2021) *Child First: The Evidence Base.* Loughborough University.

Cheney K (2023) Overcoming the adult gaze in participatory research with young people. In: Percy-Smith B, Thomas NP, O'Kane C and Twum-Danso Imoh A (eds), *A Handbook of Children and Young People's Participation: Conversations for Transformational Change.* London: Routledge.

Chhotray V and Stoker G (2009) *Governance Theory and Practice: A Cross-Disciplinary Approach.* Basingstoke: Palgrave Macmillan.

Creaney, S and Burns S (2024) Freedom from symbolic violence? Facilitators and barriers to participatory practices in youth justice. *Youth Justice* 24(1): 31–52.
Creaney S and Burns S (2025) The Achilles heel of Child First: High-risk panels in youth justice service policy and practice. *Probation Journal*. https://research.edgehill.ac.uk/en/publications/the-achilles-heel-of-child-first-high-risk-panels-in-youth-justic
Creaney S, Burns S, Douglas A-M, Brierley A, and Falconer, C (2024) Desistance through participatory practice: Involving children in decision making processes. In: Youth Justice in Alexandra Wigzell, Paterson-Young C and Bateman T (eds), *Desistance and Children: Critical Reflections from Theory, Research and Practice*. Bristol: Policy Press.
Cullen F and Bradford S (2018) Precarious practices with risky subjects? Policy and practice explorations in the UK and Europe. In: Alldred P, Cullen F, Edwards K, and Fusco D (eds), *The Sage Handbook of Youth Work Practice*. Los Angeles: Sage.
Day A-M (2023) The place of risk within child first justice: An exploration of the perspectives of youth justice practitioners. In: Case S and Hazel N (eds), *Child First: Developing a New Youth Justice System*. London: Palgrave Macmillan.
Dolaty S, Tait, N, and Brunskill H (2022) Youth participation: Models used to understand young people's participation in school and community programmes Evidence briefing #14: August 2022. Evidence Based Practice Unit / Anna Freud National Centre for Children and Families.
Farini F and Scollan A (2024) How do childhood and children's rights meanwhat they mean? Innovating the debate aroundthe social semantics of childhood and children's rights through an interdisciplinary approach. *Children & Society* 38(6): 2022–2035.
Fergusson R (2016) *Young People, Welfare and Crime: Governing Non-Participation*. Bristol: Policy Press.
Fleming S and Osborne S (2019) The dynamics of co-production in the context of social care personalisation: Testing theory and practice in a Scottish context. *Journal of Social Policy* 48(4): 671–697. https://doi.org/10.1017/S0047279418000776
Forde L (2018) Realising the right of the child to participate in the criminal process. *Youth Justice* 18(3): 265–284.
Foucault M (1977) *Discipline and Punish: The Birth of The Prison*. New York: Vintage Books.
Fox C (2024) Understanding co-creation: Strengths and capabilities. In: Baines S, Wilson R, Fox C, Narbutaité Aflaki I, Bassi A, Aramo-Immonen, H, and Prandini R (eds), *Co-Creation in Public Services for Innovation and Social Justice*. Bristol: Policy Press.
Gray P and Smith R (2024) Youth justice and social harm: Towards a 'theory of the good'. *Criminology & Criminal Justice* 26(2): 661–678.
Hampson K, Creaney S, and Burns S (2024) Transforming the balance of power? Child first collaboration: A conceptual analysis. *Societies* 14(8): Article 138.
Hastings A and Matthews P (2015) Bourdieu and the Big Society: Empowering the powerful in public service provision? *Policy & Politics* 43(4): 545–560.
Hendrick H (2015) Histories of youth crime and youth justice. 2nd ed. In: Goldson B and Muncie J (eds), *Youth Crime & Justice*. London: Sage Publications, pp. 3–16.
Hickey S and Mohan G (2004) Towards participation as transformation: Critical themes and challenges. In: Hickey S and Mohan G (eds), *Participation from Tyranny to Transformation*. London: Zed Books.

Horne M and Shirley T (2009) *Co-production in Public Services*. London: Cabinet Office.
Innes M, Davies B, and McDermont M (2019) How co-production regulates. *Social and Legal Studies* 28(3): 370–391.
Johns D, Flynn C, Hall M, Spivakovsky C, and Turner S. (2022) *Co-Production & Criminal Justice*. Abingdon: Routledge.
Larkins C, del Moral-Espín L and Stoecklin D (2023) Understanding children's participation using the capability approach. In: Percy-Smith B, Thomas NP, O'Kane C and Twum-Danso Imoh A (eds), *A Handbook of Children and Young People's Participation: Conversations for Transformational Change*. London: Routledge.
Lee N (2001) *Childhood and Society: Growing up in An Age of Uncertainty*. Buckingham: Open University Press.
Loeffler E (2016) Co-production of public services and outcomes. In: Bovaird AG and Loeffler E (eds), *Public Management and Governance*, 3rd ed. London: Routledge, pp. 319–336.
Loeffler E and Bovaird T (2019) Assessing the impact of co-production on pathways to outcomes in public services: The case of policing and criminal justice. *International Public Management Journal* 23(2): 205–223. https://doi.org/10.1080/10967494.2019.1668895.
Loeffler E and Bovaird T (2021) User and community co-production of public services and outcomes—a map of the current state of play. In: Loeffler E and Bovaird T (eds), *The Palgrave Handbook of Co-Production of Public Services and Outcomes*. Palgrave Macmillan, pp. 3–30.
Lundy L (2007) 'Voice' is not enough: Conceptualising article 12 of the United Nations Convention on the Rights of the Child. *British Educational Research Journal* 33(6): 927–942.
Karsten A (2013) A Potpourri of Participation Models [online] available at: www.youthpolicy.org/library/documents/a-potpourri-of-participation-models/ (accessed on 26 November 2025)
McCulloch T (2015) Beyond compliance: Participation, co-production and change in justice sanctions1. *European Journal of Probation* 7(1): 40–57.
McCulloch T (2016) Co-producing justice sanctions? Citizen perspectives. *Criminology and Criminal Justice* 16(4): 431–451.
Milbourne L (2009) Valuing difference or securing compliance? Working to involve young people in community settings. *Children & Society* 23(5): 347–363.
Montgomery H and Tatlow-Golden M (2018) Reconciling childhood and youth studies and developmental psychology. In: Montgomery H and Robb M (eds), *Children and Young People's Worlds*. Bristol: Policy Press, pp. 7–21
Muncie J (2005) The globalization of crime control—the case of youth and juvenile justice: Neo-liberalism, policy convergence and international conventions: Neo-liberalism, policy convergence and international conventions. *Theoretical Criminology*, 9(1), 35–64
Muncie J (2014) *Youth and Crime*. London: Sage Publications.
Osborne SP and Strokosch K (2013) It takes two to Tango? Understanding the co-production of public services by integrating the services management and public administration perspectives. *British Journal of Management* 24(S1): 31–47.
Osborne SP, Strokosch K and Radnor Z (2018) Co-production and the co-creation of value in public services: a perspective from service management. In: Brandsen T, Verschuere B and Steen T (Eds) *Co-production and Co-creation: Engaging Citizens in Public Services*. New York: Routledge, pp 18–26.

Ostrom E, Parks RB, Whitaker GP, et al. (1978) The public service production process: A framework for analyzing public services. *Policy Studies Journal* 7(1): 381–390.

Peer Power Youth (2021) *Co-creation and Participation in Practice Project.* London: Peer Power Youth/YJB.

Percy-Smith B (2012) Participation as mediation and social learning. In: Baraldi C and Iervese V (eds), *Participation, Facilitation, and Mediation Children and Young People in their Social Contexts.* London: Routledge, pp. 12–29.

Percy-Smith B and Thomas NP (2023) Introduction. In: Percy-Smith B, Thomas NP, O'Kane C and Twum-Danso Imoh A (eds), *A Handbook of Children and Young People's Participation: Conversations for Transformational Change.* London: Routledge.

Prout A (2005) *The Future of Childhood: Towards the Interdisciplinary Study of Children.* London: Routledge.

Slay J and Penny J (2014) *Commissioning for Outcomes and Co-Production: A Practical Guide for Local Authorities.* London.

Smithson H, Gray P, and Jones A (2020) "They really should start listening to you": The benefits and challenges of co-producing a participatory framework of youth justice practice. *Youth Justice* 21(3): 321–337. https://doi.org/10.1177/1473225420941598.

Smithson H and Jones A (2021) Co-creating youth justice practice with young people: Tackling power dynamics and enabling transformative action. *Children and Society* 35(3): 348–362.

Social Care Institute for Excellence (SCIE) (2022) Co-production: What it is and how to do it. [online] available at: www.scie.org.uk/co-production/what-how/ (accessed on 28 February 2025).

Sorrentino M, Sicilia M, and Howlett M (2018) Understanding co-production as a new public governance tool. *Policy and Society* 37(3): 277–293.

Thomas N (2012) Love, rights and solidarity: Studying children's participation using Honneth's theory of recognition. *Childhood*, 19(4), 453–466.

Thomson R, Bell R, Holland J, Henderson S, McGrellis S and Sharpe S (2002) Critical moments: Choice, chance and opportunity in young people's narratives of transition. *Sociology* 36(2): 335–354.

Tisdall EKM (2013) The transformation of participation? Exploring the potential of 'Transformative participation' for theory and practice around children and young people's participation. *Global Studies of Childhood* 3(2): 183–193.

Tisdall EKM (2017) Conceptualising children and young people's participation: Examining vulnerability, social accountability and co-production. *The International Journal of Human Rights* 21(1): 59–75.

Torfing J, Sørensen E, and Røiseland A (2019) Transforming the public sector into an Arena for co-creation: Barriers, drivers, benefits, and ways forward. *Administration & Society* 51(5): 795–825.

Vargas C, Whelan J, Brimblecombe J, and Allender S. (2022) Co-creation, co-design and co-production for public health: A perspective on definitions and distinctions. *Public Health Research and Practice* 32(2): e3222211.

Voorberg WH, Bekkers VJJM, and Tummers LG (2015) A systematic review of co-creation and co-production: Embarking on the social innovation journey. *Public Management Review* 17(9): 1333–1357.

Warming H (2012) Participation, facilitation, mediation. In: Baraldi C and Lervese V (eds), *Participation, Facilitation, and Mediation Children and Young People in their Social Contexts.* London: Routledge, pp. 30–48.

Weaver, B., Lightowler, C., and Moodie, K. (2019) Inclusive justice – Co-producing change: A practical guide to service user involvement in community justice. University of Strathclyde, Glasgow. Available at: www.cycj.org.uk/wp-content/uploads/2019/11/Inclusive-Justice-Guide.pdf

Wyn J and White RD (1997) *Rethinking Youth*. London: Sage Publications.

Youth Justice Board (YJB) (2016) *Participation strategy: Giving young people a voice in youth justice*. London: YJB.

Youth Justice Board (YJB) (2021) *Strategic Plan 2021–24*. London: Report, YJB.

Furtsher reading

Haines K and Case S (2015) *Positive Youth Justice: Children First, Offenders Second*. Bristol: Policy Press.

Shukra K, Ball M, and Brown K (2012) Participation and activism: Young people shaping their worlds. *Youth & Policy* 108: 36–54.

2

CO-PRODUCTION IN YOUTH JUSTICE

Power-sharing, procedural justice, and reflexive critical pragmatism

Shelley Turner

Introduction

Co-production is essentially an approach to working together that involves equal power-sharing between those who use and those who provide social services to achieve a partnership for equal benefit. Although variably defined, co-production is often conceptualised as the pinnacle of a continuum of varying degrees of participatory power (Johns *et al.* 2023). It is touted as a potentially transformative process that can upend traditional power structures and reconstruct *what* and *how* knowledge is produced and used in practice. With its roots in consumer and citizen rights movements, co-production is embraced in fields that philosophically emphasise and support the personal agency and empowerment of service users, such as health and mental health, disability, and community development. However, in criminal legal practice contexts, where the personal agency of service users is deliberately curtailed, is it realistic to imagine them in equal partnership with those explicitly holding power over their lives? Moreover, in statutory youth justice practice, where the mandated service users are children or young people and the paid service providers are adults, is genuine power-sharing or co-production even conceivable?

This chapter is a critical reflection on these questions and an exploration of the benefits and challenges of co-production and participatory approaches in statutory youth justice. It draws on the extant literature relevant to co-production and youth justice, noting the recurring and interrelated themes of *identity, time*, and *space* (see Johns *et al.* 2023) and learnings from the author's practice-based research aiming to 'give voice' to the experiences of youth justice service users (see Turner 2019; Turner 2022). Key understandings and

DOI: 10.4324/9781003602996-4

manifestations of co-production in youth justice are briefly considered, along with the key practical challenge of managing inherent disparities in power and status between adults and children, especially in this context. This highlights the current and perhaps inevitable prevalence of *individual* approaches to co-production in youth justice, which arguably are just another way of framing collaborative or person-centred practice with involuntary clients. The chapter concludes with a view to adopting a reflexive, critical pragmatic approach to help navigate the 'care and control' tensions in youth justice co-production and a call to acknowledge, rather than deny, power, as part of this.

By the end of this chapter, you will be able to:

- Articulate key tensions between participatory approaches and working with young, involuntary clients
- Describe a reflexive *critical pragmatic* approach for navigating these tensions in practice
- Understand the relevance of a procedural justice framework for enabling effective power sharing in youth justice

Co-production and youth justice

The research literature about co-production in youth justice and other criminal legal contexts is comparatively inchoate and lacks clear guidance about strategies for its application to practice. It prevails with debates about what co-production actually *is* and whether or not it is merely another buzzword or 'old wine in a new bottle' (Johns *et al.* 2023). This lack of definitional consensus, combined with the structural barriers that characterise criminal legal contexts, means that *doing* co-production in youth justice remains challenging and rarely extends beyond the individual level. Thom and Burnside (2018), for example, examined five studies on co-production in criminal justice to conclude that most represent 'individualized forms of co-production that lead to individual outcomes', including personal support for desistance (p. 1260). They conclude that many practices described as co-production might often more accurately be understood as 'different approaches to personalised offender management' (Fox *et al.* 2018). Similarly, Weaver *et al.* (2019) contend that *individual* co-production is the dominant of three distinct forms of service user involvement in criminal legal contexts. The two other forms are *group* and *collective* co-production, and in contrast to these, individual co-production benefits only the individual participants. Weaver *et al.* (2019) further contend that individual co-production corresponds with *person-centred support*, a collaborative, individual-focused approach that enables service users to have choice in and control over the services they receive and self-determination over their lives.

The tendency towards individual forms of co-production in youth justice means it is difficult to distinguish from any other strengths-based, relational, or emancipatory practice (Johns *et al.* 2023). It also seems inevitable, as certain characteristics of these systems pose a significant challenge for more collective forms of co-production. Criminal legal systems are not homogenous. Rather, they are a variety of open, intersecting, interdependent, and fragmented systems, dynamically composed of differing legislation, policies, practices, organisations, and personnel. The only unique and unifying characteristics of youth justice systems are that they involve legislation, law enforcers, and service users who are children or young people. However, exactly what constitutes a 'child' or a 'young person', especially for the purposes of determining criminal responsibility, is not agreed – not globally, nor even within and between many countries' local jurisdictions. Moreover, the aims of youth justice systems are multiple and similarly not aligned across and within global and local jurisdictions, with significant variations in their expressed and implicit intentions. While many youth justice systems foreground a rehabilitative purpose, most (if not all) are also underpinned by punitive and containment aims that are fundamentally at odds with the participatory ideals of co-production, particularly collective forms. Hence, youth justice workers understand their role as having a dual 'care and control' function, focused on both the 'needs and deeds' of the child and young person.

Managerialism, childism, and 'consumers' of youth justice services

Approaches to youth justice have tended to oscillate between the *welfare* and *justice* model, which respectively emphasise either the rehabilitation needs of the justice-involved individual or due process and accountability. Contemporary models tend to blur these focus areas to more instrumentalist ends, underpinned by principles of managerialism that emphasise efficiency, technology, and data-driven performance. The managerialism trend is evident across a range of public health and human services and uses *consumer choice* as a mechanism to frame service users as 'customers' or 'consumers' and their 'satisfaction' levels as a key performance indicator. The central tenet is that consumers have the right to choose or make decisions about services they receive. This is exemplified in the current 'consumer-directed care' approach to aged care in Australia, which requires a balanced partnership between consumers and providers to ensure and promote consumers' rights, choice, and control (Aged Care Guide 2024). However, as Weaver (2011, p. 1040) points out: 'offenders cannot un-problematically be cast as consumers', and indeed, many people might baulk at the idea of measuring the performance of a prison by the satisfaction levels of prisoners.

Rather than choose or direct services, 'consumers' of correctional and youth justice services are *involuntary*, compelled by way of a court order or threat of legal penalty into clienthood. This is compounded by the connection between consumer choice ideology and *rational choice theory*, one of several microeconomic theories that, since the 1980s, has also become popular in criminal justice (Barry 2013). Rational choice theory holds that people *choose* to commit offences based on reasoned cost–benefit analysis. Offending is thus framed as voluntaristic or as an individual's deliberate and calculated 'bad choice' that is, therefore, deserving of individual blame and punishment (De'Ath *et al.* 2018, p. 87). This, it seems, is a distinguishing feature of co-production in criminal legal contexts. Namely, it involves the rhetorically 'undeserving'; people who have *done* wrong and who some may see (especially if their offending is deemed particularly serious, persistent, or perverse) *as* wrong (Johns *et al.* 2023).

With the notable exception of substance abuse services, mandated service users in other fields, such as mental health and disability, tend to be viewed as blameless and service-involved through no fault (or rational choice) of their own. This is in stark contrast to the lived experiences of justice-involved individuals, which are always framed by the normative assumptions about crime that cast them as 'consumers' because of their own 'poor choices' (Johns *et al.* 2023). They are seen as both responsible or to blame for their justice involvement and to have forfeited the right to have a 'voice' or a say in the services they receive. Consequently, their perspectives are dismissed as unworthy of public attention. For justice-involved children and young people, this disadvantageous or undeserving position is further entrenched by the inherent power disparities between adults and children.

Aspects of the power disparities between adults and children can be understood through the lens of *childism*. Pierce and Allen coined the term in 1975, in connection to race and racism. More recently, Young-Bruehl (2009; 2012) described childism as the radical notion that, despite differences in size, experience and power, children are inherently of equal worth to adults and need to be respected as human beings. Therefore, children's and young people's perspectives and experiences should also be considered on the same merits as those of adults. Paradoxically, the significance of these ideas is evident in the imperative for contemporary youth justice systems to centre around *Child First* principles (see Case & Hazel 2023). That is, to treat children as *children*, rather than unreasonably responsibilise them for their offending behaviour by treating them as though they are adults with equal decision-making capacity and power. In Australia, for example, newly introduced 'adult crime, adult time' laws in the State of Queensland (Queensland Government 2025) mean children and young people can, for particular crimes, be sentenced as adults and placed in adult detention facilities. This is at odds with the rationale for a separate system of justice for children and young people, given they are still developing biologically, psychologically and socially, and therefore require a different approach to adults.

Power-sharing and youth justice practice

The author's research aimed at 'giving voice' to justice-involved children and young people (see Turner 2019; Turner 2022) identifies opportunities and challenges for practical ways to share power in statutory youth justice practice. Two of the more seemingly simplistic ways that adults (particularly researchers) are often advised to mitigate power disparities with children and young people are through reciprocal and group approaches. Reciprocity is fundamental to power-sharing and co-production. It speaks to the importance of genuinely and meaningfully recognising people's time, energy and contributions. This can take many forms but commonly involves financial payment or provision of a gift or service. However, debates on the ethics of reciprocal approaches in youth justice are fairly polarised, with arguments that they reward bad behaviour, are tokenistic, or are a fair and reasonable way to recognise service user contributions. In contrast, reciprocal approaches are embedded in mental health and disability practice, including in some forensic services, where consumer advisory groups and payment for their time and engagement have become the norm. In youth justice practice, such approaches are generally only evident in voluntary sector services that work with youth justice populations. In the statutory system, they typically only apply to research or specific, time-limited co-design projects that sit outside the usual mandate or reasons for a young person's service involvement (e.g. Johns *et al.* 2023; Turner 2019).

As a power-in-numbers strategy, group approaches are considered useful for shifting the power imbalance from adults to the benefit of a group of children or young people. However, in statutory youth justice practice, the risk of breaching privacy legislation and policies to protect the identity of justice-involved children often makes this impractical. Group co-production approaches, such as youth advisory groups, are therefore generally only practical in custodial settings (i.e., where young people already know one another) or in community sector organisations (i.e., where the same privacy restrictions may not apply or where young people are already involved in groups or shared accommodation). Moreover, bringing youth justice service users together as a group can pose so-called 'contamination' (Trotter 1995) and 'labelling' risks (see Turner & Trotter 2016), which are evident in diversionary strategies.

Labelling, lived experience, and identity

There is extensive literature on the 'criminal identity' and how it is developed and maintained or renounced and redeemed (Maruna 2001). Co-production can directly or indirectly challenge identity, both how participants are perceived by others, and how people perceive themselves. It can serve to interrupt unhelpful dichotomies (e.g., good/bad, offender/ex-offender) by engaging with and incorporating the expertise of those with lived and living experience (Johns *et al.* 2023). Linked to this is the ongoing rise and development of lived and living experience as its own academic discipline and discreet workforce, including in some criminal legal contexts. Engagement with co-production may enable current and former service users to create alternative narratives, or preferred stories about who they are, to act in a different role and step out of their fixed institutional identity, and to have this 'other' role acknowledged and validated (Johns *et al.* 2023). While for some criminalised adults these developments have clearly generated productive career opportunities and positive social identities, very little attention has been paid to implications for justice-involved children and young people.

Buck *et al.* (2022) examined how criminalised adults feel about activating their lived experience in criminal justice practice and found that some peer workers and lived experience academics feel trapped by their specific roles and associated identities. This sentiment is clearly articulated by one research participant: 'You are forever in the system, you never leave it, you just occupy a different position [and]...there's such a pressure to just be better than best, gooder than good' (Buck, Tomczak & Quinn 2022, p. 21). This suggests the need for a cautious approach to asking justice-involved children and young people to activate or draw on their lived experience in similar ways. Their personal and social identities are still developing, along with their capacity for rational decision-making. In fact, the same arguments used to justify a separate justice system for children and young people should inform participatory practice with that cohort. This is especially relevant for group or more collective forms of co-production that may publicly identify or label a child or young person as a current or former 'offender'. Indeed, given the relatively rapid pace of child and adolescent biological development, it seems disingenuous to suggest they can really have anything other than *living* experience. This, in turn, should be very carefully considered by adults in any participatory approach, as it is likely a period of crisis, distress, and vulnerability for the child or young person.

When interacting with a justice-involved child or young person, adults should try to be as flexible as possible in allowing conversations to evolve in a way that is child-led. This requires a complex and nuanced set of practice skills that take time to develop, involving both meta-competencies, such as judgement and critical thinking, and procedural competencies relevant to the youth justice context (Bogo 2010). It relies on the worker having a change theory in mind and being guided by a flexible, semi-structured communication framework that can adapt to the child or young person's conversation style and topic interest. At the same time, the worker should be conversing and engaging with the child or young person in a relaxed, naturalistic manner, conveying trustworthy motives and non-judgemental empathy, while continuously assessing the child or young person's needs and risks of harm to self or others. This is managing the dual 'care and control' or 'needs and deeds' component of their role that exists even in the most co-productive engagement with children and young people. In fact, it is often prescribed in legislation that the youth justice worker holds a duty of care to the safety and wellbeing of both the young person and the broader community.

Use of self and procedural justice principles

Effective power-sharing with justice-involved children and young people relies on the youth justice worker's use of self. How adults behave can influence young people's perceptions of the legitimacy of their authority, which impacts their willingness to comply with directives (Hough 2020; Ugwudike & Raynor 2013). Children and young people's experiences of encounters and interactions with authority figures are likely to be translated into trust – or distrust – of adults in general. This matters, as youth justice workers and their colleagues play a critical role in supporting the young person's desistance and community safety, and this relies on voluntary compliance by the young person. Police and probation studies show that every interaction between a young person and the police or their probation officer offers an opportunity to build trust and partnership. Colwell and Huth (2010, p. 89) found that police with '[c]ondescending, contemptuous, and disrespectful attitudes' sour these interactions and generate 'a "self-fulfilling prophesy" that affirms and hardens the contemptuousness of law enforcement'. Likewise, punitive or coercive policing strategies tend to generate perceptions of unfairness (Ugwudike & Raynor 2013), and young people who mistrust the police are more likely to defy law enforcement in general.

A substantial body of research finds that where police and worker behaviour embodies procedural justice, it improves people's perceptions of the legitimacy of their authority and, in turn, their compliance with that authority. Importantly, an Australian survey of 513 young people and 2611 adults concludes that procedural justice is even more important to young people than it is to adults (Murphy 2015). Mazerolle *et al.* (2014, p. 3) summarise the principles of procedural justice as: 'dignity and respect, trustworthy motives, neutrality, and voice'. This entails treating young people decently and politely, explaining the reasons for actions, adopting a non-judgemental approach, and listening to and fully taking into account what young people have to say (Ugwudike & Raynor 2013). These four principles clearly align with the general ethos of co-production and promote power-sharing and reciprocity between those with formal authority and those without. Translating these principles into youth justice practice relies almost entirely on the worker's effective use of self, such as their ability to engage in pro-social modelling and to clarify roles and expectations (Trotter 2022). However, the fourth principle – 'voice' – which entails listening to and fully taking into account what young people have to say, also depends significantly on a child's or young person's communication skills.

Snow and Powell (2002, 2004, 2005, 2008) compared the oral language skills of male youth justice clients to their non-offending peers and found that many are significantly disadvantaged with respect to their oral language competency. They tend to have poorer than average literacy and oral language skills, slow expressive vocabulary, poor auditory processing, and significant difficulty understanding abstract or figurative language. Importantly, this limits their ability to 'tell their story', as they struggle to construct narratives that are logical and coherent (Snow & Powell 2004, p. 223). Additionally, given their often negative prior experiences with authority figures and bureaucratic environments, some justice-involved young people can feel under pressure in interview-like situations, and this can further exacerbate their oral communication issues (Snow & Powell 2004). This means that workers wanting to 'give voice' to young people as a way to share power must consciously use more probing and structured questioning to elicit expanded responses. This relies on the worker's effective use of self, specifically their ability to use evidence-based practice skills, such as conveying non-judgemental empathy, using humour, listening reflectively, asking clarifying questions, and using non-verbal cues (Trotter & Evans 2023).

Space and time for co-production

To further encourage power-sharing, youth justice workers need to develop the skills to create a relaxed, naturalistic communication approach. Not only does the adult's way of being need to be relaxed and natural, but the context or setting for communication should also be as relaxed and natural as possible. This can be difficult to achieve in custodial or office settings, so trying to find or create space that supports this wherever possible is a challenge. While a young person's home environment might be appropriate, in most, but certainly not all, cases, locating the communication within a larger activity with which the child or young person is already familiar is a useful general approach (see Turner 2019). This can include a conversation in the car on the way to an activity, or at a local café or in a park. Of course, there are limitations to this too. Adults working with young people must consider their own safety and time availability. This limits the choice of locations, and more public spaces may compromise privacy. Nevertheless, allowing the young person, where possible, to nominate a preferred suitable time and space may be a pragmatic, direct, and effective way of sharing power.

Private and safe physical and psychological spaces are needed for effective power-sharing and co-production to occur. There are real challenges to achieving this in statutory youth justice, in detention centres, and community environments driven by risk mitigation. Questions of safety for service providers and users often revolve around spatial considerations, for example, the visibility and physical positioning of buildings, rooms, furniture, and exits (Johns *et al.* 2023). How justice spaces *feel* – through touch, sight, sound, smell, and even taste – is part of how they are experienced by both workers and clients, and how each understands their power, worth, and *identity* within these spaces. Who can get in and get out of spaces and who has to negotiate access or exit is an obvious component. Who is in the space *subject to* or *under* the terms of a legal mandate and who has *chosen* to be there and can enter or exit freely? Who has to book ahead for a visit, and who must rely on others to facilitate access to spaces? As Johns and colleagues (2023, p. 104) note: 'Having access to the 'right' people…or the institutional support to make a co-production project 'work' relies on certain kinds of power dynamics'.

Paradoxically, youth detention centres and community organisations may also be the only settings where there is adequate time and scope for more collective co-production work with youth justice clients (see Johns *et al.* 2023). Certainly a great deal of youth justice research is disproportionately carried out in custodial settings (Turner 2019), and much of the relevant co-production literature involves community, rather than statutory, organisations. Compared to adults, most children and young people spend a relatively short period of time on a legal order, as determined by the courts in accordance with sentencing and bail principles. This necessarily limits the nature and duration of a statutory youth justice worker's engagement with a child or young person, as the legal order is the *only* mandate or permission that the worker has for this. The focus of the engagement must therefore be directly relevant to the legal order and the agreed plan for addressing the young person's assessed risk of recidivism.

The tension between externally defined, linear time frames and the time needed for co-production in youth justice is not readily reconciled – if at all. Despite the typically rehabilitative focus of sentencing in youth justice, *time* to build relationships often gives way to other sentencing principles, like parsimony, proportionality, parity and totality. The time needed for and spent in building trust, within which human relationships develop and flourish, is essentially ignored. It is not often considered or measured in official youth justice metrics or mentioned in case notes or court reports. Hence, time can be a cost borne personally by those wanting to engage in co-production or power-sharing – literally, something that may be done *in your own time* (Johns *et al.* 2023). Herein lies some further pragmatic consideration. Where time does not permit the development of a trusting relationship between a youth justice worker and young person, should they instead focus on facilitating and supporting the young person to develop this elsewhere? It may be the most effective and ethical approach for a youth justice worker to take and points to the value of indirect practice, through brokerage, referral, linkage, service coordination, and advocacy. Successfully exiting the youth justice system is a main component of the rehabilitative ideal, and it may be the only way a justice-involved child or young person can have the time and space to genuinely engage in co-production.

Reflexive critical pragmatism

A reflexive approach that balances critical and pragmatic perspectives is useful and even necessary for practice in youth justice and other statutory contexts (Turner 2019). 'Practising reflexivity' (Taylor & White 2000) involves an explicit and critical examination of the kinds of knowledge used in practice and how this is applied to make sense of situations and proceedings. It is a continual and critical process of interpretation and reinterpretation to make new knowledge. Archer (2003, 2007) describes reflexivity as occurring through 'internal conversations with the self and potentially others', where we contemplate what we care about and how to bring this to fruition in contexts that are not of our own making. Reflexive practitioners must continually make 'boundary judgements' (Ulrich 1983); deciding what does and does not count as relevant facts and values. That is, determining: What *is* the case? and What *ought* to be the case? (Ulrich 2006).

Reflexive critical pragmatism is a framework that promotes the power-sharing ideal while simultaneously acknowledging the genuine power disparities that are inherent to adult–child relationships, especially within statutory youth justice practice contexts. It combines the practical, action-oriented focus of traditional pragmatism with the self-awareness and power critique inherent in critical theory and reflexivity (see Turner 2019). It blends critical, post-structural concerns about the power of discourse and representation and the socially constructed, situated, and emergent nature of knowledge with pragmatist understandings of inquiry, meaning and truth (Vannini 2008). Through a critical pragmatist lens, attention is narrowed to ethical and feasibility concerns. So, critical pragmatists must constantly ask reflective questions that stem from two lines of inquiry: (1) 'Am I being properly ethical and critical within my practice?' and (2) 'Is my practice feasible and necessarily pragmatic in nature?' (see Jordan 2012, p. 57). These questions, in attending to what *ought* to be, as well as what *is*, are core to a normative mode of reflexivity (Longhofer & Floersch 2012) and useful for navigating the ethical and practical challenges of *doing* co-production in statutory youth justice.

Acknowledging power

Co-production and its pursuit of equal power-sharing is, in and of itself, a worthy intention. There are clear ethical and legal imperatives for justice-involved children and young people to directly express and have their views heard about matters pertaining to them. It may help, for example, to realise the intentions of Article 12 of the UN Convention on the Rights of the Child, 1989, and to provide new and unique insights for youth justice policy and practice. However, the widespread adoption and diversity of co-production practices in human services settings are seen by many as a co-option and reduction of a 'truly radical and potentially powerful' concept to a 'buzzword ... rebadging ... service user involvement' (Cameron 2019, n.p.). While this may be so, the goals of service user involvement or collaborative practice – particularly with young mandated service users – are not lowly ones to aspire to. As this chapter has drawn out, there are significant challenges and complexities to sharing power in one-to-one relationships, let alone at the level of collective co-production. Arguably, this is also why co-production in youth justice typically takes an individual form.

Regardless of nomenclature, doing *with*, rather than *to* or *for*, a child or young person (Slay & Stephens 2013) has merit as both an evidence-based and ethical practice for youth justice (Trotter 2022; Turner 2019). However, ignoring or tokenistically 'mitigating' power imbalances is disingenuous, even akin to gaslighting. This is vividly illustrated by author and poet Lemn Sissay (2018) in his recounting of his personal experience as a child in statutory care:

> I was in a situation where I couldn't trust the people who were the adults who were there to care for me. They would say things to me, like um, "We need to give you a voice. We need to give you a voice so that you can tell us what you want. [...] Let me just get this right. A child who comes into care, *for* care...is then told that he or she needs a voice? So...he can tell the people that are supposed to care for him how they're supposed to care for him – and they can then get along with it? [...] Feedback is actually central...it's just that children in care are crash-test dummies quite often.

Sissay points to the important interplay between trust, participation, voice, and power and the relevance (but neglect) of practical approaches to participation, such as providing 'feedback'.

Notwithstanding opportunities, it is important to acknowledge that contextual and structural issues such as childism, managerialism, and the 'care' and 'control' tensions of statutory youth justice practice impede genuine, equal power-sharing. That is not to say these issues should simply be accepted. Rather, it is important that their existence and impact on power-sharing are made visible and transparent, especially with justice-involved children and young people. Ignoring uneven structural or relational power dynamics is at odds with procedural justice principles, such as conveying trustworthy motivations and 'voice'. As Phillips (1991, p. 134) notes: '[P]ower that is acknowledged can be subjected to mechanisms of democratic control; power that is denied can become unlimited and capricious'. Ensuring a justice-involved child or young person can *see* power is an act of emancipatory consciousness-raising that enables them to learn to use power – even if they do not have it.

References

Aged Care Guide, 2024. *Digital Publications: 25th Edition Aged Care Guide, Victoria [online]*. https://issuu.com/dpspublishing/docs/acg-vic-edition-24-complete_2_-links?fr=sMDc0YTYyOTA4Njc [Accessed 16 November 2025].

Archer, M., 2003. *Structure, Agency and the Internal Conversation*. Cambridge University Press, Cambridge.

Archer, M., 2007. *Making Our Way through the World*. Cambridge University Press, Cambridge.

Barry, M., 2013. Rational choice and responsibilisation in Youth Justice in Scotland: Whose evidence matters in evidence-based policy? *Howard Journal of Criminal Justice*, 52(4), 347–64.

Bogo, M., 2010. *Achieving Competence in Social Work through Field Education*. Toronto: University of Toronto Press.

Buck, G., Tomczak, P. and Quinn, K., 2022. This is how it feels: Activating lived experience in the penal voluntary sector. *The British Journal of Criminology*, 62(4), 822–839. https://doi.org/10.1093/bjc/azab102

Cameron, A., 2019. *Co-production – Radical Roots, Radical Results*. Blog Post. 10 November. https://allywritesblog.wordpress.com/2019/11/10/co-production-radical-roots-radical-results/

Case, S. and Hazel, N. eds., 2023. *Child First: Developing a New Youth Justice System*. Palgrave Macmillan, Cham.

Colwell, J. and Huth, C., 2010. *Unleashing the Power of Unconditional Respect: Transforming Law Enforcement and Police Training* (1st ed.). London: Routledge. https://doi.org/10.1201/EBK1420099744

De'Ath, S., Flynn, C. and Field-Pimm, M., 2018. Building knowledge of consumer participation in criminal justice in Australia: A case study. *International Journal for Crime, Justice & Social Democracy*, 7(1), 76–90.

Fox, C., Harrison, J., March, C. and Smith, A., 2018 Piloting different approaches to personalised offender management in the English criminal justice system, *International Review of Sociology*, 28(1), 35-61.

Hough, M., 2020. *Good Policing: Trust, Legitimacy and Authority*. Policy Press, Bristol.

Johns, D., Flynn, C., Hall, M., Spivakovsky, C. and Turner, S., 2023. *Co-production and Criminal Justice*. Routledge, London. https://doi.org/10.4324/9780429328657-11

Jordan, J., 2012. *Teaching Past the Test: A Pedagogy of Critical Pragmatism*. Thesis (Master of Science). University of North Texas.

Longhofer, J. and Floersch, J., 2012. The coming crisis in social work: Some thoughts on social work and science. *Research on Social Work Practice*, 22(5), 499–519.

Maruna, S., 2001. *Making Good: How Ex-Convicts Reform and Rebuild Their Lives*. American Psychological Association, Washington, District of Columbia.

Mazerolle, L. G., Sargeant, E., Cherney, A., Bennett, S., Murphy, K., Antrobus, E., and Martin, P., 2014. *Procedural Justice and Legitimacy in Policing*. New York: Springer.

Murphy, K., 2015. Does procedural justice matter to youth? Comparing adults' and youths' willingness to collaborate with police. *Policing and Society*, 25, 53–76. https://doi.org/10.1080/10439463.2013.802786

Phillips, A., 1991. *Engendering Democracy*. Polity Press, Cambridge.

Queensland Government, 2025. *Making Queensland Safer: Adult Crime, Adult Time Expands to 33 Offences [online]*. www.qld.gov.au/makingqldsafer/adult-crime-adult-time [Accessed 16 November 2025].

Sissay, L., 2018. *When All You Need is a Hug: Personal Experiences of the UK Care System*, June 2018. TEDx Liverpool. https://youtu.be/B88dCHJ9Rvg?si=PUPkQuKHql4DKa9E [Accessed 21 November 2025].

Slay, J. and Stephens, L., 2013. *Co-production in Mental Health: A Literature Review*. New Economics Foundation, London.

Snow, P. and Powell, M., 2002. *The Language Processing and Production Skills of Young Offenders: Implications for Enhancing Prevention and Intervention Strategies*. Report to the Criminology Research Council.

Snow, P. and Powell, M., 2004. Interviewing juvenile offenders: The importance of oral language competence. *Current Issues in Criminal Justice*, 16(2), 220–225.

Snow, P. and Powell, M., 2005. What's the story? An exploration of narrative language abilities in male juvenile offenders. *Psychology, Crime & Law*, 11(3), 239–253.

Snow, P. and Powell, M., 2008. Oral language competence, social skills and high-risk boys: What are juvenile offenders trying to tell us. *Children & Society*, 22(1), 16–28.

Taylor, C. and White, S., 2000. *Practising Reflexivity in Health and Welfare: Making Knowledge*. Open University Press, Buckingham.

Thom, K. and Burnside, D., 2018. Sharing power in criminal justice: The potential of co-production for offenders experiencing mental health and addictions in New Zealand. *International Journal of Mental Health Nursing*, 27, 1258–1265.

Trotter, C., 1995. Contamination theory and unpaid community work. *Australian & New Zealand Journal of Criminology*, 28(2), 163–177.

Trotter, C., 2022. *Working with Involuntary Clients: A Guide to Practice*. 4th ed. Taylor & Francis Group.

Trotter, C. and Evans, P., 2023. Developing evidence based practice skills in youth justice. *European Journal of Probation*, 15(2), 147–161. https://doi.org/10.1177/20662203231185088

Turner, S., 2019. *Case Management in Juvenile Justice: Clients' Perspectives*. Thesis (PhD). Monash University.

Turner, S., 2022. Giving voice: Communicating with young people to enhance police legitimacy and compliance. *In:* I. Bartkowiak-Théron, J, Clover, D. Martin, R. Southby and N. Crofts, eds. *Law Enforcement and Public Health: Partners for Community Safety and Wellbeing*. Springer, Cham, 75–82.

Turner, S. and Trotter, C., 2016. *Best Practice Principles for the Operation of Community Service Schemes: A Systematic Review of the Literature*. Corrections Victoria, Department of Justice, Melbourne.

Ugwudike, P. and Raynor, P. eds., 2013. *What Works in Offender Compliance: International Perspectives and Evidence-Based Practice*. Palgrave Macmillan, Houndmills, Basingstoke, Hampshire.

Ulrich, W., 1983. *Critical Heuristics of Social Planning: A New Approach To Practical Philosophy*. Haupt, Bern.

Ulrich, W., 2006. Theory and practice I: Beyond theory. (Reflections on critical pragmatism, Part 2). *Ulrich's Bimonthly*, Nov-Dec 2006. http://wulrich.com/bimonthly_november2006.html [Accessed 16 November 2025].

United Nations, 1989. Convention on the Rights of the Child, Office of the High Commissioner for Human Rights. www.ohchr.org/en/professionalinterest/pages/crc.aspx [Accessed 20 November 2025].

Vannini, P., 2008. Critical pragmatism. *In:* L.M. Given (ed.), *The SAGE Encyclopedia of Qualitative Research Methods*. Sage Publications, Thousand Oaks, 160–163.

Weaver, B., 2011. Co-Producing Community Justice: The Transformative Potential of Personalisation for Penal Sanctions. *The British Journal of Social Work*, 41(6), 1038-1057.

Weaver, B., Lightowler, C. and Moodie, K., 2019. Inclusive Justice - Co-producing Change: A Practical Guide to Service User Involvement in Community Justice. University of Strathclyde Glasgow. https://strathprints.strath.ac.uk/68901/1/Lightowler_Weaver_CYCJ_2019_Inclusive_justice_co_producing_change_a_practical_guide.pdf [Accessed 20 November 2025].

Young-Bruehl, E., 2009. Childism—Prejudice against children. *Contemporary Psychoanalysis*, 45(2), 251–265. https://doi.org/10.1080/00107530.2009.10745998

Young-Bruehl, E., 2012. *Childism: Confronting Prejudice against Children. Contemporary Psychoanalysis*. Yale, UK: University Press.

3

CHALLENGES IN CAPTURING THE AUTHENTIC VOICE OF THE 'UNCHILDLIKE CHILD'

Samantha Walker, Rebecca Oswald, and Sarah Soppitt

Introduction

Legally within the UK, 'childhood' encompasses anyone under the age of 18 (NSPCC, 2024). Yet, as a socially, politically, economically, and morally loaded concept, the notion of the child is inherently problematic in the context of youth justice (Aitken, 2001). Historical representations of childhood, as well as the persistent tensions surrounding the portrayal of children as both victims and offenders within the field of youth justice, have been widely discussed in the academic literature (see, for example, Fionda, 2005, or Hendrick, 2015). Such constructions have implications for the ways in which children's and young people's needs, experiences, and identities are understood[1]. This is particularly true of those young people whose experiences and behaviours diverge from such societal norms and who, as such, breach the boundaries between childhood and adulthood. These children and young people become what Aitken (2001) refers to as the 'unchildlike child'. While there is increased recognition that children engaged in serious violence are often *victims* of child criminal exploitation (CCE) and abuse (Marshall, 2023), children and young people involved in serious criminal activities, including serious youth violence (SYV), personify the 'unchildlike child'. While SYV is a complex issue which is often deep-rooted in a wide range of individual, interpersonal, and structural factors (Gray et al., 2021; Smith, 2019; Walker et al., 2026), and despite growing rhetoric for the need for 'Child First' approaches to working with justice-involved young people, young people engaged in SYV remain frequently subject to adultification bias and dealt with using punitive criminogenic measures (Day, 2023; Billingham and Irwin-Rogers, 2022).

DOI: 10.4324/9781003602996-5

In this chapter, we outline how children engaging in serious violence are constructed and responded to in policy and practice in England and Wales. Following a brief methodological overview of the studies which have contributed towards our discussions, we begin this chapter by exploring briefly how social constructions of childhood contribute towards ideas of the 'unchildlike child' and how children engaged in SYV – who, notwithstanding their various vulnerabilities, are often engaged in very unchildlike behaviours – come to personify this idea. Despite growing rhetoric for the need for 'Child First' approaches to working with justice-involved young people, we then move to demonstrate how young people engaged in SYV are frequently adultified. In the final section we move to explore how these complex tensions impact upon if and how the voices of these 'unchildlike children' are heard and the implications of this for co-production in youth justice.

While reflecting upon the various push and pull factors for young people into such activities, we explore the following key questions:

- What are the challenges of capturing the authentic voice of unchildlike children?
- How can we better represent childhood experiences without reinforcing stereotypes or pathologising young people and communities?
- To what extent are binary categories of 'child' and 'adult' helpful in responding to SYV?

Given the constraints of this chapter, we do not seek to provide all the answers to the above. Instead, it is hoped that the discussions presented here will act as a critical tool in thinking about how we conceptualise, understand, and co-produce work with young people engaging in unchildlike behaviours in meaningful ways that recognise their heterogeneity.

This paper draws on three research projects conducted in the North East of England between 2020 and 2024, each exploring SYV and CCE. Though independently conducted, the studies collectively aimed to understand the drivers of SYV and CCE in the region and identify effective responses to these issues. **Study 1** (2020–2022), funded by the Youth Justice Board (YJB), occurred during the COVID-19 pandemic and utilised innovative online methods (Oswald et al., 2022). **Study 2** (2023) was funded by a third-sector organisation supporting young people affected by exploitation. **Study 3** (2024) received funding from an Office for Police and Crime Commissioner and explored service provision in place for young people involved in and/or at risk of SYV and CCE. Ethical approval was granted for the projects, all of which adopted a mixed-methods approach.

The quantitative analysis across the three studies drew on service data aggregated from statutory agencies across the North East, relating to demographics, youth offending rates, social care, education, health metrics, and measures of deprivation. To deepen understanding, qualitative methods included semi-structured interviews with young people (studies 1 and 2) and stakeholders (studies 1, 2, and 3), which were supplemented by analysis of anonymised case files (studies 1 and 2). Across the three projects, 37 online interviews were conducted with frontline stakeholders who work with young people involved in and affected by SYV and CCE. These included professionals from third-sector organisations (n=9), police (n=5), youth justice services (n= 19), education (n=2), social care (n=2), and mental health services (n=1). In Studies 1 and 2, 14 young people aged 15–17 were interviewed, including thirteen males and one female. Eight participants were involved in SYV, six were at risk of involvement, and four had been victims of CCE. The analysis of 2,300 case files was used to support this data, revealing an ethnic distribution of 75% White British. In Study 1, most young people identified as White British, with an additional two identifying as White Eastern European. In Study 2, two young people identified as White Eastern European and two as Black African.

The qualitative data analysis in each of the three studies followed an inductive approach. Researchers conducted multiple readings of the raw data, developed codes, and identified key themes. The conceptualisation of children involved in or affected by SYV and CCE as the 'unchildlike child' – and the impact this has on how agencies respond to these issues – was not initially a primary focus of the projects. However, through the coding process, this emerged as a significant and distinct theme within the research findings.

We recognise the irony that, in a chapter emphasising the importance of youth participation and collaboration, direct excerpts from young people themselves are relatively scarce. This is not due to a lack of appreciation for their voices but rather reflects the nature of the research projects that informed this work. These projects were not explicitly designed to explore youth participation and collaboration, meaning that while young people's perspectives were valued, they were not the primary focus of data collection. Additionally, as this chapter will explore, the young people at the heart of these discussions often face multiple vulnerabilities and are considered marginalised, making direct engagement more challenging. As a result, while we were able to include insights from a small number of young participants, this chapter relies more heavily on the perspectives of frontline stakeholders who work closely with them.

Childhood and the 'unchildlike child': the case of SYV

Childhood is often assumed to be a natural and universal phase of life, defined primarily by biological age (Qvortrup, 1995). However, in reality, it is a socially and culturally constructed concept that varies across historical periods, geographical locations, and socio-economic contexts (James and

Prout, 1990). Social constructions of childhood also differ based on factors such as gender, class, and race, which shape the opportunities, protections, and expectations placed upon children (Zwozdiak-Myers, 2007). Although there is growing recognition that children are not a homogeneous group and that 'childhood' is neither a fixed nor universal experience (Goldson, 2004; Wagg, 1992), its construction has significant implications for how children and young people are perceived. Socio-cultural norms influence understandings of what it means to be a child and, more specifically, a 'good' child. In many contemporary Western contexts, childhood is largely framed as a period of innocence and dependency, sharply contrasted with adulthood (Goldman and Ronken, 2000). Subsequently, children – viewed as lacking self-sufficiency, agency, and intellectual capacity (Herring, 2023) – are positioned as dependent on adults for care (Fionda, 2005).

When children are seen as naturally innocent, growing up is perceived as a gradual loss of that purity, which is slowly replaced by an increasing capacity for adult tendencies towards immorality and wrongdoing (Fionda, 2005). Yet, contrary to such idealised constructions of childhood that emphasise children's vulnerability and the need to prolong their innocence, there is growing recognition of the potential threat that children pose to themselves and others. Some have even questioned the extent to which childhood has entered a state of crisis (Action for Children, 2019). This creates a paradox in which children are seen as both 'at risk' and inherently 'risky' (Brown, 2005), leading to the development of conflicting narratives in which children, as legal and moral subjects, are either the focus of welfare-based interventions aimed at safeguarding them or subjected to heightened regulation and control (Goldson, 2011). Indeed, when childhood is used as a framework for understanding broader moral and social issues, there are significant implications for how children's and young people's identities, needs, and experiences are recognised and interpreted (Aitken, 2001). Using the examples of visible working children and violent children, Aitken (2001) argues that children who disrupt traditional understandings of childhood innocence and dependency and who breach the boundaries between childhood and adulthood become the 'unchildlike child'.

While research shows that the social conditions that many child 'offenders' experience are intricate and often involve overlapping layers of social disadvantage (Goldson, 2000), justice-involved children – particularly those who engage in extreme acts of violence and criminality – personify this idea of the unchildlike child. Indeed, this contradiction between welfare responses and social control is arguably nowhere more evident than in the context of youth justice. SYV, for example, is a complex issue that is often deeply rooted in a wide range of individual, interpersonal, and structural factors (Gray et al., 2021; Smith, 2019; Walker et al., 2025). Children who perpetrate

SYV are more likely to have experienced adverse childhood experiences (ACEs), poor mental health, extreme trauma, and sexual exploitation than other justice-involved children (Children's Commissioner, 2019; Gray et al., 2021; Soppitt et al., 2022). Furthermore, there is increasing recognition that children engaged in SYV are themselves often victims of CCE and violence (Marshall, 2023; Oswald et al., 2024). Subsequently, the traditional dichotomies often drawn between the categories of 'adult' and 'child' and 'perpetrator/offender' and 'victim' do not necessarily reflect the realities of those they seek to represent.

This was acutely evident in the stories of the young people that were told as part of our research. Indeed, many young people's stories emphasised their awkward position as both 'perpetrator' and 'victim'. Young person 11, for example, who was too afraid to have their interview audio recorded for fear of repercussions, spoke about how he had been exploited and coerced into transporting substances since the age of 12. Like other young people we spoke with, he described being forced into 'trap' houses through cuckooing, where he was made to sell drugs for up to 15 hours a day. Furthermore, he and others had experienced both victimisation and perpetration of extreme violence. While many young people were on the periphery of violence, almost all spoke about violence as being something they felt was unavoidable and necessary:

> If someone's going to fight me, I'm not going to sit there and not fight back cos I think I'm going to get kicked out of college... if I don't fight back I'd look weak.
>
> *(Young person 8)*

> If I was in a situation where I thought I would be stabbed I would stab them first and kill them... I have been brought up to defend myself.
>
> *(Young person 7)*

As the next section will demonstrate, some agencies struggle to recognise violent children *as children*. However, some stakeholder interviews reinforced these experiences of harm and victimisation. As one third-sector caseworker explained:

> They [young people engaged in SYV] are often experiencing physical and sexual harm, they are being trafficked, there's threats not just to them but to their family members, people they care about.
>
> *(Stakeholder 24)*

Additionally, as we have argued elsewhere (Walker et al., 2025), all the young men we interviewed expressed a strong desire to support their families.

Reflecting a commitment to traditional masculine norms (see, for example, Ellis, 2016; O'Donnell et al., 2024), they aspired towards a very adult-centric role of 'provider':

> They talk about wanting to help out their families, they want to help mum and make sure she's not struggling, they want to help younger siblings have nice clothes, so they aren't bullied at school.
>
> *(Stakeholder 23)*

> Cause nowadays, all the teenagers, they've got someone big who got a line, they work for him for 3, 4 months, they make money [...]. Someone else who's the same age as him, he got maybe 5 pounds from his mom, and he sees his friend, going, putting food on his family's table, and he, he's taken food from his family's table, that's something what people don't like. You always like to put food on your table, you don't wanna take. So that's how people get involved.
>
> *(Young person 10)*

Ultimately, as evidenced above, children and young people involved in SYV and/or CCE are not only engaging in adult-like behaviours but are also exposed to experiences that many adults will *never* encounter. Yet, while young people who are engaged in SYV are often viewed through a lens of adult-like behaviour, they are rarely given the agency to influence the systems that govern them. As Goldson (2004) has argued, the social and political dimensions of the power relation between adult and child which feeds into decisions regarding whether and how to safeguard and control are so very often absent from analysis. To facilitate genuine co-production, power dynamics and capital deficits must be examined more closely to ensure that young people are not merely consulted but are recognised as experts in their own lives and are genuinely empowered in decision-making (Burns and Creaney, 2023). This begins with asking what agency do these unchildlike children have in deciding what policies and procedures are in place to support them? How, if at all, are their voices heard? And whose voices are we (not) listening to?

Responding to the unchildlike child: children First and offenders second?

Children who are involved in more serious crimes and encounter the youth justice system (YJS) are being recognised through CCE, and in particular, 'county lines' and illegal drug distribution, which contributes to SYV across the UK (Disley and Liddle, 2016; Home Affairs Committee, 2019; Densley et al., 2020). Marshall (2023) highlights that while the exploitation of children to commit criminal acts has a long history, the consolidation of the category of CCE can be connected to, among other factors, a broader shift in youth justice policy towards 'Child First' principles. Premised upon the notion that children should be viewed and treated as '*children first and offenders second*' (Taylor, 2016: 48), a Child First approach aims to challenge traditional adult-centric youth justice and the 'offenderisation' of children (Case and Bateman, 2020). A Child First approach forms the YJB's guiding principle for youth justice in England and Wales. The key tenets of this policy are that children who offend should be treated as 'children' by recognising their age and particular circumstances. By engaging in meaningful collaboration with children, interventions should be focused on promoting young people's strengths and capabilities to build a 'pro-social identity', which is intended to minimise criminogenic stigma (YJB, 2022).

Yet, despite this 'Child First' rhetoric, research shows that in practice, children involved in serious criminal activity, including violence, continue to be viewed from within a criminogenic lens, with the levels of social harm they have so often experienced regularly overlooked (Day, 2023; Billingham and Irwin-Rogers, 2022; Marshall, 2023). The difficulties in knowing how to place these 'unchildlike children' were evident in some of our discussions with practitioners across services:

> Police, health and social care, and education and there's some real struggles in terms of getting [some] agencies to see young people as victims when they are the ones holding the knife for example, when they're the ones who are being arrested for serious youth violence. To see them as children still, is still a struggle I think in lots of parts of the country.
>
> *(Stakeholder 29)*

As alluded to, research (Oswald et al., 2024; Soppitt et al., 2022) demonstrates that those young people who commit SYV are extremely vulnerable. However, the very serious nature of the crimes committed by these children is so antithetical to the assumptions around childhood 'innocence' that, rather than being evident of a child in extreme distress, it can lead to the responsibilisation and adultification of children who often presented the highest levels of need.

> You see a 15 year old who has seriously hurt another child—like repeatedly stabbed in the head another child—and they are on TikTok laughing about it; it is hard to hold that this is a child too and that this child is being exploited, and this child is being hurt, this child has been traumatised, and the very fact that they can do this kind of stuff without any kind of emotional impact is evidence of the trauma they've experienced.
>
> *(Stakeholder 29)*

There was further recognition in our research, as identified elsewhere, that biases influence perceptions of certain children as being more adult-like, leading to discriminatory treatment. As Davis and Marsh (2020) note, Black children are often perceived as more 'streetwise', more 'grown-up', less innocent, and less vulnerable than other children. A stakeholder also highlighted this issue during discussions about the distinctions drawn between young people identified as part of 'peer groups' and those associated with 'gangs' or 'organised crime groups', whose behaviours are more frequently viewed through a criminal and adult lens:

> Police had not recognised any organised crime groups [in this area] until about 4 or 5 years ago, and when they did they recognised two and they were both exclusively Black African. Actually, we had other groups... groups of white boys and young men who were involved in the same activities, also going by a name and they weren't receiving the same level of interest.
>
> *(Stakeholder 23)*

Despite these barriers, many agencies prioritised what they perceived to be a 'Child First' approach when working with children involved in SYV and CCE. However, they acknowledged some variation in how different agencies across the social sectors interpreted the 'Child First' principles. Recognising the extreme levels of risk associated with the activities the children had been drawn into – which often left them fearful of engaging with services or sharing information – some agencies avoided labelling them as 'difficult to engage' or 'unwilling to participate'. Instead, they refrained from placing responsibility on the children for this reluctance, acknowledging the complex circumstances they faced:

> We try to encourage all our services to think that 'we haven't been able to engage' young people as opposed to 'they chose not to engage'. So, we're not putting the responsibility back on children.
>
> *(Stakeholder 29)*

Some agencies demonstrated remarkable success in fostering engagement and participation. A notable example was a third-sector organisation that worked with young people deeply involved in SYV and gangs, where a significant proportion – one-third of their service users – were referred by peers. A critical factor in achieving this level of engagement was their nuanced approach to working with these 'unchildlike children', which embodies a flexible, needs-led model that extends support beyond the conventional legal definition of childhood. Recognising the complex and often traumatic backgrounds of the young people they support, the service avoids rigid timeframes in favour of continuity and responsiveness during young people's transition into adulthood. Central to their practice is the cultivation of trust and mutual respect. Aligning closely to the principles of co-production, young people are effectively viewed as 'partners' in creating meaningful and sustainable change. By valuing their experiential knowledge, this is achieved through the active involvement of young people when identifying risks and shaping their support pathways. Such an approach challenges traditional service delivery paradigms, recognises and prioritises individual agency, and affirms the importance of relational, participatory practice in supporting vulnerable youth.

Ultimately, while they avoided placing undue responsibility on these young people – many of whom were also victims of CCE – for circumstances beyond their control, they simultaneously showed respect for their experiences. They refrained from dismissing these young people as merely 'vulnerable children' in need of protection and making decisions on their behalf. Instead, they acknowledged their unique lived experiences and prioritised restoring a sense of agency to individuals whose autonomy had often been stripped away through exploitation:

> We take a strong safeguarding approach, and this involves believing what young people tell us, not questioning them, making sure young people know how their information will be used, writing up using young people's words… collaboratively making the most effective decisions… we don't see this approach in all agencies, not all treat young people with respect.
>
> *(Stakeholder 25)*

Crucially, therefore, our research suggests that despite being a population that might be distinctly 'unchildlike', a strong 'Child First' approach – built upon meaningful collaboration and co-production with children (Burns and Creaney, 2023) – is vital to supporting those involved in/impacted by SYV and CCE. This should involve active participation in the support they receive, with interventions informed by their voice and a recognition of the heterogeneity of their experiences – many of which are deeply upsetting and far removed from the idealised notion of childhood celebrated in Western culture. The next section shall explore how we can capture this authentic voice.

Youth participation: capturing the authentic voice of unchildlike children

As we have seen in the previous sections, for young people involved in, or at risk of involvement in, SYV, the violent perpetrator label is often more pervasive, and the condemnation greater, than the understanding given to the complex tensions that may exist in their lives. These complex tensions, which characterise the aetiology of youth crime – and serious violence in particular – can make it difficult to ensure that the voice of the child is heard and appropriately reflected in youth justice policy (Case et al., 2020). As discussed, the governments' 'Child First' approach aims to promote a justice system which sees children *as children* and places considerable emphasis on meaningful collaboration and co-production with young people (Burns and Creaney, 2023). Yet there are numerous challenges to the 'Child First' approach, not least the fact that many of the young people we look to for meaningful collaboration have experienced difficult childhoods in ways that many of us would find hard to comprehend. As the following stakeholders' comments highlight, many of these young people have found the process of looking for and securing support difficult (Burns and Creaney, 2023), subsequently eroding their trust in professionals:

> We made a deliberate attempt to invest a lot of time in a young person because we knew where he sat within the gang, we spent a long time building that relationship so he could trust us.
>
> *(Stakeholder 23)*

> Its about making sure that young person doesn't feel judged. They have a lot of distrust of professionals, often that they have been criminalised because of their exploitation.
>
> *(Stakeholder 24)*

This erosion of trust can develop from a feeling that they have not been listened to previously, that only part of their story was acknowledged, or a sense that they have not been supported appropriately by those they have shared their experiences with (Creaney, 2018). This, in addition to a fear of reprisals for speaking honestly (Ewenson et al., 2021; Scraton and Haydon, 2002), can make opening up to professionals difficult (Smithson and Jones, 2021).

Young people involved in or at risk of SYV are often involved with or have experience of a wide range of professionals. This can result in intervention fatigue and the development of a 'learnt script' (Worrall, 2012) or what McAllister and Carr (2014) refer to as 'strategies of responsibilisation' used by young people when retelling their story. As one stakeholder noted:

> I think unfortunately the young people we deal with have been dealt a lifetime of inconsistency. People that just don't stick around… or its people they can't trust.
>
> *(Stakeholder 21)*

Through discussions with peers, or by drawing upon their own experience, young people can develop a sense of mistrust, resulting in them relaying a narrative of what they *believe* others want to hear rather than what *needs* to be heard (Sandberg, 2010). Consequently, the narrative they present to professionals often doesn't reflect the totality of their lived experiences but rather the story they think they should tell.

> These young people often present as hyper-masculine, but when you get your relationship with them they're not, they are struggling with their emotional wellbeing, their self-image and identity… and a lot of times they just need someone to say it's not you, it's what's happened to you, or going on for you.
>
> *(Stakeholder 24)*

To circumnavigate this, alternative formats for young people to share their experiences have been sought. Music is one such medium that young people have used to express their lived experiences (Price et al., 2023). Throughout history, young people have consistently used music to express their lived experiences. While past examples include the Mods and Rockers of the 1960s and Punk in the 1970s, today, the genre known as 'drill' music – a sub-genre of hip-hop that emerged from the USA in the late 2010s – is popular among young people to discuss, among other things, experiences of 'gangs', violence, and crime. Through our research, we found some practitioners were utilising drill music as a medium to connect with and learn about the young people they were working with:

> It's important to ease them into conversations without it feeling threatening. [We] Might use the music as a way in. It's a medium they feel comfortable with so that we can talk about more difficult emotions and experiences.
>
> *(Stakeholder 24)*

While this is potentially helpful in breaking down those barriers, some suggest that caution is needed to avoid the misinterpretation of young people's experiences. Indeed, Ilan (2020) cautions that the literal reading of drill music by some professions can result in 'street illiteracy', which can reinforce existing suspicions and marginalisation of young people by those within the wider youth justice sector. This highlights the necessity of genuine co-production – where young people's perspectives and lived experiences shape the approach – rather than a tokenistic engagement that fails to grasp their realities. True co-production fosters deeper understanding, ensuring that support is meaningful and responsive rather than imposed from a detached professional standpoint (see, also, Johns et al., 2023).

To be successful, developing appropriate responses to SYV – which may range from reshaping public policy discourse to individual welfare interventions – requires a dialogue that is not dominated by practitioner and academic discourse but rather centres the voice of the young person and the totality of their experiences (Smithson and Jones, 2021). These voices are often difficult to hear, particularly by those who do not want to acknowledge the wider societal failures which are all too often reflected in the violent actions of young people and those who continue to work within a risk-oriented framework (Hampson et al., 2024). In our research, for example, we found that 1 in 3 young people involved in SYV were open to Children's Social Care at the time of the offence (Soppitt et al., 2022). As others have indicated (see, for example, Hampson et al., 2024), one of the more challenging aspects of co-production and co-design, then, is considering *whose* voice(s) we are aiming to capture. As alluded to previously, there is a danger that the voices of young people are seen as homogeneous. This is problematic not only in terms of how we value the narrative and life experiences of young people, but also in terms of who it is that we are listening to (Sandberg, 2010). The risk here is that co-production becomes tokenistic, capturing only the voices of young people who are seen as 'easier' to engage with at the expense of those who have relevant understanding and experience. Again, this sense of some young people being overlooked in broader dialogues was alluded to in conversations with stakeholders:

> Lots of the young people that we're working with will be young people that other people have written off as young people that they can't engage with, hard-to-reach, all those kinds of things.
>
> *(Stakeholder 29)*

There is a risk that practitioners may prioritise working with young people who are already part of formalised groups and accustomed to engagement activities, such as youth parliaments or similar programmes, or those who are more easily accessible. However, the voices of these young people are unlikely to reflect the experiences of those affected by CCE and SYV.

When considering whom we are working with and whose voices we are collecting, there are several variables we need to take into account. Developing trust with young people requires ensuring that the integrity of their story is fully acknowledged, that there is parity between what is being said and what is being heard, and, crucially, that the young person understands what will happen with the information they share. This foundation must underpin the approach to supporting them. Equally important is recognising that past experiences of being let down by professionals, family members, or carers may influence their willingness to trust and engage. Additionally, as existing research has acknowledged, many justice-experienced young people have encountered ACEs and past trauma, which are often central to understanding their offending behaviours (Fox et al., 2015; Gray et al., 2021). For some – such as those who may not be in the country legally or who are awaiting notification regarding their right to remain – the risk of fully sharing their story may feel too great. For others, the logistics of telling their story can pose challenges. For example, a disproportionate number of justice-experienced young people are neurodiverse and may struggle with concentration, social communication, and language and narrative skills (Kirby, 2021; Soppitt et al., forthcoming). In addition, English may not be their first or dominant language, further complicating their ability to share and relive experiences.

Again, these challenges were reflected in our research findings. Indeed, in Study 3, 100% of the children who had committed serious violence and undergone an assessment by youth justice professionals were identified as having speech and language difficulties. This led to practitioners raising concerns as these young people approached their eighteenth birthday. As one practitioner noted:

> We are coming from a safeguarding point of view, but then its 'ok, you're 18 now it's not safeguarding anymore you're now a perpetrator!'.
>
> *(Stakeholder 23)*

Ultimately, in whatever format the young person's story is told, it is vital that practitioners acknowledge that young people understand and make sense of the world in a unique way, reinforcing the need for co-production. As discussed above, this is crucial in avoiding the misinterpretation of young people's experiences and viewing them through the lens of a childhood we expect them to have had, rather than the one they actually lived.

Discussion: the need to capture their authentic voices

Children and young people involved in SYV and/or who have been criminally exploited not only engage in adult-like behaviours but are also exposed to experiences that many adults will never encounter. The nature of their offences and the circumstances into which they have been drawn make them 'unchildlike children', challenging typical Western notions of childhood as a time of innocence and dependence. These challenges underscore the urgent need for a co-production approach when working with young people affected by SYV and CCE. Such an approach must strike a careful balance – avoiding the undue placement of responsibility on young people for circumstances beyond their control while fostering a sense of agency and autonomy, qualities often stripped from them through exploitation.

Crucial to any attempt to work collaboratively with children impacted by SYV and/or CCE is the need to capture their authentic voices. As Aitken asserts:

> Childhood is an adult abstraction suggesting a state of being, whereas the study of children is really the study of a group of persons based on a search for the voice of those persons. But there is no authentic or just voice for childhood because the adult world dominates that of the child.
>
> *(2001: 119–20)*

Searching for the voices of young people affected by SYV and CCE requires practitioners to adopt principles of consistency, trust, and longevity in their work. Keeping these young people safe from harm, violence, and exploitation requires more than tokenistic engagement; it demands an approach shaped by and tailored towards their perspectives and lived experiences. It also necessitates recognising that so-called 'unchildlike behaviours' often stem from ACEs, trauma, and social inequalities rather than deliberate deviance.

A truly collaborative approach also hinges on relationships. As Firmin et al. (2024) and Soppitt et al. (2022) discuss, many young people who are exploited and face risks outside the home are 'known to services' – meaning they appear in the records and datasets of multiple public agencies as identifiable 'risks' requiring management. However, far fewer are genuinely 'known by professionals' in the sense of having reciprocal, caring relationships with those who work collaboratively to understand their realities and help keep them safe. A key barrier to effective engagement is the assumption that a risk-based approach is necessary for young people involved in SYV and/or CCE – where their choices are seen as needing control rather than empowerment, leaving little room for their participation and collaboration. This approach is based on a fundamental misconception – exemplified by the 'unchildlike child' dilemma discussed in this chapter – that young people involved in SYV, CCE, and associated risky behaviours have freely chosen this path and, therefore, must have their choices constrained and managed to prevent further harm. It fails to recognise that the social conditions in which many of these marginalised young people live have so severely restricted their agency that engaging in such activities may become one of their only means to meet fundamental needs.

Note

1 Reflecting the complexities of framing 'childhood', 'adolescence', and 'adulthood' and recognising the conceptual limitations of such terminology, throughout this chapter, we use 'children' and 'young people' interchangeably.

References

Action for Children (2019) *Childhood in Crisis*. Action for Children [Online] Available at: www.actionforchildren.org.uk/media-centre/childhood-in-crisis/ (Accessed 15th January 2025).

Aitken, S.C. (2001) Global crises of childhood: Rights, justice and the unchildlike child. *Area*, 33(2): pp. 119–127.

Billingham, L. and Irwin-Rogers, K. (2022) *Against Youth Violence: A Social Harm Perspective*. Bristol: Bristol University Press.

Brown, S. (2005) *Understanding Youth and Crime: Listening to Youth?* Berkshire: Open University Press.

Burns, S. and Creaney, S (2023) Embracing children's voices: Transforming youth justice practice through co-production and child first participation, in Case, S. and Neil, H. (Eds.) *Child First: Developing a New Youth Justice System*. London: Palgrave Macmillan.

Case, S. and Bateman, T. (2020) The punitive transition in youth justice: Reconstructing the child as offender. *Children & Society*, 34(6): pp.475–491.

Case, S., Haines, K., Creaney, S., Coleman, N., Little, R. and Worrall, V. (2020) Trusting children to enhance youth justice policy: The importance and value of children's voices. *Youth Voice Journal*, 2020(SI): pp. 25–40.

Children's Commissioner (2019) *Keeping Kids Safe: Improving Safeguarding Responses to Gang Violence and Criminal Exploitation*. [Online] Available at: www.childrenscommissioner.gov.uk/wp-content/uploads/2019/02/CCO-Gangs .pdf (Accessed 16th January 2025).

Creaney, S. (2018) Children's voices—are we listening? Progressing peer mentoring in the youth justice system. *Child Care in Practice*, 26(1): pp. 22–37.

Davis, J. and Marsh, N. (2020) Boys to men: The cost of 'adultification' in safeguarding responses to Black boys. *Critical and Radical Social Work*, 8(2): pp. 255–259.

Day, A. (2023) 'It's a hard balance to find': The perspectives of youth justice practitioners in england on the place of 'risk' in an emerging 'child-first' world. *Youth Justice*, 23(1): pp. 58–75.

Densley, J., Deuchar, R. and Harding, S. (2020) An introduction to gangs and serious youth violence in the United Kingdom. *Youth Justice*, 20(1–2): pp. 3–10.

Disley, E. and Liddle, M. (2016) *Local Perspectives in Ending Gang and Youth Violence Areas: Perceptions of the Nature of Urban Street Gangs*. [Online] Available at: https://assets.publishing.service.gov.uk/government/uploads/system/uploads/attachment_data/file/491802/horr88.pdf (Accessed 16th January 2025).

Ellis A (2016) *Men, Masculinities and Violence: An Ethnographic Study*. Oxon: Routledge.

Ewenson, L. and Naylor, B. (2021) Protecting human rights in youth detention: Listening to the voices of children and young people in detention. *Australian Journal of Human Rights*, 27(1): pp. 97–119.

Fionda, J. (2005) *Devils and Angels: Youth, Policy and Crime*. Oxford: Hart Publishing.

Firmin, C., Langhoff, K., Eyal-Lubling, R., Maglajlic, R.A. and Lefevre, M. (2024) 'Known to services' or 'Known by professionals': Relationality at the core of trauma-informed responses to extra-familial harm. *Children and Youth Services Review*, 160: p. 107595.

Fox, B.H., Perez, N., Cass, E., Baglivio, M.T. and Epps, N. (2015) Trauma changes everything: Examining the relationship between adverse childhood experiences and serious, violent, and chronic juvenile offenders. *Child Abuse & Neglect*, 46: pp. 163–173.

Goldman, J. and Ronken, C. (2000) The concept of childhood. [Online] *Project AXIS: Child sexual abuse in Queensland*. Available at: www.ccc.qld.gov.au/sites/default/files/2020-02/Project-AXIS-Volume-4-Selected-research-papers-Report-2000.pdf (Accessed 16th January 2025).

Goldson, B (2000) Simple toughness meets tough complexity. *Criminal Justice Matters*, 41: pp. 4–5.

Goldson, B. (2004) Children, crime and the state: An introduction, in Goldson, B., Lavalette, M. and McKechnie, J (Eds.) *Children, Welfare and the State*. London: Sage.

Goldson, B. (2011) Youth in crisis? in Goldson, B. (Ed.) *Youth in Crisis? 'Gangs', Territoriality and Violence*. Oxon: Routledge.

Gray, P., Smithson, H. and Jump, D. (2021) *Serious Youth Violence and its Relationship with Adverse Childhood Experiences*. Manchester: Manchester Metropolitan University.

Hampson, K., Creaney, S. and Burns, S. (2024) Transforming the balance of power? Child first collaboration: A conceptual analysis. *Societies*, 14(8): pp. 138.

Hendrick, H. (2015) Histories of youth crime and youth justice, in Goldson, B. and Muncie, J. (Eds.) *Youth Crime & Justice: 2nd Edition*. London: Sage.

Herring, J. (2023) Vulnerability and children's rights. *International Journal for the Semiotics of Law*, 36: pp. 1509–1527.

Home Affairs Committee (2019) *Serious Youth Violence. HC 1016*. [Online] Available at: https://publications.parliament.uk/pa/cm201719/cmselect/cmhaff/1016/1016.pdf (Accessed 15th January 2024).

Ilan, J. (2020) Digital street culture decoded: Why criminalizing drill music is street illiterate and counterproductive. *The British Journal of Criminology*, 60(4): pp. 994–1013.

James, A. and Prout, A. (1990) *Constructing and Reconstructing Childhood: Contemporary Issues in the Sociological Study of Childhood*. London: Falmer Press.

Johns, D., Flynn, C., Hall, M., Spivakovsky, C. and Turner, S. (2023) *Co-production and Criminal Justice*. Oxon: Routledge.

Kirby, A. (2021) *Neurodiversity a Whole-Child Approach for Youth Justice*. Manchester: HM Inspectorate of Probation.

Marshall, H. (2023) Victims first? Examining the place of 'child criminal exploitation within 'Child First' youth justice. *Children and Society*, 37(4): pp. 1156–1170.

McAlister, S. and Carr, N. (2014) Experiences of youth justice: Youth justice discourses and their multiple effects. *Youth Justice*, 14(3): pp. 241–254.

NSPCC (2024) *Children and the Law*. [Online] Available at: https://learning.nspcc.org.uk/child-protection-system/children-the-law#:~:text=Parents%20of%20under%2D16%2Dyear,child%20until%20they%20reach%2018 (Accessed 3rd March 2025).

O'Donnell, S., Taylor, P., Vincent, C.D., Scott-Storey, K., Wuest, J. and Malcolm, J. (2024) Masculinity and violence interconnectedness: Defining and reconciling the gender paradox among men with cumulative lifetime violence histories. *Sage Open*, 14(3): pp. 1–13.

Oswald, R., Soppitt, S., Spencer, N., Powell, L., Richardson, C. and Coombs, S. (2022) 'Safe spaces and places': The value of design-led methodologies in developing online narratives. *International Journal of Social Research Methodology*, 27(3): pp. 327–340.

Oswald, R., Soppitt, S., Walker, S. and Irving, A. (2024) *Improving the Hope of Young People Impacted by Serious Violence and Child Criminal Exploitation: Full Report May 2024*. Northumbria University: Newcastle Upon Tyne.

Price, J., Wilkinson, D. and Crossley, C. (2023) Children and young peoples' lyrics and voices capturing their experiences within youth justice services. *Safer Communities*, 22(3): pp. 186–199.

Qvortrup, J. (1995) Childhood in Europe: A new field of social research, in Chisholm, L., Buchner, P., Kruger, H.H. and du Bois-Reymond, M. (Eds.) *Growing up in Europe: Contemporary Horizons in Childhood and Youth Studies*. Berlin: Walter de Gruyter.

Scraton, P. and Haydon, D. (2002) Challenging the Criminalization of Children and Young People, in Muncie, J., Hughes, G. and McLaughlin, E (Eds.) *Youth Justice: Critical Readings*. London: Sage.

Sandberg, S. (2010) What can "lies" tell us about life? Notes towards a framework of narrative criminology. *Journal of criminal justice education*, 21(4): pp.447–465.

Smithson, H. and Jones, A. (2021) Co-creating youth justice practice with young people: Tackling power dynamics and enabling transformative action. *Children & Society*, 35(3): pp.348–362.

Smith, N. (2019) *Back to School? Breaking the Link Between School Exclusions and Knife Crime: All-Parliamentary Group on Knife Crime*. London: Barnardo's.

Soppitt, S., Oswald, R., Powell, L., Spencer, N. and Richardson, C. (2022) *Serious Youth Violence and First Time Entrants to the Youth Justice Service in Newcastle-Upon-Tyne: Serious Youth Violence Pathfinder (April 2022)*. Newcastle Upon Tyne: Newcastle City Council.

Soppitt, S., Oswald, R., Walker, S. and Cosgrove, F. (Forthcoming) *A Vision for Lasting Change: Shaping Durham and Darlington's Support for Young People*. Durham: Durham Office for the Police and Crime Commissioner.

Taylor, C. (2016) *Review of the Youth Justice System in England and Wales* [Online] Available at: https://assets.publishing.service.gov.uk/media/5a7ffc81ed915d74e622bcdb/youth-justice-review-final-report-print.pdf (Accessed 16th January 2025).

Youth Justice Board (2022) *A Guide to Child First* [Online] Available at: https://yjresourcehub.uk/images/YJB/Child_First_Overview_and_Guide_April_2022_YJB.pdf (Accessed 15th January 2024).

Wagg, S. (1992) I blame the parents: Childhood and politics in modern Britain. *Sociology Review*, 1(4): pp.10–15.

Walker, S., Soppitt, S. and Oswald, R. (2025) The role of 'place' in understanding the drivers of serious youth violence: An examination of identity, territorialism, and community, *accepted for publication in Criminology and Criminal Justice*.

Worrall, J. (2012) *Why Did You Do It?: Explanations for Offending by Young Offenders in Their Own Words*. Hampshire: Waterside Press.

Zwozdiak-Myers, P. (2007) *Childhood and Youth Studies*. London: Sage.

4

CO-PRODUCTION AND HARM REDUCTION

Collaborating *with* children assessed as 'high risk'

Sean Creaney and Samantha Burns

Introduction

The chapter aims to problematise the use of co-production in the context of risk management processes in youth justice across England, by exploring the extent to which co-production can help resolve tensions that characterise the high-risk multi-agency panel process. Co-production is a contested term, broadly describing activities that centre around co-design and joint implementation of initiatives, with a quest to create equal partnerships that potentially benefit children, professionals, and other relevant parties (Johns et al., 2022). However, tensions in youth justice mean co-production is difficult to navigate between being respectful of children's participatory rights (Yin, 2024) and using surveillance and monitoring to limit future criminality or harmful behaviours. The chapter focuses on key challenges affecting youth justice professionals, when assessing and managing risk alongside promoting children's voices and embedding participatory rights-based practices (Burns and Creaney, 2023; Day, 2023).

Youth Justice Service 'high-risk' management panels are a multi-agency coordinated approach to monitor and address concerns related to behaviour, harm, safety, and well-being (YJB, 2022; Burns and Creaney, 2023). These arrangements are multi-disciplinary, focused on public protection and harm reduction, involving senior leaders within youth justice settings and other appropriate personnel from youth justice, police, and children's social care (YJB, 2022). There is undoubtedly a degree of justification (i.e. to protect the community from harm) to sustain a community protection focus within 'high-risk' management panels.

DOI: 10.4324/9781003602996-6

Despite acknowledgement of the relevance of co-production, these arrangements are deemed necessary to manage complex, multi-faceted problems impacting on the lives of children and young people. The panels oversee the programmes of work being done to address offending behaviour, harm, and safety issues. A major issue is that these processes are still adult-centric, not only marginalising the voice of the child but also paying little regard to structural inequalities. The multi-agency arrangements appear preoccupied with public safety concerns and victims' needs, leaving children relatively powerless. The use of co-production in high-risk panels has been scarcely analysed, which denies children a role in safely and meaningfully co-producing this type of practice (Creaney and Burns, 2025). The 'high-risk' status assigned to children, decided upon through assessments, reports, and professional judgement, can legitimise their exclusion from the process and can stifle their sense of independence and agency. Within this context, they can become a passive recipient as opposed to a co-creator of knowledge. This chapter outlines key principles of co-production, including trust and safe spaces, which are pivotal when conceptualising, designing, and implementing co-production approaches and initiatives with children assessed as high risk.

Co-production could be one way to address tensions associated with deficit-based aspects of the community protection model and prosocial features of a Child First approach. The chapter offers original insight into how professionals, working within a multi-agency context, interpret and implement Child First principles within a high-risk-focused environment. The chapter aims to address the following objectives:

- Examine how professionals, working within a multi-agency context, interpret and implement Child First principles within a high-risk-focused environment.
- Problematise the use of co-production in the context of risk management processes in youth justice.
- Evaluate the benefits and challenges of a co-productive approach, as a legitimate or possible endeavour, with children assessed as 'high-risk'.

Child First in youth justice

In response to concerns that the Youth Justice System in England and Wales was operating without any consistent rationale (see, for example, Muncie, 2006: 771), Child First has now become the 'strategic approach and central guiding principle' of the Youth Justice Board (YJB, 2021). Key features include a focus on children's rights, pro-social responses, and participatory collaborative practices. Notwithstanding the lack of attention placed on the meaning and uses of these concepts in practice, Child First principles pertain to seeing children as children and working collaboratively with them in a strengths-based way to facilitate their meaningful involvement in youth justice processes (YJB, 2025). Child First was adopted by the Youth Justice Board (YJB) to ensure children's voices remain at the heart of the design, delivery, and evaluation of youth justice services (Case and Browning, 2021a, 2021b). This framework is an alternative to a deficit-based approach, especially the use of sanctions and punishments, as they can result in children feeling judged, marginalised, and disempowered (Case and Hazel, 2023). Practitioners are expected to incorporate the Child First principles into policy development at the local level, embrace the YJB vision, and apply the tenets into practice at the point of youth justice service delivery (Case and Hazel, 2023; YJB, 2021).

Tenet 3 of Child First is 'collaboration' which includes constructive, non-criminalising, and socially inclusive participative approaches (YJB, 2021). This tenet, has relatability with co-production (Brady, 2020; Loeffler and Bovaird, 2021; SCIE, 2022; Tisdall, 2017). However, Child First collaboration can be difficult to operationalise in contexts where issues of power, inequalities, and punishment weigh heavily (McCulloch, 2021). This environment can constrain opportunities for children to contribute to the decision-making process since there remains an expectation to identify and manage the risk young people pose, which can lead to judgements and labels being applied (see Smith and Gray, 2019). These issues are not confined to an English or Welsh context. Within Canadian child welfare systems, Khan and Ungar (2025: 1538) raise concern at the number of children feeling excluded from casework and decision-making processes.This is most salient when children are assessed as 'high risk' of future offending or causing serious harm, and tend to be denied the option to adopt the role of partner in the process, limiting opportunities to co-produce mutually agreed goals (Creaney and Burns, 2025; McCulloch, 2021). Thus, despite a commitment to the collaboration principle, it can be difficult to fully embrace this philosophy and implement Child First policy into youth justice practice. This difficulty reflects a hybrid culture of harm reduction, a welfare/justice binary, and the risk/public protection nexus (Day, 2023), creating challenges of working in a co-produced way with children assessed as high risk (Creaney and Burns, 2024).

High-risk management panels in youth justice

Youth justice service high-risk panels are multi-agency coordinated responses to monitor immediate concerns related to children's high-risk behaviour. These panels involve specialist workers from multiple systems and agencies working together, including youth justice services, police, social work, healthcare, and education, to minimise the likelihood of children engaging in further offending and/or engaging in self-harming behaviours (Creaney and Burns, 2024). There has been little exploration of how co-production principles can be realised within high-risk management processes. While a significant aim of high-risk panels is to ensure professional responses are guided by judgements on future risk of criminality, questions remain about the level or type of child participation in the decision-making process.

Risk assessment and professional decision making

Children assessed as 'high risk' are viewed as 'posing a risk' underpinned by a deficit-based discourse (Armstrong, 2004, 2006) which appears fundamentally at odds with the tenets associated with Child First. The term 'high-risk' is contested, and its use is potentially problematic in a Child First context due to a focus on the child's deficits. Nevertheless, it tends to be referred to when there is a high likelihood of harm being caused either to the child or the community (YJB, 2022). In other words, 'high risk' children are vulnerable and in need of youth justice supervision and/or present a significant risk of harm to the community.

Risk-averse attitudes prevail to address issues associated with the gravity of harm children have caused (Creaney and Burns, 2025). Professionals within high-risk panels have autonomy to decide upon measures that can limit or reduce the risk of harm. Meanwhile, community protection principles sit uneasily against the Child First vision and thus can obstruct co-production in practice, denying opportunities for children to adopt a key decision-maker role and meaningfully shape the design and delivery of services (Hampson et al., 2024). Consequently, this process appears to hinder the potential for children's participation, inclusion, and integration into key decision-making processes.

Implications for children assessed as 'High Risk'

There is a need to further investigate the purposes and dynamics of multi-agency high-risk panels, to uncover the factors that help or hinder the use of co-production principles within these spaces.There is a noticeable disconnect between rhetoric and reality, as co-production is difficult to square with a risk-focused mindset (Case and Smith, 2023; Gray and Smith, 2024). High-risk management panels do not appear to have the facility for the child to meaningfully take part in a co-produced endeavour (Creaney and Burns, 2024). While risk-based practices tend to focus on past behaviours and the utilisation of measures to restrict opportunities to engage in future harmful behaviours, Child First is premised on ideals of a strengths-based, forward-facing philosophy that takes account of young people's interests and perspectives (Haines and Case, 2015). For co-production to operate effectively, 'high risk' panels need to be redesigned to ensure there is a balance of power. However, there continue to be operational and strategic challenges to keeping both children and the public safe, as will be explored within the next section of this chapter.

The YJB (2022) case management guidance defines serious harm as 'death or serious personal injury, whether physical or psychological'. The guidance also states that the risk of serious harm is the likelihood and imminence of this happening and the impact if it did (see YJB, 2022). The language of risk/public protection is dominant within high-risk panels. Such discourse and associated frameworks can constrain the development of participatory practices. Risk is a contested concept (see CYCJ, 2024). Definitional clarity remains important. Risk has been separated out into key domains, including risk of reoffending, risk of harm to others, and risk of self-harming behaviours (Creaney and Burns, 2025). Professionals use the AssetPlus framework to judge the potential occurrence of future problems, determining risk levels related to serious harm to the public and/or self-harming behaviours (Smith and Paddock, 2025). In relation to children who are considered to pose a significant risk of harm to the public, a reductive approach may be adopted, resulting in a defensive practice. This can limit the scope for child involvement in the process. Certain conditions imposed in high-risk panels may violate children's participatory rights (Creaney and Burns, 2024).

While it is important to be explicit about how children can participate through prioritising their interests and preferences, levels of involvement vary depending on a myriad of factors. As alluded to, the case management guidance produced by the YJB encourages professionals to capture the perspective of the child when detecting concerns about risk of harm to the child or wider community (YJB, 2022). However, there is a lack of detail about the expected level and nature of the child's involvement in multi-agency arrangements, including how to ensure children are kept informed and consulted during the process. It is of concern that case managers may experience a sense of uneasiness about sharing power and delegating decisions to children, especially when there are complex issues at play, including an ethical and legal responsibility to manage safeguarding concerns (Creaney and Burns, 2024).

The function of high-risk panels appears to be aligned to a 'Community Protection Model' (Williamson and Connelly, 2000: 106) due to a principal focus on the use of surveillance and control alongside sanctions and punishment to prevent future victims and to satisfy the needs and perceived concerns of the harmed person (see Creaney and Burns, 2024; Kemshall and Wood, 2009). There is a degree of uncertainty regarding the extent to which Child First tenets can be applied within a high-risk management environment that is underpinned by community protection principles (i.e. regulation, surveillance, and monitoring) (Muncie, 2006: 781). For example, at times, professionals may need to invoke sanctions for non-compliance and instigate measures of control to contain potential threats to the public (Creaney, 2020), limiting opportunities for professionals to be creative, imaginative, inclusive, or participative in their risk management processes.

The issue of how to safely and meaningfully involve children within multi-agency high-risk panels has been seldom explored. There appear to be complex tensions between community protection principles and the tenets of the Child First approach. This can create challenges in terms of developing child-centred practices. Furthermore, professionals also have a responsibility to ensure the needs of the victim remain at the forefront (Gov.uk, 2025). This is especially important in the light of the new HM Inspectorate of Probation Victims' Standard, which is focused on ensuring victims remain at the heart of the process, that their needs are addressed and that they receive high-quality support and guidance from youth justice services. This can prohibit reflections on ways to involve the child in the process, as one practitioner illustrates from a study into the perspectives of professionals working with children and young people identified and assessed as 'high risk':

> *When you get into some of the practical realities of some of the young people, we have responsibility for, and are charged by the court to manage the risk the young people present and sometimes the risk present is high, like high risk of [...] violence, and we also have to be tied to the victims' code of practice to keep the victim's voice central, and usually the victims are other children themselves. Then you layer on sensitive and confidential information that might be brought into high-risk meetings, by police officers for example.*
>
> *(Youth justice practitioner, Peer Power Youth, 2021)*

Despite claims of a paradigm shift away from risk towards child-friendly practices (see Case and Hazel, 2023), child collaboration can be eclipsed by security/protection concerns, especially in the wake of a further serious offence. There may be heightened anxiety around children's safety and prioritisation of risk-reduction strategies and techniques (Tuddenham, 2000; Farrow et al., 2007), which implicitly or explicitly deny opportunities for children to exercise personal agency. Added to this, children tend to be viewed as rational beings, responsibilised, and held accountable for their actions and expected to change their behaviour, taking less account of wider social and system harms influencing their life chances (Creaney and Burns, 2025). However, children can be empowered to make decisions as part of a co-produced approach that takes account of social and economic difficulties, especially when professionals trust children to adopt a leadership role within multi-agency forums or case management processes (see Khan and Ungar, 2025). Key features of co-production include professionals embracing a facilitator role as opposed to adopting a position that instructs children to complete certain tasks decided upon by professionals (see MacLachlan et al., 2024). However, a pressing concern that warrants further investigation is how to nurture a child's sense of autonomy and navigate or address dynamics of power between professionals and children within multi-agency environments.

Opportunities for co-producing 'high-risk' panels

Mutual trust between the child and practitioner is key in terms of a co-produced approach (Social Care Institute for Excellence, 2022). Yet, it is necessary to note that children and young people may hold a distrust of authority, having previously experienced system harms (Creaney et al., 2024; Moore et al., 2025; Weaver et al., 2024). However, practitioners may be anxious about managing the risk of harm due to children being viewed as a danger to society. In this climate, such attitudes or cultures can contribute to the development of a risk-averse practice, spawning restrictive as opposed to enabling strategies (Creaney and Case, 2021; Goldson, 2011: 4). In principle, advocates for a co-produced practice with children argue that it can lead to power redistribution, democratise the decision-making process, and present golden opportunities to actualise their participatory rights (Tisdall, 2017; Burns, 2019). Yet, this can be undermined by a process that excludes young people from participating directly in processes. Such risk-averse mentalities may persist, especially following a death or serious injury, limiting opportunities for the child to express their own narratives and ideas (Burns and Creaney, 2023). One professional, interviewed as part of the Peer Power Youth (2021) study into how children perceive and experience participation, or lack thereof, in decision-making processes, reflected upon the importance of creating a safe space for children to feel confident exercising agency:

> *I have learnt we need to create safe spaces for people to talk, and it's the high risk [children] who are really the most important to get feedback from – why are they high risk in the first place or what would have helped them within the situation, or what intervention, or when would it have been useful? – you can't plan your services effectively around it otherwise.*
> *(Youth justice practitioner, Peer Power Youth, 2021)*

It is important to note that inviting children into high-risk panels may not always be the most appropriate action. For example, the experience may cause further harm in children's lives due to the process being adult-centric and retraumatising as opposed to child-friendly and person-centred (Burns and Creaney, 2023). The high-risk panel process could feel like a form of punishment, contrary to Child First principles, which may adversely affect children's self-concept, generating feelings of being 'othered' (Goldson, 2010). Therefore, it appears changes to the processes and procedures of high-risk panels are urgently needed to ensure they are democratic and inclusive, enabling children to engage in a supportive environment and feel able and motivated to exercise agency. It has long been argued that (see Turnbull and Spence, 2011) children can feel judged when viewed as a 'risk to others' and thus reticent to exercise agency within such spaces. That said, involving the child in the process can potentially have a profound impact on the child and make the process more meaningful, as one professional within a youth justice service illustrates:

> *I managed a nasty case with a child... and he actually received a custodial sentence and because of the risk being so great he actually came into a therapeutic section of custody, and he had been in this community placement for about 12 months and I went into the most amazing meeting that was chaired by him [child] which was amazing! I couldn't get over it! And he said I realise that whilst I am in this environment my risk is medium because I am safe, but I will not be safe at Christmas, and they [practitioners] said why is that? And I said, that is because my [relative] is at home and I can't be there, therefore I am at greater risk, and it was a bit of an eye opener really that they had got to that stage where he could chair his own meeting, which took an awful lot of energy and therapeutic work and a lot of support, but his risk was more manageable because he was part of the whole process and he understood it, and well, it's his risk isn't it, it's about him and that is the bit about it's not being done to him, it is acknowledging it for himself. I don't think we have got the energy or the ability or the time to be able to do it in that manner with all of our young people, BUT I would LOVE it! Wouldn't it be lovely!*
>
> *(Youth justice practitioner, Peer Power Youth, 2021)*

It appears that the decision on whether to involve the child or not in the process is left to the discretion of the professional. Without national guidance, there is inevitable variation in how participatory or co-production principles are constructed and applied in practice. Thus, there is a lack of clear evidence on which 'child-centred' approaches are most impactful or appropriate within multi-agency meetings or forums, for whom, and under what circumstances (Muncie, 2006; Peer Power Youth, 2021; Creaney and Burns, 2025). Nevertheless, the above account captures professional experiences of children's involvement in decision-making within risk panels. While there is little documented research on the impact of child involvement in risk panels, the above account illustrates a possibility of children becoming partners in the process of managing risk of harm, including the option for children to set the agenda and guide discussions on their terms. Indeed, when children are viewed in a positive way and encouraged to play a role in discussions about types of support suitable to address their needs, this can help to motivate them to participate in the process (Smithson et al., 2022). The above account also indicates that children have the capability and expertise to co-produce with practitioners during high-risk meetings but that they also require support and guidance during the process. It is important to cultivate a safe environment that does not retraumatise or (re)ignite system harms.

Despite this account of potentially progressive practice, there is a lack of empirical research into how these processes are understood and experienced by children and young people identified and assessed as 'high risk'. Alas, it is difficult to progress a co-produced endeavour within the confines of criminal justice sanctions. Considerable uncertainty remains about whether or how youth justice services should facilitate child collaboration, in a safe and ethical manner, within 'high risk' panels. Professionals may be too risk-averse and refrain from enacting Child First principles into practice due to the danger that this approach could compromise commitments towards keeping victims and communities safe (HMIP, 2025). For example, there may be confidential/sensitive police intelligence shared about victims or other matters disclosed about surveillance techniques to monitor the whereabouts of children under the supervision of youth justice services (Creaney and Burns, 2023). It can be distressing/upsetting for a child to observe professionals within a multi-agency setting discussing ways to minimise their risk level and/or reduce the likelihood of them engaging in further serious offending. They may even perceive this experience as dehumanising if they are pathologised, resulting in contextual factors being downplayed or sidelined. They may not be viewed as an active contributor, and this can be due to a reluctance among professionals to listen to them and value their insights. There may be a lack of acknowledgement that they have experienced – continue to experience – 'social harms', including but not limited to social and economic disadvantage, adversity, and childhood trauma, which limit their life chances (Day et al., 2023). Therefore, professionals must actively cultivate child-friendly and safe environments that foster trusting relationships and enable children to participate meaningfully in decision-making processes.

Conclusion and implications for practice

While the overarching or principal purpose of the youth justice system to prevent offending remains unchanged, Child First guidance positions an alternative to deficit-based practice across England. Child First policy discourse has therefore increased opportunities for inclusive and meaningful forms of co-production approaches with children and young people. Despite this discernible shift towards a principled Child First youth justice, there is a gap between intentions and action. This approach struggles to impact or influence multi-agency high-risk panels. There has been little research or debate focused on this issue. Therefore, this chapter demonstrates the lack of co-production in multi-agency risk panels.

While the Child First collaboration principle appears compatible with the concept of co-production, there is a need to develop more effective ways of involving children in high-risk management processes. Children may not be willing or feel able to contribute their views or articulate their future aspirations due to the process appearing to privilege adult-centric risk/public protection agendas over power sharing/relational building. This limits opportunities for reciprocal exchange of ideas between child and multi-agency professional. Perhaps, the lack of child/young person involvement in this process is somewhat unsurprising, given there is a paucity of guidance available that is fit for use within this space, capable of mobilising a shift towards co-production.

Existing mechanisms may need to be disrupted, challenged, and transformed to democratise the decision-making process, allowing the child to share unique insights and participate more meaningfully in proceedings that affect them. It is important that their participation is safe and meaningful. Professionals have to take great responsibility to ensure they cause no harm and actively seek to minimise the impact of system/social harms by recognising and responding to any trauma/adversity children have experienced in their lives and help them to thrive within their communities (Day et al., 2023; Peer Power Youth, 2021).

There is reference made to high-risk panels within the most recent case management guidance (YJB, 2022). For example, they are described as necessary to monitor ongoing and significant public protection and safety and well-being concerns (YJB, 2022). However, there is a paucity of detail or insight into the potential value of including them in the decision-making process. In terms of key areas to consider for future work, it has to be reiterated that not enough is known about how to address the risk/public protection/Child First/co-production nexus. The design or application of co-production principles within a youth justice context (and wider services) is still in its infancy (see Dixon et al., 2018). While translating research evidence into practice can be challenging, these principles can support a shift towards recognising children labelled 'high risk' as experts on their own lives, capable of sharing their ideas and experiences.

The child or young person may be reticent, of the view that they are not deserving of a voice or unsure if they have a right to influence proceedings and processes that affect them (Hart and Thompson, 2009; Creaney, 2020). Therefore, the onus is on professionals to cultivate welcoming organisational cultures, prioritise the implementation of co-production principles premised on ideals of children as rights holders and equal partners, and to forge opportunities for children to participate in safe and meaningful ways. While it varies in definition, co-production foregrounds children's perspectives throughout their contact with the system, and the framework can be utilised to ensure their perspective is given due weight by professionals who act as facilitators within the decision-making process (MacLachlan et al., 2024: 309; see also Boyle et al., 2010, 2013; Boyle and Harris, 2009). Accordingly, children can add new or differing insights and broaden or challenge definitions and meanings of risk classifications devised and constructed by professionals (Peer Power Youth, 2021). However, for them to feel comfortable offering their unique insights, their safety must remain a priority, whereby they are not only listened to but also taken seriously.

Future projects could explore whether the underpinning principles of community protection models align with children's participation rights and considerations around their 'best interests' being paramount. Such studies could investigate the voice of the child within public protection agendas and opportunities for co-production principles to be applied within this space, where children are engaged and involved throughout the process. It may not be possible (or appropriate) to fully recognise children as equal contributors within multi-agency panels or other related decision-making arrangements when the priority is to protect them from harm or from inflicting injury on others. These children are undertaking an order and sanctioned to comply and engage with the service, which creates complexities in terms of power sharing and reciprocal relationship building. Examining perspectives on forms of co-creation and types of co-production in practice, with particular reference to listening to the voices of children who are labelled 'high risk', could assist the development of evidence-based practice for multi-agency panels in youth justice settings.

References

Armstrong, D. (2004). A risky business? Research, policy and governmentality and youth offending. *Youth Justice*, 4(2), 100–16.

Armstrong, D. (2006). Becoming criminal: The cultural politics of risk. *International Journal of Inclusive Education*, 10(2/3), 265–78.

Boyle, D., Coote, A., Sherwood, C., et al. (2013). *Right Here, Right Now. Taking Co-production into the Mainstream.* London, UK: NESTA. https://media.nesta.org.uk/documents/right_here_right_now.pdf

Boyle, D. and Harris, M. (2009). The challenge of co-production. How equal partnerships between professionals and the public are crucial to improving public services. https://neweconomics.org/uploads/files/312ac8ce93a00d5973_3im6i6t0e.pdf (Accessed 01 May 2024).

Boyle, D., Slay, J. and Stephens, L. (2010). Public services inside out. Putting co-production into practice. https://media.nesta.org.uk/documents/public_services_inside_out.pdf (Accessed 01 May 2024).

Brady, L. (2020). *Embedding Young People's Participation in Health Services New Approaches.* Bristol: Policy Press.

Burns, S. (2019). Young people as co-producers in policing across England. An evaluation of the 'Youth Commission' on police and crime. *Children & Society*, 33(4), 347–362.

Burns, S. and Creaney, S. (2023). Embracing children 's voices: Transforming youth justice practice through co-production and child first participation. In: Case, S. and Hazel, N. (eds.) *Child First: Developing a New Youth Justice System*. London: Palgrave Macmillan.

Case, S. and Browning, A. (2021a). Child first justice: The research evidence-base [Full report]. Loughborough University.

Case, S. and Browning, A. (2021b). The child first strategy implementation project: Realising the guiding principle for youth justice [Full report]. Loughborough University.

Case, S. and Hazel, N. (eds.). (2023). *Child First: Developing a New Youth Justice System*. London: Palgrave Macmillan.

Case, S. and Smith, R. (2023). Child first and the end of 'bifurcation' in youth justice? *Journal of Children's Services*, 18(3/4), 180–194. https://doi.org/10.1108/JCS-02-2023-0005

Children and Young People's Centre for Justice (CYCJ). (2024). Children and young people in conflict with the law: Policy, practice and legislation. www.cycj.org.uk/resource/youthjusticeinscotland/

Creaney, S. (2020). "Game playing" and "docility": Youth justice in question. *Safer Communities*, 19(3), 103– 118.

Creaney, S. and Burns, S. (2024). Freedom from symbolic violence? Facilitators and barriers to participatory practices in youth justice. *Youth Justice*, 24(1), 31–52. https://doi.org/10.1177/14732254231156844

Creaney, S. and Burns, S. (2025). The Achilles heel of Child First: High-risk panels in youth justice service policy and practice. *Probation Journal*. Online First. 1-21. https://doi.org/10.1177/02645505251353719

Creaney, S. and Case, S. (2021). Promoting social inclusion: Participatory rights alternatives to risk discourses in youth justice. In: Liamputtong, P. (ed.) *Handbook of Social Inclusion Research and Practices in Health and Social Sciences*. Singapore: Springer.

Day, A-M. (2023). The place of risk within child first justice: An exploration of the perspectives of youth justice practitioners. In: Case, S. and Hazel, N. (eds.) *Child First: Developing A New Youth Justice System*. Cham: Palgrave MacMillan.

Day A, Malvaso C, Butcher L, O'Connor J, McLachlan K (2023), "Co-producing trauma-informed youth justice in Australia?". Safer Communities, Vol. 22 No. 2 pp. 106–120, doi: https://doi.org/10.1108/SC-08-2022-0030

Dixon, J., Ward, J. and Blower, S. (2018). "They sat and actually listened to what we think about the care system": The use of participation, consultation, peer research and co-production to raise the voices of young people in and leaving care in England. *Child Care in Practice*, 25(1), 6–21. https://doi.org/10.1080/13575279.2018.1521380

Farrow, K., Kelly, G. and Wilkinson, B. (2007). *Offenders in Focus*. Bristol: Policy Press.

Goldson, B. (2010). The sleep of (criminological) reason: Knowledge– policy rupture and New Labour's youth justice legacy. *Criminology and Criminal Justice*, 10(2), 155–178.

Goldson, B. (2011). Youth in crisis? In: Goldson B. (ed.) *Youth in Crisis? 'Gangs', Territoriality and Violence*. London: Routledge.

Gov.uk. (2025). Code of practice for victims of crime in England and Wales (Victims' Code). www.gov.uk/government/publications/the-code-of-practice-for-victims-of-crime/code-of-practice-for-victims-of-crime-in-england-and-wales-victims-code

Gray, P. and Smith, R. (2024). Youth justice and social harm: Towards a 'theory of the good'. *Criminology & Criminal Justice*, 26(2), 661–678. https://doi.org/10.1177/17488958241254446

Haines, K. and Case, S. (2015). *Positive Youth Justice: Children First, Offenders Second.* Bristol: Policy Press.

Haines, K. and Drakeford, M. (1998). *Young People and Youth Justice.* London: Macmillan.

Hampson, K., Creaney, S. and Burns, S. (2024). Transforming the balance of power? Child first collaboration: A conceptual analysis. *Societies*, 14(8), 138. https://doi.org/10.3390/soc14080138

Hart, D. and Thompson, C. (2009). *Young People's Participation in the Youth Justice System.* London: National Children's Bureau.

HMIP (2025) Youth Justice Inspection Guidance Manual. Available online at https://hmiprobation.justiceinspectorates.gov.uk/document/youth-justice-inspection-guidance-manual/

Johns, D., Flynn, C., Hall, M., Spivakovsky, C. and Turner, S. (2022). *Co-Production & Criminal Justice.* Abingdon: Routledge.

Kemshall, H. and Wood, J. (2009). MAPPA: Learning the lessons for young offenders. In: Sutherland, A. and Baker, K. (eds.) *Multi-Agency Public Protection and Youth Justice.* Bristol: Policy Press.

Khan, A. and Ungar, M. (2025). Un/heard, un/informed, un/involved: Meaningful participation for young people receiving child welfare services. *The British Journal of Social Work*, 55(4), 1536–1553. https://doi.org/10.1093/bjsw/bcaf003

Loeffler, E. and Bovaird, T. (2021). User and community co-production of public services and outcomes—A map of the current state of play. In: Loeffler, E. and Bovaird, T. (eds.) *The Palgrave Handbook of Co-Production of Public Services and Outcomes.* Cham: Palgrave Macmillan, pp. 3–30.

MacLachlan, A., Pemmasani, P., Jamieson-Mackenzie, I., McMellon, C., Cunningham, E., Lewis, R. and Tisdall, E.K.M. (2024). Applying co-production principles in research: Reflections from young people and academics. *Childhood*, 31(3), 309–328. https://doi.org/10.1177/09075682241269692 (Original work published 2024)

McCulloch, T. (2021). Co-producing desistance: The role of peer support. In: Loeffler, E. and Bovaird, T. (eds.) *Palgrave Handbook on Co-production of Public Services and Outcomes.* Cham: Palgrave Macmillan, pp. 409–426. https://doi.org/10.1007/978-3-030-53705-0_21

Moore, K., Ahern, E., O'Meara Daly, E. et al. (2025). Youth justice services: Relationships, rehabilitation and the reality of the young people involved—A meta-synthesis of the qualitative literature. *Clinical Child and Family Psychology Review*, 28(3), 631–649. https://doi.org/10.1007/s10567-025-00534-6

Muncie, J. (2006). Governing young people: Coherence and contradiction in contemporary youth justice. *Critical Social Policy*, 26(4), 770–793. https://doi.org/10.1177/0261018306068473 (Original work published 2006)

Peer Power Youth. (2021). *Co-creation and Participation in Practice Project.* London: Peer Power Youth/ YJB.

Smith, H. and Paddock, E. (2025). Does AssetPlus facilitate effective assessment of children within the youth justice system?: A critical evaluation. *Probation Journal*, 73(1), 70–89.

Smith, R. and Gray, P. (2019). The changing shape of youth justice: Models of practice. *Criminology & Criminal Justice*, 19(5), 554–571. https://doi.org/10.1177/1748895818781199

Smithson, H., Lang, T. and Gray, P. (2022). From rhetoric to reality: Participation in practice within youth justice systems. In: Frankel, S. (ed.) *Establishing Child Centred Practice in a Changing World, Part A (Emerald Studies in Child Centred Practice)*. Bingley: Emerald Publishing Limited, pp. 111–122.

Social Care Institute for Excellence (SCIE). (2022). Co-production: What it is and how to do it. [online]. www.scie.org.uk/co-production/what-how/ (accessed on 28 February 2025)

Tisdall, E.K.M. (2017). Conceptualising children and young people's participation: Examining vulnerability, social accountability and co-production. *The International Journal of Human Rights*, 21(1), 1–13. https://doi.org/10.1080/13642987.2016.1248125.

Tuddenham, R. (2000). Beyond defensible decision-making: Towards reflexive assessment of risk and dangerousness. *Probation Journal*, 47(3), 173–183.

Turnbull, G. and Spence, J. (2011). What's at risk? The proliferation of risk across child and youth policy in England. *Journal of Youth Studies*, 14(8), 939–959. https://doi.org/10.1080/13676261.2011.616489

Weaver, B., McCulloch, T. and Vaswani, N. (2024). Envisioning social justice with criminalised young adults. *British Journal of Criminology*, 64(3), 675–692.

Williamson, S. and Connelly, C. (2000). Review of the research literature on serious violent and sexual offenders. Project Report. Scottish Executive Central Research Unit, Edinburgh, UK. https://content.iriss.org.uk/throughcare/files/pdf/longterm/lt4_risk2.pdf

Yin, M. (2024). Ascribed agency, denied influence: How adult narratives shape and constrain the right of children in the justice system to be heard. *The International Journal of Children's Rights*, 32(4), 998–1026.

Youth Justice Board (YJB). (2021). Strategic plan 2021–24. Report. London: YJB.

Youth Justice Board (YJB). (2022). *Case Management Guidance*. London: YJB.

Youth Justice Board (YJB). (2025). *Youth Justice Statistics*. London: YJB.

Further reading

Picken, N., Baker, K,. d'Angelo, B., Fays, C. and Sutherland, A. (2019). Process evaluation of AssetPlus. RAND Europe. www.rand.org/pubs/research_reports/RR3177.html (Accessed 7th December 2020).

5

CO-PRODUCTION OR EXPLOITATION?

Mind the exploitation trap!

Kierra Myles

Introduction

The Youth Justice Board (YJB) for England and Wales set out Child First as the guiding principle for youth justice practice in their 2021–2024 strategic plan (YJB, 2021). The YJB repeated this again in their 2024–2027 strategic plan (YJB, 2024), continuing to make a commitment to implementing the four Child First tenets across youth justice services (YJS). This commitment includes influencing policymakers and services that work with children in conflict with the law; '*collaboration with children*' is the third of four Child First tenets (Case and Browning, 2021). Children have legal rights, regardless of any strategic plan and criminal jurisdiction. The UK signed up to the United Nations Convention of the Rights of the Child (UNCRC), which came into force in 1992. Article 12 of the UNCRC clearly states that children have the right to be included, heard, and involved in decisions being made about their lives. Participation should be respectful, transparent and monitored to ensure it is safe, fair, and without barriers (UNICEF, 1989). Furthermore, the Children's General Comment No. 24 (2019) on children's rights in the child justice system puts emphasis on children's ability to participate throughout the child justice process.

Nationally, YJS have focused on '*collaborating with children*' by not only listening to children's views and experiences but also including children as equal partners to co-produce workshops, service delivery, and diversionary activities that they enjoy. More broadly, there is also evidence regarding involving children as co-creators in the design of service delivery, which creates a more fair and equal power dynamic between professionals and children in conflict with the law (Peer Power/YJB, 2021; Creaney et al.,

DOI: 10.4324/9781003602996-7

2024). Johns et al. (2023) found that, when used properly, co-production allows *'new stories to be told, and for new purposes to be found' (p. 131).* Co-production creates the opportunity for children to see their experience through a new lens. They are now the storyteller, the creator of new ideas or the lead for a part of the co-produced activity or project they are working on. Importantly, children need to understand how they are equal partners, how this is being measured and how they are benefiting from co-production (Johns et al., 2023; Case et al., 2024).

This chapter focuses on the importance of trauma-informed collaboration with children in conflict with the law. Trauma-informed principles do not solely depend on attending training or creating strategies and policies that adopt a trauma-informed approach; it's about embedding this into youth justice practice. Significantly, practitioners need to be adept with the skills and knowledge to recognise the symptoms of trauma, responding in a way that is compassionate, strengths-based, and causes no further harm (Vaswani et al., 2024; SAMHSA, 2014). Furthermore, adult professionals and practitioners are responsible for ensuring children are supported to fully understand the process, in an environment they feel comfortable in, with care and consideration given to their lived experiences, which have often been traumatic (Case et al., 2024; Creaney et al., 2023). Collaboration is recognised as one of the key principles of trauma-informed practice *(safety, trustworthiness, choice, collaboration and empowerment as well as respect for diversity)* (Kezleman, 2014). Collaboration, partnering, and the removal of disproportionate power to create a power-sharing relationship would be considered trauma-informed (Vaswani et al., 2024) and a key principle in collaboration with children, along with trust and safe spaces (Burns et al., 2023; Creaney et al., 2024). This approach respects and harnesses children's human rights, not only to participate in decisions being made about their lives, but also their right to play and be protected from abuse (UNICEF, 1989), providing an intention that children's participation will not be exploitative, tokenistic, or harmful.

What does this concept mean for children in conflict with the law? How do they understand what this 'power' means when they are participating in co-production (Day et al., 2023)? Ultimately, the YJS still hold power and control over children who are open to their services (John's et al., 2023). Therefore, it is the role of adult professionals or practitioners collaborating with children to ensure there is fair and equal power sharing and an ethical and non-exploitative approach is taken. By focusing on activity-based methods of trauma-informed collaboration and co-production with children, focusing on developing relationships through creative activities, this chapter affirms research which highlights the importance of creative co-production through sport, arts, and peer mentoring when seeking to maximise positive child outcomes (Smithson and Gray, 2021; Case et al., 2024; Creaney,

2020a; Austria and Peterson, 2017). Providing children with opportunities to be involved in co-designing YJSs as co-creators recognises children's capabilities, skills, and knowledge (Creaney and Burns, 2023; Creaney et al., 2023). By discussing these forms of creative co-production, this chapter proposes that if used correctly, these methods can be utilised further across YJS practice for meaningful collaboration, creating a safe space where they can share their views and experiences to shape policy and practice. For these forms of co-production practices to be implemented, this chapter will firstly discuss concerns over the potential harms of co-production in youth justice before addressing how peer mentoring, sports, and creative arts provide three clear examples of ways to overcome potential harms of co-production.

Collaboration or exploitation?

Care and ethical considerations are needed to foster co-production in a youth justice context, since children who enter formal YJSs have often suffered multiple and prolonged traumas with little or inconstant relational attachments (Wright et al., 2016). Children who are neurodivergent, have speech and communication difficulties, have challenges with drugs and alcohol, and/or their mental health are continuously over-represented in the YJS (Day, 2022; 2025). Children from low-income households, who are often excluded from school and suffer from structural disadvantage (White and Cunneen, 2015), are labelled as offenders and then treated as 'outsiders' (Creaney, 2012) throughout the formal justice process, causing additional trauma (Case et al., 2024; Brierley, 2021; Day, 2022; Wright et al., 2016; Bateman, 2016; Haines and Case, 2015). Subsequently, it is important to recognise children need to be adequately supported so they are included throughout the formal justice process. Developing relationships based on trust and transparency creates an environment where they feel safe and understand what is being asked of them (Creaney et al., 2024; Day et al., 2023; Vaswani et al., 2024).

Although the Child First policy has been promoted across the YJS alongside trauma-informed principles, youth justice practitioners may still struggle to recognise the power imbalance between practitioner and child (Peer Power/YJB, 2021). Including children but not consulting with them, asking but not listening, or promising things that cannot be delivered can be harmful and mirror behaviours seen in child criminal exploitation (Brierley and Myles, 2024). There is currently no statutory definition for child criminal exploitation. However, there are many evolving definitions which follow the theme of children being manipulated through deception, coercion, and control for personal gain – even if it appears consensual (Home Office, 2018; 2019; James, 2021). Using collaboration as a tick-box method encouraging '*passive compliance*' (Creaney et al., 2024, p. 213) without listening to or valuing the views and experiences of children can be described as manipulation. This happens when professionals misuse their power to manipulate children into believing they have a say in a plan that has been created without them (Arnstein, 1969). Furthermore, this unequal power dynamic could be considered a type of 'symbolic violence' (Creaney and Burns, 2023) since children may also be unaware of their exploitation. Using coercive language, including threats of a breach due to 'non-compliance', without considering who holds the power, who is benefiting from the co-production, and who the consequences fall on if the child does not want to participate, could indeed be exploitative practice (Creaney, 2020b; Johns et al., 2023). This adult-centric approach often used in youth justice invites children to be included but then their experiences, views, and opinions are still marginalised (Case et al., 2020). Often it is the case that practitioners are not intentionally abusing their power to assert control over children, but their practice may not be inclusive, allowing bias to inform their practice (Day, 2023). Hence, the environment that practitioners are working in can result in them acting in exploitative ways with justice-involved children.

The YJB's steer is in the direction of collaborating with children as equal partners. However, professionals are *still* not collaborating with children as equals; their voices are not seen as valuable (Creaney and Burns, 2024); and *'systemic neglect of children's views'* (Smithson and Grey, 2021, p. 4) continues to be problematic, preventing meaningful participation from taking place. For children to collaborate fully in a meaningful way, policies, procedures, and methods of engagement cannot be designed for and by adults (Case et al., 2024). Additionally, adult professionals and practitioners need to consider ways to address power sharing; this might mean sitting in a less formal environment such as a community centre, sports hall or art house. Children might want to use up some energy boxing before speaking about how they feel. Some might want to express themselves through lyric writing, painting, or perhaps even colourful language to express themselves. While we must discourage pro-criminal behaviour, we must understand that we need to allow children to be children (Haines and Case, 2015). It is only when we accept children for who they are that we can respectfully listen to them, supporting them to identify their own strategies and belief in their ability to achieve their goals (Case et al., 2024).

Child-centred approaches to overcome exploitation

Children have proven repeatedly that they are knowledgeable and very capable of understanding not only their own experiences but also the strengths and limitations of YJSs. Children can advocate very well for themselves (Burns, 2019), as they are best placed to share insights into their own individual experiences (Myles, 2022). Taking a trauma-informed approach to co-production would involve creating a safe space for children to form relationships with practitioners in an attempt to foster trust (Day et al., 2023). Supporting or empowering children to identify their own strengths and aspirations for the future (Case et al., 2024) enhances their sense of agency while continuing to develop a pro-social identity and life away from harmful and stigmatising YJS (Case and Browning, 2021).

Encouraging and supporting children to identify and achieve their aspirations requires the recognition that they are children in need of care and guidance, rather than 'mini adults' who need to be held responsible for their actions (Haines and Case, 2015). Children want to be treated with respect by professionals who trust them to participate in meaningful activities (Creaney, 2015; Case et al., 2024). Drawing on children's natural curiosity to learn through play and adventure builds on their strengths and capabilities. This approach is participatory and inclusive; with careful consideration, it can even be a non-criminal-justice practice-focused one (Case and Haines, 2021; Case and Browning, 2021). Taking time to focus on what children want to achieve from their lives and how they can be supported to get there requires listening and maintaining an empathetic and non-judgemental approach. This is where the development of relationships through sports, arts, and peer mentoring removes the focus from offender-focused or punitive discourses onto how they can move towards their future. One way to achieve this is through peer mentoring, privileging their narratives, and lived experiences.

Peer mentoring

Peer mentoring in youth justice is still a relatively new concept in practice and research. Peer mentors have overcome their own personal challenges by creating positive change in their lives (Lenkins et al., 2023; Buck, 2020). Peer mentors in youth justice have managed to navigate a challenging path away from the YJS and have accumulated experiential knowledge or 'know-how' (Creaney, 2020a) that professionals may not fully understand (Brierley, 2023; Myles, 2022). Furthermore, peer mentors understand the deep feeling of hopelessness while trying to overcome the stigma and shame attached to criminal justice involvement, including the social barriers and emotional challenges of fear, rejection, and abandonment (Lenkins, 2020; Brierley, 2023; Myles, 2022; 2023). Peer mentors have demonstrated their inherent ability to embody compassion and empathy, which they utilise through relational practice (Buck, 2020; Brierley, 2021). They provide a safe space and carefully listen to mentees while acting as role models, inspiring hope for a positive future (Creaney, 2020a; Myles, 2023).

Creaney (2020a) found that children feel like people who have lived experience of YJS are best placed to work with them in YJS. They believe they understand the challenges children face. One child said, '*unless you've experienced that, you cannot tell them … you cannot relate to them*' (p. 28). Interestingly, this research highlighted that when children were asked about peer mentoring, they were inspired. If they had a peer mentor, there's a possibility that they too could develop into peer mentors in the future. Elsewhere in research, Bussu et al. (2024) interviewed peer mentors developing into their role. Peer mentors really valued the opportunity to use their lived experiences to support positive change with children still experiencing the system. The peer mentors recognised the need to be self-aware, manage boundaries, and face professional challenge. The very skills they learnt to navigate away from services could now be shared or used to help others (Myles, 2023).

In terms of barriers and limitations to peer mentoring, it must be recognised that not all children will want a peer mentor. They might not want to meet additional people or may be cautious of other people's offending histories (Creaney, 2020a). The main identified barriers and limitations are by professionals, although it must be noted that they were incredibly positive too, recognising peer mentors' strengths (see Bussu et al., 2024; Porteous and Goodman, 2023). The challenges identified were risk-averse, punitive responses (Creaney, 2020b) by professionals that are not ready to accept peer mentors as equals (Porteous and Goodman, 2023). Some identified that it might be difficult for professionals that previously worked with peer mentors to move on from their past, which may include a history of violent behaviour as a child (Bussu et al., 2024). To create an equal power dynamic, peer mentors need to be accepted and have their experiences valued (Creaney and Burns, 2023). Myles (2022) critically explores why this type of thinking does not create hope for children still experiencing YJSs. How can children be hopeful and inspired when adults who are no longer in conflict with the law, who have forged a positive life for themselves, are still being rejected by services?

Collaborating with children is both about creating a safe space and an equal power-sharing relationship (Burns et al, 2023; Creaney et al, 2024), as well as about how we support children to achieve their future goals (Case et al, 2024), which can be difficult to balance. Peer mentors have demonstrated they can develop reciprocal, trusting, non-hierarchical relationships (Creaney et al, 2024), supporting children's involvement in YJS and the wider professional support network (Smart, 2023; Porteous and Goodman, 2023; Bussu et al, 2024). Peer mentors have demonstrated their willingness to work in partnership, promoting positive change (Bussu et al., 2024). The positive impact of relational attachment through nonjudgemental, empathetic and compassion-led practice has been received well by mentees (Creaney, 2020a; Myles, 2023). Creating hope that they too can be mentors creates an environment for children to expand on their own aspirations. Peer mentors are well placed to encourage children to have a say in the support they are receiving. Something children are not always willing to do due to the threat of consequence, or in other words, coercion (Creaney, 2020b). Children may also find value in the mentorship, or meaningful, non-judgemental relationships that come with sporting activities (Kelly, 2012).

Sport

Sport has long been promoted by government to encourage children's participation, develop confidence and encourage community involvement – widening children's social network (Department for Culture, Media & Sport, 1999). In 2022 the Ministry of Justice announced the allocation of 5 million pounds to the Youth Justice Sport Fund (YJSF), funding 220 voluntary and community sports schemes to actively divert children from criminal activity and the formal YJS (MOJ, 2023). This fund brought together Street Games, The Alliance of Sport in Criminal Justice, and the Sport for Development Coalition to deliver this important programme.

Mason et al. (2023) were commissioned to produce an external report reviewing the impact of the sport-based activities; a massive 7,832 children took part. The programme has now been evidenced as effective in promoting positive outcomes and engaging children in meaningful activities. The report does not differentiate between diversionary activities and children already criminalised through contact with the formal YJS. However, the report identified that 39% of referrals came via YJSs. Mason et al. (2023) found that YJSs need to have a better understanding of the impact of sport as an intervention. Sport-based activities create an environment where learning from mistakes, teamwork, and having to keep going even when it is hard (resilience) support children to have improved self-esteem and develop a pro-social identity.

However, it is not clear from the report if the initial co-development of any of the projects included children, which is regarded as a more enhanced form of co-production. Mason et al (2023) do highlight that children's voices are mainly absent; it is a key recommendation for future planning to involve children more. It would seem the timescales provided by the government-run YJSF scheme did not allow adequate time to actively involve children from the beginning, a missed opportunity driven by adult-led thinking (Haines and Case, 2015; Creaney and Burns, 2023; Case et al., 2024). Regardless of a lack of children's involvement in the setup, the programmes were widely beneficial for children. They were allowed to choose the activities they wanted to participate in; football and boxing were the most popular. Children who were not in mainstream education gained certificates providing them hope and belief that they can achieve their aspirations. Children felt included and empowered and found a sense of belonging and community, all of which are key themes in trauma-informed co-production (Day et al., 2023; Creaney et al., 2023; 2024). Through the 'plus' programme, on top of the sports-focused activities, children were able to access additional support through mentorship and workshops, important spaces for them to share without judgement.

Mason et al. (2024) further recommended the need to strengthen partnerships between YJSs and organisations that offer sports-based activities for children, ensuring referrals are sent in a timely manner. There is clearly further development that is required in this area; sports-based activities are something children have identified as a positive, safe space for personal development (Smithson et al., 2021; Mason et al., 2023; Case et al., 2024). Furthermore, sports-based activities align with the Child First policy (see Case and Browning, 2021; YJB, 2024). Children need physical activity; it is essential for healthy development (tenet 1). Children really enjoyed the opportunity to participate in a non-formal environment (tenet 3) with non-YJS practitioners. They were able to build empathic relationships that recognised and harnessed children's strengths (Mason et al., 2023). Building on children's strengths and abilities promotes the development of social skills, encourages positive behaviours (tenet 2), and improves overall well-being (Eime et al., 2013; Meek, 2018). Importantly, sports-based activities, especially the enhanced 'sports plus' programme, presented the opportunity to deliver important targeted diversionary workshops away from the stigmatising YJS environment (tenet 4). Children felt like they benefited from the workshops; they were able to share their invaluable views and experiences of YJSs while learning and developing their skills without the threat of sanction.

Creative arts

The creative arts are another child-centred approach which can enhance forms of co-production with children in YJS. Between 2019 and 2021, the YJB funded research into creative arts at Sandwell Youth Offending Service (YOS). During this research, Caulfield et al (2019) found that using creative arts as a form of participation left children feeling inspired and connected, and they felt included. Some of the activities included drawing, music production, and creative writing. Children were involved from the initial stages of the project. They decided what was important to them and what activities they would like to take part in, making the experience fair and equal from the beginning. The relationships between practitioners and children improved, providing practitioners with the opportunity to really understand what was going on for the children. With the activities being child-led, they took place in an informal environment that was not overly structured. Children who wanted to continue with creative arts were introduced to community projects, supporting them to widen their social networks (Case and Browning, 2021), in the hope that they may find a sense of belonging and feel safe enough to express themselves in an environment they feel comfortable (Burns et al, 2023) – key principles in trauma-informed co-production with children (Creaney et al, 2023; 2024; Day et al., 2023; Vaswani et al., 2024).

Sandwell YOS started to use creative arts alongside offending programmes such as their motoring offence programme and knife crime. It is not clear if children were involved in the decision-making behind this method of participation. This is an improvement from most offending-related programmes; however, offending programmes are not favoured or respected by children. In fact, children often do not understand the key objectives or how it helps them move on with their life (Case et al., 2024). They are favoured and respected by the punitive, adult-focused aspect of YJS. This is where well-meaning and effective methods of participation move towards coercion and control. If a child does not want to take part in offence-related work, they can be further punished by the system. The opportunity for children to participate as equals is removed by adults who choose to focus on risk, creating barriers to participation (Burns et al., 2023; Day et al., 2023). Instead of harnessing children's valuable expertise, further reminding children that practitioners have disproportionate control over them until they complete their order (Creaney and Burns, 2023; Creaney et al., 2023).

During a participatory research project involving arts-based methods, Smithson et al (2021) highlighted that practitioners need to recognise that not all children are able to fully participate due to their traumatic experiences or because they do not feel like they have the skills to contribute. This should not be a barrier to meaningful participation, as they are still capable and have developed knowledge that professionals are not able to attain (Myles, 2022; Brierley, 2023). It is important that their needs are recognised and responded to with careful consideration, ensuring the environment is inclusive so children do not feel disempowered during the process (Creaney, 2021). Relationships and trust need to be developed, and children need to be given the right information so they understand the purpose of their involvement (Case et al, 2024; Burns et al, 2023; Johns et al, 2023).

During this project children identified themes that were important to them to create a fair and equal space for them to participate. One of the themes was *'try to avoid threats and sanctions'*, another *'remember that it's ultimately their choice'* (Smithson and Grey, 2021: p. 8). Children are clearly feeling the pressure of coercion and control; they want to participate in a way that is meaningful. This continues to be problematic when they are on supervision orders or do not feel like they have a choice in the interventions they are subject to (Smithson et al., 2022; Creaney, 2020b). This project allowed children space and time to think about what they were interested in, and they had a choice (Day et al., 2023; Creaney et al., 2024; Vaswani et al., 2024). Significantly, this research highlighted the importance of creating the right environment for children to feel trusted, empowered, and safe enough to choose what they would like to do (Creaney et al., 2024; Day et al., 2023; Case et al., 2024). The children involved decided on boxing, lyric writing, and urban arts, leading to a series of workshops being co-created and delivered with children. The focus of the workshops and activities was not on offending, but rather on identity, second chances, and children's frustrations with not feeling like their voices are being heard. The workshops were delivered outside of the formal YOT, in settings where these activities would usually take place (Smithson et al., 2021). Creating an informal learning environment that increases confidence and social skills promotes a life away from the YJS (Caulfield et al, 2022; Case et al, 2024).

Conclusion: environment matters for co-production in youth justice

The purpose of this chapter was to consider how sport, creative arts, and peer mentoring can all be used as non-exploitative, creative methods to evoke effective co-production in YJS. Encouraging participatory activities that allow children to recognise their own strengths, supporting the development of a pro-social identity, in line with Child First policy. The Child First collaboration principle in policy does not align with the deficit-based undertones of offence-related work that often occur in formal youth justice environments. The focus should be on engaging with a child-centred approach within a non-formal environment to understand what children enjoy and what they want to achieve from their lives and encouraging them to identify a way they can work towards achieving their aspirations. Importantly, children need to believe they are equals and trusted and their experiences and unique perspectives will be valued and listened to.

Co-production is a relatively new approach in a youth justice context; an identified barrier to fair co-production is the afterthought of children being involved. If children are involved in an environment of their choice from the beginning, they will be more invested and feel empowered to influence aspects of their lives – all of which are key themes of trauma-informed co-production (Creaney et al., 2023, 2024; Case et al., 2024; Vaswani, 2024; Day et al., 2023; Johns et al., 2023). Arguably, focusing on listening to children and creating the right environment for learning enables children to develop self-confidence and promote desistance (Creaney et al., 2024; Creaney et al., 2023).

Another identified barrier that needs further consideration is that, regardless of co-production taking place in a non-exploitative way, in non-formal environments and being led by non-YJS practitioners, children will still need to meet YJS practitioners to comply with the statutory demands of their order. With this carries the challenge of children's human rights being upheld within YJS; they are continuously ignored and neglected by practitioners who struggle to recognise how children are being exploited through the formal youth justice process (Creaney and Burns, 2023; Smithson et al., 2022). One way to mitigate this would be to allow youth justice practitioners the opportunity to be more creative with how they work with children. Day (2023) highlighted that enthusiastic practitioners are under pressure from management to focus on risk. Risk-focused interventions being led by YJS practitioners do not allow for equal power sharing (Burns et al, 2024) or for equal benefit (Johns et al, 2023) within their relationship with children.

This chapter has demonstrated that when children are engaged in creativity while developing relationships, they increase their human and social capital (Creaney et al., 2023), and they feel trusted, empowered, and capable (Caulfield et al., 2022). Children were able to join community creative arts networks outside of the formal YJS after the intervention had finished. Children found peer mentoring created hope; they met people with lived experiences of YJSs who offered their time and asked for nothing in return. Peer mentors have demonstrated their ability to develop trusting, meaningful, and non-hierarchical relationships. Children still experiencing the system felt inspired to make positive changes so they too could become peer mentors (Creaney, 2021; Bussu et al, 2024; Myles, 2023). During the sports plus project, children chose activities they wanted to do while developing a relationship with a mentor who listened and did not pass judgement. They completed important workshops educating children on relationships, gangs, and trauma. These methods of co-production did not use manipulation, coercion, or control to engage children in activities; they had a choice, and they were able to co-produce activities and develop relationships that were not based on compliance, coercion, or control.

References

Arnstein, S. R. (1969) A ladder of citizen participation. *Journal of the American Institute of Planners*, 35(4), 216–224.

Austria, R. and Peterson, J. (2017) *Credible Messenger Mentoring for Justice-Involved Youth*. New York: The Pinkerton Foundation.

Bussu, A., Creaney, S., Price, J., Burns, S. and Myles, K. (2024) 'It's A Sixth Sense… I See You, You See Me, and We've Been There': Benefits and challenges of developing a peer mentoring scheme with young people in youth justice services. *British Journal of Community Justice*, 19(2), 4–19. Available at: https://doi.org/10.48411/4c2h-hc54

Bateman, T. (2016) *The State of Youth Custody-2016*. National Association for Youth Justice. Available at: https://thenayj.org.uk/wp-content/uploads/2016/10/NAYJ-Briefing-State-of-Youth-Custody-Sep16.pdf.

Brierley, A. (2021) *Connecting with Young People in Trouble: Risk, Relationships and Lived Experience*. Hook, Hampshire: Waterside Press.

Brierley, A. (2023) Experiential peers cultivate a participation culture in youth justice. *Safer Communities*, 22(2), 78–90. https://doi.org/10.1108/SC-07-2022-0024
Brierley, A. and Myles, K. (2024) In conversation: An inside perspective of youth justice practice and experience. *Probation Journal*, 71(2), 179–185, https://doi.org/10.1177/02645505241241586
Buck, G. (2020) *Peer Mentoring in Criminal Justice*. London: Routledge.
Burns, S. (2019) Young people as co-producers in policing across England. An evaluation of the 'Youth commission' on police and crime. *Children & Society*, 33(4), 347–362.
Burns, S., Creaney, S., Hampson, K. and Case, S. (2023) Child First: Seeing children as the solution, not the problem. CYCJ. www.cycj.org.uk/ resource/ info- sheet- 110/
Caulfield, L. (2021) The role of arts in the criminal justice system. In D. A. Crighton and G. J. Towl (eds) *Forensic Psychology*. Chichester: Wiley-Blackwell. https://doi.org/10.1002/9781394260669.ch23
Caulfield, L., Jolly, A., Simpson, E. and Devi-McGleish, Y. (2022) 'It's not just music, it helps you from inside': Mixing methods to understand the impact of music on young people in contact with the criminal justice system. *Youth Justice*, 22(1), 67–84.
Caulfield, L., Sojka, B. and Massie, R. (2019) An evaluation of Sandwell Youth Offending Service–a creative approach to working with young people.
Case, S. and Browning, A. (2021) *Child First Justice: The Research Evidence*. Loughborough: Loughborough University.
Case, S., Creaney, S., Coleman, N., Haines, K., Little, R. and Worrall, V. (2020) Trusting children to enhance youth justice policy: The importance and value of children's voices. *Youth Voice Journal*, 2020(Special issue), 25–40. www.rj4allpublications.com/product/trusting-children-to-enhance-youth-justice-policy-the-importance-and-value-of-childrens-voices/
Case, S. and Haines, K. (2021) Abolishing youth justice systems: Children first, offenders nowhere. *Youth Justice*, 21(1), 3–17.
Case, S., Hampson, K. and Nisbet, A. (2024) Child First? Examining children's perspectives of their 'effective' collaboration in youth justice decision-making. Aberystwyth: Aberystwyth University. Available at: https://doi.org/10.17028/rd.lboro.27968766.v1
Creaney, S. (2012) Targeting, labelling and stigma: Challenging the criminalisation of children and young people: Sean Creaney reports on how children involved in youth justice processes are unable to overcome the negative 'outsider' label attached them. *Criminal Justice Matters*, 90(1), 16–17. https://doi.org/10.1080/09627251.2012.721967
Creaney, S. (2015) Youth justice, participation and radical moral communitarianism. *British Journal of Community Justice (BJCJ)*, 13(2), 125–139.
Creaney, S. (2020a) Children's voices – are we listening? Progressing peer mentoring in the Youth Justice System. *Child Care in Practice*, 26(1), 22–37. https://doi.org/10.1080/13575279.2018.1521381
Creaney, S. (2020b) "Game playing" and "docility": Youth justice in question. *Safer Communities*, 19(3), 103–118.
Creaney, S. and Burns, S. (2023) Freedom from symbolic violence? Facilitators and barriers to participatory practices in youth justice. *Youth Justice*, 24(1), 31–52.
Creaney, S., Burns, S. and Day, A. (2023) Theory and practice of co-production and co-creation in youth justice. *Safer Communities*, 22(3), 149–155. https://doi.org/10.1108/SC-07-2023-054

Creaney, S., Burns, S., Douglas, A. M., Brierley, A. and Falconer, C. (2024) 'Desistance through participatory practice: Involving children in decision-making processes in youth justice'. In Wigzell, A., Paterson-Young, C. and Bateman, T. (eds.) Desistance and children: critical reflections from theory, research and practice. Bristol: Bristol University Press, pp. 212–227.

Day, A., Malvaso, C., Butcher, L., O'Connor, J. and McLachlan, K. (2023) Co-producing trauma-informed youth justice in Australia? *Safer Communities*, 22(2), 106–120.

Day, A. M. (2022) Disabling and criminalising systems? Understanding the experiences and challenges facing incarcerated, neurodivergent children in the education and youth justice systems in England. *Forensic Science International: Mind and Law*, 3, 100102.

Day, A. M. (2023) 'It's a hard balance to find': The perspectives of youth justice practitioners in England on the place of 'risk' in an emerging 'Child-First' world. *Youth Justice*, 23(1), 58–75.

Day, A. M. (2025) Kids 'at risk' of school exclusion and youth justice involvement? Or neurodivergent children and families in need of trauma-informed support? *Emotional and Behavioural Difficulties*, 1–16. https://doi.org/10.1080/13632752.2025.2499788

Department for Culture, Media, & Sport. (1999) *Policy Action Team 10: Arts and Sport*. London, UK: HMSO.

Eime, R. M., Young, J. A., Harvey, J. T., Charity, M. J. and Payne, W. R. (2013) A systematic review of the psychological and social benefits of participation in sport for children and adolescents: informing development of a conceptual model of health through sport. *International Journal of Behavioural Nutrition and Physical Activity*, 10, 1–21.

Haines, K. and Case, S. (2015) *Positive Youth Justice: Children First, Offenders Second*. Bristol: Policy Press.

Home Office. (2018) Serious violence strategy. Home Office. https://assets.publishing.service.gov.uk/government/uploads/system/uploads/attachment_data/file/698009/serious-violence-strategy.pdf

Home Office. (2019) Child exploitation disruption toolkit. Home Office. https://assets.publishing.service.gov.uk/media/63106669e90e076ebfb7f419/Child_Exploitation_Disruption_Toolkit_082022.pdf

James, E. (2021) Exploited and criminalised what can the police, crime, sentencing and courts bill do to ensure that children who are criminally exploited receive the care and support they need? Barnardo's.

Johns, D., Flynn, C., Hall, M., Spivakovsky, C. and Turner, S. (eds) (2023) Now what? In *Co-production and Criminal Justice*. London: Routledge.

Kazleman, C. (2014) Trauma-informed practice. https://mhaustralia.org/general/trauma-informed-practice

Kelly, L. (2012) Sports-based interventions and the local governance of youth crime and antisocial behaviour. *Journal of Sport and Social Issues*, 37(3), 261–283. https://doi.org/10.1177/0193723512467193

Lenkens, M., Rodenburg, G., Schenk, L., Nagelhout, G. E., Van Lenthe, F. J., Engbersen, G., Sentse, M., Severiens, S. and Van De Mheen, D. (2020) "I need to do this on my own" resilience and self-reliance in urban at-risk youths. *Deviant Behaviour*, 41(10), 1330–1345.

Lenkens, M., van Lenthe, F. J., Schenk, L., Sentse, M., Severiens, S., Engbersen, G. and Nagelhout, G. E. (2023) Experiential peer support and desistance from

crime: A systematic realist literature review. *Psychology, Crime & Law*, 30(10), 1421–1451.
Mason, C., Morgan, H., Walpole, C. and Meek, R. (2024) Getting on track: Reducing youth offending and re-offending through sport and physical activity. Sport for Development Coalition.
Mason, C., Walpole, C., Morgan, H. and Meek, R. (2023) Youth justice sport fund external evaluation report. Street Games.
Meek, R. (2018) A sporting chance. An independent review of sport in youth and adult prisons. *Ministry of Justice*, 333.
Ministry of Justice. (2023) Youth Justice Sport Fund. Available at: www.gov.uk/guidance/youth-justice-sport-fund
Myles, K. (2022) Youth justice practice and lived experience: Inclusion or exclusion? Howard League for Penal Reform ECAN Bulletin Issue 51. https://howardleague.org/wp-content/uploads/ 2022/08/ECAN-summer-2022- FINAL.pdf
Myles, K. (2023) I have never met a child that healed in a cell. In A. Brierley (ed) *The Good Prison Officer* (pp. 63–75). London, Routledge.
Peer Power/Youth Justice Board. (2021) *Co-Creation and Participation in Practice Project*. London: Peer Power/YJB.
Porteous, D. and Goodman, A. (2023) "If I had had a me": The benefits and challenges of involving children with lived experience in youth justice services. *Safer Communities*, 22(3), 172–185.
SAMHSA. (2014) Substance Abuse and Mental Health Services Administration's concept of Trauma and Guidance for a Trauma-Informed Approach, SAMHSA, Rockville, MD.
Smart, J. (2023) Using ex-gang members as peer youth workers. In Andell, P. and Pitts, J. (eds.) *The Palgrave Handbook of Youth Gangs in the UK*. Cham: Springer International Publishing, pp. 587–614.
Smithson, H., Gray, P. and Jones, A. (2021) 'They really should start listening to you': The benefits and challenges of co-producing a participatory framework of youth justice practice. *Youth Justice*, 21(3), 321–337. https://doi.org/10.1177/1473225420941598
Smithson, H. and Gray, P. (2021) Supporting children's meaningful participation in the youth justice system. HM Inspectorate of Probation.
Smithson, H., Lang, T. and Gray, P. (2022) From rhetoric to reality: Participation in practice within youth justice systems. In S. Frankel (ed) *Establishing Child Centred Practice in a Changing World, Part A, Emerald Studies in Child Centred Practice* (pp. 111–122). Bingley: Emerald Publishing.
UN Committee on the Rights of the Child. (2019) *General Comment No. 24 on Children's Rights in the Child Justice System. CRC/C/GC/24*. Geneva: Switzerland.
UNICEF. (1989) *United Nations Convention on the Rights of the Child 1989*. Geneva: United Nations.
Vaswani, N., Moodie, K. and McEwan, D. (2024) Children's experiences of police custody and the implications for trauma-informed policing. *Youth Justice*, 25(1), 108–125. https://doi.org/10.1177/14732254241282503
White, R. and Cunneen, C. (2015) Social class, youth crime and justice. In B. Goldson and J. Muncie (eds) *Youth, Crime and Justice* (2nd ed., pp. 17–30). London: Sage. ISBN 9781446210833.
Wright, S., Liddle, M. and Goodfellow, P. (2016) Young offenders and trauma: Experience and impact: A practitioner's guide. Beyond Youth Custody.
Youth Justice Board (YJB). (2021) Strategic plan 2021–24. Report, YJB, London.
Youth Justice Board (YJB). (2024) Strategic plan 2024–27. Report, YJB, London.

PART II

Values and policy implications

Co-production approaches and evidence-informed policymaking

6

CHILDREN'S RIGHT TO PARTICIPATE IN YOUTH JUSTICE RESEARCH

Opportunities and challenges in Irish youth justice

Louise Forde

Introduction: children's rights and co-production

Article 12 of the UN Convention on the Rights of the Child ("UNCRC") provides that any child capable of forming his or her own views should have a "right to express those views freely in all matters affecting the child", and to have these views accorded "due weight" in accordance with their age and maturity. Referred to as one of the "pillars" of the UNCRC, the guarantee is broad in scope (UN Committee on the Rights of the Child, 2009, para. 26), and applies to all aspects of children's lives, across multiple domains (UN Committee on the Rights of the Child, 2009). This encompasses a requirement to consult with children on '*all* matters' affecting them (emphasis added), and this extends to including children in the design, implementation, development, and evaluation of policies relevant to them, and to their involvement in research (UN Committee on the Rights of the Child, 2009; Byrne & Lundy, 2019). Article 12 is equally applicable in justice settings, where children come into conflict with the law (UN Committee on the Rights of the Child, 2009, paras. 57–61; UN Committee on the Rights of the Child, 2019, para. 44) and has a central importance in this context where a child's ability to participate meaningfully becomes central to the realisation of their due process rights. In addition, it has been posited that ensuring that children have the opportunity to have their voice heard through their interactions with justice mechanisms is crucial to supporting positive engagement with children and, through this, to promoting more positive outcomes (Creaney, 2015; Smithson et Al., 2021; Brierley, 2023).

Article 12 requires that children should have the opportunity to make their views known in the development and evaluation of youth justice policies, and

DOI: 10.4324/9781003602996-9

in research relating to the operation of the youth justice system and its impact on young people in conflict with the law. While effecting change within the youth justice system is often driven by a range of different concerns and considerations, including political considerations (Fergusson, 2007; Case & Hampson, 2019), there is significant potential in centring children's voices and experiences of their rights to advocate for more child-centred, rights-compliant changes in law and policy. Experiences of children participating in public decision-making processes have demonstrated the potential for children to contribute to meaningful change in law, policy, and practice at national and local levels (Forde et al., 2020) and can provide a means for young people who may be marginalised to make their voices heard in a powerful way (Pleysier & Kilkelly, 2023; Smithson & Jones, 2021). In recognising children in conflict with the law as 'experts by experience' (see, e.g., Smithson & Jones, 2021; Creaney & Burns, 2024), there is a valuable opportunity to understand how the rights of children in conflict with the law are impacted by their interactions with the justice system and to imagine improvements to youth justice law, policy, and practice with children's voices as a central guiding influence.

The child's right to participation under Article 12 shares some characteristics with 'co-production' principles which have recently gained prominence in some youth justice systems (see, e.g., Burns & Creaney, 2023; Smithson et al., 2020; Day et al., 2023). While it is beyond the scope of this chapter to conduct an in-depth consideration of the extent to which the child's right to participation under Article 12 and principles of co-production align or diverge, it is worth noting that a number of important features of these approaches are shared. These include recognition of the importance of the inclusion of and engagement with 'experts by experience' in the co-design, co-delivery, and co-evaluation of services and activities, and recognition of their capacities and of the value of their experience and insights in shaping and enhancing these interactions (see further Social Care Institute for Excellence, 2022; Creaney *et al.*, 2024; Burns & Creaney, 2023; Day *et al.*, 2023; Morgan *et al.*, 2025). From a children's rights perspective, it is important that participation is not something which is bestowed on children by benevolent adults but is a right which all children are entitled to and which States Parties to the UNCRC have concrete duties to ensure are respected and upheld (Committee on the Rights of the Child, 2009). It is 'about agency, dignity and respect for children as individuals worthy in their own right, with a voice and a right to have a say' (Kilkelly, 2023, pp. 125–6), and has relevance in all stages of a child's contact with the youth justice system, including in research and evaluation (UN Committee on the Rights of the Child, 2019).

This chapter aims to consider, from a children's rights perspective, how children in conflict with the law can be supported to make their voices heard through participatory research and how the lived experiences of children can contribute to better realisation of children's rights within the youth justice system, drawing on examples from research with young people in the Irish youth justice system.[1] Despite an increased emphasis on hearing the voices of children in conflict with the law in national policy in recent years, this cohort of young people is still sometimes described as 'hard to reach' in the Irish context, and it has been suggested that, more generally, participatory research with children in conflict with the law is still rare (Pleysier & Kilkelly, 2023). This paper will draw on the experiences of the author in conducting research with children in the Irish youth justice system, based on the Lundy model of child participation. It will highlight the importance of including children in youth justice research, discuss the benefits and opportunities inherent in ensuring children's voices are at the centre of this research, reflect on some of the practical challenges in conducting this type of research, and consider some means for further enhancing research with children in this area. The chapter will begin by discussing the scope of Article 12 in the context of youth justice before considering some of the key insights gained from three children's rights-based participatory studies with young people in the Irish youth justice system.

Children's right to participate in youth justice systems under international human rights law

Article 12 of the UNCRC guarantees to all children a right to express their views on matters affecting them and to have these views be given due weight. This unambiguous statement is broad in scope (UN Committee on the Rights of the Child, 2009, para. 26) and 'constitutes one of the fundamental values of the Convention' (UN Committee on the Rights of the Child, 2009, para. 2). It is a right which belongs both to individual children and to children as a group (UN Committee on the Rights of the Child, 2009, Part III) and includes a right to be heard in relation to policy development and evaluation relevant to children's lives (UN Committee on the Rights of the Child, 2009; Byrne & Lundy, 2019). It is a right of all children, including those in conflict with the law (UN Committee on the Rights of the Child, 2019). In considering what the child's right to participation means within the justice system, it is necessary to take a multi-faceted approach. It has been suggested that participation is a somewhat contested term within youth justice (Creaney & Burns, 2024). Children's participatory rights within the youth justice context have at least three distinct dimensions.

Firstly, the right to participate has a direct bearing on the realisation of children's due process rights. Article 12, read together with Art. 40(2), has been interpreted by the UN Committee on the Rights of the Child to afford the child a right to 'effective participation' in all stages of the proceedings (UN

Committee on the Rights of the Child, 2019, para. 46). Initially developed by the European Court of Human Rights (*T. v. the United Kingdom* and *V. v. the United Kingdom*), the concept has been embraced by the UN Committee on the Rights of the Child, and concepts of 'effective participation' and 'child-friendly justice' have become important dimensions of a child-rights-based approach to youth justice (Forde, 2018; Daly & Rap, 2017; Liefaard, 2020). This requires not only that adequate protection is given to children's due process rights within the youth justice system but also that adaptations are made to youth justice processes to ensure that they are meaningful and effective for children in practice (Daly & Rap, 2017; Forde, 2018). Despite this, research across jurisdictions has demonstrated that children nonetheless continue to experience significant challenges in realising their right to effective participation in justice proceedings (Daly & Rap, 2017; Forde, 2018; Kilkelly, 2008; Carr, 2024).

The second important dimension of Article 12 within the youth justice system relates to their interactions with professionals, programmes, and in their experiences of diversion processes, or other interventions within the system. Creaney and Burns have raised questions about the extent to which children's participation in non-voluntary processes such as mandated youth justice interventions can constitute 'meaningful' participation (Creaney & Burns, 2024). Nonetheless, research has highlighted the significance of young people's engagement and of participatory practices in supporting positive outcomes for young people (Creaney et al., 2024; Creaney & Burns, 2024; Burns & Creaney, 2023). In addition, the ability to participate meaningfully is a prerequisite for certain processes within youth justice systems, such as restorative justice processes (Marder & Forde, 2023; Lynch, 2010). In England and Wales, the increased focus on engagement of young people as a central aspect of the 'Child First' approach to youth justice has brought new attention to the need to promote the active and meaningful engagement in practice to support positive outcomes for children within this system (Case & Haines, 2015). Studies have indicated that a lack of meaningful or active participation with youth justice services can reduce the overall effectiveness of these engagements (Creaney, 2015).

The third aspect of children's right to participation within the youth justice system – which is the central focus of the remainder of this chapter – relates to children's right to have their voice heard in research and in the development and evaluation of policy. In addition to this being a key aspect of the Article 12 guarantee (UN Committee on the Rights of the Child, 2009, para. 12; Bryne & Lundy, 2019), the Committee has emphasised the importance of ensuring that children with experience of contact with the youth justice system are involved in evaluation and in research relating to it (UN Committee on the Rights of the Child, 2019, para. 115). In light of this, participatory research with children and meaningful consultation with children in relation to the development of law and policy relevant to them is seen as increasingly central to a children's rights-based approach, including for children in conflict with the law (Byrne & Lundy, 2019; Pleysier & Kilkelly, 2023).

However, several barriers continue to impact the number of participatory research and consultations which take place with children. For example, it has been noted that research *on* children is still more common than research *with* children, particularly in a justice context (Pleysier & Kilkelly, 2023). Further, research into children's participation in public decision-making processes has demonstrated the need for special attention to ensuring that spaces are accessible and inclusive to children who may already be marginalised within society (Forde et al., 2020). This is also a key feature of co-production (Social Care Institute for Excellence, 2022; Creaney and Burns, 2024; Smithson & Jones, 2021). Further, children who are from 'seldom heard' groups may experience difficulties in expressing their views in research and consultations to develop policy, and therefore an adapted approach may be required in order to facilitate these young people in having their voices heard (McEvoy, 2015).

A children's rights approach to participatory research with children requires both that the process of carrying out the research is child rights-compliant and that the central focus is on children's experiences of their rights in practice with a view to contributing to debates relevant to policymakers so that children's rights can be better realised and implemented in practice (Lundy & McEvoy, 2012a; Lundy & McEvoy, 2012b; Byrne & Lundy, 2019). This means, firstly, that ethical standards must be of the highest priority, with a focus on ensuring that no harm is done to children in the course of the research, minimising any vulnerability young people may experience, and ensuring that adequate information is provided both to children and to their parents or guardians about the purpose and aims of the research, as well as what will be done with it (Pleysier & Kilkelly, 2023; McEwan et al., 2025). Both children's best interests and matters related to the safeguarding and protection of children need to be a central aspect of the design of this research from the outset; however, it has also been argued that issues related to protection should not be allowed to override children's right to participation but instead should be considered alongside it (Pleysier & Kilkelly, 2023).

In addition, a UNCRC-informed approach requires acknowledgement of the mutually reinforcing nature of Convention rights, and in particular the relationship between other Convention provisions and Article 12 (Lundy, 2007). For example, ensuring that children have access to adequate information, as required by Article 17, is a crucial first step in ensuring that children are able to formulate, develop, and express their views (Lundy and McEvoy, 2012b). The principle of children's evolving capacities (Article 5 UNCRC) requires acknowledgement that young people may require help from parents or guardians in the exercise of these rights (Kilkelly, 2020; Charles et al., 2024); this can be important to ensure children understand the aims and purpose of the research, the process involved, and to ensure consent is sought from both the young people themselves and their parents or guardians. The Lundy model of child participation sets out a process for a children's rights-based approach to implementation of Article 12, encompassing Voice, Space, Audience, and Influence (Lundy, 2007). This model of participation is particularly suited to children's rights-based participatory research, given its emphasis on including children in the design of the research as well as research participants, and on ensuring that children can make their voices heard and that these views are communicated effectively, especially to those with responsibility for decision-making (Lundy & McEvoy, 2012a). The next section reflects on the process involved in carrying out research with children with experience of contact with the justice system in Ireland utilising the Lundy model of participation and of the significant benefits for research and advocacy that inclusion of these voices can bring to bear.

Reflections on children's rights-based youth justice research in Ireland – opportunities and challenges

The remainder of this chapter reflects on some of the key insights gained from the author's involvement, together with colleagues, in three participatory research projects involving children with experience of the youth justice system in Ireland, utilising a children's rights approach based on the Lundy model of participation (Lundy, 2007; Lundy & McEvoy, 2012a; Lundy & McEvoy, 2012b). These included a study on young people's pathways into conflict with the law and their experiences of contact with the youth justice system in Ireland (Kilkelly et al., 2021); a study on young people's experiences of their rights while being interviewed by An Garda Síochána[2] (Kilkelly & Forde, 2020; Forde & Kilkelly, 2023); and a study on young people's experiences of engagement in arts-based approaches within the Irish youth justice system and the impact of these activities on their rights (Forde, forthcoming). While these studies each had a different focus, key unifying elements in all three projects included a focus on the implementation and realisation of children's rights within the youth justice system – with children's lived experiences of these rights as a central concern of the research – and the use of a participatory methodology which included children both as advisors in relation to the design of the research and as research participants.

For context, it is worth considering briefly the national position related to youth justice, child participation, and children's rights in Ireland. Arguably, there has been an increased recognition for these principles in recent years, with the value of both children's rights and child participation being acknowledged within the youth justice system (Department of Justice, 2021; Forde and Swirak, 2022). The Irish government adopted its first

National Youth Participation Strategy, based on the Lundy method, in 2015 (Department of Children and Youth Affairs, 2015), and this has since been followed by a second iteration (Department of Children, Equality, Disability, Integration and Youth, 2024). This has been accompanied by a series of initiatives to develop processes to support regular consultation with children across a range of areas (see further Lundy & O'Donnell, 2022; Department of Children, Equality, Disability, Integration and Youth, 2024). This national focus on systematically consulting children has had an impact on the development of youth justice policy. The *Youth Justice Strategy 2021–2027* commits to delivering, assessing, and monitoring youth justice policy in light of the rights set out under the UNCRC (Forde & Swirak, 2022) and makes a commitment to upholding the right of children to be heard and to effective participation within their interactions with the youth justice system and 'development of policies, programmes and systems [which are] informed by the voices of children and young people (including those who have and who have not had contact with the criminal justice system)' (Department of Justice, 2021). This represents a significant statement of commitment to the implementation of Article 12 rights for children in the development of policy and in research at a national level.

This focus on participation can also be seen in practice in key areas within the youth justice system; for example, Oberstown Children Detention Campus has developed its own Participation Strategy (Oberstown Children Detention Campus, 2017) and has sought to embed meaningful participation of young people in everyday practice and in important decisions in the institution through the establishment of consultative mechanisms and has sought the participation of young people in the development of its internal policies and in hiring processes for key personnel within the institution, including the Director (Kilkelly & Bergin, 2022). While these efforts have undoubtedly brought very positive changes in the extent to which children are being consulted across a range of areas at national level, in some areas, further attention is needed to ensure better understanding among adults of the value of youth participation, better representation of children in participatory mechanisms, better follow-up and feedback, and to address barriers to participation (Department of Children, Equality, Disability, Integration and Youth, 2024).

As a researcher carrying out research on children's rights within the Irish youth justice system, recognising the importance of participation and children's rights within national policy provides a valuable starting point. International research demonstrates that children's rights protection tends to be enhanced in jurisdictions which accord children's rights legal status in a systematic way (Lundy, Kilkelly & Byrne, 2013), and the focus on child participation and children's rights in Irish national policy meant that there was acknowledgement of the value of participatory research with children among both policymakers and practitioners working in Irish youth justice. While this does not mean that the process of carrying out participatory research with young people in youth justice settings is without challenges, it does mean that there is an acceptance of the value of this type of research in principle. To build on this opportunity, however, there remains a need to be intentional and reflexive in developing approaches to research which seek to enhance children's rights, both in the process of carrying out the research and in advancing children's rights through the outcomes of the research. The remainder of this section highlights some key aspects of research, reflecting on the role of Youth Advisory Boards, the need to pay attention to participation and representation, insights which can be gained from young people, and the value of this research for both young people and for developing child-centred recommendations for changes in law and policy.

Youth Advisory Groups

In all three studies, Youth Advisory Groups (YAGs)[3] were a key aspect of the study design. The establishment of YAGs is an important step to ensure both that the aims of the research and the methodology for the research are reflective of the needs of children and in order to ensure that the key principles of Voice, Space, Audience, and Influence can be incorporated into the research design from the outset (Lundy & McEvoy, 2012a; Lundy & McEvoy, 2012b). To this end, YAGs were established in all three studies at the outset to provide input into the aims of the study, the most important issues the research should consider, and the research methodology to ensure that children were enabled to express their views in a safe, friendly, and non-judgemental environment (Kilkelly et al., 2021; Kilkelly & Forde, 2020; Forde & Kilkelly, 2023; Forde, forthcoming). This approach shares characteristics with co-production approaches, wherein service users are involved in the design of the service and in co-produced research with children (see further Social Care Institute for Excellence, 2022; Smithson & Jones, 2021; Smithson *et al.*, 2021).

In establishing these YAGs, the research teams took steps to ensure that the composition of the YAG could represent the concerns of young people generally and of young people with experience of contact with the justice system. This was also reflective of the overarching aims of the studies; in two of the studies (on young people's pathways into and experiences of the youth justice system and young people's experiences of arts-based approaches), part of the central aims of the research involved inquiry into aspects of children's lives which were not directly related to contact with the justice system (e.g. children's experiences of avoiding getting into trouble or their experiences of engagement in the arts generally), and therefore establishing this mix of experience on the YAGs was important. In each study, YAGs were made up of a mixture of young people who had direct experience of contact with the youth justice system and young people who did not have such contact.

In the early phases of each study, 1-3 meetings were held with each YAG. While the amount of time spent with each YAG was partially dependent on practical constraints, in each case, advice was sought on three key areas. First, young people were informed about the purpose of the study, were given background information about the topic under study, and were asked to review drafts of information sheets and consent forms which the researchers proposed to use in later data collection phases. Providing young people with sufficient information is key to ensuring that young people are supported to participate and is vital to ensuring that research processes are fully informed, safe, and voluntary (Lundy & McEvoy, 2012b). Where YAGs made suggestions to alter or amend the wording, these were implemented by researchers in subsequent drafts. Second, YAG members were invited to contribute to the substantive aspects of the research. While initial draft question frames were prepared in advance based on analysis of the UNCRC, other relevant international guidelines, and existing research, YAGs were asked to suggest what issues might be most important to young people about the topic under study before being presented with pre-prepared material. This ensured that YAGs could have influence on the aims and key themes to be addressed by the research without undue influence by the research teams. Following on from this, YAGs then engaged in more detailed consideration of some of the pre-prepared materials and provided feedback on their relevance and appropriateness for young people, as well as provided input on any aspects that the adult researchers may have overlooked. Thirdly, YAG members were invited to advise on the research methodology to be used. This involved providing input on whether researchers should use methodologies such as focus groups or one-on-one interviews as the most appropriate way to support children in expressing their views on the different topics under discussion. It also involved providing advice and feedback to researchers on their approach to engaging with young people and how they could best support them to feel safe and free to make their views known. It also involved reviewing the proposed methodologies researchers had planned and providing feedback on whether these were appropriate and if they needed amendment. Where this feedback was provided, it was subsequently adopted in the final design of the research for use later in the study.

The experience of working on these studies demonstrated that YAGs are a vital component of research that aims to be children's rights-centred in the aims, process and outcomes produced. The insights provided by the YAGs gave essential guidance on the issues of most importance to young people, allowing researchers to shape their approach to reflect the concerns of young people and to allow space for inclusion of any issues not captured by researchers in the initial design; this substantially enhanced the research team's ability to ensure that the voice of young people could be heard in a meaningful way which sought to avoid tokenism (Lundy, 2018). In addition, the YAGs provided invaluable input on the research methodologies. As a researcher working with young people, it is necessary to adopt a reflexive stance and to acknowledge the potential disparity in power between the young people who participate in research and the researcher (Shier, 2022; McEwan et al., 2025). In seeking the views of YAGs on the research methods, we aimed to address some of this potential disparity in power and to ensure that children could be confident that both the space and the audience promoted children's ability to express their views in a full, free, and safe manner. Finally, a key component emphasised by the YAGs was to ensure that young people understood what would happen to their views and how this would be communicated both within research outputs and to policymakers – both vital aspects of ensuring that children's voices have influence (see further, e.g., Barron, 2022). From a practical perspective, this resulted in steps being taken by the research teams in each study to include clear information about what would be done with the information for research participants and to ensure that activities included questions about their views about what policymakers or practitioners should know or what they could do differently to better protect and promote children's rights.

Ensuring participation and representation

A second key reflection relates to the participation and representation of young people within the studies. Young people in youth justice systems often experience multiple challenges (see further Kilkelly et al., 2024; Case & Browning, 2021; Day et al., 2023; van der Laan et al., 2009), which have a negative impact on their opportunities to make their voices heard (see further, e.g., McEwan et al., 2025; McMahon & Jump, 2017; Creaney et al., 2024). Research has shown that specific efforts are needed to ensure that children who may be marginalised are included in consultative mechanisms (Forde et al., 2020). Therefore, attention was given – within the practical constraints of each individual research study – to reducing any barriers to participation and to ensuring that there was representation of a spectrum of young people's views within the studies.

It is worth noting that all research studies have practical constraints in relation to time, funding, and availability of researchers and research participants, which can influence the extent to which participatory practices can be carried out. All three of the projects cited were relatively small-scale studies – and while all exceeded initial targets for the numbers of young people included – their ability to be fully representative of the wide spectrum of experiences that young people may have within the youth justice system was constrained by the small-scale nature of the studies (see further Kilkelly et al., 2021; Kilkelly & Forde, 2020; Forde, forthcoming). Although relatively small numbers of young people were included in each study, in all cases an effort was made to include children with a wide spectrum of experiences. In order to ensure as much diversity as possible within the research cohort, in all studies, efforts were made to recruit research participants from across all stages of the youth justice system – within diversion/early intervention projects, community-based probation projects, and in detention – to include a variety of urban and rural locations, and to include a mix of both boys and girls among the research participants.

While this approach was generally successful, there were nonetheless limitations to each study which highlighted the need for further, more specific inquiry into key issues. For example, while all studies included both boys and girls, a comparatively small number of girls participated as compared to boys. This was both reflective of the over-representation of boys within the Irish youth justice system and highlighted to researchers that there may be a need for further research studies which consider the specific gendered experiences of young people of these issues. Similarly, international research has highlighted that research may also need to take specific issues relevant to the cultural backgrounds of young people into consideration (McEwan et al., 2025; Butcher et al., 2020). In light of the fact that these specific questions were not the core focus of any of the three research studies described, particular attention was not given to how experiences of being from a minority group – such as children from immigrant or Traveller backgrounds, for example – might have experiences which were different from those of other children. While the potential for these differences was noted as part of the research process, further research is needed to consider these issues in a more in-depth manner.

A further barrier can sometimes arise where it is contended that children's expressed views are not representative of the views of all children, and therefore that they may not be seen as legitimate (Hanna et al., 2024). In line with a children's rights-based approach, while researchers acknowledged that the views collected in these studies could not be representative of every single child's experience, the views and experiences of each individual participant were treated as being important, valid, and worthy of serious consideration in enhancing our understanding of children's experiences of their rights, and therefore of relevance to important issues relating to reform of youth justice law, policy, and practice (Lundy & McEvoy, 2012a). In line with research on co-production with children, which has highlighted the importance of trust and non-hierarchical, mutually respectful relationships between researchers and young people to assist young people in expressing their views (Creaney & Burns, 2024; Smithson & Jones, 2021), researchers sought to establish safe, friendly, and non-judgemental approaches to young people to enable them to express their views and to ensure that they were aware that their views were taken seriously and were valued within the research.

Insights from young people

Participatory research with children has the potential to establish a wealth of knowledge about the operation of the youth justice system and children's experiences of their rights (Smithson & Jones, 2021). In each study, rich insights were gained from young people about their experiences when they came into contact with the youth justice system and of their experiences of their rights in practice. These experiences were extremely valuable in shaping recommendations relating to reform of law, policy, and practice in these studies. Without the direct involvement and participation of children, it would have been extremely difficult – if not impossible – for these perspectives to be included, and the findings, conclusions, and policy recommendations generated from the studies would have been poorer for it.

While it is beyond the scope of this piece to detail the findings of these studies, a number of common themes emerged (Kilkelly et al., 2021; Kilkelly & Forde, 2020; Forde, forthcoming). First, the perspectives of young people led to an enhanced understanding of how children enjoy their rights in practice. Given that there is often significant divergence between the aims expressed in law and policy and the lived experience of individuals of their rights, the views expressed by young people provided valuable opportunities to understand how rights are accessed – or not – by young people in practice. Similar to rights-based research with children in conflict with the law in other jurisdictions (e.g. McEwan et al., 2025; McAlister & Carr, 2014), our research highlighted the diversity of views and experiences among young people, even when discussing similar issues and events. For example, in the study of young people's experiences of police questioning, young people reported a wide variety of experiences of police questioning, with some reporting very straightforward experiences and others reporting much more negative experiences. It was also interesting that, despite the different areas of concern in each study, common themes emerged consistently; for example, all studies demonstrated the central importance of supportive and respectful relationships and interactions between adults and young people to support greater realisation of children's rights and noted that young people's experiences were often significantly shaped by the approach of the adults involved.

Secondly, children's contributions brought a number of issues into consideration which would not otherwise have found their way into the research. In some cases, young people raised issues which had not been anticipated by researchers and which had not otherwise been raised by adult participants in the study. For example, in the study of young people's experiences of being questioned by the police, a number of young people raised issues (unprompted by researchers) relating to poor treatment which they experienced in their interactions with members of An Garda Síochána (Kilkelly & Forde, 2020; Forde & Kilkelly, 2023). As this was not something which had been anticipated by researchers or by the YAGs in advance of the interviews with young people in this study, this vitally important issue would have been missed had the voices of young people not been included.

Thirdly, the inclusion of young people – often in addition to adult professionals working within the youth justice system – helped to shed light on differences in understanding which can arise between young people and adults. For example, again in the study of young people's experiences of questioning, members of An Garda Síochána who took part in the study highlighted their approach to interviewing children, which involved rapport-building, where Gardaí sought to engage young people in general conversation to help establish a relationship and also to help to put them at ease in a stressful situation. While this would generally be considered an important aspect of child-centred and developmentally appropriate practice by many adults, many young people in the study spoke about feeling as though they were being 'tricked' by this type of practice (Kilkelly & Forde, 2020; Forde & Kilkelly, 2023). The experience of the author within these studies strongly reinforced the value of including both young people and adult professionals in studies of this sort, as it can highlight areas where the understanding and experiences of adults and young people diverge. This is key to understanding not only how processes and practices can be made more child-centred, but also can help us to better understand children's experiences and expectations of their rights in these contexts.

Fourthly, these studies can shed light on matters of general relevance which – though not *prima facie* connected to youth justice processes – can nonetheless shape their experiences in important ways. For example, the study on young people's experiences of arts-based interventions identified that many young people in the study had had variable access to arts-based activities outside of their contact with the justice system; this provides important insights not only into the rights young people are entitled to as a result of their contact with the justice system but can also help us to understand how well children's other UNCRC rights – such as the right to participate in arts and cultural life (Article 31) – are protected and upheld in practice (see further Forde, forthcoming). Similarly, the study on young people's experiences of coming into conflict with the law in Ireland provided important insights into how young people's ability to access leisure activities, education, and employment, and their interactions with their peers could help to shape whether they came into contact with the youth justice system (see further Kilkelly et al., 2021). Given that the rights of general application under the UNCRC often receive limited attention for children in conflict with the law (Kilkelly et al. 2024), the young people's expressed concerns about a wide range of areas in their lives reinforce the need for an approach to youth justice which takes a holistic approach and which acknowledges them as children with needs and interests across all areas of their lives, and not just those needs which arise as a result of their contact with the justice system.

Finally, in each study, the conclusions and recommendations reached were substantially enhanced and informed by the contributions of children and added significant value to the perspectives brought by adults and the analysis of the legal texts and existing research in the area. Research studies involving children have noted the need for adult facilitators to assist them to present their views clearly and in a way that would be convincing and compelling for decision makers so that these can be taken seriously in any future consideration of changes to law, policy, and practice (Lundy, 2018). The experience in these studies demonstrates that this is not only necessary as part of ensuring that children's Article 12 rights are realised, but also that ensuring this is done brings significant benefits for the research findings. Across all three studies, the findings and the policy recommendations generated were substantially influenced by what we were told young people. As researchers with an interest in developing further respect for children's rights and advocating for better realisation of children's rights, ensuring children's voices form a central component of the development of these recommendations is essential.

Conclusion

Participatory approaches which involve children both as advisors and participants in research hold vast potential to enhance our knowledge of what is meant by a children's rights approach to youth justice system, and can add significantly to debates about the development of children's rights-based law, policy and practice. These approaches can also complement and assist efforts to develop co-produced approaches in other areas of youth justice research, policy design and service delivery. Through acknowledging children's inherent right to participate, there is the potential to place children's voices and experiences at the centre of these efforts and give greater attention to the variety of rights children are entitled to under the UNCRC and which States Parties have a duty to protect, respect, and uphold. It has been noted that failing to adequately respect the right of children in conflict with the law under the UNCRC to participation can have 'system-wide consequences' (Charles et Al., 2024). Conversely, supporting positive, rights-based participatory practice in research and policy development equally holds the potential to influence the development of practice in youth justice systems, which can equally have wide-ranging impacts. Scholars such as McAra have highlighted the need for academics to look for multiple avenues for entry into discussion and debate with politicians, policymakers, and the wider public to affect change within criminal justice law, policy, and practice (McAra, 2017); seeking to promote methods to enhance the participation of children within this research, and to bring their voices and experiences to bear in policy debates, may be one particularly fruitful avenue to support arguments related to the need to change aspects of the youth justice system.

There are a number of challenges inherent in carrying out research with children in conflict with the law. They may be 'hard to reach', and additional efforts are required on the part of researchers to access these young people and to ensure that the research is as inclusive and representative as possible. In addition, there is a special need to ensure that children are adequately safeguarded within these approaches and to ensure that protection and participation are balanced (Pleysier & Kilkelly, 2023). Further, where there is a lack of acknowledgement of the value that the inclusion of young people's voices in a meaningful way can bring to debates about the transformation of law, policy, and practice related to youth justice by policymakers, this can present a significant barrier to the development of more child-centred and rights-compliant approaches (Smithson et al., 2021). It has also been suggested that in some youth justice systems, participation and engagement are given relatively low priority as compared with other concerns, such as punishment and retribution (Creaney, 2015). However, it is worth noting that the context in which these studies were carried out – where there was a substantial emphasis placed both on children's rights under the UNCRC and the importance of child participation in national policy in Ireland – was of significant benefit in setting an expectation that child participation is desirable and of value to the development of policy and practice at national and local levels.

As the experience in carrying out participatory research in Ireland demonstrates, there are substantial benefits to be gained from including children both as research participants and as advisors in relation to the design of the research. Building on Lundy's model of participation (Lundy, 2007; Lundy & McEvoy, 2012a; Lundy & McEvoy, 2012b), these studies have reinforced the many benefits which can be gained from including young people meaningfully in research. The insights gained from these studies enriched our understanding of what a children's rights approach looks like, how children experience and understand their rights, and contributed to the development of conclusions and policy recommendations which hold the potential to develop youth justice systems that are more responsive to the lived experiences and needs of the children who are most affected by them. These studies may also bring other benefits; for example, Lundy has highlighted that children who have been involved in participatory research have reported a range of benefits from this participation, including personal learning, gaining skills and confidence, and increased awareness of their rights (Lundy, 2018). In our experience of young people's participation in these studies, young people were often eager to talk about their experiences with adults who they felt would listen, and keen to ensure that their views and experiences would form part of the message which was communicated through the conclusions of the research to a wider audience and to policymakers and decision-makers with responsibility for developing the youth justice system.

The obligation set out in Article 12 of the UNCRC is one which we would do well to take seriously in youth justice research. While there are often challenges inherent in this research, and researchers will often experience barriers and limitations related to logistical arrangements, the availability of time and funding to support this work, and in ensuring that processes both safeguard children and promote their ability to participate meaningfully, these should not be reasons to avoid undertaking this type of research with children (Lundy, 2018; Pleysier & Kilkelly, 2023; Barron, 2022). As children's rights researchers, it is incumbent on us to respect children's rights in the process of carrying out research – including recognising children's entitlement to participate under Article 12 – as well as in promoting the realisation of children's rights through the aims pursued and conclusions reached throughout research. The inclusion of children in the research – in line with the Lundy method of participation to ensure research processes are appropriate and relevant for children – and the significant value which this can add to our understanding of children's rights in practice, and to our debates around the development of law and policy, hold the potential to contribute greatly to our knowledge about children's rights within the context of youth justice

Notes

1 This article draws on three previous studies, carried out by the author and with colleagues. Thanks and acknowledgement is owed both to the original co-authors of these studies and to the Youth Advisory Group members, research participants, and all who contributed to the completion of these studies, as well as to those who generously funded the research. The studies referred to include: 1) the Irish Research Council/DYCA COALESCE-funded study on children's pathways into and experiences of the Irish youth justice system, led by Prof. Ursula Kilkelly, published as Kilkelly, U., Forde, L., Hurley, E., Lambert, S., Swirak, K., Kelleher, D. & Buckley, S., *Ensuring the collaborative reform of youth justice in Ireland in line with international research and evidence-based approaches* (2021); 2) the Policing Authority-funded study on children's experiences of their rights in police questioning, led by Prof Ursula Kilkelly and the author, originally published as Kilkelly U. & Forde, L, Children's Rights and Police Questioning: A Qualitative Study of Children's Experiences of being interviewed by the Garda Síochána (Dublin: Policing Authority, 2020); and 3) the Brunel Research Initiative Enterprise Fund study, led by the author on children's experiences of creative arts in the youth justice system, reported in Forde, forthcoming.

2 The Irish police.

3 The terms "Youth Advisory Group" (YAGs) and "Children's Research Advisory Group" (CRAGs) have been used interchangeably in publications associated with these studies; both terms refer broadly to the same process and use broadly the same methodology.

Bibliography

Barron, C. (2022). 'Are they going to do anything with this info?': Implementing children's perspectives on play and recreation policies. In D. Horgan & D. Kennan (Eds.), *Child and youth participation in policy, practice and research* (pp. 57–70). Oxon & New York: Routledge.

Brierley, A. (2023). Experiential peers cultivate a participation culture in youth justice. *Safer Communities, 22*(2), 78–90.

Burns, S., & Creaney, S. (2023). Embracing children's voices: Transforming youth justice practice through co-production and Child First participation. In S. Case & N. Hazel (Eds.), *Child First: Developing a new youth justice system* (pp. 333–365). Palgrave Macmillan.

Butcher, L., Day, A., Kidd, G., Miles, D., & Stanton, S. (2020). Community engagement in youth justice program design. *Australian & New Zealand Journal of Criminology, 53*(3), 369–386.

Byrne, B., & Lundy, L. (2019). Children's rights-based childhood policy: A six-P framework. *International Journal of Human Rights, 23*(3), 357–373.

Carr, S. (2024). Who's in charge of children's equality? Children's participation in their youth justice. *British Journal of Community Justice, 19*(2), 84–87.

Case, S., & Browning, A. (2021). *Child First justice: The research evidence-base* [full report]. Loughborough University.

Case, S., & Haines, K. (2015). Children First, offenders second: The centrality of engagement in positive youth justice. *The Howard Journal of Criminal Justice, 54*(2), 157–175.

Case, S., & Hampson, K. (2019). Youth justice pathways to change: Drivers, challenges and opportunities. *Youth Justice, 19*(1), 25–41.

Charles, A., Hampson, K., Case, S., & Brown, A. (2024). Challenging notions of children's "participation" in the youth justice system: The United Nations Convention on the Rights of the Child, Article 12. *The International Journal of Children's Rights, 32*(1), 9–44.

Creaney, S. (2015). Still working with 'involuntary clients' in youth justice. *British Journal of Community Justice, 13*(1), 41–54.

Creaney, S. (2018). Children's voices—are we listening? Progressing peer mentoring in the youth justice system. *Child Care in Practice, 26*(1), 22–37.

Creaney, S., & Burns, S. (2024). Freedom from symbolic violence? Facilitators and barriers to participatory practices in youth justice. *Youth Justice, 24*(1), 31–52.

Creaney, S., Burns, S., Douglas, A. M., Brierley, A., & Falconer, C. (2024). Desistance through participatory practice: Involving children in decision making processes in youth justice. In A. Wigzell, C. Paterson-Young, & T. Bateman (Eds.), *Desistance and children: Critical reflections from theory, research and practice* (pp. 212–227). Bristol: Policy Press.

Daly, A., & Rap, S. (2017). Children's participation in youth justice and civil court proceedings: Have states made sufficient progress? In U. Kilkelly & T. Liefaard (Eds.), *International law on the rights of the child*. Springer.

Day, A., Malvaso, C., Butcher, L., O'Connor, J., McLachlan, K. (2023, 27 March). Co-producing trauma-informed youth justice in Australia?. *Safer Communities, 22*(2), 106–120.

Department of Children and Youth Affairs. (2015). *National strategy on children and young people's participation in decision-making 2015–2020*. Dublin: Department of Children and Youth Affairs.

Department of Children, Equality, Disability, Integration and Youth. (2024). *Participation of children and young people in decision-making: Action plan 2024–2028*. Dublin: Department of Children, Equality, Disability, Integration and Youth.

Department of Justice. (2021). *Youth justice strategy 2021–2027*. Dublin.

Fergusson, R. (2007). Making sense of the melting pot: Multiple discourses in youth justice policy. *Youth Justice, 7*(3), 179–194.

Forde, L. (2018). Realising the right of the child to participate in the criminal process. *Youth Justice, 18*(3), 265–284.

Forde, L., & Kilkelly, U. (2023). Children and police questioning: A rights-based approach. *Criminology & Criminal Justice, 24*(3), 648–669.

Forde, L., Kilkelly, U., Lundy, L., & Kelleher, D. (2020). *The right of children to participate in public decision-making processes*. London: Save the Children.

Forde, L., & Swirak, K. (2022). The development of the Irish youth justice system: Towards a children's rights model of youth justice? *Journal of Contemporary Criminal Justice, 39*(1), 114–132.

Hanna, A., Kane, J., Savage, C., & Lundy, L. (2024). We are who we represent: A theory of "immersive" representation in student activism. *The International Journal of Children's Rights, 32*(3), 560–584.

Kilkelly, U. (2008). Youth courts and children's rights: The Irish experience. *Youth Justice, 8*(1), 39–56.

Kilkelly, U. (2020). "Evolving capacities" and "parental guidance" in the context of youth justice: Testing the application of Article 5 of the Convention on the Rights of the Child. *The International Journal of Children's Rights, 28*(3), 500–520.

Kilkelly, U. (2023). Child First and children's rights: An opportunity to advance rights-based youth justice. In S. Case & N. Hazel (Eds.), *Child First: Developing a new youth justice system* (pp. 109–133). Palgrave Macmillan.

Kilkelly, U., & Bergin, P. (2022). *Advancing children's rights in detention: A model for international reform*. Bristol: Bristol University Press.

Kilkelly, U., & Forde, L. (2020). *Children's rights and police questioning: A qualitative study of children's experiences of being interviewed by the Garda Síochána*. Dublin: Policing Authority.

Kilkelly, U., Forde, L., Hurley, E., Lambert, S., Swirak, K., Kelleher, D., & Buckley, S. (2021). *Ensuring the collaborative reform of youth justice in Ireland in line with international research and evidence-based approaches*. Department of Children, Equality, Disability, Integration and Youth, Dublin.

Kilkelly, U., Forde, L., Lambert, S., & Swirak, K. (2024). *Children in conflict with the law: Rights, research and progressive youth justice*. Switzerland: Palgrave Macmillan.

Liefaard, T. (2020). Child-friendly justice and procedural safeguards for children in criminal proceedings: New momentum for children in conflict with the law? *Bergen Journal of Criminal Law and Criminal Justice, 8*(1), 1–17.

Lundy, L. (2007). 'Voice' is not enough: Conceptualising Article 12 of the United Nations Convention on the Rights of the Child. *British Educational Research Journal, 33*(6), 927–942.
Lundy, L. (2018). In defence of tokenism? Implementing children's right to participate in collective decision-making. *Childhood, 25*(3), 340–354.
Lundy, L., Kilkelly, U., & Byrne, B. (2013). Incorporation of the United Nations convention on the rights of the child in law: A comparative review. *International Journal of Children's Rights*, 21(3), 442–463.
Lundy, L., & McEvoy, L. (2012a). Childhood, the United Nations Convention on the Rights of the Child, and research: What constitutes a 'rights-based' approach? In M. Freeman (Ed.), *Law and childhood studies: Current legal issues (Vol. 14)*. Oxford: Oxford University Press.
Lundy, L., & McEvoy, L. (2012b). Children's rights and research processes: Assisting children to (in)formed views. *Childhood, 19*(1), 129–144.
Lundy, L., & O'Donnell, A. (2022). Partnering for child participation: Reflections from a policy-maker and a professor. In D. Horgan & D. Kennan (Eds.), *Child and youth participation in policy, practice and research* (pp. 15–29). Oxon & New York: Routledge.
Lynch, N. (2010). Restorative justice through children's rights lens. *International Journal of Children's Rights, 18*(2), 161–184.
Marder, I. D., & Forde, L. (2023). Challenges in the future of restorative youth justice in Ireland: Minimising intervention, maximising participation. *Youth Justice, 23*(2), 201–225.
McAlister, S., & Carr, N. (2014). Experiences of youth justice: Youth justice discourses and their multiple effects. *Youth Justice, 14*(3), 241–254.
McAra, L. (2017). Can criminologists change the world? Critical reflections on the politics, performance and effects of criminal justice. *The British Journal of Criminology, 57*(4), 767–788.
McEvoy, O. (2015). *A practical guide to including seldom-heard children and young people in decision-making*. Dublin: Department of Children and Youth Affairs.
McEwan, A., Price, L., Suzuki, M., Pascoe, V., Lorenza, L., Bloomfield, C., Power, D., & Stanton, L. (2025). Rural youth participation in youth justice research: Towards a rights-based approach. *Youth Justice*, 25(2), 242–261.
McMahon, G., & Jump, D. (2017). Starting to stop: Young offenders' desistance from crime. *Youth Justice, 18*(1), 3–17.
Morgan, G., Jones, D., Walker, C., Prideaux, G., & Jones, E. (2025). Co-production in the criminal justice system: Introducing the DEVICES principles. *The Howard Journal of Crime and Justice*, 64, 162–180.
Oberstown Children Detention Campus. (2017). *Strategy for the participation of young people in decision-making*. Dublin: Oberstown Children Detention Campus.
Pleysier, S., & Kilkelly, U. (2023). The right to participation in youth justice research. *Youth Justice, 23*(3), 263–268.
Shier, H. (2022). Locating the (adult) researcher in participatory research with children. In D. Horgan & D. Kennan (Eds.), *Child and youth participation in policy, practice and research* (pp. 157–167). Oxon & New York: Routledge.
Smithson, H., Gray, P., & Jones, A. (2020). 'They really should start listening to you': The benefits and challenges of co-producing a participatory framework of youth justice practice. *Youth Justice, 21*(3), 321–337.

Smithson, H., & Jones, A. (2021). Co-creating youth justice practice with young people: Tackling power dynamics and enabling transformative action. *Children & Society, 35*(3), 348–362.

Social Care Institute for Excellence (2022). Co-production in social care: What it is and how to do it. Available from: www.scie.org.uk/co-pro duction/what-how

United Nations Committee on the Rights of the Child. (2009). *General comment No. 12: The right of the child to be heard* (CRC/C/GC/12).

United Nations Committee on the Rights of the Child. (2019). *General comment No. 24 on children's rights in the child justice system* (CRC/C/GC/24).

van der Laan, A. M., Blom, M., & Kleemans, E. R. (2009). Exploring long-term and short-term risk factors for serious delinquency. *European Journal of Criminology, 6*(5), 419–438.

7

CO-PRODUCING A CHILD FIRST POLICY FRAMEWORK FOR THE WEST YORKSHIRE VIOLENCE REDUCTION PARTNERSHIP

Georgia Watkinson

Introduction

Child First is the central guiding principle in the Youth Justice Board's strategic plan centred around creating a system that sees children as children, treats them fairly, and builds on their strengths (Youth Justice Board, 2024a). The theory and evidence underpinning Child First is summarised into four tenets: As Children, Building Pro-social Identity, Collaborating with Children, and Diverting from Stigma (Youth Justice Board, 2022). Although designed in the context of Youth Justice, there has been a recent shift towards its application beyond the justice system (Youth Justice Board, 2024b). The core principles of Child First are applicable to all organisations that impact the lives of children. Embedding these principles across the whole system to create a consistent and coordinated approach could help to recognise and respond to the unmet needs of children (Watkinson, Marshall & Kewley, 2024). This chapter will outline the work at the West Yorkshire Violence Reduction Partnership on their journey to implement Child First across the region and how this links to the existing Child First evidence base. Discussion will then focus on barriers and enablers to effective co-production, lessons learned, and key takeaways for collaborative working with children. While co-production can be a time- and resource-intensive process (Cunningham & Wakeling, 2022), it empowers children to increase their agency while transforming how professionals view children and to challenge power imbalances (Burns & Creaney, 2023).

The West Yorkshire Violence Reduction Partnership (VRP) is one of twenty Violence Reduction Units (VRUs) across the UK. They were first established in 2019 by the Home Office to respond to rising trends in serious violence

DOI: 10.4324/9781003602996-10

and to bring together key partners, including police, health, local authorities, education, and community leaders, to create multi-agency responses to violence reduction (Home Office, 2020). By adopting a public health approach, VRUs put a focus on early intervention and prevention, highlighting the need to understand the underlying causes of serious violence (Public Health England, 2019). There are three core measures that VRUs are required to report on, all with a focus on under 25s (Craston et al., 2020). These are:

- A reduction in hospital admissions for assaults with a knife or sharp object, especially among those victims aged under 25,
- A reduction in knife-enabled serious violence, especially among those victims aged under 25,
- A reduction in all non-domestic homicides, especially among those victims aged under 25 involving knives.

Both the age specification outlined by the Home Office and recent research outlining the prevalence of violence in the lives of children (Youth Endowment Fund, 2024) meant implementing Child First into our work was a necessary change. Child First places a focus for practitioners on prevention and diversion from formal contact with the Youth Justice System (Hazel & Williams, 2023), which suggests that by combining this with a public health approach, it would better equip VRUs to achieve their aims and better understand and respond to the specific needs of children.

Initial changes made in the work included a review of language used throughout core documents and breaking down the focus from under 25s to children (under 18s) and young adults (18–25s). In West Yorkshire, the VRP sits within the Mayoral Combined Authority, which has devolved powers from the government around skills, education, and jobs; transport and housing and planning; and Police and Crime Commissioner functions (Ministry of Housing, Communities and Local Government & Department for Levelling Up, Housing and Communities, 2024). These are all areas that impact the lives of children, either now or in the future. Given our positioning in the Combined Authority, we began to understand our valuable position to influence wider system change to benefit children. Embedding Child First into the Combined Authority would impact policies and delivery in these areas while influencing the five local authorities we collaborate with. The Mayor of West Yorkshire, Tracy Brabin, committed to adopting a Child First approach when re-elected in 2024 (Brabin, 2025).

Developing a West Yorkshire Child First Framework

Adopting a Child First approach was discussed within the VRP team, and while they agreed with the principles, they felt it needed more operational and localised guidance to embed Child First both internally and within our wider partnership. The existing guidance on Child First is youth justice-centric, given its origins, but it was felt it may not directly translate to our wider partnership, such as education or local authorities. Furthermore, while current guidance offers extensive justification for *why* Child First is effective for practice, it lacks clarity on *how* it can be applied day to day (Hampson, Nisbet & Case, 2023). It was therefore agreed that the VRP would develop a West Yorkshire Child First Framework to provide guidance to all professionals who work with or for children on how Child First can be applied in the context of their roles.

In keeping with Tenet 3 of Child First, collaborating with children, it was essential we involved children in shaping this work from the very start of the framework development process. We decided to co-produce a framework that outlined how children wanted Child First to be put into practice. Co-production sessions were facilitated by the Research and Evaluation Specialists and Program Delivery Managers within the VRP. The purpose of this document was to communicate how Child First should be incorporated at every level of an organisation, including those who do not interact with children directly, such as those in policy development or management roles.

Due to the lack of universal model, there are varying definitions of what co-production means (Ikhile et al., 2023). However, co-production can be broadly defined as creating an equal relationship between people who use services and those responsible for services. This fosters a process of working together to inform decision-making, policy development, and delivery (Local Government Association, n.d.). Key principles of co-production include reducing power imbalances to create equal and reciprocal relationships while engaging with a diverse group in an accessible way (Social Care Institute for Excellence, 2022). To inform our co-production activities, we utilised the Lundy model of participation (2007) due to its alignment with the United Nations Convention on the Rights of the Child. The model outlines four key elements to ensure meaningful collaboration is achieved; these are Space, Voice, Audience, and Influence. Workshops were conducted with children across the region to give children the opportunity to shape the framework. Below is an outline of how these sessions aligned to the Lundy model.

Space: We ensured we went to spaces where children already felt safe and comfortable to express their views. This included youth clubs, football pitches, schools, and alternative provisions.

Voice: All workshops started with introductions of who the facilitators were, both professionally and personally. We explained the framework we wanted to create and that children in the session were the experts who could shape it, but they did not have to stay if they did not want to.

Audience: Facilitators explained to children that their views were going to create a framework along with lots of other children. They were told that we would share the draft with them so they could check we had understood and interpreted their views correctly.

Influence: As a team, we are continuing to communicate with the children we engaged with about the impact their work has had. They were invited to our launch event to celebrate their contributions, and we have gone back to groups to tell them where their work continues to go.

To respond to the varying needs of children, it was vital to incorporate a number of engagement methods to ensure all children were able to participate. Hampson et al. (2023) highlight the importance of *choice* in participatory research with children, ensuring children are able to decide whether or not to take part without external influence from professionals. This should extend to choice over *how* children would like to participate rather than assuming one approach will be appealing to all (Caulfield, Sojka & Devi-McGleish, 2021). To balance this with consistency, all activities were centred around four statements agreed by our multi-agency working group for children to consider:

- We work together
- We see you as an individual
- We build trusted relationships
- Right place, right time, right person, and right reason

The working group was established in November 2023 with representation from sectors across West Yorkshire who are responsible for working with or for children. This included Youth Justice, the youth sector, local authorities, education, social care, probation, and academics. Membership was voluntary, and members identified themselves after membership details were circulated to our partnership via email and through our VRP newsletter. The statements outlined above were suggested due to concerns that the Child First tenets would not be easily understood by children. Instead, statements were chosen that the group felt captured the ethos of what we needed to understand to effectively implement Child First.

Discussions were facilitated by VRP staff or by children in the group. This peer-led approach enhanced the quality of feedback as children were able to use their lived experience to facilitate conversations in a way professionals could not. This was achieved through them using knowledge not possessed by professionals and asking questions in more child-friendly ways due to their shared experiences (Brady et al., 2023; Brierley, 2023). Children had the option to write their responses themselves or discuss it and have the facilitator note it down. There were other resources available to encourage participation, including mind maps, to organise their thoughts either as a group or independently. All information was recorded on flip chart paper, so children were able to see what was being written and correct it or elaborate if needed. Literature suggests that children are more likely to engage if the activity is centred around something they enjoy, with creative methods creating a less formal environment that aids relationship building (Caulfield et al., 2019). In our groups, some children wanted to participate but did not want to take part in group discussions or write their answers. In this scenario, children were able to draw answers to their responses and explain these to their facilitator at the end of the session on a one-to-one basis. We also incorporated games to make sessions more interactive. For example, we facilitated a giant game of snakes and ladders with questions to be answered when landing on different squares.

Effective co-production relies on a foundation of trust between children and professionals as this helps create a judgement-free environment for children to share their views (Burns & Creaney, 2023; Social Care Institute For Excellence, 2022). Where an existing relationship was needed to facilitate meaningful engagement, workshops were conducted by partner organisations. This was supported by the creation of facilitator packs, which included briefings, session plans, resources, and guidance on capturing children's views. Throughout the engagement process, we spoke to 455 children in 30 different settings, including schools, youth clubs, and youth justice. Children's input was recorded on flipchart paper either by the children or by session facilitators before being transcribed digitally. This ensured we were capturing content in children's words and children could check facilitators had understood them, as being misunderstood by professionals can be detrimental to children's future engagement (Cunningham et al., 2024). To ensure compliance with ethical considerations, all contributions were anonymised, and children were made aware that their involvement was voluntary and they were able to leave whenever they wanted.

Organising children's voices

We identified themes from the workshops which are outlined below:

Think big picture – This section highlighted the need for us to consider the whole child, not just the aspect that relates to our priorities. Initially, we need to understand *how* children are impacted by our work, considering different needs and experiences. Children should be valued as equal stakeholders, with a focus on reciprocal and long-lasting relationships, which is a key principle of effective co-production (Social Care Institute for Excellence, 2022).

All them people who come and talk to us really should come back and see us, but they never turn up again.

You say, we're listening – Children felt they had creative solutions to problems and could offer valuable insight. They wanted to know there are tangible outcomes, including the specific actions that have been taken as a result of their input. This section highlighted the need for joined-up working and knowledge sharing between professionals so children do not have to repeat themselves. This aligns with recognised best practice within youth justice (see Byrne & Brooks, 2015).

Professionals should know my story, so I don't have to repeat my story.

Right person and right place – Children spoke to us about the right person to engage with them and what made the physical environment right. They wanted someone who *genuinely* wants to hear their views. They valued professionals being upfront about who they are and why they want to speak to them; not sharing anything that had been discussed without telling them beforehand; and a sense of humour goes a long way too! There was a preference for professionals going to spaces where children already were, and they noted the empowering nature of the physical environment if it is safe, welcoming, and comfortable.

Actually showing genuine interest.

TEXTBOX 7.1 ENGAGEMENT SHOULD BE ENGAGING – TEN STEPS FOR SUCCESSFUL ENGAGEMENT

1. Tailor the engagement to the group, considering learning styles and what effective communication looks like
2. At the start of the session, establish boundaries, explain why you are there, and how children's feedback will be used
3. Be curious and ask questions while respecting the boundaries set out
4. Be mindful of the space you are in
5. Be open to children asking you questions too, demonstrating you're on an equal footing
6. Make the engagement activities interesting
7. Be an active part of the conversation
8. Consider different methods to engage children
9. Capture what is said in a respectful way, allowing children to see what has been recorded
10. Give feedback to children after the session so they know the impact they have had

Listen – that's most important.

Quotes were taken directly from the engagement with children and are also used throughout the framework to ensure their voices are central to this project. Draft copies were sent back to every group that fed into the framework to get their feedback. We went back to sessions to showcase the framework and allow children to choose which quotes they wanted featured, highlighting what they thought was most important. We also tested the framework with partners to ensure that the recommendations offered realistic challenges, rather than suggesting changes that were unfeasible in practice.

Developing links to Child First

Child First is summarised into four tenets and aligns with an international evidence base on children's rights and child-centred approaches to justice (Case and Browning, 2021). In this section, we explore how our approach to co-production and the findings of our work align with existing literature.

As children – The aim of the framework was to highlight the responsibility of *all* adults and professionals in implementing Child First, not just frontline workers. The evidence base around Child First recognises the importance of understanding children's unmet needs (Hazel & Williams, 2023). Children wanted to be part of the process to identify their needs rather than professionals making assumptions about what the problem is.

Professionals trying to problem solve instead of listening to what I've got to say.

Building pro-social identity – Workshops were designed to empower children to share their thoughts on how professionals should work with them, reinforcing the narrative that children belong in decision-making roles. The importance of relationships was clear, with children discussing ways professionals can develop them. This included participating in activities together or finding mutual interests. Children wanted more opportunities to be involved in decision-making and understand the impact they have made. Our framework encourages children's involvement at all levels of an organisation and the need to demonstrate their impact, as this can help build a pro-social identity.

Listening and putting answers together to improve things.

Collaborating with children – We wanted to involve children from the earliest stage and maintain their involvement throughout the process. Children felt they had a lot to contribute in decision-making roles, offering creative solutions to problems. If their ideas could not be taken forward, children understood this but still wanted to be part of the conversation to find a compromise.

Explain why and say this is what we can do, what other ideas do you have?

Diverting from stigma – The impact of stigma was discussed broadly by children and reached beyond criminogenic stigma. This included stigma about where they lived and their families. Children felt that adults often misinterpreted them or made assumptions about them, which negatively impacted their relationships with professionals. We wanted the framework to help challenge these negative perceptions of children and encourage children from *all* backgrounds to be involved in co-production activities.

> *Not think that cos I've been in trouble I'm no good.*

Overcoming barriers to effective co-production with children

It is well established in literature that the existence of a power imbalance can act as a barrier to meaningful co-production (Hampson et al., 2023). This is particularly prevalent during collaborative work between children and professionals, but the impact of this can be mitigated by empowering children to share their views and experiences (McGinnis & O'Shea, 2022). This power imbalance often means children are distrustful of professionals, meaning we have a responsibility to create an environment that is welcoming and empowering for children to share their views (Burns & Creaney, 2023). This helps to reinforce that children have the ability to shape the future of policy and practice. Smithson and Jones (2021) suggest that a power imbalance can be reduced by conducting engagement in an environment that children thrive in but professionals lack expertise in. To limit the impact of power imbalances in our engagement, we prioritised going to spaces where children already felt safe and able to express their views. As we knew children might be hesitant to talk to us, we used our existing relationships with their trusted adults, such as teachers and youth workers, as a foundation to develop relationships ourselves.

When explaining who we were and why we wanted to speak to the group, we focused on empowering children to take part in conversations. We explained that, as children, they were the experts, and by sharing their views with us, they had the potential to influence how children were involved in decision making and how professionals interacted with them moving forward. This was further enabled by going to spaces where we lacked expertise as professionals. Our engagement conducted at a football session was a good example of this, as it allowed children the opportunity to demonstrate their strengths to us through a penalty shoot-out! This type of activity also allowed us to give back to the children involved by giving up our time to engage in something they enjoyed.

Delivery should be tailored to the specific context of a session and to the needs of the group (Sicilia, Sancino, Nabatchi & Guarvini, 2019). At times, it may even be necessary to tailor activities during a session to meet the needs of individuals. This includes adaptations to meet the needs and circumstances of individuals, but also their interests to make engagement fun (Peer Power Youth, 2021). In our delivery, we found that group-based work was not the best way for all children to express their views. This meant we had to tailor the sessions to allow children to work 1:1 with a facilitator or independently, while still enabling group discussions. By allowing children to draw their responses to questions or feeding our questions into games, children were able to contribute in a way that worked best for them.

Meaningful co-production can be time intensive and requires the adequate allocation of resources (Cunningham & Wakeling, 2022). Participatory methods often come with additional costs to cover child-friendly activities, incentives, travel, and venues (Mawn Welsh, Kirkpatrick, Webster & Stain, 2016). We also incurred additional costs around staffing and overtime due to the need to meet with children outside of perceived 'standard working hours'. Time must also be allocated to facilitate relationship building between children and facilitator, as co-production requires two-way trust (Afifi, Makhoul, El Hajj & Nakkash, 2011). This results in a longer process than when working exclusively with professionals. To minimise costs, we made sure to seek formal commitment to the project from our senior leadership team. This included allocation of a budget to deliver sessions and staff availability. A timeline was drafted for the various stages of engagement, including buffers, to allow for delays in delivery. While the benefits of co-production and participation are well understood within this context (see Smithson, Gray and Jones, 2021), the associated costs need to be balanced with the sensitivities of public sector funding.

There were two further barriers we expected to encounter during our project: partnership buy-in and recruiting children. However, we experienced overwhelming support from partners who facilitated engagement opportunities for us, enabling us to involve 455 children in the project. While this chapter is focused on collaboration with children, it is important to note the importance of collaboration with key partners and stakeholders. Through establishing a multi-agency working group, we were able to gain partnership buy-in early and draw on the expertise of those in the group. This also gave partners a sense of ownership over the project, as they were able to shape the direction it took.

Future directions

Children told us they '*want professionals to communicate*' more so they do not have to repeat themselves. To try and prevent this over-consulting in West Yorkshire, we set up a local network of professionals from varied backgrounds who come together to share learning across the sector. Conversations are focused on thematic topics, such as creating child-friendly products or communicating with children, and the group discusses best practices, challenges, and solutions. This learning is summarised into infographics and shared widely to ensure we are putting what children have told us into practice.

Since creating the local network, it has become clear we would benefit from this level of knowledge exchange on a national level too. This led us to convening a National Child First Delivery Group with representation from the Youth Justice Board for England and Wales, Offices of Police and Crime Commissioners, and Violence Reduction Units. The purpose of this group is to encourage collaboration and learning across regions to avoid localised pockets of good practice in relation to children and the criminal justice system. In the inaugural meeting, several themes for discussion were identified, including sharing learning from HM Inspectorate of Probation (HMIP) and HM Inspectorate of Constabulary (HMIC) inspections, children's scrutiny panels, and meaningful engagement with children.

There was a desire for children to have more creative ways to express themselves and share their voices, beyond surveys and focus groups. We used this as the basis for our launch of the framework by hosting an art exhibition with pieces focused on children's experiences of growing up in West Yorkshire. In total, we received over sixty exhibits and three live performances for the exhibition, including photography, poetry, rap, sculpture, collage, and paintings. They focused on several themes, such as education, community safety, gangs, and knife crime. We found by taking this creative approach we were able to engage with groups of children who had not wanted to participate in our workshops to develop the framework, allowing them to share their experiences with professionals in a different way. Positive feedback was also received from professionals who attended the exhibition, as they felt they were given an insight into children's lives through their creative work, which brought the framework to life.

Safe spaces and community safety were some of the key areas children wanted to influence. This identified a great opportunity to incorporate creative methods into a collaborative project with children. To understand what children perceive to be 'safe spaces' and what makes children feel safe, we use a creative research methodology called Photovoice, which uses photography to capture views, followed by qualitative interviews about the content of the photos captured (Wang & Burris, 1997). This methodology aims to enable people to record the strengths and concerns of their local area and promote a dialogue about community improvement with key decision makers. The creative and collaborative elements of this methodology are appealing to children while also providing an opportunity to feed their voices directly to decision makers (Williams, Wyatt & Peter, 2023). This project allows us and other professionals working directly with the children, such as youth workers, to develop children's pro-social identity through offering praise for their photographs and involving them in the project design. Once all the photographs have been collated, the aim is to co-produce an exhibition with children to showcase their work and the learnings from the project with professionals and their families.

Reflections and lessons learned

Creating our framework in this collaborative way has meant we have a product we can rely on, as children's voices are at the heart of it. It has become a first port of call for colleagues within the VRP and for our partners when wanting to improve how they work with children. This helps to embed a more consistent approach with a strong evidence base as decisions are made based on children's views. Not only has this process allowed us to develop a framework to inform our work, but it has also opened up more opportunities for meaningful engagement with children. This is in part due to our strengthened relationships with key stakeholders and increased trust from children. This allows us to continuously learn from children and demonstrate our commitment to transform their views into tangible actions.

The main barrier encountered during the course of this project was time. While we were able to engage with a diverse group of children across West Yorkshire, there were some communities who were not represented in the framework, including children in custody. This was due to the lengthy ethics process required for us to speak to children in custody and the time often needed to develop trust and build relationships. The deadlines in place also limited the number of children we could revisit in person. While all groups received a draft copy of the framework to provide feedback on, time restraints meant we were unable to go back in person to collect this feedback from all groups face to face. This is likely to have limited how many children are aware of the influence their inputs had, a core component of the Lundy model of participation (Lundy, 2007), as we were relying on this being communicated by partners. With this learning in mind, any similar projects should ensure that deadlines in place are flexible to best accommodate the groups you are engaging with and factor in sufficient time to communicate the impact of involvement in the project.

The framework is now a core document for the VRP and has been shared with teams throughout the Combined Authority and with our strategic partners across West Yorkshire. On a national level it has been showcased as good practice with other VRUs and by the Youth Justice Board to help influence decision-making. There is an accompanying offer of support from the VRP for any organisations wanting to use the framework, whether that be joining our network for peer support or meeting with the team to discuss its application in more detail.

Key takeaways

Throughout this process, we identified three key takeaways from children that should be considered for all collaborative work with children.

1. ***Give us flexibility*** – There is never going to be a one-size-fits-all approach to co-production with children. As professionals, we need to be prepared to adapt our approaches and be guided by the specific needs and interests of the children we are working with.
2. ***Listen and show you are listening*** – Listening to children is obviously an important part of co-production with children, but it is what we do with their input that counts. We need to go back to children and prove that we have listened! This allows us to check our understanding, ensuring we have not misunderstood what they have told us or put a professional spin on their words. It also gives us the opportunity to let them know the impact they have had and what changes are being made as a result.
3. ***Don't be boring!*** – Arguably the most important consideration! When working with children, it's vital we do our best to make sure the activities are fun and engaging and link back to their specific interests where possible.

Conclusion

Co-producing our West Yorkshire Child First framework with children offered us invaluable insight into children's lives and how we can best support them. Incorporating a range of engagement methods such as drawing and mind maps allowed us to tailor sessions to meet the needs and interests of the children involved. It was clear that children want a say in decisions that impact them and feel they could offer creative solutions that professionals may not have considered. The framework now guides all our decisions that impact children in the West Yorkshire Violence Reduction Partnership, ensuring we are capturing and amplifying their voices in the best ways possible. In turn, this enhances our ability to support our communities by recognising and responding to their needs.

Co-production allowed us to build positive relationships, both with children and professionals, opened up avenues for future collaborative working, and increased our confidence in adopting creative methodologies to create engaging interactions. The process of developing and sharing our framework has also facilitated positive conversations around child-friendly practices and the importance of involving children on both regional and national levels.

Attention should be given to exploring how children can be continuously involved in the work of the VRP rather than on project-based agendas, such as the design and commissioning of services. This should involve a transition to more creative and participatory methods that reduce professional involvement and empower children to direct our spending and focus. Due to the challenges caused by the time-consuming nature of co-production, future projects should have more flexible deadlines allowing for delivery based on the needs of the children involved. Schedules should also include sufficient time to close the feedback loop and ensure children are aware of the impact they have made.

References

Afifi, R.A., Makhoul, J., El Hajj, T. and Nakkash, R.T., 2011. Developing a logic model for youth mental health: Participatory research with a refugee community in Beirut. *Health Policy and Planning*, *26*(6), pp.508–517.

Brabin, T. 2025. *My manifesto – Tracy Brabin for West Yorkshire mayor*. Available at: https://tracybrabin.com/manifesto/ (Accessed 22 May 2025).

Brady, L.M., Miller, J., McFarlane-Rose, E., Noor, J., Noor, R. and Dahlmann-Noor, A., 2023. "We know that our voices are valued, and that people are actually going to listen": Co-producing an evaluation of a young people's research advisory group. *Research Involvement and Engagement*, *9*(1), p.11.

Brierley, A., 2023. Experiential peers cultivate a participation culture in youth justice. *Safer Communities*, *22*(2), pp.78–90.

Burns, S. and Creaney, S., 2023. Embracing children's voices: Transforming youth justice practice through co-production and child first participation. In Case, S. and Hazel, N. eds. *Child First: Developing a new youth justice system* (pp.333–365). Cham: Springer International Publishing.

Byrne, B. and Brooks, K., 2015. Post-YOT youth justice. *Howard League for Penal Reform*. Available at: https://howardleague.org/wp-content/uploads/2016/04/HLWP_19_2015.pdf (Accessed 14 April 2025).

Case, S. and Browning, A., 2021. *Child first justice: The research evidence-base [full report]*. Loughborough: Loughborough University. Available at https://yjresourcehub.uk/wp-content/uploads/media/YOT_Talk_Full_Report_European_Journal_of_Criminology_March_2021.pdf (Accessed 14 April 2025).

Caulfield, L., Sojka, B. and Devi-McGleish, Y., 2021. *Follow-on evaluation of Sandwell Youth Offending Service – a creative approach to working with young people*. Wolverhampton: University of Wolverhampton. Available at: https://yjresourcehub.uk/wp-content/uploads/media/follow-on%20evaluation%20of%20Sandwell%20Youth%20Offending%20Service%20%E2%80%93%20a%20creative%20approach%20to%20working%20with%20young%20peopl.pdf (Accessed 11 April 2025).

Caulfield, L., Sojka, B. and Massie, R., 2019. *An evaluation of Sandwell Youth Offending Service–a creative approach to working with young people*. Wolverhampton: University of Wolverhampton. Available at: https://wlv.openrepository.com/server/api/core/bitstreams/596b5101-2504-44a0-8462-7c1c7f2cc645/content (Accessed 11 April 2025).

Craston, M., Balfour, R., Henley, M., Baxendale, J. and Fullick, S., 2020. *Process evaluation of the violence reduction units*. London: Home Office.

Cunningham, E., Jamieson-MacKenzie, I., McMellon, C., McCallin, M., Eltiraifi, M., Smith, L. and Hepburn, K., 2024. "Don't tell me how to tell my story": Exploring young people's perceptions around what it means to 'feel (mis) understood' by adults in supporting roles. *Children and Youth Services Review*, *156*, 107361.

Cunningham, N. and Wakeling, H., 2022. Engagement and co-production with people with lived experience of prison and probation: A synthesis of the evidence base. *Prison Service Journal*, *262*, pp.3–11.

Hampson, K., Nisbet, A. and Case, S., 2023. Child First participatory research-The challenges of involving children in youth justice decision-making. *British Journal of Community Justice (BJCJ)*, *19*(2), pp. 45–65.

Hazel, N. and Williams, P., 2023. Developing Child First as the guiding principle for youth justice. In Case, S. and Hazel, N. eds. *Child First developing a new youth justice system*. Cham: Springer International Publishing., (pp.169–201).

Home Office. (2020). *Violence Reduction Unit (VRU) interim guidance*. [online] GOV.UK. Available at: https://assets.publishing.service.gov.uk/media/5e7de2cfe90e0706ef2db559/12VRU_Interim_Guidance_FINAL__003_2732020.pdf (Accessed 11 April 2025).

Ikhile, D., Glass, D., Frere-Smith, K., Fraser, S., Turner, K., Ramji, H., Gremesty, G., Ford, E. and van Marwijk, H., 2023. A virtuous cycle of co-production: Reflections from a community priority-setting exercise. *Health Expectations*, *26*(6), pp.2514–2524.

Local Government Association. no date. *Co-production, Local Government Association*. Available at: www.local.gov.uk/topics/devolution/devolution-online-hub/public-service-reform-tools/engaging-citizens-devolution-7 (Accessed 11 April 2025).

Lundy, L., 2007. 'Voice' is not enough: Conceptualising Article 12 of the United Nations Convention on the Rights of the Child. *British Educational Research Journal*, *33*(6), pp.927–942.

Mawn, L., Welsh, P., Kirkpatrick, L., Webster, L.A. and Stain, H.J., 2016. Getting it right! Enhancing youth involvement in mental health research. *Health Expectations*, *19*(4), pp.908–919.

McGinnis, E. and O'Shea, J., 2022. Lessons learned in meaningful collaboration with justice involved young adults. *Journal of Participatory Research Methods*, *3*(3), pp.1–12.

Ministry of Housing, Communities and Local Government and Department for Levelling Up, Housing and Communities. 2024. *English institutions with devolved powers: Plain English guidance*. GOV.UK. Available at: www.gov.uk/government/publications/english-institutions-with-devolved-powers-plain-english-guidance/english-institutions-with-devolved-powers-plain-english-guidance (Accessed 11 April 2025).

Peer Power Youth. 2021. *Co-creation and participation in practice project*. London: Peer Power/YJB.

Public Health England. 2019. *Multi-agency approaches to tackling serious violence: A review of the effectiveness of multi-agency working and the factors that support it*. [online] GOV.UK. Available at: https://assets.publishing.service.gov.uk/government/uploads/system/uploads/attachment_data/file/862794/multi-agency_approach_to_serious_violence_prevention.pdf (Accessed 11 April 2025).

Sicilia, M., Sancino, A., Nabatchi, T. and Guarini, E., 2019. Facilitating co-production in public services: Management implications from a systematic literature review. *Public Money & Management*, *39*(4), pp.233–240.

Smithson, H., Gray, P. and Jones, A., 2021. 'They really should start listening to you': The benefits and challenges of co-producing a participatory framework of youth justice practice. *Youth Justice*, *21*(3), pp.321–337.

Smithson, H. and Jones, A., 2021. Co-creating youth justice practice with young people: Tackling power dynamics and enabling transformative action. *Children & Society*, *35*(3), pp.348–362.

Social Care Institute for Excellence (2022) *Co-production: What it is and how to do it*. SCIE. Available at: www.scie.org.uk/co-production/what-how/#:~:text=back%20in%20exchange.-,Principles%20of%20co%2Dproduction,putting%20co%2Dproduction%20into%20practice. (Accessed 11 April 2025).

Wang, C. and Burris, M.A., 1997. Photovoice: Concept, methodology, and use for participatory needs assessment. *Health Education & Behavior*, *24*(3), pp.369–387.

Watkinson, G., Marshall, D. and Kewley, S., 2024. 'If you just look at risk, people look horrific' Youth Justice Practitioners' Perspectives of Child First Practice. *British Journal of Community Justice*, *19*(2), pp.30–45.

Williams, A., Wyatt, K. and Peter, J., 2023. *To be seen and heard: Developing photovoice as a method for the police to engage with young people in under-served communities*. Scottish Institute for Policing Research. Available at: www.sipr.ac.uk/wp-content/uploads/2023/04/Williams-Russell-Wyatt-Peter-Hughes_merged.pdf (Accessed 1 March 2025).

Youth Endowment Fund. 2024. *Children, violence and vulnerability 2024: Summary of findings*. [online] Youth Endowment Fund. Available at: https://youthendowmentfund.org.uk/wp-content/uploads/2024/11/CVV24_R1_OverallViolence.pdf (Accessed 11 April 2025).

Youth Justice Board for England and Wales. 2022. *Child First: Overview and guide*. Available at: https://yjresourcehub.uk/wp-content/uploads/media/Child_First_Overview_and_Guide_April_2022_YJB.pdf (Accessed 17 January 2025).

Youth Justice Board for England and Wales. 2024a. *Youth justice board strategic plan 2024–2027*. Available at: https://assets.publishing.service.gov.uk/media/6603e2ecc34a860011be7607/2024_03_26_-_6.8802_YJB_Strategic_Plan_2024_FINAL_v07_WEB.pdf (Accessed 17 January 2025).

Youth Justice Board for England and Wales. 2024b. *What is Child First?*. Available at: https://yjresourcehub.uk/wp-content/uploads/2024/12/What-is-Child-First.pdf (Accessed 17 January 2025).

8

OPPORTUNITIES FOR PROGRESSING TRAUMA-INFORMED YOUTH JUSTICE CASE MANAGEMENT THROUGH CO-PRODUCTION PRINCIPLES

Catia Malvaso, Andrew Day, and Lorna Robinson

Introduction

In response to the high prevalence of maltreatment, trauma, and adversity experienced by children and young people with experience of the youth justice system (Fagan & Novak, 2017; Hamilton, Malvaso, Day, Delfabbro, & Hackett, 2024; Levenson et al., 2017; Malvaso et al., 2021; Malvaso et al., 2022; Mendez, Mozley, & Kerig, 2020; Turner et al., 2020; Vitopoulos, Peterson-Badali, Brown, & Skilling, 2019; Wolff, 2017), there have been increasing calls to implement more trauma-informed approaches across youth justice services (Butcher, Day, Malvaso, & Fernandez, 2024; Clancey, Wang, & Lin, 2020; Day, Malvaso, Butcher, O'Connor, & McLachlan, 2023; Levenson & Willis, 2018; Malvaso, Day, & Boyd, 2024; Modrowski, Chaplo, & Kerig, 2022; Skinner-Osei, Mangan, Liggett, Kerrigan, & Levenson, 2019). Trauma-informed practice (TIP) is best thought of as a broad philosophy or set of values that prioritise the operationalisation of a set of key principles across all levels of a service: safety (physical, psychological and cultural); trustworthiness, choice; collaboration; and empowerment; as well as respect for the ways in which historical, structural, cultural and gender-related factors influence developmental pathways (Kezelman, 2014). A trauma-informed approach also emphasises the need to *realise* how trauma impacts behaviour, to *recognise* signs of trauma, to create systems that are effective in *responding* appropriately, and to outline an approach to employing service models that are effective in *resisting re-traumatisation*. Fundamentally then, trauma-informed youth justice is concerned with understanding when and how children most feel safe, ensuring their physical and psychological safety at

DOI: 10.4324/9781003602996-11

all times, and with building trust, choice, collaboration, and empowerment into all professional relationships. It is predicated on listening to, and understanding, the experiences and perspectives of those who receive a service, in this case children and young people under youth justice supervision (Day et al., 2023). In this chapter we illustrate how children and young people can meaningfully contribute to decisions about service delivery, drawing on work completed as part of a larger project that aimed to strengthen youth justice case management. This involved aligning practice with these trauma-informed principles, which emphasise the critical role of co-production with children in a youth justice context. We begin by outlining the context for this work before sharing what children and young people who are currently receiving case management had to say about how it might be improved. By the end of this chapter, you will have learnt how;

- To progress a trauma-informed approach to youth justice case management by inviting children and young people with experience of the youth justice system to contribute their ideas relating to concepts of safety, trust and transparency, collaboration, choice, and empowerment;
- To demonstrate that engaging with, and listening to, children and young people is central to the development of more responsive services;
- To provide insight into the ways in which the views of children and young people are similar, or different, to those of service providers and to understand their ideas about how to resolve differences in opinions relating to support needs.

Adversity and trauma among children in youth justice

Numerous studies have confirmed the high prevalence of exposure to adverse and potentially traumatic events among children and young people who have experience of the youth justice system (Astridge, Li, McDermott, & Longhitano, 2023; Malvaso et al., 2021). In our local jurisdiction, South Australia, of those under Youth Justice supervision interviewed in 2019 (N=184), 9 in 10 reported multiple adverse events during their childhood, including experiences of maltreatment and household challenges (Malvaso et al., 2022). The prevalence of both individual and the cumulative number of adverse experiences was as much as four times higher than those reported in the international literature (Malvaso et al., 2021). Nearly everyone was assessed to have trauma symptoms indicative of clinically significant problems in at least one of the following domains: posttraumatic stress, dissociation, anxiety, depression, and anger. Furthermore, more than 3 in 4 scored in the problematic range for substance use, indicative of a clinical-level disorder, with almost all children and young people also in the symptomatic range for externalising problems and approximately two-thirds for internalising problems. The majority (~80% across different subgroups) had a new conviction 12 months post interview.

These data were used to support arguments that the local agency should develop a more trauma-informed model of practice; one that prioritised an understanding of how life events impact on the developmental needs and behaviour of children and young people under supervision, including how these experiences influence the development of different trauma-based coping mechanisms, such as dissociation and substance misuse. As the current approach to case management is driven by a risk assessment and risk management model of practice, we quickly realised that for a new, trauma-informed model of care to be adopted, comprehensive screening of adversity and trauma was necessary if referrals were to be made for more in-depth, holistic assessments (that go beyond an assessment of risk of 're-offending'), as well as case planning activities that connected children with appropriate support services and programmes. While these might include the provision of specialist trauma treatment services, there was also a need to improve the recognition of and responses to signs and symptoms of trauma in everyday case management. In line with the principles that underpin the trauma-informed approach (notably choice, collaboration, and empowerment), this meant talking not only to professionals about their current practice but also to children and young people about their lived experience and engagement with the service. This aligns with a key purpose of co-production; that is, to uphold children's participatory rights in ways that can influence decision-making processes (Burns & Creaney, 2023).

Co-production as a key part of a trauma-informed response to service delivery

Co-production, as a participatory approach in public services, is considered key to service improvement across health, human service and criminal justice agencies (Verschuere, Brandsen, & Pestoff, 2012) and has been described as occurring along 'a continuum of opportunities for participation' (Weaver, Lightowler, & Moodie, 2019). A simple definition of co-production, 'equal partnership and for equal benefit' (Johns, Flynn, Hall, Spivakovsky, & Turner, 2022), is useful here as it draws attention to the power differentials that exist in youth justice settings. It encourages us to ask 'who is in this partnership, on whose terms, for whose benefit, and "equal" by whose measure?' – all questions that are particularly important in settler-colonial countries such as Australia, where the ongoing impact of colonisation continues to shape the experience of First Nations[1] peoples today. First Nations children continue to be grossly over-represented in the Australian youth justice system; while accounting for less than five percent of the general community, First Nations children account for half of the population of children under youth justice supervision (Australian Institute of Health and Welfare, 2024). Personal, familial and community-based trauma is widely seen as a key driver of this over-representation (as a result of the enduring impacts of colonisation: the loss of spiritual, land-based and cultural wealth; kinship disconnection and fractured identity; grief and loss; racism; discrimination; and structural inequality (Blagg, 2016), and has been described as 'a national crisis', with the need to address the adverse impacts of intergenerational disadvantage considered both 'critical' and 'urgent' (Australian Child Rights Taskforce, 2018, p. 13). The National Closing the Gap[2] reform in Australia, for example, calls for a 'structural transformation of mainstream government organisations' to improve accountability and respond to the needs of First Nations people, with the expectation that public organisations will invest in ensuring a better understanding of First Nations communities and their unique historical, social, and political contexts before developing any policy of practice. It is through this process of engagement that the community's cultural knowledge, cultural authority, governance structures, and decision-making protocols can be better understood, and genuine partnerships formed that recognise community self-determination (The Magnolia Project and the Aboriginal Legal Rights Movement South Australia, 2023). This is, of course, consistent with the ethos of participatory practice and resonates strongly with the need to uphold the right to self-determination as part of reconciliation efforts.

Although, broadly speaking, different opportunities are potentially available for children and young people to meaningfully contribute to decision-making, they are rarely utilised. These include a range of different 'partnership' activities, from participation and collaboration to co-planning, codesign, co-delivery and co-evaluation in research and practice, and even 'co-governance' or 'co-management'. In practice, however, most approaches that involve co-production are based simply on 'service users' coming together to discuss their experience of services and identify how they might be improved (Day et al., 2023). In youth justice systems, these opportunities are typically limited, especially in those jurisdictions where no clear policy or practice commitment exists that prioritises participation.

In what follows we describe a series of focus groups and one-on-one consultations with children and young people under Youth Justice supervision across both community and custodial settings, whereby children and young people were invited to speak to a researcher and 'expert by lived experience' consultant about the services they receive and to offer their views on how engagement with the service could be enhanced. These are an example of efforts to encourage 'participation', with a particular focus on assessment and case planning activities in the community. Community-based supervision (or probation) is the most common court disposition for justice-involved children and young people in our jurisdiction (and similarly in most jurisdictions across Australia as well as in the United Kingdom), with case management the principal method of providing services and support. However, a lack of clarity about the very purpose and goals of community-based dispositions (The Annie. E. Casey Foundation, 2018), the absence of any clearly articulated theory of change (Esthappan et al., 2020), and youth justice policies that legitimate and endorse a wide range of different services and programmes (Day & Malvaso, 2024), have resulted in considerable variation in the day-to-day practices of individual case managers and practitioners (Viglione & Labrecque, 2021). This is in a context in which the number of children and young people who come into contact with the justice system continues to decline in Western countries (Tuttle, 2024), and where an increasing proportion of children with intersecting needs across health, disability, education, welfare and child protection are being identified (Malvaso, 2024; Taylor et al. 2018). And in relation to the increasing pressure placed on youth justice services to better respond to more complex health, social, and often trauma-based needs (Clancey et al., 2020), genuine questions have been asked about what casework with justice-involved children and young people should look like (Haines & Case, 2015).We therefore sought to obtain, first-hand, information about how children and young people understand case management, what they identify as qualities of good supervision, how they conceptualise safety (physical and psychological), the most pressing areas of support needs, and how they think children and young people can best be engaged in order to ensure that their ideas are prioritised. Their views were then used to inform recommendations to the Youth Justice agency about how case management services might be more trauma-informed.

Approach

After receiving ethics approval from the University of Adelaide HREC (#H-2024-150), we invited children and young people currently under Youth Justice (YJ) supervision aged 14 or older, either in the community or custody, who had experienced a supervision order which included case management service delivered in the community. We liaised with Community Youth Justice (CYJ) staff and the state's only custodial centre, Kurlana Tapa leadership, in consultation with case managers and coordinators, to identify children and young people who met these eligibility criteria and then organised session times and locations to meet. Each session was facilitated by the lead author and supported by a Lived Experienced Consultant who was engaged as a support person to further enhance the safety of the children and young people, as well as offer advice from a lived experience perspective. In particular, advice was provided about how to best ensure the wellbeing of children, minimise risk, ensure processes (e.g., the phrasing of questions) were suitable for children under supervision, and to offer reflections on the interpretation of key findings. Questions broadly focused on the topics outlined in Table 8.1.

We conducted three separate focus groups (one in Kurlana Tapa, two in CYJ) and three individual interviews (two in Kurlana Tapa, one in CYJ), with a total of nine children and young people aged 16–18 years participating across community and custodial settings (summarised in Table 8.2). This included five males and four females, six First Nations children and young people, and six children and young people who had dual involvement with Youth Justice and the Department for Child Protection.

TABLE 8.1 Focus group topics and example questions

Domain	*Example questions*
Understanding case management	• Do you know who your case manager is? • Do you know what your case manager's job is? • Do you have a case plan?
Qualities of good supervision	• What characteristics make a good worker? • Should young people choose their workers? • How often and where should you meet?
Conceptualising safety	• How can workers help young people feel safe?
Identifying support needs	• What do young people most need help with? • What should we do if young people and workers disagree? • Would you change your advice if the young person was engaging in harmful behaviours?
Prioritising young people's participation	• Should we do more things like this – inviting young people to share their ideas? • Should YJ talk to young people more often about their ideas?

TABLE 8.2 Description of children and young people who participated in the study

#	*Sex*	*Age*	*First Nations*	*Dual DCP*	*Location*	*Group*
1	M	16	Y	Y	Custody	With 2
2	M	16	N	Y	Custody	With 1
3	M	18	Y	Y	Custody	1:1
4	F	16	Y	Y	Custody	1:1
5	F	16	Y	Y	Community	1:1
6	M	16	N	Y	Community	With 7
7	M	17	N	N	Community	With 6
8	F	18	Y	N	Community	With 9
9	M	18	Y	N	Community	With 8

Findings

Understanding case management

Although none of the children and young people who participated in this study were familiar with the terms 'case management', 'case manager' or 'case plan', when prompted they were able to identify their 'workers' and elements of community 'supervision' such as sitting down with their worker to identify and progress goals. When asked about their workers' roles, all of the children and young people suggested that the role related to monitoring mandates and compliance with conditions (e.g., to 'keep track' of young people). Some suggested that a large part of the role was about writing reports for the Youth Court, and two suggested the workers' role was to provide transportation to appointments. Only one identified the worker's primary role as a support person. One young person elaborated on the utility of the 'case plan', suggesting that it was too generic with broad goals such as 'going to school'. Despite this, numerous examples were given of workers acting in supportive roles in response to other questions raised.

Qualities of good supervision

Despite the focus on compliance in their understanding of case management, most children and young people suggested that those workers who focused less on compliance were better able to build a better rapport with the children and young people that they worked with. Young people identified a number of different personal qualities of a 'good' worker, including: organised; persistent; consistent; flexible; non-authoritative; relaxed; and collaborative. All children and young people spoke about the importance of 'trust', which included: building relationships and 'bonds' with their worker before being willing to share personal information about their thoughts and needs and the importance of being 'believed' by their worker. One example given about rapport building was about how a particular worker always spent the first part of supervision meetings focusing on the young person, for example, by asking how the young person is feeling and if anything has happened since the last time they spoke, rather than immediately focusing on matters relating to compliance.

Other examples of 'good' supervision were also provided. Three children and young people spoke about the importance of family support, with examples of 'good' workers being those who supported family members too (e.g., nanna, little brothers). Two spoke about the importance of being challenged and 'pushed' by their workers, and appreciating workers who set boundaries and explained clearly why some requests are not able to be fulfilled. One spoke about their case manager as a 'mother figure' who gave the impression that being a worker wasn't 'just a job'.

Most children and young people stated that they preferred workers who provided outreach, with only one indicating that he preferred to come to the metropolitan CYJ office. All but two indicated they would like to choose their worker, or aspects (e.g., gender) of those they worked with, with all agreeing that children and young people should be able to change workers if they were not working well together. In most of the sessions there was discussion about differences between workers in custodial versus community settings, with some children and young people indicating they had better relationships with custodial staff. Examples were given about the importance of 'teamwork' and having workers follow young people through custodial and community settings, as well as workers attending court to advocate for children and young people.

Diverse views about the frequency of supervision meetings were expressed, with some children and young people suggesting fortnightly meetings would be sufficient, and others suggesting meetings should be scheduled on a needs basis. Two young people spoke about the idea of 'purposeful engagement' and that the purpose should determine the frequency of meetings. Two young people expressed views about their case managers' workloads; while these young people acknowledged the need for their worker to support other children and young people, it was suggested that case managers should work with fewer young people more intensively.

Conceptualising safety

The children and young people who participated in this project identified a number of ways that 'safety' might be enhanced. This included further discussion about the benefits of outreach, with children and young people offered choices about where and when they meet with their case manager. Young people also spoke about safety in relation to rapport building, suggesting that case managers who took the time to listen and 'get to know you' able to create a sense of psychological safety in supervision. Transparency was also important, with young people suggesting that case managers who took the time to explain the purpose of every meeting and making the effort to accommodate and follow up on preferences were possible. Advocacy was raised as particularly important to psychological safety, particularly in court proceedings. Three young people spoke about the importance of having their thoughts and behaviour challenged by their case managers but in a respectful way where differences in opinion or point of view were clearly explained.

Identifying support needs

Children and young people identified a range of areas in which supports are required, including education (with home detention identified as a barrier to attending school), employment, housing, Centrelink (access to government benefits), independent living skills, mental health and wellbeing, transport, family supports, health (e.g., quitting smoking), recreation and hobbies (e.g., sports), and substance use. Three young people spoke about mentoring and the need to be 'shown different opportunities' and that 'life can be different'. One example given was a young woman talking about the moment she realised she wanted 'to be normal, just get a job and be normal' in describing seeing a young girl she used to babysit enter custody and realising she wanted something different for herself and her friend. One suggested there should be more youth centres where young people can drop in, stay occupied, meet new people, and participate in 'fun' activities. When prompted about who should be running this type of service, the young person suggested Youth Justice could create a safe space like this.

All dual-involved children and young people spoke about deficiencies in care from the Department for Child Protection (DCP). DCP was viewed as 'the problem' and that they need to 'stop taking kids from families' and separating siblings. Two young people spoke about the need to deescalate situations, particularly in residential care homes. Examples given were a reduced reliance by staff on pressing duress buttons or calling police to help manage behaviour. One young person said, 'I get more support in here [Kurlana Tapa] than I do from them [DCP]'. All suggested that Youth Justice and DCP could work better together to meet the needs of dual-involved children, especially around exit planning as they approached their eighteenth birthdays.

When asked about situations in which case managers and young people disagreed, for example, on priorities and goals to work on during supervision, all children and young people agreed that the view of the young person should be prioritised. It was explained by one young person that this is important because it is the young person who has to be motivated to change or to engage in certain activities. Other young people also recognised the need for balance and to reach agreement between worker-suggested and young-person-identified priorities. One example given was a young person describing how he felt he was being set up to fail through his obligation conditions on home detention, which he continues to breach because of failed drug tests. The young person explained that he smokes cannabis to stay calm and out of trouble and, despite not feeling ready to give up, he indicated wanting support to try rather than being punished for failing.

Prioritising young people's participation in service development

All children and young people thought that talking with and listening to the ideas and views of individuals impacted by the justice system is important, and that Youth Justice should be consulting more frequently with young people in the service. One young woman stated, 'they should keep talking with us until they listen'. This young woman also explained that consultation needs to be more than a once off to enable the development of trusting relationships so that young people feel comfortable and confident in sharing their views and experiences. This resonates strongly with calls to create organisational climates where meaningful participation is explicitly encouraged and valued, and where children and young people can feel confident that their contributions are having influence (Burns & Creaney, 2023).

Discussion

These focus groups and one-on-one interviews in which children and young people under youth justice supervision were invited to speak to a researcher and lived experience consultant about the case management services they receive in the community provided a range of insights into the ways in which case management could become more trauma-informed. The knowledge and experiences of the participants were organised into five topic areas, with their views and ideas then collated to inform recommendations about how case management activities could be more responsive and attuned to children's needs. The identified strategies and suggestions are summarised in Table 8.3, but four priorities are highlighted for immediate implementation: the use of more child-friendly language across case management with greater transparency relating to the roles of case managers and clear and consistent documentation of children's wishes and views about their case plan; co-producing safety plans in collaboration with every child under supervision to ensure their physical, psychological and cultural safety needs can be met; inviting young people to comment about how safe they feel in every assessment and review meeting; and, introducing governance structures that allow children and young people (and/or their representatives) to participate in the development of planning and policy in relation to case management and ensure that there are opportunities for formal consultation about the types of services and programmes that they think are needed.

While the research approach described in this chapter illustrates how tangible ideas and advice can be harnessed from a one-off engagement, ongoing opportunities to capture the views of children and young people who experience the youth justice system are clearly needed to open up pathways for more regular and meaningful contribution to youth justice decision-making. While there are other consultation processes already in place, such as the Training Centre Visitor Scheme overseen by an independent body (i.e., the South Australian Office of the Guardian for Children and Young People),[3] this is provided only to children and young people in custody and is typically concerned only with matters relating to human rights rather than specific features of service delivery such as case management. It offers, for example, an opportunity to advocate for those in custody, manage complaints, and

TABLE 8.3 Opportunities for strengthening case management practice based on the views and ideas of children and young people

Domain	*Opportunities for strengthening practice*
Understanding case management	• Use of more child-friendly language across case management service delivery • Greater transparency relating to the roles of case managers, e.g., terms such as 'case manager' are changed to 'worker' and case plans to explicitly be labelled to 'Goals, aspirations and legal requirements'. • Children are given and/or talked through a child-friendly position description that clearly outlines what they can reasonably expect from their case managers and the service. • Case managers are provided with ongoing guidance about how to develop meaningful and attainable goals in collaboration with children. • Mandatory aspects of a case plan (e.g., legal order conditions) are distinguished from goals in which the child can reasonably have meaningful input (e.g., personal aspirations).
Qualities of good supervision	• Practitioners can be effective agents of change when they draw on the principles of coproduction in everyday practice, focus on listening to children and young people, help them to feel safe and to avoid re-traumatisation, and when they work in ways that promote positive childhood experiences. • Youth Justice staff should be supported through ongoing training and professional development opportunities in basic counselling skills and supporting adaptive coping skills, the use of universal trauma screening as well as assessing positive childhood experiences, and psychoeducation. • Clear guidance is provided to case managers about outreach, with resources and supports in place to facilitate this approach (e.g., access to vehicles, smaller caseloads and/or reduced administrative duties to ensure that time and competing priorities are not a barrier). • Arbitrary frequency of contact should be reconsidered and replaced by individualised and tailored arrangements to meet the needs of both the child as well as statutory obligations. • The purpose of every meeting is made clear to the child.

TABLE 8.3 (Continued)

Domain	*Opportunities for strengthening practice*
Conceptualising safety	• Case managers regularly ask children and young people about how safe they feel and use this information to develop safety plans in collaboration with the child to ensure their physical, psychological, and cultural safety needs are being met. • Case managers are provided with a practice guideline about practical ways to enhance safety, drawing on the suggestions made by children, e.g., guidance on how to structure a supervision meeting and how to advocate effectively in court. • Transparency around roles and expectations and a focus on casework skills suggested to support children's understanding of case management and effective supervision can also help to enhance children's sense of safety.
Identifying support needs	• Child-friendly guidelines are developed and include what children may expect from their case manager in terms of interactions with other agencies, such as health, education and child protection. • Memoranda of Understanding are developed between agencies, with child-friendly versions shared – and co-produced – with young people and their families. • Case managers are provided with ongoing support and guidance about advocating for children and young people who require support from other agencies, e.g., ensuring transition from out-of-home care plans are in place. • Specific, tailored and collaborative supports are developed for dual-involved children. • Goals are developed in collaboration with the child or young person, and with the input and support of other agencies involved in their care. • All supervision meetings involve reviewing progress towards goal attainment using validated frameworks.
Prioritising young people's participation	• A co-produced engagement strategy is developed which gives careful consideration to the inherent power imbalance that exists to reduce the likelihood of services perpetuating cycles of trauma. • Governance structures are introduced to consider opportunities for justice-involved children (and/or their representatives) to participate in the development of planning and policy in relation to case management. • Children and young people, and those with lived experience and/or their representatives, are formally consulted about the types of services and programmes that they think are needed.

make systemic recommendations related to the provision of quality care. Nevertheless, such schemes, along with consultations of the type reported in this chapter and other opportunities for co-production demonstrate that children and young people are willing and able to contribute ideas for creating more responsive and effective systems that can help others in the future. These processes can also empower children and young people and restore their confidence in service systems (assuming that change results from their engagement), and this can be reinforced through the opportunities that ongoing and sustained consultation provides for skills and resilience building, and for encouraging teamwork, problem solving and responding to difficult situations. Accordingly, we see the need to advance more consistent and robust forms of co-production for routinely listening to children and young people impacted by the youth justice system and acting upon the advice that they offer.

In this chapter we describe an important first step towards developing a more participatory approach to enhancing service development in youth justice services that align with trauma-informed principles, but there are opportunities to introduce more formal structures to ensure the views and experiences of those with living experience are prioritised in service improvement. For example, as this was a once off engagement, a next step may involve the formation of a collective or councils that offer ongoing guidance and collaboration to further advance co-production opportunities (Weaver et al., 2019). Care needs to be taken when attempting to set up these groups, which are not common in justice settings, particularly relating to rebalancing inherent power dynamics to ensure that participation is meaningful, inspiring and based on the development of trust (Burns & Creaney, 2023). Indeed, one striking similarity between consultations with children and young people described in this chapter and those with Youth Justice staff in the same jurisdiction (see Malvaso & Day, 2025) was the importance placed on engagement and relationship building in effective case management. Both children and practitioners consistently told us how important the relationship formed between them is for successful outcomes, and we have argued elsewhere that practitioners can only be effective agents of change when they successfully engage children and young people in the case management process (Day & Malvaso, 2024). Through these pieces of research, as well as work completed in other jurisdictions (Burns & Creaney, 2023), it has become clear that both youth justice staff and justice-involved children and young people view meaningful and authentic engagement as key to enhancing both a trauma-informed and co-production approach in youth justice.

Staff training, recruitment and selection offer additional opportunities for lived experience participation, such as in staff performance management and review processes. This could be achieved through simple measures, such as by incorporating children and young people's perspectives and feedback in staff supervision review meetings and exit interviews but could also be extended to invitations to participate in staff interview panels and other selection processes after a certain period has passed since their own youth justice involvement. The views of children and young people could also be included in staff training and programme development (Willmot & Jones, 2022), and there may be opportunities to involve children and young people in the development of staff resources, further enhancing opportunities for them to co-produce materials.

Finally, we see a role for children and young people to become involved in agency governance structures. This would require the establishment of power-sharing arrangements to enable co-production of policies to reduce the likelihood of services perpetuating cycles of trauma. This can be particularly challenging to implement within risk- and deficit-focused systems and will inevitably require a cultural shift towards a trauma-informed and child-centred approach. Despite the challenges that arise from the inherent power inequalities that exist in a criminal justice system (i.e., where there are statutory obligations to contain and control individuals), basic human rights principles (such as those outlined in the United Nations Riyadh Guidelines) act as an important reminder that social control should only be used as a means of last resort, and that the wellbeing of children and young people should be the focus of intervention efforts. Trauma-informed youth justice practice is compatible with these principles and reminds us that adopting a 'child-centred orientation' will inevitably require partnering and co-producing knowledge with children and young people. But this also means statutory agencies and adults making the active and conscious effort to relinquish control and create an authorising environment that facilitates, legitimises and embraces the views and ideas of children and young people (Burns & Creaney, 2023; Creaney & Case, 2021).

An important consideration is that many of the opportunities identified in this chapter are predominantly administrative and serve agency priorities and goals. It is important to think about the experience of the child to find ways to best engage those of different ages, gender, cultural background, and developmental capacity. This will encourage participation from those with different experiences and perspectives and ensure that children and young people can meaningfully exert influence over issues that are important to them. It is also important to recognise, however, that some young people will not want to participate in service development activities, while others may desire a more active role (Hampson, Creaney, & Burns, 2024). As a minimum though, feedback mechanisms can be introduced that can highlight common themes derived from the individual's experience of the service (e.g., by routinely inviting feedback about how 'listened to' the child or young person was in each session; see Duncan et al. (2003).

In conclusion, we see trauma-informed youth justice as inherently concerned with prioritising the concerns and views of those with lived experience of the youth justice system, and with encouraging participation in shared decision-making processes (Day et al., 2023), which aligns with the intentions of co-production as a participatory approach in youth justice. This means recognising the knowledge, capabilities and experiences of those with current or historical involvement in youth justice systems and the contribution they can make to the development of strong service delivery systems. Engaging with, and listening to, the perceptions and views of children and young people impacted by the youth justice system is essential for understanding the current and future directions of trauma-informed youth justice.

Notes

1 In Australia, First Nations is a term used to refer to a person or group of people who identify themselves as being of Aboriginal and/or Torres Strait Islander. We respectfully acknowledge their diversity and autonomy and recognise that the preferred language and terminology may differ among individuals, families, and communities.

2 Closing the Gap is a formal Australian government commitment to reduce, and eventually eliminate, the disparity in life outcomes between Indigenous and non-Indigenous Australians. See www.closingthegap.gov.au/

3 The Office of the Guardian for Children and Young People advocates for the rights and best interests of children and young people in care and youth detention in South Australia. https://gcyp.sa.gov.au/what-we-do/training-centre-visitor/#:~:text=Shona%20Reid%20is%20the%20Training%20Centre%20Visitor

References

Astridge, B., Li, W. W., McDermott, B., & Longhitano, C. (2023). A systematic review and meta-analysis on adverse childhood experiences: Prevalence in youth offenders and their effects on youth recidivism. *Child Abuse Neglect, 140*, 106055. doi:10.1016/j.chiabu.2023.106055

Australian Child Rights Taskforce. (2018). *The Children's Report: Australia's NGO Coalition: Report to the United Nations Committee on the Rights of the Child.* Retrieved from Sydney:

Australian Institute of Health and Welfare. (2024). *Youth Justice in Australia: 2022-23*. Retrieved from Canberra:

Blagg. (2016). *Crime, Aboriginality and the Decolonisation of Justice*. Australia: Federation Press.

Burns, S., & Creaney, S. (2023). Embracing children's voices: Transforming youth justice practice through co-production and child first participation. In S. Case & N. Hazel (Eds.), *Child First: Developing a New Youth Justice System* (pp. 333–365). Cham: Palgrave MacMillan.

Butcher, L., Day, A., Malvaso, C. G., & Fernandez, M. (2024). An exploration of two different models of leadership for youth justice reform. *Journal of Applied Juvenile Justice Services*, 39–56. doi:10.52935/24.22120.5

Clancey, G., Wang, S., & Lin, B. (2020). Youth Justice in Australia: Themes from recent inquiries. *Trends & Issues in Crime & Criminal Justice, 605*, 1–19.

Creaney, S., & Case, S. (2021). Promoting social inclusion: Participatory rights alternatives to risk discourses in youth justice. In P. Liamputtong (Ed.), *Handbook of Social Inclusion Research and Practices in Health and Social Sciences*. Singapore: Springer.

Day, A., & Malvaso, C. G. (2024). 'Back to basics': A practice approach to reforming youth justice. *Child & Youth Services*, *46*(3), 536–560. doi:10.1080/0145935x.2024.2372790

Day, A., Malvaso, C. G., Butcher, L., O'Connor, J., & McLachlan, K. (2023). Co-producing trauma-informed youth justice in Australia? *Safer Communities, 22*(2), 106–120. doi:10.1108/sc-08-2022-0030

Duncan, B. L., Miller, S. D., Sparks, J. A., Claud, D. A., Reynolds, L. R., Brown, J., & Johnson, L. D. (2003). The Session Rating Scale: Preliminary psychometric properties of a "working" alliance measure. *Journal of Brief Therapy, 3*(1), 3–12.

Fagan, A. A., & Novak, A. (2017). Adverse childhood experiences and adolescent delinquency in a high-risk sample. *Youth Violence and Juvenile Justice, 16*(4), 395–417. doi:10.1177/1541204017735568

Hamilton, H. N., Malvaso, C. G., Day, A., Delfabbro, P. H., & Hackett, L. (2024). Understanding trauma symptoms experienced by young men under youth justice supervision in an Australian jurisdiction. *International Journal of Forensic Mental Health, 23*(4), 333–348. doi:10.1080/14999013.2024.2323939

Hampson, K., Creaney, S., & Burns, S. (2024). Transforming the balance of power? Child First Collaboration: A conceptual analysis. *Societies, 14*(8), 138–155. doi:10.3390/soc14080138

Johns, D., Flynn, C., Hall, M., Spivakovsky, C., & Turner, S. (2022). *Co-Production & Criminal Justice*. Abingdon: Routledge.

Kezelman, C. (2014). Trauma-informed practice. Retrieved from https://mhaustralia.org/general/trauma-informed-practice

Levenson, J. S., Baglivio, M. T., Wolff, K. T., Epps, N., Royall, W. C., Gomez, K. C., & Kaplan, D. (2017). You learn what you live: Prevalence of childhood adversity in the lives of juveniles arrested for sexual offenses. *Advances in Social Work, 18*(1), 313. doi:10.18060/21204

Levenson, J. S., & Willis, G. M. (2018). Implementing trauma-informed care in correctional treatment and supervision. *Journal of Aggression, Maltreatment & Trauma, 28*(4), 481–501. doi:10.1080/10926771.2018.1531959

Malvaso, C. G., Cale, J., Whitten, T., Day, A., Singh, S., Hackett, L., … Ross, S. (2021). Associations between adverse childhood experiences and trauma among young people who offend: A systematic literature review. *Trauma, Violence, & Abuse*, *23*(5), 1677–1694. doi:10.1177/15248380211013132

Malvaso, C. G., Day, A., & Boyd, C. M. (2024). The outcomes of trauma-informed practice in youth justice: An umbrella review. *Journal of Child & Adolescent Trauma*, *17*(3), 939–955. doi:10.1007/s40653-024-00634-5

Malvaso, C. G., Day, A., Cale, J., Hackett, L., Delfabbro, P., & Ross, S. (2022). Adverse childhood experiences and trauma among young people in the youth justice system. *Trends & Issues in Crime & Criminal Justice, 651*, 1–19.

Mendez, L., Mozley, M. M., & Kerig, P. K. (2020). Beyond trauma exposure: Discrimination and posttraumatic stress, internalizing, and externalizing problems among detained Youth. *Journal of Interpersonal Violence, 37*(3–4), 1825–1851. doi:10.1177/0886260520926314

Modrowski, C. A., Chaplo, S. D., & Kerig, P. K. (2022). Advancing Our Understanding of the risk factors associated with crossover youth in the child welfare and juvenile justice systems: A trauma-informed research agenda. *Clinical Child and Family Psychology Review, 25*(2), 283–299. doi:10.1007/s10567-021-00370-4

Skinner-Osei, P., Mangan, L., Liggett, M., Kerrigan, M., & Levenson, J. S. (2019). Justice-involved youth and trauma-informed interventions. *Justice Policy Journal, 16*(2), 1–25.

The Magnolia Project and the Aboriginal Legal Rights Movement South Australia. (2023). *A Practice Guide for Preparing Mental Health PreSentence Reports with Aboriginal People in the Criminal Justice System in South Australia*. Retrieved from Adelaide:

Turner, D., Wolf, A. J., Barra, S., Muller, M., Hertz, P., Huss, M. T., & Retz, W. (2020). The association between adverse childhood experiences and mental health problems in young offenders. *European Child and Adolescent Psychiatry*. 30(8), 1195-1207. doi:10.1007/s00787-020-01608-2

Verschuere, B., Brandsen, T., & Pestoff, V. (2012). Co-production: The state of the art in research and the future agenda. *VOLUNTAS: International Journal of Voluntary and Nonprofit Organizations, 23*(4), 1083–1101.

Vitopoulos, N. A., Peterson-Badali, M., Brown, S., & Skilling, T. A. (2019). The relationship between trauma, recidivism risk, and reoffending in male and female juvenile offenders. *Journal of Child & Adolescent Trauma, 12*(3), 351–364. doi:10.1007/s40653-018-0238-4

Weaver, B., Lightowler, C., & Moodie, K. (2019). *Inclusive Justice: Co-Producing Change – A Practical Guide to Service User Involvement in Community Justice*. Retrieved from Scotland:

Willmot, P., & Jones, L. (2022). *Trauma-Informed Forensic Practice*. Oxon: Routledge.

Wolff, K. T., Baglivio, M. T., Piquero, & A. R. (2017). The relationship between adverse childhood experiences and recidivism in a sample of juvenile offenders in community-based treatment. *International Journal of Offender Therapy and Comparative Criminology, 61*(11), 1210–1242. doi:10.1177/0306624X15613992

9

USING CREATIVE ARTS APPROACHES FOR CO-PRODUCTION IN YOUTH JUSTICE

Laura Caulfield and Dean Wilkinson

Introduction

Many children involved in the justice system have experienced social marginalisation, exclusion from or difficulties with education, and adverse childhood experiences (Gray, Jump, and Smithson, 2023), making them less likely to respond positively to conventional intervention approaches that might mirror traditional education. There are, notably, high numbers of children in contact with the youth justice service (YJS) who have speech, language, and communication needs, requiring ways of working that meet these needs (Royal College of Speech and language Therapy, 2024).

Traditional interventions in youth justice have often relied on structured rehabilitative approaches, which may not resonate with children who feel disengaged from formal institutions such as schools. Approaches and interventions that mirror traditional education are unlikely to be attractive in engaging children with complex needs. Arts-based interventions, including music production, lyric writing, and other creative activities, have emerged as an alternative means of supporting children in the YJS. Given the challenges faced by this group of children, there has been growing interest in creative approaches as a way to encourage participation and engagement, support well-being, and promote positive behavioural change (Mansfield, O'Connell and White, 2024).

Music and the arts can offer accessible engagement methods, allowing children to express themselves, build confidence, and develop social skills. There is a growing, international body of research demonstrating the impact of the arts in adult criminal justice (Gardner and Caulfield, 2024), and research has shown that participation in arts-based activities in youth

DOI: 10.4324/9781003602996-12

justice settings can enhance emotional regulation, increase self-esteem, and strengthen relationships with professionals. Creative interventions align with current approaches in youth justice in England and Wales with a Child First approach – which prioritises children's needs, strengths, and capacities to develop pro-social identities – by providing services that are legitimate and authentic to children.

This chapter presents a synthesis of findings from studies and practice across three YJSs in England. The studies investigate the impact of arts-based methods on engagement, emotional well-being, identity development, and relationships with practitioners, while also highlighting the practical challenges and best practices for integrating creative approaches into youth justice settings. By drawing on research and practice with three youth justice teams, these studies provide valuable insights into the effectiveness of co-produced arts interventions and their potential for long-term impact. This chapter has two key aims; (1) to discuss the evidence of the impact of arts-based approaches to co-production in youth justice; (2) to share key learning about the practice of working in this way.

Creative arts and youth justice

Through engaging activities and safe spaces, arts-based activities have been found to support increased well-being, motivation, and improved social and interpersonal skills for children in youth settings justice, and there is emerging evidence of impact on medium- and longer-term outcomes such as educational engagement and sentence compliance (Caulfield, Jolly, Simpson and Devi-McGleish, 2022; Caulfield and Sojka, 2023). This emerging evidence demonstrates the benefits of the arts for children in contact with, or at risk of contact with, the youth justice system.

Often activities in the criminal justice space are assessed through quantifiable outcomes, and the arts are no exception (e.g. Mansfield et al., 2024). However, the value of the arts goes beyond quantifiable outcomes, providing an important tool for implementing participatory approaches (Caulfield, Botham and Smith, 2023) which have broader social and educational value. Our research on music making and lyric writing with children in YJS settings highlights how this can provide the opportunity for meaningful activity, purposeful conversations, and a tool for children and young people to communicate, express their emotions, and experience a sense of achievement (Caulfield et al., 2022; Wilkinson, Price and Crossley, 2022). Such activities create opportunities for children and young people to take ownership and directly input into the co-creation and production process (Price, Wilkinson and Crossley, 2023). Creative methodologies in research and evaluation have enabled a process of co-production and co-designed approach when working with young people, allowing them to input in the shape, nature and trajectory of the creative space (Wilkinson, Price and Crossley, 2022). We assert this methodological approach is aligned with the 'Child First' framework, leading to legitimate and authentic services for children and young people across youth justice settings.

This chapter has two key aims. First, to discuss the evidence of the impact of arts-based approaches to co-production in youth justice. Second, to share key learning about the practice of working in this way. The chapter will include examples from our experiences working with three YJS teams in England through research and evaluation and service design and redesign. The chapter will highlight the benefits and challenges of implementing arts-based approaches in youth justice.

By the end of this chapter, you will be able to:

1 Understand how creative arts are used as a method to hear children's voices in youth justice.
2 Consider the variety of ways creative arts can be used in youth justice – as methods to support co-production/co-creation, engagement with YJSs, and as a research method.
3 Understand key principles in implementing creative arts practice in YJS.

The role of the arts in three youth justice settings in England

The chapter focuses on work undertaken by the authors of the chapter with three YJSs: two studies undertaken with Birmingham YJS' music programme (Caulfield et al., 2022; Caulfield and Sojka, 2023); one practice-based research project with Birmingham YJS and Cheshire YJS (Price et al., 2023; Wilkinson et al., 2022); and the development of a good practice guide that captures learning from Sandwell YJS' experience developing a 'creative service' (Caulfield et al., 2023). We briefly outline each YJSs' approach below:

Birmingham YJS has, for over a decade, run a music programme for children in contact with their service. The project is open to any child in contact with the YJS and referrals are made by a child's caseworker. Initially the programme was externally funded, before being brought 'in-house' following a number of years of successful activity. Periodically, when specific external funding has been secured, the music programme has also been made available to children referred by external partners including Social Emotional and Mental Health (SEMH) schools, Pupil Referral Units, or referred from care homes by social workers. For those children in contact with the YJS, the music programme forms part of their individualised sentence plan. The aims of the programme are to develop the creative, expressive and musical ability of children and young people and improve children and young people's confidence and well-being. For YJS participants, the aim is also to improve the level of compliance and successful completion of court orders among project participants. Sessions run on a one-to-one basis between the music leader and child – with their caseworker present where appropriate – typically in one two-hour session per week over a 12-week period. The programme is run in a professional studio space near central Birmingham, and children can work on a variety of music-making activities, ranging from production skills and composition to performance skills and music tuition.

During the COVID-19 pandemic, Cheshire YJS sought innovative ways to engage with young people and ensure their voices were heard despite restrictions on face-to-face contact. One such approach was the use of lyric writing as a creative and expressive medium. This initiative provided young people with an opportunity to articulate their thoughts, emotions, and experiences in a format that resonated with them, fostering both individual reflection and collective dialogue. By embedding this practice within Cheshire YJS's broader framework of participation and desistance-focused work, lyric writing became a powerful tool for capturing authentic youth perspectives. It enabled practitioners to listen in a meaningful way, amplifying young voices in a system where they are often marginalised. This approach not only offered an outlet for self-expression, but importantly, directly informed service development by highlighting the realities and concerns of those involved in the justice system, and accounting for their support needs during a period of unprecedented disruption.

In January 2019, Sandwell YJS were awarded funding from the Youth Justice Board's Serious Youth Violence Grant to help increase the use of arts with their cohort. Between 2019 and 2021, Sandwell designed, implemented, and grew a creative service. Sandwell had noted that although the size of their YJS population was decreasing, the complexity of needs of children in contact with their service was increasing: often with speech, language, and communication difficulties, vulnerable to exploitation, and significant experiences of trauma. Sandwell recognised that the resulting distrust of authorities could seem insurmountable and that to really meet the needs of these children, they needed to take a different approach. The resulting development of a service with creativity and the arts embedded throughout – a 'creative service' – required engaging children, staff, and leaders, a focus on building staff confidence and capability with new ways of working, and to keep listening to children. Sandwell developed links with external arts partners, sought arts accreditations, as well as making fundamental shifts to their day-to-day work with arts interventions and creative approaches to statutory programmes.

The studies focused on the impact of the arts on children in contact with the YJSs (Caulfield et al., 2022; Caulfield and Sojka, 2023), exploring the role of the arts in capturing children's voices and experiences (Price et al., 2023; Wilkinson et al., 2022), and documenting the coproduced nature of some of the arts provision (Caulfield et al., 2023).

Impact of the arts in youth justice

An established body of research highlights the positive impact of arts-based interventions in youth justice (for a summary see Caulfield, 2024). Engagement with creative activities such as music, drama, visual arts, and creative writing has been shown to foster attributes such as self-expression, emotional regulation, and positive identity formation (e.g., Jean-Berluche, 2024; Caulfield et al., 2022). Arts-based interventions also enhance engagement, motivation for education, improve compliance with justice services, personal agency, and strengthen social connections, ultimately aiding desistance (Cheliotis and Jordanoska, 2016; Caulfield et al., 2022). Other systematic reviews and studies in community settings have highlighted that music programmes can enhance the engagement of individuals from a range of backgrounds and with diverse needs, by aligning with participants interests, and fostering a sense of belonging, allowing individuals to take ownership of their activities. For example, marginalised young people (Parker et al., 2018), the specific cultural needs of black detained young people (Thompson, 2014), and for risk factors including housing (Eagle, 2008).

Moreover, autonomy/agency plays a crucial role in arts interventions. When young people co-create music or other artistic work, they are more engaged and motivated than when given rigidly structured tasks (Caulfield et al., 2022; Price et al., 2023). The ability to shape their creative expression increases investment in their work, encouraging personal growth and sense of achievement. Collaborative music-making builds trust, teamwork, and a sense of belonging, while also encouraging aspirations and skill development (Hargreaves and Lamont, 2017). Here we present some specific outcomes/processes of arts-based methods in youth justice on justice-involved children and young people.

Music as a tool for well-being, emotional and social development

Caulfield et al. (2019) found that participation in youth justice music programmes increased young people's confidence, improved their communication skills, and fostered stronger relationships with justice professionals by breaking down barriers.

Given the prevalence of trauma, mental health difficulties, and adverse childhood experiences among young people in the justice system, well-being is a key concern. Research consistently demonstrates the therapeutic benefits of arts engagement, helping young people build resilience and develop coping strategies. Viggiani et al. (2013) found that participation in creative projects reduced stress and anxiety while providing a safe, non-judgemental environment for engagement. Music is an effective tool to assist with and engage individuals with rehabilitation in youth justice settings, offering a non-verbal outlet for self-expression, which is particularly beneficial for young people with communication difficulties, trauma histories, or low self-esteem. Hargreaves and Lamont (2017) note that music allows young people to process emotions constructively. Caulfield and Sojka (2023) found that young people who engaged in music activities reported greater self-confidence, enhanced emotional regulation, and increased resilience. Music provided a safe and empowering outlet for processing emotions and articulating personal struggles.

Arts and identity development in youth justice settings

Music, and specifically lyric writing, can lead to transformation for young people, as they use it to reclaim their identities and resist negative labels (Price et al., 2023; Hargreaves and Lamont, 2017). The cultural relevance of music genres such as grime and rap allowed participants in one study to construct personal narratives that challenged stigmatising perceptions of young people who offended (Price et al., 2023). Equally, music making can act as a medium to facilitate culturally relevant and creative, approaches to interventions, enabling activities that are more meaningful and impactful on the young people's journeys and lives (Wilkinson et al., 2022).

The arts, relationships, and engagement and compliance with justice services

Creative activities play a crucial role in strengthening relationships between young people and YJS practitioners (Caulfield et al., 2019; Price et al., 2023). Many young people value the support of YJS workers who encourage their creative development, particularly when provided with access to music studios and spoken word projects. In these circumstances, the activities reflect the co-production principles (Social Care Institute for Excellence, 2022) by working in equal partnership with mutual respect, breaking down barriers, by sharing power and creating more inclusive, effective, and mutual outcomes that build on individuals existing capability. However, some young people have previously expressed their concerns about over-surveillance, particularly during the COVID-19 pandemic, perceiving frequent remote check-ins as intrusive rather than supportive (Price et al., 2023). These findings highlight the importance of relationship-based practice models that prioritise trust, mutual respect, and co-production over control. Therefore, a key challenge in youth justice is ensuring young people engage with services and comply with interventions. Research suggests that arts-based programmes increase compliance by making justice services more engaging and meaningful. Caulfield et al. (2022, 2023) found that participation in music programmes significantly improved attendance at YJS appointments, suggesting that creative engagement fosters commitment and responsibility. Meaby (2019) explored how arts interventions reshape young people's perceptions of justice professionals, fostering relationships built on mutual understanding rather than authority. Lyric writing, in particular, has been an effective means of encouraging self-expression, allowing young people to communicate their experiences in a way that feels natural and empowering (Wilkinson et al., 2022; Price et al., 2023).

The role of arts in rehabilitation and desistance from crime

Arts-based interventions support desistance from crime by helping young people build pro-social identities and develop agency over their futures. The National Criminal Justice Arts Alliance (NCJAA) study (Bilby et al., 2013) found that engagement with the arts allows individuals to redefine their identities beyond the offender label, fosters high levels of engagement, and is linked to increased compliance with justice orders. The presence of professional artists in these interventions further enhances success, as young people respect their expertise and mentorship. Wigzell et al. (2024) explore the theoretical and conceptual principles that underpin desistance for children and young people. The arts (Stephenson, 2024) and participatory practice (Creaney et al., 2024) are highlighted as key tools for application when engaging resistant thinking in children and young people.

Viggiani et al. (2013) found that young people engage more when they have ownership over creative projects rather than following rigid interventions. Similarly, Eagle (2008) evaluated the Misspent Arts programme and found that artistic activities that reflected young people's lived experiences were more effective in fostering meaningful engagement. Lyric writing enabled young people to articulate their views more effectively than traditional interview methods. Young people reported feeling more comfortable expressing their experiences through music, leading to greater engagement with YJS staff and researchers (Wilkinson et al., 2022; Price et al., 2023). Overall, arts-based interventions provide a valuable platform for rehabilitation by empowering young people to develop personal agency, engage with support services, and move towards desistance from crime.

Challenges with methodologies and gathering the evidence

Evaluating the impact of arts programmes in criminal justice presents several challenges, particularly in measuring their effectiveness and long-term influence. Unlike traditional interventions with clear, quantifiable outcomes, arts-based programmes often produce initial, subjective benefits such as improved well-being, self-expression, and social connection. Often these are captured through qualitative studies, which are valuable for understanding personal experiences but do not contribute to the longitudinal impact studies capturing desistance – which often we are looking for. Establishing a causal link between participation in the arts and key justice outcomes – such as reduced reoffending, improved probation attendance, or lower rates of police encounters – requires robust longitudinal data, which is often fragmented across different agencies. Data-sharing restrictions, inconsistencies in record-keeping, and ethical concerns around privacy further complicate efforts to track participants over time. Overcoming these barriers requires interdisciplinary collaboration, standardised data collection methods, and innovative evaluation frameworks that combine quantitative justice metrics with qualitative insights into behavioural and psychological change. The lack of robust quantitative and statistical data presents challenges when looking to secure long-term funding and convince policymakers to integrate arts interventions into mainstream YJSs.

Principles for co-creating and implementing creative arts in youth justice

While the studies above discuss findings relating to specific arts programmes or interventions and the challenges around research in this area, some YJSs have moved towards a 'creative service' with the arts and creativity embedded throughout. Rather than being treated as optional or extracurricular activity, there is likely to be merit in embedding arts-based interventions into case management and rehabilitation programmes. There are early indicators of the benefits of this approach, but further research is needed to explore the impact on outcomes for children (Caulfield et al., 2019; Caulfield et al., 2021). Although not all services will wish to become a 'creative service' integrating arts-based methods into statutory YJSs can ensure that these interventions are sustained and widely accessible.

One of the authors of this chapter worked with Sandwell YJS to explore their innovative approach to developing a 'creative service'. Caulfield worked in collaboration with the YJS manager and creative lead from the YJS to write a good practice guide so that other professionals can learn from the Sandwell experience. The good practice guide contains a checklist for practitioners and youth justice services seeking to develop a creative approach (see Table 9.1). Caulfield et al. (2023) demonstrate how youth justice teams can successfully integrate creative arts into their service design, underpinned by a grounding in the needs of children and young people. This part of the chapter outlines key principles from the good practice guide alongside key implementation lessons from research with other YJSs.

The importance of co-production in arts-based youth justice

Co-production and youth-led approaches should be central to the development of arts-based interventions and services. When young people

TABLE 9.1 A checklist for developing creative approaches to youth justice

Caulfield et al. (2023: 28) have developed a checklist for practitioners and youth justice services seeking to develop a creative approach:

- Have you listened to feedback from the children you work with?
- Are you clear about the evidence? I.e. why a creative approach might work well in your YJS?
- Have you identified the creative person/people in your team?
- Have you engaged your senior leaders and your board? Have you identified your key local partners?
- Have you identified potential sources of funding?
- Have you considered ongoing work to engage colleagues and build confidence?
- Have you built in monitoring and evaluation to understand if what you're doing is successful?
- Have you got mechanisms to keep listening to feedback from the children you work with?

shape creative activities, they develop a greater sense of ownership and are more likely to engage meaningfully. The research also indicates that co-production fosters more positive relationships between young people and practitioners. Wilkinson et al. (2022) found that when young people worked collaboratively, through co-production and co-creation, with facilitators to develop music and lyrics, they felt more respected and valued within the youth justice system. This collaborative approach was associated with higher levels of trust, engagement, and a willingness to participate in the services. In this study, the lyricist led the conversation with the young people, where music was used as a medium for exploration and communication, allowing the lyricist to discuss with the young people through culturally relevant conversations and expressions, that allowed the development of lyrics that presented the young people's experiences as well as their desires for the future.

Sandwell YJS engaged children right from the beginning of their journey towards developing a creative service. Initially they sent out a questionnaire, via case managers, asking children involved with the YJS about what creative arts activities appeal to them. Sandwell really listened to what children wanted and designed the service around this, but they also tested out some creative options that the children hadn't talked about 'to broaden young people's experiences' (Chad Smith, Sandwell YJS, 2023 – quote from Caulfield et al., 2023). It is important to highlight that Sandwell kept listening and learning as the creative service evolved and became embedded through their new Youth Council.

Research has also emphasised the importance of autonomy and choice in focused arts interventions and activities in youth justice. Young people respond best when they have agency over their creative work, allowing them to explore their interests and strengths. Caulfield et al. (2022) highlight the success of youth-led lyric writing and music production, where participants were actively involved in shaping the direction of their creative work. This approach empowered young people to challenge negative societal labels and begin to develop positive identities. Children were also more engaged and motivated compared to when they were simply given structured tasks.

However, Price et al. (2023) highlight that while co-production can be highly effective, it requires flexible working structures and committed facilitators who are willing to adapt to young people's needs. Often the nature of the criminal justice system can instil power imbalances and constraints, and indeed some young people expressed frustration when they felt their contributions were not taken seriously, emphasising the need for genuine youth agency in decision-making. Other factors around risk and safeguarding can limit openness and flexibility needed for genuine co-production and creative expression. Creative methods often provide valuable tools and flexibility required to encourage inventive and imaginative processes. In some cases, this approach can break down institutional barriers between young people and their mentors or workers. However, the arts can facilitate the development of supportive relationships with young people, empowering them to make positive contributions to wider society.

How to successfully deliver co-created creative approaches to youth justice

Our experiences working with a number of YJSs have highlighted how important it is to engage senior leaders at boards early in the journey towards creative youth justice. Birmingham YJS, for example (see Caulfield et al., 2022) secured external funding and built a strong evidence base for their music programme, which eventually resulted in the music programme becoming integrated into the service. For Sandwell YJS and the development of their 'creative service', they needed senior buy-in from the start. As Mike Botham (the then service lead) sets out:

> We wouldn't have been able to get sign off on a creative lead within our service, had we not put a lot of effort into our Board's understanding and agreeing to our aspiration. Our initial approach included having Arts Connect and Professor Caulfield come to a meeting of our Board to set the context of why our direction would be innovative. We grounded it in the feedback from the children we work with, which of course adds weight to any initiative, and a consideration of the needs of our cohort in terms of speech and language. We also set out with an intention of evaluation from

the outset (i.e. we think this would work, can we try it and evaluate). This gained enough momentum to allow us to start....

(Mike Botham in Caulfield et al., 2023: 11)

Once initial support has been secured, for arts-based interventions to be successful, it is vital that YJS practitioners are supported to engage with creative activities and to feel confident with these too. This is important when considering the role of case managers in referring children into creative interventions and becomes crucial when developing innovative 'creative services' where staff right across the service should have an active role to play. For the latter, staff – who may well not have existing skills to deliver creative work – need adequate training and support. In their journey developing and embedding a creative service, Sandwell YJS, perhaps unsurprisingly, found that some staff lacked confidence in delivering creative interventions. Sandwell not only focused on training and supporting staff but also on creating partnerships between the YJS and professional artists. YJSs should explore collaborations with experienced musicians, lyricists, and artists, although it is important that groups and individuals have professional skills and knowledge to engage children with high levels of need.

Flexibility and adaptation through creative and statutory programmes

When thinking about creative work in youth justice, what most readily comes to mind is often 'extra-curricular' arts programmes. However, it is possible to adapt statutory programmes to be delivered in creative ways. Sandwell YJS give the example of their Motoring Offence programme, where children are encouraged as part of the programme to write a fictional story and design a driving safety poster – activities that the team at Sandwell have found are more likely to engage children than simply working through a workbook. Indeed, there is research evidence that children and young people respond best to informal, adaptable creative sessions, rather than rigid, school-like structures, and Wilkinson et al. (2022) found that tailoring sessions to young people's musical interests significantly increased engagement.

The flexibility and adaptability achieved through creative approaches can also enable YJSs to respond to the significant numbers of children in contact with their services who have speech, language, and communication needs. There are emerging examples of research with children in youth justice settings where creative approaches have been successfully employed to support children to discuss sensitive experiences. Meaby (2019), for example, utilised an approach that combines ethnography and arts-based approaches, called ethno-mimesis (O'Neil, 2002), to talk to children in contact with YJSs about loss. Devi-McGleish, Caulfield and Puttick (2024) worked with one YJS to explore Child First approaches to youth justice and wanted to hear directly from the children about their experiences. They designed an in-person, arts-based focus group to gather experiences and feelings from children that could be challenging to explain through textual or oral mediums. Although the project report is not publicly available, a detailed description of the method can be found in Caulfield and Hill (2025: 213–214). Learning directly from children supported their agency and ensured their voices meaningfully contributed to evidence-based practice developments within the YJS (Burns and Creaney, 2023).

Challenges in implementing arts-based approaches

Despite the promising research and practice findings, several barriers to implementing arts interventions in youth justice settings have been identified. One of the most significant challenges is funding and sustainability. Many arts programmes rely on short-term grants, which makes it difficult to ensure long-term delivery. Without consistent funding, even successful interventions may struggle to continue, limiting their ability to have a sustained impact.

Staff training and engagement can also present challenges. Many youth justice professionals may be unfamiliar with creative methodologies and require additional support to effectively and confidently integrate them into their practice. Without adequate training, some practitioners may feel ill-equipped to deliver arts-based interventions, potentially reducing their effectiveness. Some young people may also initially resist arts interventions due to low confidence, scepticism, or negative past experiences with education. Overcoming this resistance requires building trust, ensuring activities are relevant to their interests, and demonstrating the personal value of participation.

Finally, variability in delivery is a concern. The success of arts-based interventions can vary significantly depending on facilitator expertise, participant engagement, and organisational support. Without clear frameworks for standardising best practices, the effectiveness of creative interventions may be inconsistent across different YJS teams. Learning from others, particularly the good practice shared by Sandwell YJS (Caulfield et al., 2023), is important to minimise some of these potential challenges.

By embedding co-created arts-based interventions into youth justice policy and practice, services can create more engaging, rehabilitative, and empowering experiences for young people in the justice system. Co-created arts practice in youth justice directly aligns with the third principle of the Youth Justice Board's definition of Child First: 'Encourage children's active participation, engagement, and wider social inclusion. All work is a meaningful collaboration with children and their carers' (YJB, 2021, p. 11).

Conclusion and recommendations for the future

The existing literature provides strong evidence that arts-based interventions offer an innovative and effective method of engaging young people in co-production activities in youth justice settings. Research highlights the importance of music, lyric writing, and other creative activities in fostering positive identity development, emotional well-being, and improved compliance with youth justice orders. Importantly, arts provide a medium for culturally relevant activities for children to co-design and engage with that allow meaningful outputs for young people and allow young people to take control of the activity.

Research highlights the transformative potential of music and creative arts, showing that they can enhance self-expression, strengthen social relationships, and provide meaningful opportunities for personal development. However, there is a need for further research on long-term behavioural outcomes, as well as greater efforts to integrate creative approaches into mainstream youth justice practices.

While existing research provides compelling evidence of the benefits of arts-based interventions, there are still gaps in understanding their long-term impact. Future research should focus on:

- Longitudinal studies tracking whether arts participation reduces reoffending over time.
- Comparative studies examining which art forms (e.g., music, drama, visual arts) are most effective in different justice settings.

There remain challenges around funding, evaluation design, and staff training in arts-based interventions and activities in the criminal justice setting.

To maximise the benefits of arts-based interventions used for co-production, YJSs should:

1 Co-produce and embed flexible and culturally relevant arts-based approaches within statutory YJS practice, ensuring shared ownership between children, practitioners, and artists.
2 Develop and deliver training through co-designed sessions involving staff, children, and professional artists to build capacity and mutual understanding.
3 Co-design and conduct longitudinal research with children, practitioners, and researchers to evaluate long-term outcomes on reoffending and personal development.
4 Establish sustainable funding models that support co-produced, arts-based initiatives and embed them as core elements of YJS provision.

By embedding arts-based interventions into youth justice policy and practice, services can co-create more engaging, rehabilitative, and empowering experiences for young people in the justice system.

References

Bilby, C., Caulfield, L. and Ridley, L. (2013). *Re-Imagining Futures: Exploring Arts Interventions and the Process of Desistance*. London: The Arts Alliance. Available at: https://artsincrimjustice.s3.eu-west-2.amazonaws.com/wp-content/uploads/2016/07/13114242/Re-imagining_Futures_Research_Report_Final.pdf

Burns, S. and Creaney, S. (2023). Embracing children's voices: Transforming youth justice practice through co-production and child first participation. In: Case, S. and Hazel, N. (eds.) *Child First*. Palgrave Macmillan, pp. 333–366.

Caulfield, L., Sojka, B. and Massie, R. (2019). *An Evaluation of Sandwell Youth Offending Service –A Creative Approach to Working with Young People*. Wolverhampton: University of Wolverhampton.

Caulfield, L. S. (2024). Developing methodologies to evidence the impact of the arts in criminal justice. In: Gardner, A. and Caulfield, L. S. (eds.) *Arts in Criminal Justice and Corrections: International Perspectives on Methods, Journeys, and Challenges*. London: Routledge, 29–47.

Caulfield, L. S., Botham, M. and Smith, C. (2023). *Developing Creative Approaches in Youth Justice: A Guide for Youth Justice Professionals*. Wolverhampton: Institute for Community Research and Development.

Caulfield, L. S. and Hill, J. (2025). *Criminological Skills and Research for Beginners: A Student's Guide*, 3rd Edition. London: Routledge.

Caulfield, L. S., Jolly, A., Simpson, E. and Devi-McGleish, Y. (2022). 'It's not just music, it helps you from inside': Mixing methods to understand the impact of music on young people in contact with the criminal justice system. *Youth Justice, 22*, 67–84.

Caulfield, L. S. and Sojka, B. (2023). Exploring the impact of music on children at risk of contact with the criminal justice system. *Safer Communities, 22*, 121–132.

Caulfield, L. S., Sojka, B. and Devi-McGleish, Y. (2021). *Follow-on Evaluation of Sandwell Youth Offending Service – A Creative Approach to Working with Young People*. Wolverhampton: Institute for Community Research and Development.

Cheliotis, L. and Jordanoska, A. (2016). The arts of desistance: Assessing the role of arts-based programmes in reducing reoffending. *The Howard Journal of Crime and Justice*, 55, 25–41.

Creaney, S., Burns, S., Douglas, A., Brierley, A. and Falconer, C. (2024). Desistance through participatory practice: Involving children in decision-making processes in youth justice. In: Wigzell, A., Paterson-Young, C. and Bateman, T. (eds.) *Desistance and Children*. Bristol, UK: Policy Press, 212–227. https://doi.org/10.51952/9781447369127.ch01

Devi-McGleish, Y., Caulfield, L. S. and Puttick, M. (2024). *Implementing Child First: Dudley Youth Justice Service*. Dudley, UK: Report for Dudley Council.

Eagle, S. (2008). Evaluation of the miss spent programme 2008 (online). Available at: www.artsevidence.org.uk/media/uploads/evaluation-downloads/clean-break-miss-spent-2008.pdf

Gardner, A. and Caulfield, L. S. (2024). *Arts in Criminal Justice and Corrections: International Perspectives on Methods, Journeys, and Challenges.* London: Routledge.

Gray, P., Jump, D. and Smithson, H. (2023). *Adverse Childhood Experiences and Serious Youth Violence.* Bristol: Bristol University Press.

Hargreaves, D. and Lamont, A. (2017). *The Psychology of Musical Development.* New York: Cambridge University Press. https://doi.org/10.1017/9781107281868

Jean-Berluche, D. (2024). Creative expression and mental health. *Journal of Creativity, 34*(2). https://doi.org/10.1016/j.yjoc.2024.100083

Mansfield, L., O'Connell, N. and White, H. (2024). *Arts Programmes: Toolkit Technical Report.* London: Youth Endowment Fund.

Meaby, V. (2019). *Nothing to Lose? Using Ethno-Mimesis to Explore Loss in the Lives of Young People Who Offend.* University of Durham: Unpublished PhD thesis.

O'Neill, M., Giddens, S., Breatnach, P., Bagley, C., Bourne, D., & Judge, T. (2002). Renewed methodologies for social research: Ethno-mimesis as performative praxis. *Sociological Review, 50*(1), 69–88.

Parker, A., Marturano, N., O'Connor, G. and Meek, R. (2018). Marginalised youth, criminal justice and performing arts: Young people's experiences of music-making. *Journal of Youth Studies, 21*(8), 1061–1076. https://doi.org/10.1080/13676261.2018.1445205

Price, J., Wilkinson, D. and Crossley, C. (2023). Children and young people's lyrics and voice capturing their experiences within youth justice services. *Safer Communities, 22*(2), 186–199.

Royal College of Speech and Language Therapy. (2024). *RCSLT NI BRIEFING: The Links Between Speech, Language, Communication and Swallowing Needs and People in Contact with the Criminal Justice System.* RCSLT Northern Ireland.

Social Care Institute for Excellence. (2022). Co-Production: What is it and how to do it. [Online]. Social Care Institute for Excellence. Last Updated: July 2022. Available at: www.scie.org.uk/co-production/what-how/ [Accessed 27 May 2025].

Stephenson, M. (2024). Summer arts colleges: Using the arts to promote educational engagement and desistance. In: Wigzell, A., Paterson-Young, C. and Bateman, T. (eds.) *Desistance and Children* (pp. 194–211). Bristol, UK: Policy Press.

Thompson, J. D. (2014). Towards cultural responsiveness in music instruction with black detained youth: An analytic autoethnography. *Music Education Research, 17*(4), 421–436. https://doi.org/10.1080/14613808.2014.930117

Viggiani, N., Daykin, N., Moriarty, Y., and Pilkington, P. (2013). *Musical Pathways: An Exploratory Study of Young People in the Criminal Justice System, Engaged with a Creative Music Programme.* Bristol: University of the West of England.

Wigzell, A., Paterson-Young, C. and Bateman, T. (2024). *Desistance and Children: Critical Reflections from Theory, Research, and Practice.* Bristol: Policy Press. https://doi.org/10.51952/9781447369127

Wilkinson, P., Price, J. and Crossley, C. (2022). Developing creative methodologies: Using lyric writing to capture young peoples' experiences of the youth offending services during the COVID-19 pandemic. *Journal of Criminological Research, Policy and Practice, 8*(2), 105–119.

Youth Justice Board (YJB). (2021). *Strategic Plan 2021–2024. Report.* London: YJB.

10

BLACK SPACE MAKING

Co-creating hope for Black and Mixed heritage boys in and outside the Criminal Justice System

John Wainwright

Introduction

This chapter will discuss how institutional responses to Black and Mixed heritage boys in the Criminal Justice System require a radical rethink. It will do this by putting forward a case for Black space making both within the Criminal Justice System and beyond (Du Bois, 1899). In particular, it will suggest that Black space making is co-created with Black and Mixed heritage boys to provide both a vision and practices oriented towards desistance and pathways to opportunities through embracing Africanness (Obasi, 2019).

Before exploring co-creative Black space making, it is important to acknowledge the contexts of everyday experience of Black and Mixed heritage boys in wider society in the United Kingdom in comparison with the United States. This must acknowledge the experience of being Black in the United Kingdom and African/American in the United States and the impetus of the Black Lives Movement for society to acknowledge the everyday trauma of racism (McCoy, 2020; Bates, 2023).

The brutal killing of George Floyd, and Eric Garner before him, by New York and Minneapolis police officers respectively, through strangulation with them both gasping for breath with the heartrending words 'I can' t breath', was a watershed moment for Black people across the globe (Wainwright and Larkins, 2019; Tedam and Cane, 2022). The subsequent impulse to make a stand against the everyday and many manifestations of racism asserts that Black Lives (actually) do matter. Thus, the Black Lives Matter (BLM) movement united Black people and their communities in protests, spreading like a wave of liberation across the United States, United Kingdom and Europe. This resistance has shone a bright light across the West

DOI: 10.4324/9781003602996-13

on the experience of being Black or Brown; being of African heritage (Joseph-Salisbury et al, 2021). It highlights how Black people, Black communities often must contend with direct and indirectly transmitted hatred from white society. This includes the vexed psycho-social contestation of occupying the same space as white people (Anderson, 2015; Bates, 2023).

Everyday racism

The visceral dehumanisation, demonisation, denigration and outright hatred through racism that Black people experience manifests itself in a multitude of ways, consisting of micro-, meso- and macro-aggressions in their everyday lives (Wainwright et al, 2024). Microaggressions are sometimes unspoken but are still communicated strongly to Black people and we are made to feel not welcome in the same spaces as (some) white people. For instance, this may be through public transport, catching a bus, or a train when white people may be reticent or even physically resistant to sit next to Black people. This is not always the case, but it is emblematic of the feeling of worth (lessness) that Black people often experience in public spaces (Harries, 2014; Anderson, 2021). In a similar way, meso exclusion can involve the discriminatory experience of Black people and the wider Black community accessing public services, which could be the Criminal Justice System, education, housing and immigration, or in the private sector, access to banking services, and utilities (HMIP, 2019; Wainwright et al, 2020). Meso everyday racism presents to Black and Brown people a more begrudging, exclusionary or punitive service, in contrast to one that should be delivered with equal quality and proportional responses to need. Thirdly, there is the macro experience for Black people as citizens in the United Kingdom or United States; that of being excluded from positive representation in the media, Government, and the Judiciary (Bourabain and Verhaeghe, 2021). With Black lives punctuated by microaggressions, meso discrimination and macro exclusion, we experience, irrespective of whether born in the country, or not, a citizenship that is at best 2nd class (Wainwright et al, 2024).

There are many complex and intersecting reasons for the antipathy towards the Black community felt in mainstream (white) society in the United States and United Kingdom. There is, however, one common denominator that underpins all of them: racism. I contend in this chapter that much of the antipathy towards Black and Brown people as individuals and the Black community, is an unspoken belief, an ideology that presents Black people as lesser humans. That is, not as capable, of less intellect and being more emotional, easily angered and more defined in terms of physicality than white people (Mirza, 1998; Miles and Brown, 2004; Eddo-Lodge, 2020; Lala et al, 2025). This stereotype is, of course, rooted in the pseudo-scientific racism of 19th-century colonialists. However, it is suggested here that much social policy, institutional treatment and disadvantage that Black people experience emanates from such racist belief systems (Osbourne et al., 2023).

Whiteness is underpinned by power and assumptions by white society that there are entitled rights for white people in society in the Criminal Justice, health, education and immigration system, that are not accessible to Black and Brown people (Earl, 2023).

Discriminatory representations and exclusions of Black and Brown people are reinforced and refracted through a corollary belief that whiteness is normal: to be white, or present as European is the natural order of things (Clarke, 2021). All else, to be Black, of African heritage, South Asian or Chinese heritage is to be of less worth, significance and not the norm (Said, 2016; Bowler, 2017). Whiteness, then, manifests in Black people's everyday experiences in micro-, meso- and macro-structures (Joseph-Salisbury, 2019). With regard to the subject matter of this chapter, meeting the needs of young Black people in relation to the Criminal Justice System can be, at least in part, understood through this lens (Cuneen and Tauri, 2019).

All of these many factors contribute to the present climate of normalising antipathy towards Black and Asian communities and migrants of colour through the 'stop the boats' movement in both the United States and the United Kingdom (Bonansinga and Forrest, 2025). Along with the demonisation of Muslims by Trump and Farage and vocal hostility to Black and Brown people by the 'America First; and 'raise the (English/British) Flag' movements, quite literally sweeping across both countries (Harris, 2025). If Black people and communities of colour were ever in any doubt regarding the depth of racism that engulfs them, Trump, Farage, Reform and English nationalists flying their Union Jack and St George flags have made matters crystal clear (Addley, 2025). This is the world that Black and Mixed heritage boys, their families and wider communities have experienced all of their lives, and now have outright, explicit, institutional confirmation of it (Meechan et al, 2021).

Disproportionality for Black and Mixed heritage boys

First, at every point of contact in the Criminal Justice System Black and Mixed heritage boys are disproportionately represented (HMIP, 2021a; YEF, 2025). These disparities between Black and Mixed heritage boys and their white peers in the Criminal Justice System are also widening (HMIP, 2019; MOJ, 2020; HMIP, 2021b; 2022; YEF, 2025). Second, from the first point of contact in the Criminal Justice System, there are disproportionate numbers of Black boys entering the system because of discriminatory police stop and search practices. More broadly, Black children between the ages of 10 and 17 constitute 6% of the population in England and Wales, yet, in 2023/24, they represented 10% of arrests, 15% of stop and searches and 24% of the monthly youth custody population (YEF, 2025). Third, Black and Mixed heritage children are five times more likely to be placed in custody for homicide and more likely to be victims as well (YEF, 2025). Fifth, boys of Black and Mixed heritage are twice as likely to be excluded permanently from school compared to their white peers (HMIP, 2021a; IRR, 2022). Thus, in sum, at the sharp end of the state, in England and Wales, Black and Mixed heritage boys are disproportionately over-represented in the Criminal Justice System and are more likely to commit and be the victim of a violent crime (Bateman et al., 2023).

Adultification

This suggests that there is something quite distinct regarding the experiences of Black and Mixed heritage boys and the way those in positions of authority respond to the racism they experience, exclusion, from school, lack of education and training and being pathologised. Within this context, it is important to discuss the experience of Black and Mixed heritage boys in the Criminal Justice System and their contact with other agencies of the state, their local community, and familial experiences. Black boys are, by definition, children, but it is suggested that because they may present as physically older than their age, a process of adultification takes place. This is the process whereby people in authority in education, health, and the Criminal Justice System perceive and treat Black and Mixed heritage boys as if they are much older than their actual age. This may involve children as young as 12 or 13 being treated as young adults, effectively as if they are 18, 19, or 20. This adultification brings with it an implicit assumption of adult responsibility leading to harsher and more punitive treatment by the police, the courts, youth justice services, and in schools. In many ways, criminalising Black boys is a failure to protect and safeguard them as children through the most challenging time of their lives: adolescence. (Davis and Marsh, 2020).

Exclusion from education

Black and Mixed heritage boys are often treated differently and detrimentally in school settings. This can manifest in a lack of ambition that the school, or particular teachers, hold for Black and Mixed heritage boys' academic potential and ability (Boyd, 2019). Some schools can perceive the process of educating Black and Mixed heritage boys as mostly containing and managing perceived 'challenging' behaviour, rather than having aspiration for their academic success. The unspoken process of adultification can inform an institutional response of fear and antipathy from education authorities and teachers in response to any alleged challenging behaviour (Stewart-Hall et al, 2023). One such example of the institutional (mis)management of Black boys (and girls) has been the incidence of strip searches and arrests by police on school premises, facilitated and supported by teachers without the knowledge of children's parents. This practice of strip searching Black and Mixed heritage children was starkly highlighted in the case of Child Q, which received intensive media coverage (Ibrahim, 2025). This was not an isolated incident, as despite Black and Mixed heritage children constituting only 5% of secondary pupils, they account for 17% of strip-searches in England and Wales (BBC, 2022). Further, in the last few years, children who are of Black and Minority ethnic heritage were three times more likely to be strip searched after arrest than white children (BBC, 2022; Ibrahim, 2025). It is acknowledged that the highlighted case of strip searching that gained national publicity was concerning a Black girl, however, these practices of abuse on children apply equally to Black boys as girls (Duff and Kemp, 2025).

Pupil referral units

It could be argued that within schools Black children, Black boys, are often given a clear message that they are the problem, and any ambition of a formal education is now over as they need to be *contained* in an alternative facility. As one Mixed heritage boy put it in a study in Liverpool:

> *they didn't want to know why I had the fight, the fact that this kid was calling my family. They said I started it and was to blame and then I was out ….*
>
> *(Wainwright et al, 2020)*

This experience is not uncommon as in another recent study 60% of Black and Mixed heritage boys who were subject to court orders were seen as disruptive and excluded from school, often permanently (HMIP, 2021a). This process of school exclusion contributes significantly to Black and Mixed heritage boys becoming criminalised and drawn into the Criminal Justice System. Once they are excluded from formal education, there is a detrimental psycho-social and physical effect of them being outside of the education system, with very little structure or support offered (HMIP, 2021a; b; IRR, 2022; YEF, 2025). As the Institute of Race Relations (IRR) suggests, pupil referral units effectively become:

> *[a] prison pipeline for working-class black children.*
>
> *(IRR, 2022)*

Once placed in pupil referral units Black and Mixed heritage boys often have to negotiate fractured family lives where the only space to spend more time with their peers is in their local neighbourhoods, or places some distance from where they live, where everyday life can be much more perilous (Pitts,

2020). Either way, these spaces are often contested, more threatening with adults and older children coercing them into repeat and/or serious offending behaviour involving, drugs, violence and gangs (Pitts, 2020).

The Black and Mixed heritage boys who are excluded from school often live in the most socio-economically deprived parts of cities or towns that present a challenging environment for them to grow up. The concept of a childhood for them can be understood as another world, another place, separate from the spaces that they must negotiate in their everyday lives (Brodie et al, 2025). They are in a place where spaces are contested: for many, stepping outside of their home feels like they are entering into a 'war zone' (HMIP, 2021a), not a place of community or safety where children can grow, thrive and play. These contested spaces are often linked to gangs or groups of children and young people that belong to or live in the specific area (Pitts, 2020; Palmer, 2023). For some Black and Mixed heritage boys these gangs are constituted of Black and white boys. For others, they are groups of mainly Black and Mixed heritage children. The contested spaces can be focused on territory, over a space for drugs, or caught up in the milieu of county lines both within their own city, or town or farther afield in another town (Pitts, 2020).

Black and Mixed heritage boys excluded from school then have limited options and may find themselves joining gangs as a replacement for family. Where family trauma, socio-economic conditions and poverty mean that (step) parents and carers are often absent at home, in work or elsewhere, this provides a vacuum that groups of children and adults, or gangs, can fill (Palmer, 2009). Whiteness and the various three levels of structural racism can contribute to Black and Mixed heritage boys needing to spend more time out of the family home because of these socio-economic and psycho-social pressures on families. If the child's family is a place of trauma because of the pressures of racism, poverty and exclusion from having a stake in society, then local streets, spaces, and further away places will become the boys' everyday environment (Pitts, 2020; Wainwright, 2024). However, Black and Mixed heritage boys may not have the psycho- social resilience to negotiate these contested terrains, where older adults often coerce them into gang membership or county lines offending (Pitts, 2020).

It is an awareness of the way whiteness excludes Black and Brown families from a material full stake in society that can inform an understanding of the experiences of Black and Mixed heritage boys. It embodies an anti-Blackness racism that perpetually places Black people out of place with little or no space of their own (Dancy et al, 2018; Gilborn, 2018). For many, the only space they can exist in is that of their local community, which is often one of poverty, gangs contesting spaces and further away places, where, for many, violence is the only currency that matters (Palmer, 2009; Pitts, 2020). To belong to a gang may be a relatively safer prospect than existing alone within environments denuded of the means for supporting ordinary childhood play, learning, growth and development. Theirs is an everyday existence of survival, the threat of violence, gangs and spectre of older adults providing routes into criminality (Palmer, 2009). These possibilities are not opportunities for the boys to thrive but often involve petty and increasing levels of crimes; for instance, initially carrying soft drugs, but soon being sent farther afield to other towns to be involved in county line dealings with hard drugs. This is the world of many Black and Mixed heritage boys (and girls) pulled into the Criminal Justice System (Palmer, 2023).

The evidence is compelling that there needs to be a radical rethink concerning Black and Mixed heritage boys' experiences before, during, and after they enter the Criminal Justice System. This is where co-creating Black space making with Black children can provide possibilities for a different kind of future for them: A better type of youth justice (Wainwright, 2024).

A word on co-creation

In essence, co creation enables children, and in this context Black and Mixed heritage boys, to have a voice and reduces the power imbalance in decision making in their lives (Wainwright et al, 2020; Creaney, 2014). Creative co-production with Black and Mixed heritage children can provide opportunities to reimagine and create a different world, a better world. The co-creation suggested here will privilege the (counter) voices of Black and Mixed heritage children and explore with them how to develop ways of moving away from offending. Their stories, challenges and aspirations need to be heard and placed at the centre of any transformational plans for change in their lives (Dixson, 2018; Wainwright and Larkins, 2019; Wainwright et al, 2020). Black space making will be discussed alongside co-creation with Black and Mixed heritage boys and the concrete example of a peer action collective with Black children in London and Birmingham is illustratively drawn upon. Before moving to the specifics of co-creating Black spaces, it is important to understand the philosophy, sociology and politics of Black space making.

Black spaces – a world that embraces Africanness

The idea of a Black revolution where communities of African descent have eschewed whiteness, colonialism and the dehumanising of Black people has long been proselytised by several Black scholars (Fanon, 1970; Robinson, 1983; hooks, 2000; Du Bois, 2011). Particularly, Black commentators have argued that people of African descent have been (dis)placed from Africa through trans-Atlantic slavery and forcibly moved to the United States, the United Kingdom and Europe. Over time they have been systemically excluded from mainstream society to live in the marginal spaces in cities and towns

(Gilroy, 1993; hooks, 2000). A political economy of capitalism prevails that has been built for centuries on the violence inflicted on and exploitation of Black bodies through their exclusion from spaces of economic prosperity, democratic participation and citizenship (Robinson, 1983; McKittrick, 2011; Hawthorne, 2019). More recently there have been studies proposing the idea of a Black economy, Society and Politics, that are quite separate from the whiteness that systemically discriminates and oppresses peoples of African heritage (Clarke, 2021; Gordon-Nembhard, 2023).This suggests that even within Western societies, the United States, United Kingdom, or Europe, Black communities would prosper more by establishing separate economies, arrangements for political governance and physical demarcation from mainstream white society (Robinson, 2000; Du Bois, 2011).

Perhaps the forms of more equitable social provisions envisaged by such anti-colonial thinking would result in far less entanglement of Black boys and girls with the Criminal Justice System. But the realisation of such an ideal state of affairs may be a long time coming, so the spirit of these ideas for separate arrangements could be applied to the justice system and associated institutions as we find them in the present (Fanon, 1967; 1970; Cuneen, 2019; Hossein, 2019).

Correspondingly, a case can be made that to make co- creation with Black and Mixed heritage boys in general and youth justice in particular meaningful it needs to move away from the whiteness that has engulfed their lives and the intergenerational trauma of racism that has damaged their families and communities. Thus, there needs to be a shift in thinking and practice that develops a world for them that reflects and celebrates Black children and young people's reality of Blackness, a celebration of Africanness (Obasi, 2021; Kolajo, 2025).

To do this, it is important to provide the space for Black boys to explore the micro-realities of how they feel about being Black and what it means to them. This can be done by co-creating a completely different world or space for them that is separate and safe away from the trauma of whiteness and its consequential racism. In other words, providing a space that is safe and protected from whiteness, with its assumed privilege and power, to enable Black and Mixed heritage children to explore their identity, their world, free from the debilitating effects of racism (Kolajo, 2025). So, we need to take a step back and think of a counterpoint, an alternative that does not portray Black children as all the negative images of being angry, disengaged and/or violent (Dache-Gerbino and White, 2016; Meechan et al, 2021). Rather, Black space making must result in co-created space(s) where an understanding of the philosophy of Africanness is an altogether different and celebratory thing. There needs to be a movement for Black and Mixed heritage boys to understand and to be able to articulate their democratic voice. Black and Mixed heritage boys' voices are those that are silenced, and/or pathlogised as being inherently criminal and violent. Co-creating Black space making should provide a space where their counter – narrative of Africanness, Blackness has a legitimate hearing (Dixson, 2018). A counter-narrative that eschews the St George and Union Jack flag waving, a voice that provides serious attention to their experiences of those in authority and the wider state. This can be done by enabling Black and Mixed heritage boys to have a space, a platform to discuss in a broad sense their experiences of racism (Harries, 2014; Williams and Clarke, 2018). This articulation, this counter narrative, will probably not talk to the intergenerational trauma of trans-Atlantic slavery (McKittrick, 2011), of being displaced and misplaced through (post) colonialism (Bruno, 2021). Yet, it will probably express an anger, a visceral feeling of exclusion, of familial pain and emptiness caused often by the tangled web of racism(s) (Barnes et al, 2001; Meechan et al, 2021).

Specifically, to explore their micro-realities those that co-work these ideas, these spaces need to be of African heritage not only in body, but in mind (Fanon, 1967). They need to understand their own reality of being of African heritage and share a space with Black and Mixed heritage boys that is revolutionary and liberatory in outlook. Black practitioners, community workers and/or Community Champions (mentors) need to co-design and create spaces that have as a first point of principle the idea that Africanness is a virtue (Wainwright, 2024). Community Champions can be those people that model the qualities of being of African heritage, of the Black community, that are perhaps not immediately apparent to Black boys (Brown et al, 2023). Blackness in children, adults, families and heterogeneous communities needs to be revered and celebrated. This provides an opening for a counter-narrative that moves away from silencing Black and Mixed heritage boys in a denial of their experiences and feelings. Celebrating Africanness and giving voice to Blackness can provide a tangible route to Black and Mixed heritage boys feeling, thinking, hoping that they belong, that they are equal citizens and can have an understanding of democratic co-participation in their lives and their future (Tulino, 2019).

Second, that Blackness, or Africanness can mean many things to Black and Mixed heritage boys in any way they want. To create a space they want means a philosophy, a politics, a culture that acknowledges heterogenous and multi-dimensional views of Blackness, of Africanness (Hall, 1993). There are a plurality of expressions, articulations and possible creations of a Black identity (Gilory, 1993). The important thing is the space and then safety and creativity within this space. So, instead of focusing solely on, for instance, the standard youth justice assessment models used with children which talk absolutely nothing to a Black reality? Why not encourage, poetry, drawing, music, argument, discussion, humour, about Black Mixed heritage boys' everyday existence (Hunter et al, 2016)?

The space as and of itself is important, as this is the environment that can be the genesis of hope, exploration and opportunities for Black and Mixed heritage children (Allen, 2020). The Space Making in many ways is part of the journey as it is co-creating it encourages the children to envisage what this space making may be. The space can be in the minds of Black and Mixed heritage children, or it can be a physical space inside a building. Just as importantly, the Space making may talk to an area, a zone, or wide space in their locality that enables them to feel safe and comfortable in their Blackness (Hawthorn, 2019). It can, of course, be a fluid manifestation of many of these and much more. It can be a spiritual, emotional, psychosocial and physical space, incorporating complexities of relationality and materiality. These spaces resonate with Black scholars' articulations of a Black geography, not on the margins of their universe, but at the centre (hooks, 2000). Such safe spaces can be informed by democratic co-participation of Black and Mixed heritage boys, where they feel loved, cared for and enabled to make the right choices for themselves, in contrast to the brutal, threatening world that often engulfs them in a physical and emotional sense (Kolajo, 2025).

This democratic co-creation encourages children to explore their micro and meso reality with an optimistic and generative lens. The goal is ultimately a space where Blackness, Africanness, can be collectively created; in music, dance, drama, education, philosophy that is meaningful to them and reflective of their lives (Mace, 2024):

- A space that gives them the opportunity to explore their intersectional and multi-dimensional identity, what their Africanness means to them. How a Black World is for them.
- A space that eschews and challenges the trauma of violence, drugs and/or repeat offending, rather offering tangible solutions to the contested neighbourhoods in their lives (Palmer, 2009, Pitts, 2020).
- Space that is safe and encourages the children to create a pathway to opportunity that they can own and be proud of.

The process by which this is achieved may be to understand the philosophy of Blackness of being from Africa: To explore its rich and diverse cultures, religions, music and languages and how this connects with their sense of Africanness in their world (Obasi, 2019). Importantly, these explorations of identity must enable moving from negative forms of gang membership, drugs and violence, which for many Black and Mixed heritage boys is their unfortunate reality. Instead, there can be a shift to understanding the centuries of culture, knowledge and history of African successes (Apena, 2007; Obasi, 2021). There is absolutely no point co-creating with Black and Mixed heritage boys in a vacuum, a bubble of whiteness and exclusion (Robinson, 2000). Likewise, this cannot be fully realised within an

> education, psycho-social, Criminal Justice, social care and welfare system that has done nothing but pathologise and marginalise their Africanness and their Blackness (Williams and Clarke, 2016; Wainwright et al, 2019).

Authentic co-creation thus means creating tangible concrete steps to enable Black and Mixed heritage boys to move slowly away from gangs, violence, drugs and making quick, but precarious and dangerous money. This movement embraces a vision, a world, where they can visualise, aspire and achieve something tangible in their lives, through confronting violence and gangs with an assertive and physical rejection of forms of Black identity manifested in the destructiveness of gangs, of violence, of anger and hopelessness (Dixson, 2018; Wainwright, 2024). This is tough. It is a long haul. It is at the centre of Black space making and if it is to be meaningful to Black and Mixed heritage boys caught up in all of this, they need to be able to realise there is another direction. Not on the margins of space, physical and pyscho-social but at the centre (hooks, 2000). A centre that talks to Black spaces, A Black economy; a Black politics. What it is not is acquiescing and trying to squeeze Black boys into a white Criminal Justice System, that it can be argued has done nothing but damage them since birth (Williams and Clarke, 2018).

The ideal space can create a vision of the African diaspora that is relevant to Black boys' everyday experiences. Such spaces must emphasise the abilities that each child or young person has and encourage them to express their identity and creativity in a way that opens up a world of opportunity. It is fundamentally a psycho-social space in their minds that is creative, liberatory, with practical solutions offering a better life for them and their families (de St Croix and Doherty, 2023). There are many examples of Black space making where Black children, young people and adults feel in a safe space. These spaces are co-created by Black people for Black people. These spaces are the inverse of whiteness and focus on the positives of being of African heritage. This can be in conversations, the displaying of African, evoking stories of history ingrained in their local communities (Hunter et al, 2016; Allen et al, 2019; Wainwright et al, 2020).

It should be acknowledged that some of this work is already occurring within Black Communities of England and Wales (for instance, Voyage Youth London, 2025: UK Youth, 2025). But, the work is local with little coherence or grand vision regarding Black space making or how to design bespoke spaces for the very different ever-changing heterogenous communities that our children and families inhabit. It is, therefore, a psychosocial space in Black children's minds, a range of potential imaginaries, that provide a liberatory vision, a framework for Black and Mixed heritage children to move from the trauma of violence, of being pathologised, criminalised and excluded from the education system. This can transform children's potential to a place where anything is possible, that the very essence of their Africanness provides hope, where too often there has been none. But, instead, it proves a pathway of opportunities to a horizon of a diaspora that is celebrated (Allen et al, 2019).

Further, Black space making would encourage children and young people to create space that was safe, yet limitless in its possibilities. For instance, what about a Black judiciary, a Criminal Justice System that looked like the children that they so disproportionately drag Black children into? It needs to be acknowledged that Black court officials and judges, in and of themselves do not just reproduce an oppressive system they have been inducted and socialised into. They need to be Black in the political and revolutionary sense (Fanon, 1970; Robinson, 2000; Du Bois, 2011). In other words, there needs wholesale attention to underpinning values and prejudices underpinning the established (post) colonial and class-based system that is at the very epicentre of the exclusion and marginalisation of Black and Mixed heritage boys (Fanon, 1970; Hall, 1993). Preventative measures must also address broader institutions associated with the structural and psycho-social processes that cause criminal behaviours, such as providing for a Black education system that explores Africanness not in a superficial way, but in depth: exploring the philosophies of the many tribes and cultures of Africa and those peoples that now reside in the United Kingdom. Moreover, we might envisage an economy and employment system that the children designed and that worked for them. Taken together, such a mixture of abolition and generation would be encouraging children to co-create a Black world, a space that met their ambitions and hopes (Hunter et al, 2016). Ultimately, to co-create a space that in every way embraced change that eschewed the structural and institutional racism that traumatised them and does so much damage to their everyday lives (Wainwright, 2024).

Co-creating Black space making provides limitless and fluid opportunities. How would a Black economy work for Black and Mixed Heritage Children, their families and their communities? What about the Criminal Justice System that worked for Black People, was run by Black people? Imagine an education service that revered African scholarly knowledge? That was exciting and revelatory for Black and Mixed heritage children. (Baldridge et al, 2011). What about an economy that does not place Black children and their families in the lowest-paid jobs with the least status in every workplace or industry? Imagine a space where Black young men and Women had genuine, authentic power to change things (Hawthorne, 2019; Hosseine, 2019); that demonstrably celebrates anti-racism, equality and the African Diaspora in its many, varied and heterogeneous forms. This is a co-created Black space making that is transformative for Black children and provides possibilities for youth justice that is not performative but can be life-changing.

An example of this is one recent study with 23 Black and Mixed heritage children in London, England, who co-created a research project as a peer action collective with their peers identified housing, poor education and lack of opportunities as the key determinants contributing to their experience of violence in their everyday lives. The Black and Mixed heritage children and young people in this London project brought their peers together to listen to them about the outcomes of their own research, raising awareness of the issues they may have been otherwise facing alone, and to build a narrative of common experiences (Sharpe et al, forthcoming)

The Black peer action collective presented a clear set of ambitious but achievable demands to young people in the community, based on their peer research, and to shape a set of policy recommendations for local young people to build their energy around. These included celebrating the minority ethnic diversity of the children and young people in their local area; having a space to discuss the violence they experience and providing a platform to disseminate their authentic voices and ensuring local agencies of the state listened to and reported to them on any tangible change both on preventing the violence that blights their lives and opportunities and broader horizons to move away from it. Most importantly, they argued for a safe space where their Blackness, their identity, can be explored in a positive way. Whilst developing some tangible strategies to challenge and refute the everyday violence that they endure. This is a practicable example of Black space making at a local level, where Black and Mixed heritage children co-create possibilities and opportunities in their own psycho-social and physical space (Dixson, 2018; Sharpe et al, forthcoming).

Conclusion

Whiteness and assumptions about entitlement and superiority of white people and society inform an understanding of white privilege and by implication, the necessity of challenging a perceived relative worthlessness of Black people. This challenge must occur at a fundamental human level and for Black and Mixed heritage boys (children) to understand there is a place for Black space making, and that this has emancipatory and transformational potential. Central to this is developing a psycho-social environment and Black economy that persuades Black and Mixed heritage children that there is a practicable way to achieve their financial ambitions in a legitimate way. This is in contrast to being coerced and/ or seduced, into finding alternative 'families' by being a gang member, involved in drugs, violence and contested spaces in their communities. Hence, the context in which an idealised co-creative endeavour can be brought into must be grounded in a Black economy, A Black Psychology, A Black Philosophy. Ideally, all of this is made by Black and Mixed heritage children so that it works for them (Gordon-Nhembard, 2023).

What this all means when co-creating with Black and Mixed heritage boys is that there needs to be an acknowledgement of the pervasiveness of whiteness, of exclusion and marginalisation on micro, meso and macro levels. That Black and Mixed heritage boys and their families are often failed by the state through structural poverty, poor housing, and education system that diminishes and excludes them and a Criminal Justice System the pathologies and criminalises them. The co-creative process implicitly offers a space whereby alternative space-making can be enacted, and this ought to be the goal of progressive change.

Questions to consider

How can Black and Mixed heritage children meaningfully be engaged in co-participation?

What does youth justice need to do to change the way Black and Mixed heritage children experience it?

What would Black space making look like in your community/service?

References

Addley, E. (2025). A dangerous moment: The emboldening of Britain's far right; the Observer. June 2025. www.theguardian.com/news/ng-interactive/2025/aug/24/britain-far-right-emboldened-migration-nationalism accessed 3rd October 2025.

Allen, D., Lawhon, M., & Pierce, J. (2019). Placing race: On the resonance of place with black geographies. *Progress in Human Geography*, *43*(6), 1001–1019. https://doi.org/10.1177/0309132518803775 (Original work published 2019)

Allen, D. L. (2020). Asserting a black vision of race and place: Florida A&M university's homecoming as an affirmative, transgressive claim of place. *Geoforum*, *111*, 62–72.

Anderson, E. (2015). The white space. *Sociology of Race and Ethnicity*, *1*(1), 10–21. https://doi.org/10.1177/2332649214561306

Anderson, E. (2021). *Black in White Space: The Enduring Impact of Color in Everyday Life*. University of Chicago Press. https://doi.org/10.7208/chicago/9780226815176

Apena, F. (2007). Being Black and in trouble: The role of self-perception in the offending behaviour of Black youth. *Youth Justice*, *7*, 211–228.

Baldridge, B. J., Lamont Hill, M., & Davis, J. E. (2011). New possibilities: (Re)engaging Black male youth within community-based educational spaces. *Race Ethnicity and Education*, *14*(1), 121–136. https://doi.org/10.1080/13613324.2011.531984

Barnes, B., Palmary, I., & Durrheim, K. (2001). The denial of racism: The role of humor, personal experience, and self-censorship. *Journal of Language and Social Psychology*, *20*(3), 321–338.

Bateman, T., Brodie, I., Day, A. & Osidipe, T. (2023). 'Race', disproportionality and diversion from the youth justice system: A review of the literature. www.nuffieldfoundation.org/wp-content/uploads/2022/10/%E2%80%98Race-disproportionality-and-diversion-from-the-youth-justicesystem-a-review-of-the-literature.pd

Bates, D. (2023). 'This is Britain, get a grip': Race and racism in Britain today. In: Sikka, T., Longstaff, G. & Walls, S. (eds) *Disrupted Knowledge: Scholarship in a Time of Change*. Haymarket/Brill, pp. 97–113.

BBC. (2022). Thousands more children strip searched by police. www.bbc.co.uk/news/articles/c0k1gd44revo accessed 6th July 2023.

Bonansinga, D., & Forrest, C. (2025). "Stop the boats": Populist contagion and migration policymaking in the UK. *Ethnic and Racial Studies*, 1–19. https://doi.org/10.1080/01419870.2025.2465513

Bourabain, D., & Verhaeghe, P-P. (2021). Everyday racism in social science research a systematic review and future directions. *Du Bois Review: Social Science Research on Race, 18*(2), 221–250. https://doi.org/10.1017/S1742058X21000102

Bowler, R. (2017). *Whiteness, Britishness and the Racist Reality of Brexit.* Working Paper. University of Sunderland.

Boyd, R. (2019). *"Nothing Much Has Changed:" Black Boys' Experiences of Exclusion and Reintegration in Mainstream Secondary Schools.* Other thesis, University of Essex & Tavistock and Portman NHS Trust.

Brodie, I., Day, A., Kiff, J., Osidipe, T., Pitts, J., & Batemen, T. (2025). Exploring racial disparity in the youth justice system in England and Wales - Youth Justice Resource Hub. https://yjresourcehub.uk/exploring-racial-disparity-in-diversion/ accessed 4th October 2025.

Brown, L., Samuel, L., & Parke, S. (2023). The Black adoption project: Phase 1. www.google.com/search?q=black+adoption+project+phase&oq=black+adoption+project+phase&gs_lcrp=EgRlZGdlKgYIABBFGDkyBggAEEUYOTIICAEQ6QcY_FXSAQg5NDQ3ajBqMagCALACAQ&sourceid=chrome&ie=UTF-8

Bruno, T. M. (2021). *Environmental Injustice and Black Sense of Place in the Social and Biophysical Afterlife of Slavery.* University of Oregon.

Clarke, A. (2021). Recognising British bodies: The significance of race and whiteness in 'post-racial' Britain. *Sociological Research Online*, *28*(1), 279–295. https://doi.org/10.1177/13607804211032232

Creaney, S. (2014). The benefits of participation for young offenders. *Safer Communities*, *13*(3), 126–132.

Cunneen, C. (2019). Youth justice and racialization: Comparative reflections. *Theoretical Criminology*, *24*(3), 521–539. https://doi.org/10.1177/1362480619889039

Cunneen, C., & Tauri, J. M. (2019). Indigenous peoples, criminology, and criminal justice. *Annual Review of Criminology*, *2*(1), 359–381.

Dache-Gerbino, A., & White, J. A. (2016). College students or criminals? A postcolonial geographic analysis of the social field of whiteness at an urban community college branch campus and suburban main campus. *Community College Review*, *44*(1), 49–69.

Dancy, T. E., Edwards, K. T., & Earl Davis, J. (2018). Historically white universities and plantation politics: Anti-blackness and higher education in the Black lives matter era. *Urban Education*, *53*(2), 176–195.

Davis, J., & Marsh, N. (2020). Boys to men: The cost of 'adultification' in safeguarding responses to Black boys. *Critical and Radical Social Work*, *8*(2), 255–259. https://doi.org/10.1332/204986020X15945756023543

de St Croix, T., & Doherty, L. (2023). 'It's a great place to find where you belong': Creating, curating and valuing place and space in open youth work. *Children's Geographies*, *21*(6), 1029–1043. https://doi.org/10.1080/14733285.2023.2171770

Dixson, A. D. (2018). "What's going on?": A critical race theory perspective on Black lives matter and activism in education. *Urban Education*, *53*(2), 231–247.

Du Bois, W. E. B. (1899). *The Philadelphia Negro: A Social Study*. University of Pennsylvania.

Du Bois, W. E. B. (2011). *Dusk of Dawn: An Essay Toward an Autobiography of a Race Concept*. Transaction Publishers. (Original work published 1940).

Duff, K., & Kemp, T. (2025). Strip-searching as abjectification: Racism and sexual violence in British policing. *Theoretical Criminology*, *29*(1), 65–90.

Earle, R. (2023). Tackling whiteness as a decolonising task in contemporary criminology. In: Cuneen, C., Deckert, A., Porter, A., Tauri, J., & Webb, R. (eds) *The Routledge International Handbook on Decolonizing Justice*. Routledge, pp. 516–525.

Eddo-Lodge, R. (2020). *Why I'm no Longer Talking to White People about Race*. Bloomsbury Publishing.

Fanon, F. (1967). *Wretched of the Earth*. Trans. Constance Farrington. Grove Press.

Fanon, F. (1970). *Black Skin, White Masks*. Paladin, pp. 13–30.

Gillborn, D. (2018). *Heads I win, tails you lose*: Anti-Black racism as fluid, relentless, individual and systemic. *Peabody Journal of Education*, *93*(1), 66–77. https://doi.org/10.1080/0161956X.2017.1403178

Gilroy, P. (1993). *The Black Atlantic: Modernity and Double Consciousness*. Harvard University Press.

Gordon-Nembhard, J. (2023). Black political economy, solidarity economics, and liberation: Toward an economy of caring and abundance. *Review of Radical Political Economics*, *55*(4), 525–538. https://doi.org/10.1177/04866134231163216 (Original work published 2023).

Hall, S. (1993). Culture, community, nation. *Cultural Studies*, *7*(3), 349–363.

Harries, B. (2014). We need to talk about race. *Sociology*, *48*(6), 1107–1122.

Harris, J. (2025). Flags as symbols of prejudice, not pride – and a distinct air of menace. Welcome to England 2025. The Observer. Sunday 24th August. www.theguardian.com/commentisfree/2025/aug/24/flag-hard-right-prejudice-england accessed 10th October 2025.

Hawthorne, C. (2019). Black matters are spatial matters: Black geographies for the twenty-first century. *Geography Compass*, *13*(11), e12468.

HMIP. (2019). Black and minority ethnic service users—effectiveness of rehabilitative services. www.gov.uk/guidance/Black-and-minority-ethnic-serviceusers-effectiveness-of-rehabilitative-services accessed 3rd February 2020.

HMIP. (2021a). *The Experiences of Black and Mixed Heritage Boys in the Youth Justice System*. HMIP.

HMIP. (2021b). Race equality in probation: The experiences of black, Asian and minority ethnic probation service users and staff: A thematic inspection by HM Inspectorate of Probation. March 2021. HMIP. Manchester.

HMIP HM Inspectorate of Probation. (2022). *2021 Annual Report: Inspections of Youth Offending Services*. HMIP.

hooks, b. (2000). *Feminist Theory: From Margin to Center*. Pluto Press.

Hossein, C. S. (2019). A Black epistemology for the social and solidarity economy: The Black social economy. *The Review of Black Political Economy*, *46*(3), 209–229. https://doi.org/10.1177/0034644619865266 (Original work published 2019).

Hunter, M. A., Pattillo, M., Robinson, Z. F., & Taylor, K.-Y. (2016). Black placemaking: Celebration, play, and poetry. *Theory, Culture & Society*, *33*(7–8), 31–56. https://doi.org/10.1177/0263276416635259 (Original work published 2016).

Ibrahim, Y. (2025). Strip search on black children: Institutional racism, sexual violence and blackness. *Social Identities*, 1–16. https://doi.org/10.1080/13504630.2025.2524177

Institute of Race Relations. (2022). How Black working class youth are criminalised and excluded in the English school system: A London case study. https://irr.org.uk/article/beyond-the-pru-to-prison-pipeline/

Joseph-Salisbury, R. (2019). Institutionalised whiteness, racial microaggressions and black bodies out of place in Higher Education. *Whiteness and Education*, *4*(1), 1–17. https://doi.org/10.1080/23793406.2019.1620629

Joseph–Salisbury, R., Laura Connelly, L., & Wangari-Jones, P. (2021). "The UK is not innocent": Black lives matter, policing and abolition in the UK. *Equality, Diversity and Inclusion: An International Journal*, *40*(1), 21–28. https://doi.org/10.1108/EDI-06-

Kolajo, S. (2025). *Young Black People's Geographies of Comfort: Home, Daily Living and Becoming Un/comfortable*. Diss. Loughborough University.

Lala. K. N., Brown, G., Twyman, K., & Feldman, M. W. (2025). Impediments to countering racist pseudoscience. *Evolutionary Human Sciences, 7*, e24. https://doi.org/10.1017/ehs.2025.10012

Mace, J. A. (2024). Transformative Reframing of the Blues Epistemology. *Kalfou, 11*(2), 156–181. www.proquest.com/scholarly-journals/transformative-reframing-blues-epistemology/docview/3222371261/se-2

McCoy, H. (2020). Black lives matter, and yes, you are racist: The parallelism of the twentieth and twenty-first centuries. *Child Adolescolent Social Work J*, *37*, 463–475. https://doi.org/10.1007/s10560-020-00690-4

McKittrick, K. (2011). On plantations, prisons, and a Black sense of place. *Social & Cultural Geography*, *12*(8), 947–963. https://doi.org/10.1080/14649365.2011.624280

Meechan, H., John, M., & Hanna, P. (2021). Understandings of mental health and support for Black male adolescents living in the UK. *Children and Youth Services Review, 129*, 106192, ISSN 0190-7409, https://doi.org/10.1016/j.childyouth.2021.106192

Miles and Brown. (2004). *Racism*. Routledge.

Ministry of Justice (MOJ). (2020). *Tackling Racial Disparity in the Criminal Justice System*. Ministry of Justice. https://assets.publishing.service.gov.uk/government/uploads/system/uploads/attac hment_data/file/881317/tackling-racial-disparity-cjs-2020.pdf acccessed 1st October 2020.

Mirza, H. S. (1998). Race, gender and IQ: The social consequence of a pseudo-scientific discourse. *Race Ethnicity and Education*, *1*(1), 109–126. https://doi.org/10.1080/1361332980010108

Obasi, C. (2019). Africanist sista-hood in Britain: Creating our own pathways. In: Emejulu, A. & Soband, F. (eds) *To Exist is to Resist: Black Feminism in Europe*. Pluto Press, pp. 229–242. ISBN 9780745339474, 9780745339481, 9781786804570.

Obasi, C. (2021). Identity, language and culture: Using Africanist Sista-hood and deaf cultural discourse in research with minority social workers. *Qualitative Research*, *22*(3), 353–368. https://doi.org/10.1177/1468794120982827 (Original work published 2022).

Osbourne, L., Barnett, J., & Blackwood, L. (2023). Black students' experiences of "acceptable" racism at a UK university. *Journal of Community & Applied Social Psychology*, *33*(1), 43–55. https://doi.org/10.1002/casp.2637

Palmer, S. (2009). The origins and emergence of youth 'gangs' in a British inner-city neighbourhood. *Safer Communities*, *8*(2), 17–26.

Palmer, S. (2023). Race and gangs: Towards a Black criminology. In: Andell, P., & Pitts, J. (eds.) *The Palgrave Handbook of Youth Gangs in the UK*. Palgrave Macmillan, pp. 323–345. https://doi.org/10.1007/978-3-030-99658-1_14

Pitts, J. (2020). Black young people and gang involvement in London. *Youth Justice*, *20*(1-2), 146–158.

Robinson, C. J. (1983). *Black Marxism: The Making of the Black Radical Tradition*. University of North Carolina Press.

Robinson, C. J. (2000). *Black Marxism: The Making of the Black Radical Tradition* (2nd edn). University of North Carolina Press

Said, E. W. (2016). Orientalism. In: Longhofer, W. & Winchester, D. (eds) *Social Theory Re-Wired*. Routledge, pp. 402–417.

Sharpe, D., Wainwright, J., Morocza, N., Larkins, C., Roy, A., Farrelly,, Tatham, S., Nowland, R., Ennis, C., & Rooney, C.. (forthcoming). *Child Sexual Abuse: Structural Violence and Co-Creation: Black and Mixed-heritage Youth in Diverse Urban Spaces*. University of East London/ University of Lancashire.

Stewart-Hall, C., Langham, L., & Miller, P. (2023). Preventing school exclusions of Black children in England–a critical review of prevention strategies and interventions. *Equity in Education & Society*, *2*(3), 225–242.

Tedam, P., & Cane, T. (2022). "We started talking about race and racism after George Floyd": Insights from research into practitioner preparedness for anti-racist social work practice in England. *Critical and Radical Social Work*, *10*(2), 260–279.

Tulino, D, S., Madjiguene Fall, M. & Browne, S. (2019). Resisting anti-blackness through counternarratives. *English Journal*, *109*(2), 32–38.

UK Youth (2025). Young Change Makers www.ukyouth.org/what-we-do/our-programmes/young-changemakers/ accessed 1st October 2025.

Voyage youth London. (2025). www.voyageyouth.com/ accessed 27th August 2025

Wainwright, J. (2024). Black and mixed-heritage boys: Desistance through a co-creative Critical Race and postcolonial lens. In: Wigzell, A., Paterson-Young, C., & Bateman, T. (eds) *Desistance and Children: Critical Reflections from Theory, Research and Practice*. Policy Press, pp. 128–146. ISBN 978144736912

Wainwright, J., Burke, L., & Collett, S. (2024). 'A lack of cultural understanding and sometimes interest': Towards half a century of anti-racist policy, practice and strategy within probation. *Probation Journal*, *71*(2), 116–138.

Wainwright, J., & Larkins, C. (2019). Race, ethnicity, young people and offending: The elephant in the room. *Social Identities*, *26*(1), 128–144. https://doi.org/10.1080/13504630.2019.1684887

Wainwright, J., Robertson, L., Larkins, C., & Mckeown, M. (2020). Youth justice, Black children and young men in Liverpool: A story of rac (ism), identity and contested spaces. *Genealogy*, *4*(2), 57.

Williams, P., & Clarke, B. (2016). Dangerous associations: Joint enterprise, gangs and racism—an analysis of the processes of criminalisation. www.crimeandjustice.org.uk/sites/crimeandjustice.org.uk/files/Dangerous%20assoc ations% accessed 6th May 2021.

Williams, P., & Clarke, R. (2018). The Black criminal other as an object of social control. *Social Sciences*, 7(11), 234.

YEF. (2025). *Racial Disproportionality in Violence Effecting Children and Young People*. YEF. https://youthendowmentfund.org.uk/wp-content/uploads/2025/02/YEF_Racial_Disproportionality_FINAL.pdf accessed 1st October 2025.

11

INTERDISCIPLINARY METHODOLOGICAL INNOVATIONS FOR ENHANCING CO-PRODUCTION WITH PROFESSIONALS AND CHILDREN IN SECURE SETTINGS

Stefan Kleipoedszus, Caroline Andow, Raymond Arthur, Rachel Dunn, and Nicola Wake

Introduction

This chapter provides novel insight into a methodological approach used by a multi-disciplinary research team from Bournemouth, Northumbria, and Leeds Becket Universities in multiple projects to explore the design of Secure children's homes (SCHs). Secure accommodation refers to locked facilities within the childcare system designed to provide a safe and secure environment for those who require it (Milligan and Smith, 2006). Secure accommodation is defined by section 25 of the 1989 Act as '*accommodation provided for the purpose of restricting liberty*' and includes SCHs. It is a form of out-of-home placement used for various reasons, including protection, punishment, or rehabilitation (Ellis, 2016). Within youth justice, children can receive a custodial sentence and be sentenced to detention in an SCH. SCHs are typically used for children and young people who are perceived as more vulnerable due to their age, the risk of harm to themselves or others, and/or because they are deemed to be a danger to society (McKeown et al., 2022). Alternatively, section 25 of the Children Act 1989 (the '1989 Act') gives the local authority power to detain a looked-after child in secure accommodation if the child has a history of absconding and is likely to do so and suffer significant harm, or if they are likely to injure themselves or other people when residing in any other type of accommodation. Despite the high stakes and costs involved in providing secure care – the most recent data available indicates an economic cost of £628 per day for a youth justice placement, and £1008 per day for a welfare placement (Williams et al., 2020), with the difference between the costs being accounted for by differences in contracting beds – this is a field that is under-researched. The gap in knowledge is partly due to how difficult

DOI: 10.4324/9781003602996-14

it is to reach this vulnerable demographic and those involved in their care. We highlight the development of new approaches to conducting research that can contribute knowledge in this area and demonstrate how innovative methodologies can operate as pathways to impact.

Our research engaged several objectives, such as, exploring perceptions of 'ideal' models of secure care and identifying unresolved issues in design such as how to design a space that is flexible and adaptable to the changing needs of the occupants. These objectives were co-created between the research team and key stakeholders such as providers of secure care (considered further below). The objectives are linked through adoption of the Child First approach. The Child First approach sees the child at the centre, recognises their autonomy and strengths and considers how interventions can be tailored individually to support the development of a pro-social identity (see Andow et al., 2024). Child First has been adopted as a central guiding principle of the English and Welsh youth justice system (Youth Justice Board, 2020). We engage with this youth justice principle as a lens through which we critically explore the design of SCHs. A Child First youth justice system is 'based on positive strengths-based working, privileging collaboration with children and working *towards* positive outcomes', is child-focused, developmentally informed and acknowledges structural barriers and meets responsibilities towards children (Case et al., 2023: 205). Our ultimate aim was to achieve impact in the design of new SCHs. As a team we considered from the outset that co-creation with professionals involved in the delivery of care in SCHs was necessary to generate knowledge about how to make SCHs child-focussed and developmentally informed.

This chapter focuses on our innovative methodological journey which engages with those who work in secure care in the first instance, to support co-production with professionals working within youth justice, who are often not considered in discussions about co-production, before working with children through co-creative methods. To access stakeholders, it is often necessary to depart from traditional modes of research, with interdisciplinary models providing new opportunities to generate knowledge. To achieve impact, defined here as change in practice because of new knowledge, it is necessary to reach stakeholders in a meaningful way with scaffolded approaches to data gathering designed specifically for the participants. Engaging stakeholders in the planning and design of research can assist, but methodological tools should be both accessible and used reflexively. Some methods adopted by the research team have been used with young people, aiming to be inclusionary and provide the young people with a voice in our research. We used a mixed-methods participatory approach with the goal of co-production of results. Participants engaged in several data collection activities, including the Diamond-9 ranking tool, Lego Serious Play, solution sketchpads, and the Kawa Model. This chapter first outlines the methodological interdisciplinary research (MIR) framework before explaining the models adopted and the benefits of using these methods, which allow participants to think more deeply about the research topics and encourage participation. Second, this chapter discusses the analytical approach adopted for these methods and how data is presented. Finally, the authors highlight some of the challenges and logistical elements of the methods and how to overcome them. This includes how these methods can be adapted for use with children in secure settings.

The key objectives of the chapter are:

- To demonstrate the importance of involving and empowering professionals in the research process using innovative methodological approaches to improve collaboration and co-creation with children.
- To provide description and analysis of the various research methods adopted and how they each individually formed pathways to impact.
- To invite readers to reflect upon what co-production means for youth justice settings, and the importance of involving and empowering professionals in the research process to improve collaboration with children, alongside the use of a range of creative methodologies.

We start by outlining the framework underpinning our research.

Quasi-co-creation as a methodological framework

Our research followed the MIR framework as members of the research team have practice experience and academic expertise in social work, social pedagogy, youth justice, children's rights, access to justice and social sciences, and first-hand involvement in research in secure residential childcare. In this respect, an interdisciplinary approach was adopted in relation to all aspects of the research. Interdisciplinary in this context is defined as:

> any study or group of studies undertaken by scholars from two or more distinct scientific disciplines. The research is based upon a conceptual model that links or integrates theoretical frameworks from those disciplines, uses study design and methodology that is not limited to any one field, and requires the use of perspectives and skills of the involved disciplines throughout multiple phases of the research process.
>
> *(Aboelela et al., 2007)*

Our approach also adopted co-production as a collaborative approach to research, whereby researchers, participants, and stakeholders work together throughout the research process from the beginning of the project to its completion. Co-production aims to empower participants by recognising their expertise and lived experiences as valuable contributions to the research process. Price et al. (2022) highlights that this shift from a researcher-driven model to one of co-production allows for the identification of research needs by participants in research. This participatory approach enhances the quality of the research and promotes inclusivity, ensuring that the voices of marginalised groups are heard and respected. Though staff working in SCHs, for example, may not be considered vulnerable, they are marginalised in the sense that their voices are rarely heard, or heard fully, whether that is because of the difficulties researchers face in accessing locked institutions, and/or the time pressures staff face while at work (see Andow, 2020).

Although we use the term co-production to define the overall approach of the research process, it is more realistic to define our approach as a form of 'quasi co-creation' in line with the definition of Bettinson et al. (2024):

> Co-creation involves 'the collaborative generation of knowledge by academics working alongside stakeholders from other sectors' and should shape the project design. We have termed our approach 'quasi co-creation' as it differs from the definition of co-creation because our participants were not involved from the outset with the design. We use the term 'quasi cocreation' to denote the collaborative way the researchers worked with stakeholders during part of the design process.

Co-production ensures that research is based in the real-world experiences and needs of participants (Staley et al., 2019). By involving users in the research process, the resulting evidence is more likely to address the actual needs of the participants and their social context, making it more applicable and impactful. This aligns with community priorities and enhances the likelihood that research findings will be applied in practice.

While co-production offers many benefits, it also presents challenges. Duggan et al. (2024) discuss the complexities of co-production, highlighting the need for reflexivity among researchers to critically examine their roles and the power dynamics at play. The research team are aware that their positionality as researchers has the potential to impact the research process from study design to analysis. Researcher identities and perspectives were therefore disclosed to our partners in meetings, during sessions and in our research. For example, Andow spent 400 hours over seven months immersed in a SCH for her ground-breaking doctoral ethnographic study of the experiences of children's lives in a SCH. Kleipoedszus has 25 years' experience in practice and research with children and young people in out-of-home care; Arthur, Dunn and Wake have adapted and applied innovative child-friendly research methodologies to children in an SCH to allow the children to communicate in creative ways their own lived experience of secure care, which resulted in the children becoming more engaged with staff, improving academically, and some children benefited from reduced time in custody. The approach was embedded by staff and subsequently the SCH was judged 'outstanding' by OFSTED for the first time (Arthur et al.,

2019). This demonstrates how co-production of research with young people provides impacts for service governance and delivery beyond the individual outcomes for young people, creating systemic and long-lasting benefits.

We also agreed that bi-directional approaches to research – deductive, in drawing on previous experience, and inductive in being open to new and emerging data – would not only be necessary but would have to be purposefully built into the technical design of the research given the team's positionality. Reflexive practice is, therefore, essential for ensuring that co-production is genuinely collaborative and does not reinforce existing power imbalances: 'relational awareness … an inter-dependent awareness of how I as a researcher am influencing my research participants' perceptions and a simultaneous and interdependent awareness of how they are influencing me' (Warin, 2011: 809). To aid such a collaborative process, our innovative methodological framework recognises the influence the researcher has on the research process but enables participants to take ownership of the research process and, more importantly, on the knowledge creation that takes place in each research session.

Ethical considerations

To address the perspectives of the entire research team, cognisant of different ethical sensitivities across disciplines (Tobi et al., 2018), the team co-created the ethical approval documentation. The ethical principles and procedures of the British Society of Criminology were followed, and ethical approval was granted through the respective institutional Ethics Committees of each of the researchers. Ethics applications were duplicated across each University to ensure institutional compliance for each of the researchers. Participation was voluntary and based on informed consent. Anonymity was guaranteed, and we asked for permission to audio record the focus group discussions. Participants were made aware at the outset that it would not be possible to withdraw their data from focus group discussions where individuals are unidentifiable. This research involved only adults. This included adults who had previously been residents in a SCH. This approach enabled us to obtain views from those with care experience as a young person but avoided the ethical sensitivities around researching with young people/children currently in secure care.

'Scheduled unsessions' with professionals

Fundamental to our methodological design was the opportunity for participants to come together and explore relevant topics as a group, setting the parameters of the research questions themselves. We used the notion of a 'scheduled unsession' framework combined with a variety of novel visual methodologies (discussed further below).

We targeted stakeholders involved in secure care since engaging more people generates more creative thinking and impact potential. Participants responded to invitations through the Secure Accommodation Network, legal and education networks as well as direct personal invitations. Those involved in our sample included staff working in SCHs (including both residential care staff and managers), mental health practitioners, policymakers, professionals from third-sector organisations and representatives from local authorities involved in children's social care.

The sample was generated using a mixed approach involving purposive and non-probability snowball sampling (Ahmed, 2024). Such sampling is less expensive, and resource intensive than probability sampling, which is costly, takes longer and engages more resources (Ahmed, 2024). Non-probability sampling is a method where 'the sample populate is selected in a non-systematic process that does not guarantee equal chances for each subject in the target population' (Elfil and Negida, 2017, p.1). It is generally considered optimal for exploratory and time-pressured studies, whereas probability sampling has the benefit of generalisability depending on how the research is conducted. The way we accessed the participants for our study also represents a challenge to the probability sampling model. Though we identify non-probability sampling as a potential limitation of our study, in that it is argued in this sampling method those who take part are often unrepresentative of the studied population (Boyd et al., 2023), we note that the purposive dimension to our sampling meant we were successful in accessing significant stakeholders.

As such, the rich qualitative data we obtained provides significant insight to policy change that could be applied across the sector, as well as providing an opportunity to demonstrate the value of the innovative methodological approach.

We held workshops on Design and Build of SCHs (in London and Wolverhampton n=53 over 2 days), Staff Perceptions and Experiences (in Bournemouth (n=25) and Leeds (n=18)) and the future of Secure Accommodation (in Glasgow (n=32)). Each event engaged participants in five to six focus groups forming our '(un)sessions". We used a central facilitator to lead each event. The central facilitator (Stefan Kleipoedszus) was supported by one facilitator from the research team per focus group, whose task it was to keep the group focused on the topic/ task and maintain an audio record of the discussion. Additionally, we undertook one mini focus group (see Kamberelis and Dimitriadis, 2005) online with adults who had experienced secure care as children (n=2, aged 18–25).

In relation to the scheduled unsessions, we sought saturation, i.e. the point at which no new themes or insights emerge from more focus groups, at each of our events. Guest et al. (2017: 22) noted that 'a sample size of two to three focus groups will likely capture at least 80% of themes on a topic – including those most broadly shared – in a study with a relatively homogeneous population using a semi structured guide. As few as three to six focus groups are likely to identify 90% of the themes'. According to Guest et al. (2017), saturation can also be achieved when the diversity of perspectives among participants is adequately represented, allowing for a thorough exploration of the topic at hand. This is echoed by Häberlein and Hövel (2023), who highlight the importance of including a diverse range of experts and stakeholders to ensure that different viewpoints are captured, thereby enhancing the richness of the data collected. We considered that for the topics explored and as an insight into the work conducted in secure care we had sufficient diversity, though we recognise that future studies seeking to emphasise a specific facet of secure care might require greater homogeneity and specificity in sample selection.

Conducting research with larger groups of people at the same time can be difficult for various reasons, such as difficulties in recording (verbal, visual), processing (transcription) and analysing the data in a coherent way. Over some iterations, which explored the perspectives of our individual disciplines and planning how we would analyse the data in advance, we established a flexible research protocol that effectively generates data but also presents meaningful opportunities for participants to come together and not just be subjects of research but active participants in a joint learning and development event. This pre-planning is essential to engage in meaningful interdisciplinary research which optimises the utility of expertise from across disciplines (Tobi et al., 2018). For these events, we used the idea of a so-called un-session, further considered below, as a container for applying different visual methodologies that facilitate discussion and deep thinking.

Measurement plan: the scheduled (un)session

The use of scheduled (un)sessions avoided predetermining the contents of what would be explored at these events, which allowed us to engage in inductive analysis of new and emerging themes. The idea is to emphasise to the participants that they are active participants and collaborators and that they are invited because they are the 'brightest, sparkiest minds' in their field and experts in the area due to their professional experience.

Example of invitation

> **Calling all bright sparks.** In this Unsolved Problems Unsession you will be active participants and collaborators. We are gathering 60 of the brightest, sparkiest minds in the provision of secure homes for children and young people to debate the open questions in our field, and create new approaches to solving them. The outcome will be a list of real problems that affect our daily work as professionals. *Come and help shed some light.*

These events follow some simple yet inspiring principles which are shared with the participants ahead of the event.

- Conferences are too one-way, too passive. We want more action.
- We want open, honest conversations about secure provision for children and young people.
- Bring your most courageous, opinionated, candid self.
- The stuff you're scared to mention, or you'd only talk about over a beer? Bring that.
- The minute you think you're right, you've checked out of the conversation.
- Listen with an open mind.
- This is an experiment.
- Failure is an option; it's just the least desirable one.
- Conversely, perfection is the least likely.
- Whoever shows up are the right people.
- What happens is the only thing that could have happened.
- There is no finish line.
- What we are doing is not definitive.
- Move fast and break things.

These principles spell out the essence of the idea behind these sessions, which is that while there is a focus for the event, this only provides a backdrop for the discussions at each event that can develop into directions chosen by the participants.

Scheduled un-sessions are flexible gatherings of research participants which actively seek to generate an atmosphere that is informal. That allows for a more organic interaction among participants and aims to establish an environment that generates rich discussions and insights. The collaborative nature of these sessions can lead to deeper insights into participant experiences and is particularly useful at the explorative stage of research. The methodological flexibility of scheduled unsessions allows for innovative approaches to data collection which facilitates the (desired) possibility of participants playing with the research questions, changing the focus and exploring lines of enquiry that we as a research team did not contemplate.

Despite the informal nature of these sessions, planning and facilitation is essential to ensure that discussions remain productive and focused, and to maximise the utility of the expertise of the interdisciplinary team. As noted by Stahl et al. (2011), the dynamics of group interaction can significantly influence the outcomes of group discussions, such as the scheduled unsessions, for example, necessitating a structured approach to guide the conversation while allowing for organic contributions from participants.

Visual methods

Rather than simply inviting participants to have a verbal discussion about the different aspects of the research question, we used a variety of visual methods to allow participants to be more actively involved in shaping their own interpretation of the research question and co-producing the research by adding more dimensions at this explorative phase of our research agenda. These methods have been primarily used with professionals working in, or in connection to, SCHs. The Diamond9 has been used with both professionals and young people (aged 18–25) who have experience of being a resident in secure care, which will be explored further in that section.

One significant advantage of visual methods is their capacity to engage participants and involve them in the research process. Pera et al. (2021) highlight that the co-creation of research through visual contributions allows participants to become more actively engaged. Visual methods enhance critical thinking skills (Dewi et al., 2023). They also promote a more inclusive research environment by allowing participants to express their ideas in non-verbal ways (Clark et al., 2013). Vindrola-Padros et al. (2016) note that creative and arts-based approaches, such as participatory photography, make research enjoyable and facilitate communication. Another benefit is that these methods can stimulate cognitive engagement and reflection. Kahlke and Eva (2018) found that using visual elicitation techniques helped participants articulate their thoughts more openly, avoiding rehearsed narratives. This approach encourages participants to think critically about their responses and fosters a more genuine exploration of the research question.

In our sessions, visual methods enhanced participant engagement and influenced the way individuals think about research questions. We used Lego Serious Play; Solution Sketchpads, the Kawa Model, Photo Elicitation, and Diamond-9s, in different combinations at the different events to facilitate communication and reflection among participants.

LEGO serious play

We used LEGO Serious Play (LSP) because of this method's effectiveness to facilitate engagement, creativity, and communication among participants. This approach uses LEGO bricks as a means to express thoughts and ideas metaphorically. Kriszan and Nienebar (2024) highlight that LSP serves as a methodological enrichment for participatory research, enabling the generation of transformative knowledge. The tactile and visual nature of LEGO allows participants to articulate their experiences and perspectives in a non-threatening manner, thus filling a significant methodological gap in social research. Schön, 1971 as cited by James (2013) described LSP as 'a set of activities combining metaphorical modelling, building with Lego and peer discussion to explore complex issues'. These metaphors can prove very useful for 'creating radically different ways of understanding things'.

LSP has been shown to foster creativity and collaboration in research environments. McGehee (2022) explores how engagement with LSP can inspire creative confidence among participants, suggesting that the collaborative nature of building with LEGO can lead to enhanced creative outputs. This notion is supported by Wheeler et al. (2020), who found that LSP promotes psychological safety within teams, encouraging open communication and collaboration. The ability of LSP to create a safe space for dialogue is crucial in research contexts, as it allows for the exploration of diverse perspectives and ideas. Barton and James (2017) found that LSP can change the nature of group interactions to overcome hierarchies and other barriers to expression and facilitate equality of voice among participants in an environment which encourages authentic non-hierarchical communication of diverse opinions and approaches creating new insights into the development of equitable partnerships among students.

LSP is an effective tool to understand and represent complex concepts. Kirby and Pawlikowska (2019) discuss the use of LEGO to revise core concepts in pharmacology, demonstrating how play can serve as a powerful learning tool. This aligns with the findings of Cox (2021), who outlines how LSP can be employed to articulate and share mental models, thereby facilitating deeper understanding among participants.

LSP has been applied in various fields, including mental health research, where it has been used to gather insights into service users' experiences. Vusio et al. (2022) illustrate how LSP can facilitate engagement and stimulate critical thinking among participants, making it a valuable tool for exploring sensitive topics in research. This versatility of LSP across different domains underscores its potential as a robust research methodology.

One of the foundational aspects of LSP is its alignment with constructivist and constructionist theories of learning. Kirby and Pawlikowska (2019) argue that LSP serves as a powerful tool for revising core concepts, allowing participants to engage in active learning through the physical manipulation of LEGO bricks. This hands-on approach enables a deeper understanding of abstract concepts, as participants can visualise and construct their thoughts in a tangible form.

The role of LSP in enhancing creativity and collaboration is well-documented. McGehee (2022) explores how LSP can inspire creative confidence among participants by placing them in collaborative environments where they can express their ideas freely. This notion is further supported by Wheeler et al. (2020), who found that LSP fosters psychological safety within teams, encouraging open communication and collaboration. The ability to approach conflicts as collaborative opportunities rather than adversarial situations is a hallmark of effective team dynamics, which LSP effectively promotes.

LSP has been recognised for its capacity to facilitate the articulation of mental models. Cox (2021) discusses how LSP can be used to explore individual worldviews and combine them into a shared understanding, akin to consensus modelling techniques. This ability to visualise and negotiate different perspectives is particularly valuable in settings where diverse viewpoints must be integrated, such as in organisational decision-making processes.

In the context of research, LSP has been applied to engage vulnerable groups effectively. Nienaber and Kriszan (2023) highlight LSP's low-threshold approach, which allows participants, particularly young migrants, to express their thoughts and ideas in a supportive environment. This participatory aspect of LSP is crucial for generating transformative knowledge and fostering inclusivity in research settings, as noted by method's adaptability to various contexts, which underscores its potential as a methodological enrichment for participatory research.

Additionally, LSP has been utilised in exploring complex emotional and psychological concepts. Wężyk et al. (2020) demonstrate how LEGO can be employed to externalise and communicate abstract ideas such as stress, providing participants with a playful yet profound means of discussing their experiences. This exploration of emotional landscapes through LSP not only aids in individual reflection but also fosters group discussions that can lead to collective insights.

Solution sketchpad

The idea for a solution sketchpad is taken from an unsession at the Canadian GeoConvention in Calgary in 2013 shared by Agile Geoscience (agilegeoscience.com). The idea is to get participants to work on an unsolved problem that was identified by the group and start thinking about a solution together with a diverse group of people who all bring different experiences to the table that can help to express the first simple steps to a solution.

This solution-focused approach is effective because it allows participants to identify and develop solutions rather than dwelling on the problem, which is what often happens in more traditional focus group discussions. We used this method during our stakeholder events with professionals who work within, or close to, SCHs.

The solution sketchpad acknowledges the problem by getting participants to clearly define the challenge but also create a visual representation of the problem. The latter facilitates a more in-depth and reflective thought process about the details of the problem. By asking who cares about the problem, the systemic nature of challenges faced in real world contexts is emphasised.

In itself, a solution sketchpad is a visual representation of the discussion which acts as a focused summary of the thoughts shared by the group. In addition to this, the verbal presentation of the work to the plenary and the discussions that occurred when completing the solution sketchpad provide a rich source of data for analysis.

The Kawa Model

Another visual tool we used to explore staff perceptions of professionals working in SCHs is the Kawa Model. The Kawa Model, developed by a team around Michael Iwama, is a framework used in occupational therapy to represent the complexities of life and the interplay between individuals and their environments. Using this model, we wanted to understand the circumstances, context, and the barriers those involved in secure care for children face in achieving their occupational goals. At its core, the Kawa Model visualises a river, where the water represents the flow of life. The riverbanks and riverbed represent the environment and context in which a person lives, while obstacles such as rocks and driftwood signify challenges and personal assets that influence their occupational engagement (Iwama et al., 2009; Ching and Ammon, 2020). According to Naidoo et al. (2023), this metaphor helps to understand a person's narratives and experiences in a holistic manner. That creates a deeper understanding of their unique situations (Naidoo et al., 2023).

The Kawa Model is used mainly within occupational therapy. Research around the Kawa Model focuses mostly on its application in practice (Carmody et al., 2007; Ching and Ammon, 2020; Hsiao, 2024). There does not seem to be any application of Kawa as a research tool itself. However, there are some ideas that highlight the usefulness of this model for research with a group of professionals and people with living experience. For example, Lape et al. (2019) conducted a pilot study to assess the Kawa Model's effectiveness in promoting interprofessional collaboration among healthcare professionals. Their findings suggest that the model can serve as a valuable tool for enhancing communication among diverse practitioners. Naidoo et al. (2023) examined the Kawa Model as a self-reflection tool for occupational therapy students during practice placements. Their study found that this model can help with increasing awareness of cultural lenses and enhancing an understanding of practice.

In our stakeholder sessions with professionals, we used the model to explore what everyday life in secure looks like and understand what facilitates a good day and what challenges occur at different times of the day. By using the Kawa method, the participants worked together to find commonalities and differences in their experiences. As a visual method, Kawa enables participants to approach these kinds of research questions in a more kinaesthetic way, which has many benefits. Pera et al. (2021) show that the co-creation of research through visual contributions allows participants to become more actively engaged. By revisiting visual materials, participants can reflect on their experiences and values and how these link with the research topic. According to Söderlund and von Schoultz (2024), the visual outputs generated during participatory research can access participants' thoughts and feelings on a deeper level. The use of metaphors and visual metaphors can help participants articulate complex ideas that may be difficult to express verbally. The results from these methods can be very rich, which is evident not only in the actual drawings the groups produced but also the narratives when these drawings are explained and the discussions that take place while the group works together on producing a drawing of a river, the riverbed, rocks, and driftwood.

Photo elicitation

In our sessions, we asked participants to take photos of aspects that symbolise important themes relevant for the research question with an instant camera. These photos can be glued onto a flipchart or annotated using cards to write an explanation of why they took this photo. This added another dimension to the discussions. As defined by Johnson et al. (2010), photo elicitation enables researchers to encourage exploration of participants' experiences and recover unarticulated aspects of their narratives. One of the primary advantages of photo elicitation is its ability to engage participants more effectively than traditional verbal methods, triggering participants' views so as to evoke reflections and generate rich data' (Kyolo et al., 2023: 22) that may not have been feasible with conventional interview methods.

The Diamond9

The Diamond9 was developed for use in primary education studies, and is referred to as a 'thinking skills tool' (Clark et al., 2013, p.6), to encourage and facilitate discussion. It collects both quantitative and qualitative data, easily adaptable to the research aims and needs. The purpose of the Diamond9 is for participants to place cards in a hierarchy, forming a ranking system, on a diamond-like shape. Those placed at the top of the board are the 'highest' with those at the bottom of the board the 'lowest'. Any placed on the same row carry the same weight of importance to each other. This opens up the relationship between the ranking of the cards, and differentiates the middle categories more from just the highest and the lowest. Though it is a simple tool, and may seem rigid, the Diamond9 'can become flexible and fluid, creating ways to collect data and opinions from participants and be adapted for whatever the research purpose is' (Dunn, 2020, p.39). The Diamond9 can be categorised as a visual method of participant-generated data (Wall et al.,

2013, p.3). The benefits of using the Diamond9 include enhancing the richness of the data, used for member checking and validity to add to the reliability of the data, easily replicable with other populations (Glaw et al., 2017). Further, its use can be more effective than using interviews alone, as the visual aids can prompt participants to 'reveal more than they were expecting to share with the researcher' (Pain, 2012, p.313), and visual methods can help to alleviate participant anxiety about the research process (Bailey and Harken 2014).

Participants are either given cards or can develop their own to be placed on the board, or a mix of both. The cards can contain words, statements or images relating to what the researcher is measuring. For example, participants could be asked to rank in terms of preference, importance, feelings or understanding. Whatever it is, the participants take often simple cards and make 'overarching relationships by which they organise knowledge' (Niemi, Kumpulainen and Lipponen 2015, p.140).

The Diamond9 can be done with an individual participant or a group. When done with a group, members are required to talk to each other and come to a final decision as to the placement of the cards on the board. Cards will often be moved to a different rank until consensus has been reached. This allows the researcher to capture discussions around the creation and placement of cards, providing more depth to the data set. If done individually, we usually ask the participant questions around the placement, to gain those qualitative comments. There is no right or wrong answer to the Diamond9, and the 'process of discussion, negotiation, accommodation to other perspectives, and consensus-seeking' (Clark, 2012, pp.223–24) as well as the final placement is what is important.

To analyse the Diamond9, each part of the board is split into different sections and given a numerical value (Woolner et al., 2012). The top of the board has the highest numerical value, decreasing in value to the bottom, as shown on the below diagram:

Having the top of the board carry the higher numerical value helps with the representation of the data on resulting graphs, and seeing which card was deemed to be the highest in the category. When collecting data across several participant groups, the addition of the numerical values helps to see which cards were placed more consistently in which sections of the board, and what the overall score for that card was (for more information on the presentation of Diamond9 data, please see Andow et al., 2024). The qualitative data is analysed using thematic analysis.

We have utilised the Diamond9 several times during our previous research, with both stakeholders and adults who had experienced secure care as children. In both instances, we have asked participants to create their own cards prior to the Diamond9. When in person, this was done on Post-It notes. When online, we did this using Padlet. We did not restrict the number of cards participants could make, but at the start of the Diamond9 they had to choose their most important 9 cards. This adds another element to the data

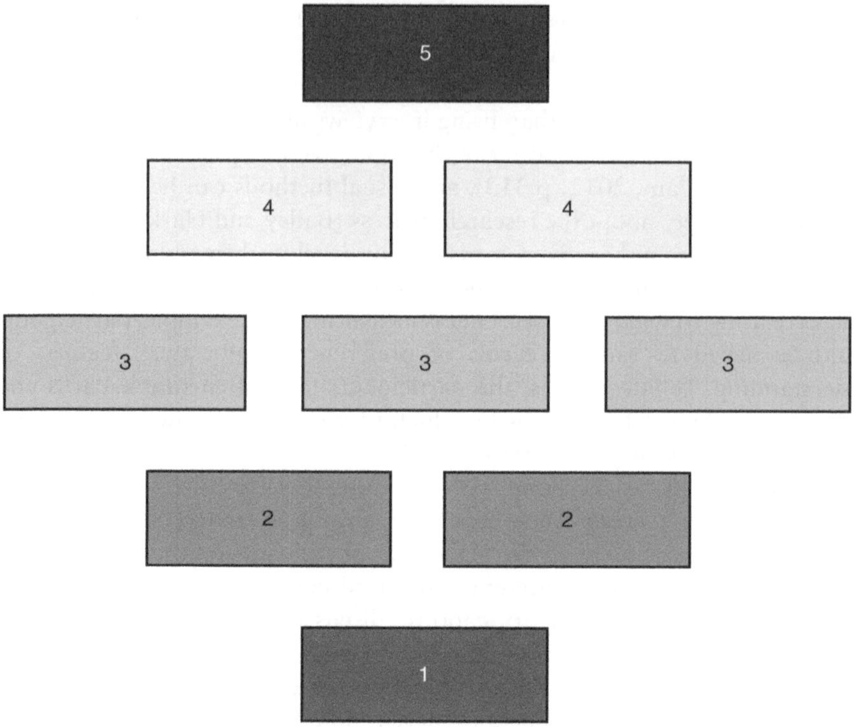

FIGURE 11.1 Diamond9.

collection process, asking participants to carefully think about what needs to be represented on the final placement on their board.

The above example shows data collected with adults who had been in secure and residential care as children. This was done through online data collection using Teams. The participants were first asked to list what they liked and did not like about their care experiences. As they were talking, the researcher typed them into Padlet, sharing their screen with the participants. Once the lists were complete, the participants were asked to pick the 9 most important to them and then place them on the Diamond9 board. Conversations were captured, and the final board is a representation of what they felt was important during their care placement. This enabled the research team to identify what was most important to them, and check their meaning with participants as they are ranking them.

When doing this with stakeholders, we went through the same process but in-person, asking them to write on Post-It notes what works well in secure care and the issues they face. As we were seeking to identify these issues and how they can be resolved, we asked participants to select 9 cards from their issues pile. Once all Diamond9 boards were complete, the researchers took a photograph of all Diamond9 boards and the whole group viewed them

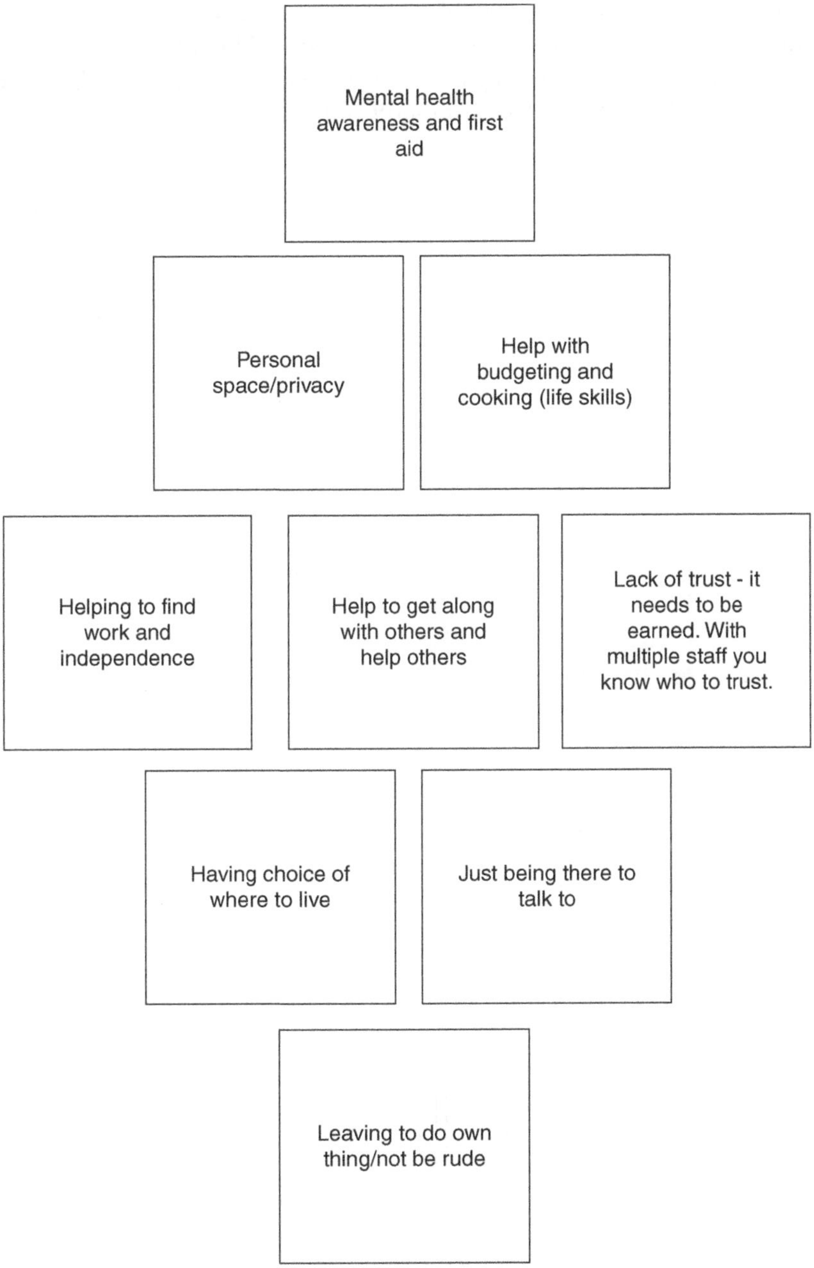

FIGURE 11.2 Example showing data collected with adults.

on the projector. Groups were able to comment on other boards, and make comments as to the similarities and differences. This allowed us to collect more qualitative data, and engage with participant validity of the data set. An example of a stakeholder Diamond9 is displayed below:

FIGURE 11.3 Stakeholder Diamond9.

FIGURE 11.3 (Continued)

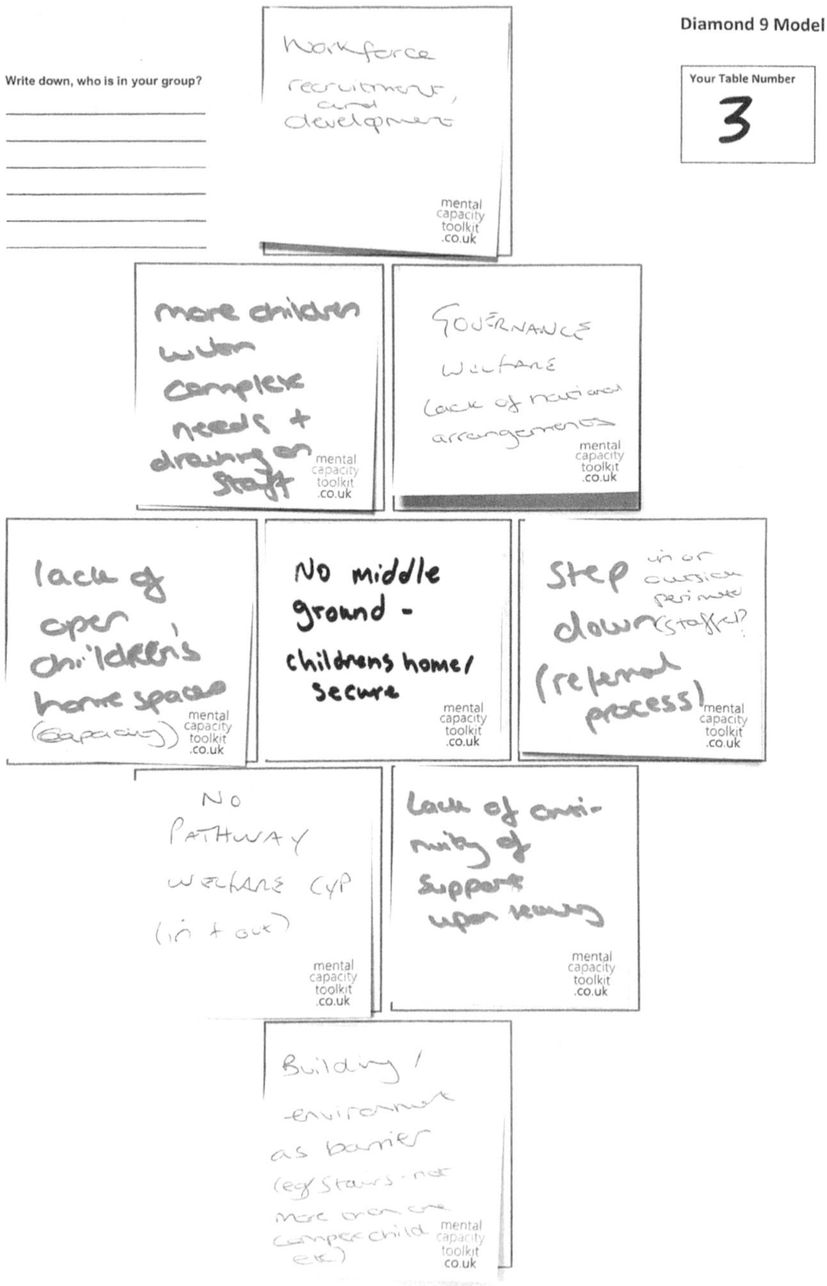

FIGURE 11.3 (Continued)

FIGURE 11.3 (Continued)

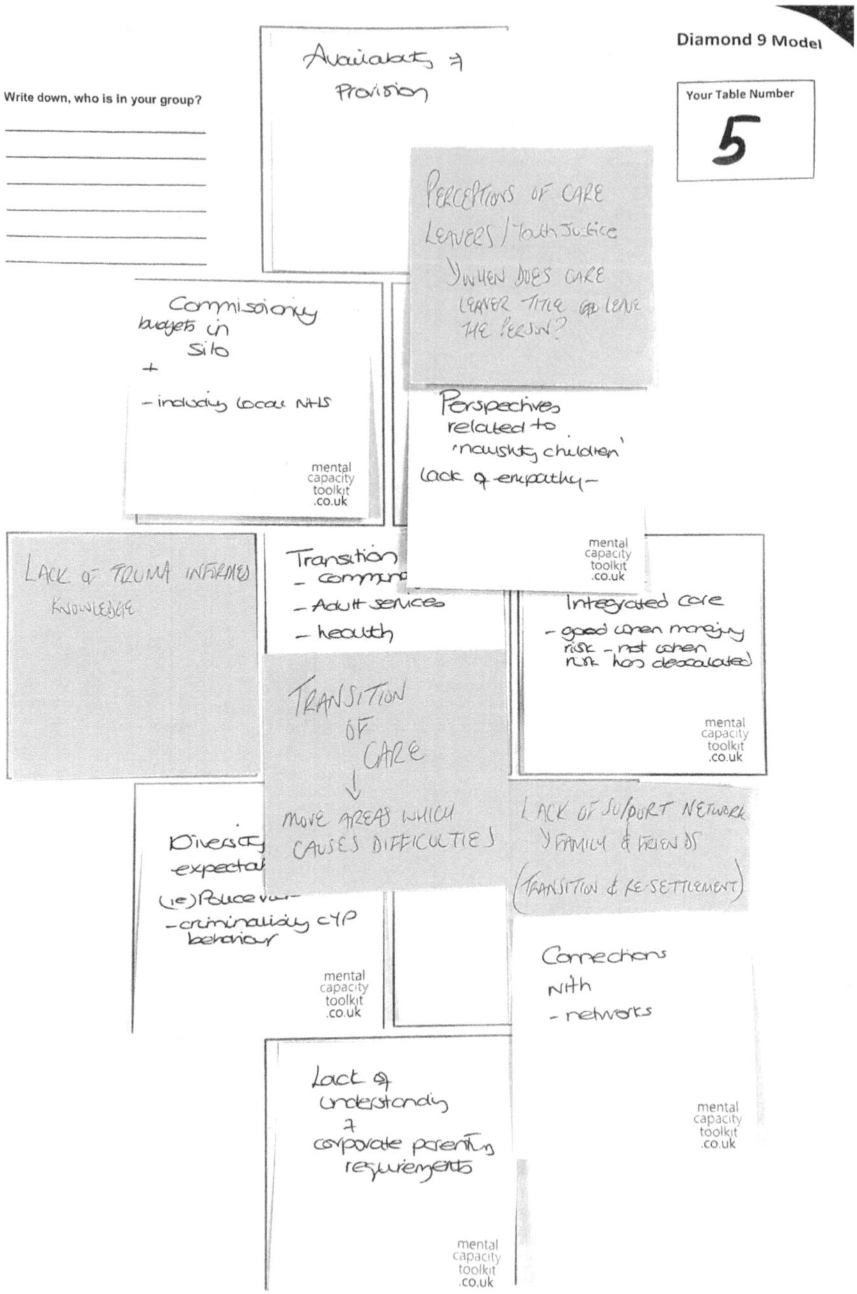

FIGURE 11.3 (Continued)

Having many groups complete the Diamond9 across several stakeholder events allowed us to identify what are common issues faced by those working in, or connected to, secure care for children. This has helped to direct our future research plans, with further exploration on the issues most raised. Used in conjunction with other data collection methods, the Diamond9 has allowed for a rich data set, which is simple to use and participatory in nature.

Analysing the data

In interdisciplinary contexts, it is essential to agree on a data plan at the outset to ensure optimal input from those involved and because different disciplines have diverse experience of training in methods and analysis (Tobi et al., 2018). At the outset, we agreed to adopt Braun and Clarke's (2006) six-stage Thematic Analysis framework for the analysis of qualitative data due to its theoretical freedom and flexible approach 'which can potentially provide a rich and detailed, yet complex account of data' (Braun and Clarke, 2006: 78). This approach is appropriate in interdisciplinary contexts given the diverse perspectives of researchers involved. A strength of thematic analysis is that the data can be situated within relevant contexts, such as social, political and policy, for deeper contextualising. Further, Braun and Clarke (2022) highlight how the flexibility and accessibility of this analysis method can be useful for community and inclusive research, which relates to our own research. We wanted to ensure that the data analysis allowed for a collaborative approach, and thematic analysis enabled us to be more reflexive and sense-check ideas about codes and themes as we went through the process. This enabled a rich interpretation of the data and its meaning and to consider the voice and data creation of our participants in more depth (Byrne, 2021).

Our thematic analysis plan involved a research team debrief following each event, with the discussion of emerging themes. After data had been transcribed and uploaded to NVivo, we met in person to do the first round of coding. This involved individual coding on paper transcripts and then coming together to discuss and refine the codes. Once we had an initial codebook, we added them to NVivo to continue the coding remotely. We had regular meetings to discuss the adding and removal of codes, before then meeting to organise them into themes. These themes were reviewed continuously before and during the write-up stage, and it is normal for them to change and shift until publication (Trainor and Bundon, 2020). This is a benefit of reflexive thematic analysis. As Braun and Clarke (2022) highlight, good thematic analysis is not linear, but instead a continual process of ensuring the codes generated reflect the data.

While the thematic analysis of textual data is relatively straightforward, the additional thematic analysis of photographs or drawings adds a significant level of complexity. Our research collated a great amount of data which can be challenging to manage and bring together (i.e. linking the explanation of a LSP model with the right element of the transcript). It can be a complex process to get from the data that exists in different formats to the point of doing a thematic analysis. Braun and Clarke (2022, p.27) make it clear that thematic analysis allows for a lot of flexibility of dataset size and composition, and it is suitable analysis for a range of data collection methods, including visual. There is a need, however, to be systematic in the approach to the data, using a 'deliberate and thought-through strategy'. Our analysis involved identifying, analysing, and reporting patterns (themes) within visual and oral material. The starting point is that the researchers familiarise themselves with the available data. As Braun and Clarke (2012) emphasise, this familiarisation is essential for developing a nuanced understanding of the material. We used a hybrid thematic analysis (inductive and deductive) (Swain, 2018; Fereday & Muir-Cochrane, 2006), that includes triangulation of photographic images and interview transcripts to develop themes. The research team's approach to the data analysis, outlined above, helped us to familiarise ourselves with the mass of data, and be strategic in the analysis process to ensure a robust process. This thematic organisation helps to identify connections between different elements of the data. Sharma (2022) emphasised that textual-visual thematic analysis is valuable for understanding complex visual material by identifying common threads across the dataset.

Learning from research practice with adults to inform co-production with children

Prior first-hand experiences within our team of attempting to do research with children in secure settings made us very aware of challenges, not only in terms of initial access, and engagement in the research, but also in terms of finding ways to empower children in co-producing knowledge. Children in secure settings are repeatedly assessed by adults and may consider any research encounter as a form of assessment (Milham et al., 1978; Goldson, 2002). They might not want to engage in research, or participate only to a limited extent. This inhibits the generation of in-depth, quality data.

Aware of these limitations in relation to using interviews in this context, Andow (2016) spent a long-time planning to use non-verbal methods with children in her doctoral ethnography of an SCH. This turned out to be unsuccessful as her planned methods required items such as pens and glue, which posed a risk to children resident at the time who were concealing items with which to later self-injure. Arthur, Wake and Dunn (2019) had more success in using the Diamond 9 approach detailed above in their work with children in a SCH, as all they needed was the Diamond9 Board and cards, and wrote statements on the blank cards for the young people. This simple method allowed to collect data in a participatory way, empowering the young people involved, but was suitable for the SCH setting.

Our research using the range of methods outlined above has not only enabled us to generate in-depth data with a range of stakeholders involved in secure care – which is of value in itself – but it has also generated a methodological toolkit for us to draw from when engaging children in secure settings in research. We needed to co-create data with stakeholders first to understand how these methods might work best with children. This toolkit gives us the opportunity to empower participants by offering them a range of methods to choose from, and we can restrict the range of choices if it is not appropriate to be using equipment such as LEGO for example. Alternatively, we can adapt LSP method and use a material such as plasticine. The research process does not have to imposed but rather can be led by the participants. Children, as stakeholders themselves, should be afforded this autonomy and potential for co-creation and collaboration.

Conclusion

This chapter details how we have developed a repertoire of methods to use to engage stakeholders in our research on issues relating to secure accommodation. The success of these methods is demonstrated by the engagement of the participants during our events, and the quality data generated. Our stated aim at the beginning of the chapter was to illustrate the importance and practice of using innovative methodological approaches to engage with adult stakeholders of secure care which can then be adapted to enable co-creation with children. Our research has prompted consideration about what co-production means in youth justice and child welfare settings, which includes involving and empowering professionals in the research process to improve collaboration with children through a range of creative methodologies.

The following are some of the key messages that have emerged from our work:

- The methodological innovation, and the combination of different methods, offer a means of overcoming the barriers that traditional interviews pose – to adults and children alike – and offer research participants more opportunities for ownership and co-creation in the research process.
- There is a significant need to empower and co-create with professionals to manage power dynamics and empower them, also to build trust and gain research access to children.
- Using innovative methodological approaches promotes a Child First approach as Child First privileges collaboration with children, acknowledges structural barriers and is developmentally informed.

References

Aboelela, S. W., Larson, E., Bakken, S., Carrasquillo, O., Formicola, A., Glied, S. A., and Gebbie, K. M. (2007). 'Defining Interdisciplinary Research: Conclusions from a Critical Review of the Literature' *Health Services Research* 42(1), 329–346.

Ahmed, S. K. (2024). 'How to Choose a Sampling Technique and Determine Sample Size for Research: A Simplified Guide for Researchers' *Oral Oncology Reports* 12, 100662.

Andow, C. (2016). 'Everyday Life in a Secure Children's Home: A Goffmanesque Analysis.' Unpublished PhD thesis: University of Southampton.

Andow, C. (2020). 'The Institutional Shaping of Children's Educational Experiences in Secure Custody: A Case Study of a Secure Children's Home in England' *International Journal of Educational Development* 77.

Andow, C., Kleipoedszus, S., Dunn, R., Wake, N., Arthur, R., Shafi, A., and Gibson, D. (2024). 'Re-Designing Secure Children's Homes Through a Child-First Lens' *Societies* 14, 217. https://doi.org/10.3390/soc1411021

Arthur, R., Dunn, R., and Wake, N. (2019). 'Empowering Young People, Multi-Disciplinary Expressive Interventions Utilising Diamond9 Evaluative Methods to Encourage Agency in Youth Justice' *International Journal of Mental Health and Capacity Law* 25, 124–148.

Bailey, N. M., and Van Harken, E. M. (2014). 'Visual Images as Tools for Teacher Inquiry' *Journal of Teacher Education* 64(3), 241–260.

Barton, G., James, A. (2017). 'Threshold Concepts, LEGO SERIOUS PLAY and Whole Systems Thinking' *Practice and Evidence of the Scholarship of Teaching and Learning in Higher Education* 12(2), 249.

Bettinson, V., Crofts, T., and Wake, N. (2024). Preparing a public perceptions study on the use of violent resistance as self-defence in domestic abuse cases. In M. Burton, V. Bettinson, K, Richardson, and A. Speed (Eds.), *Research Handbook on Domestic Violence and Abuse*, (pp. 346–365). Edward Elgar Publishing.

Braun, V., and Clarke, V. (2006). 'Using Thematic Analysis in Psychology' *Qualitative Research in Psychology* 3, 77–101.

Braun, V., and Clarke, V. (2012). Thematic analysis. In H. Cooper, P. M. Camic, D. L. Long, A. T. Panter, D. Rindskopf, and K. J. Sher (Eds.), *APA Handbook of Research Methods in Psychology,* Vol. 2. *Research Designs: Quantitative, Qualitative, Neuropsychological, and Biological* (pp. 57–71). American Psychological Association. https://doi.org/10.1037/13620-004

Braun, V., and Clarke, V. (2022). *Thematic Analysis: A Practical Guide*. London: Sage.

Boyd, Robin J., Powney, Gary D., and Pescott, Oliver L. (2023). 'We Need to Talk about Nonprobability Samples' *Trends in Ecology and Evolution* 38(6), 521–531.

Byrne, D. (2021). 'A Worked Example of Braun and Clarke's Approach to Reflexive Thematic Analysis' *Quality and Quantity* 56(2), 1391–1412.

Carmody, S., Nolan, R., Ni Chonchuir, N., Curry, M., Halligan, C., and Robinson, K. (2007). 'The Guiding Nature of the Kawa (river) Model in Ireland: Creating Both Opportunities and Challenges for Occupational Therapist' *Occupational Therapy International* 14(4), 221–236.

Case, S., Browning, A., and Hampson, K. (2023). 'The Child First Strategy Implementation Project – Translating Strategy Into Practice' *Youth Justice* 24(2), 204–230.

Ching, E., and Ammon, A. (2020). 'Navigating the Tide: Health Science Student Faculty of Color Academic Experiences' *Diversity & Equality in Health and Care* 17(1), 101–106.

Clark, J. (2012). 'Using Diamond Ranking as Visual Cues to Engage Young People in the Research Process' *Qualitative Research Journal* 12(2), 222–237.

Clark, J., Laing, K., Tiplady, L., and Woolner, P. (2013). *Making Connections: Theory and Practice of Using Visual Methods to Aid Participation in Research*. Newcastle: Research Centre for Learning and Teaching, Newcastle University.

Cox, S. (2021). 'Using Lego® Serious Play® to Articulate Understanding and Share Mental Models. In *EDULEARN21 Proceedings* (pp. 6173–6180). IATED.

Dewi, I. G. A. T. S. U., Padmadewi, N. N., Marsakawati, N. P. E., Artini, L. P., Ratminingsih, N. M., and Utami, I. L. P. (2023). 'Students' Perception of Infographics: A Visualization Tool on Strengthening Critical Thinking Skills' *Jurnal Penelitian Dan Pengembangan Pendidikan* 7(1), 135–141. https://doi.org/10.23887/jppp.v7i1.55866

Duggan, J., Clement, S., Cvitanovic, C., and Van Putten, I. (2024). Incorporating sense of place into the management of social-ecological systems: The researchers' perspectives' PLoS One 19(9), e0308726.

Dunn, R. (2020). 'Diamonds are a Girl's Best Friend…And a Great Data Collection Tool' *International Journal of Clinical Legal Education* 27(3), 33–76.

Elfil, M., and Negida, A. (2017). 'Sampling methods in Clinical Research; an Educational Review' *Emergency* 5(1), e52. https://doi.org/10.22037/emergency.v5i1.15215

Ellis, K. H. (2016). 'He's got some nasty impression of me he has: Listening to Children in the Secure Estate' *The British Journal of Social Work* 46(6), 1553–1567.

Fereday, J., and Muir-Cochrane, E. (2006). 'Demonstrating Rigor Using Thematic Analysis: A Hybrid Approach of Inductive and Deductive Coding and Theme' *Development. International Journal of Qualitative Methods* 5(1), 80–92 https://doi.org/10.1177/160940690600500107

Glaw, X., Inder, K., Kable, A., and Hazelton, M. (2017). 'Visual Methods in Qualitative Research: Autophotography and Photo Elicitation Applied to Mental Health Research' *International Journal of Qualitative Methods* 16, 1–8.

Goldson, B. (2002). *Vulnerable Inside: Children in Secure and Penal Settings*. London: The Children's Society.

Guest, G., Namey, E., and McKenna, K. (2017). 'How Many Focus Groups Are Enough? Building an Evidence Base for Nonprobability Sample Sizes' *Field Methods* 29(1), 3–22. https://doi.org/10.1177/1525822X16639015

Häberlein, L., and Hövel, P. (2023). Importance and Necessity of Stakeholder Engagement. In E. Gonzales-Esteban, R. A. Feenstra, and L. M. Camrinha-Matos (Eds.), *Ethics and Responsible Research and Innovation in Practice: The Ethna System Project*, (pp. 38–53). Cham: Springer Nature Switzerland.

Hsiao, H. Y., Wang, T. Y., Lee, C. H., Lu, Y. C., Huang, Y. C., Chien, Y. C., Potenza, M. N., and Lin, C. Y. (2024). 'Advancing Readiness for Change in Substance Use for People with Substance Use Disorders Using the Kawa Model Based Intervention Program: A Quasi-Experimental Study' *The Hong Kong Journal of Occupational Therapy* 37(2), 91–101.

Iwama, M. K., Thomson, N. A., and Macdonald, R. M. (2009). 'The Kawa Model: The Power of Culturally Responsive Occupational Therapy' *Disability and Rehabilitation* 31(14), 1125–1135.

James, A. (2013). 'Lego Serious Play: A Three-Dimensional Approach to Learning Development' *Journal of Learning Development in Higher Education* 6. https://doi.org/10.47408/jldhe.v0i6.208

Johnson, C. M., Sharkey, J. R., McIntosh, A. W., and Dean, W. R. (2010). '"I'm the Momma": Using Photo-Elicitation to Understand Matrilineal Influence on Family Food Choice' *BMC Women's Health* 10(1), 21.

Kahlke, R., and Eva, K. (2018). 'Constructing Critical Thinking in Health Professional Education' *Perspectives on Medical Education* 7(3), 156–165.

Kamberelis, G., and Dimitriadis, G. (2005). Focus Groups: Strategic Articulations of Pedagogy, Politics, and Inquiry. In N. K. Denzin, and Y. S. Lincoln (Eds.), *The Sage Handbook of Qualitative Research*, 3rd ed. (pp. 887–907). Thousand Oaks, CA: Sage Publications Inc.

Kirby, Brian P., and Pawlikowska, T. (2019). 'Pharmacology through Play: Using Lego® to Revise Core Concepts for Undergraduates' *MedEdPublish* 8, 201.

Krisnan, A., Nienebar, B. (2024). 'Researching Playfully? Assessing the Applicability of LEGO Serious Play for Researching Vulnerable Groups' *Societies* 14(2), 15. https://doi.org/10.3390/soc14020015

Kyololo, O. M., Stevens, B. J., and Songok, J. (2023). 'Photo-Elicitation Technique: Utility and Challenges in Clinical Research' *International Journal of Qualitative Methods* 22. https://doi.org/10.1177/16094069231165714

Lape, J. E., Lukose, A., Ritter, D. R., and Scaife, B. D. (2019). 'Use of the Kawa Model to Facilitate Interprofessional Collaboration: A Pilot Study' *Internet Journal of Allied Health Sciences and Practice* 17(1), 3.

McGehee, W. D. (2022). 'Constructing Creative Confidence with LEGO(R) Serious Play(R)' *Journal of Behavioral and Applied Management* 22(2), 278–306.

McKeown, A., MacMillan, G., Watkins, E., Caveney, D., Smith, A., Kennedy, P. J., ... and Lee, R. (2022). 'Reduction in Incidents during COVID-19 in a Secure Children's Home: An Opportunity for Learning' *Journal of Aggression, Conflict and Peace Research* 14(3), 259–271.

Millham, S., Bullock, R., and Hosie, K. (1978). *Locking Up Children: Secure Provision Within the Childcare System*. Farnborough, Hants: Saxon House.

Milligan, I. M., and Smith, M. (2006). 'From Welfare to Correction: A Review of Changing Discourses of Secure Accommodation' *Educational and Child Psychology* 23(2), 75–86.

Naidoo, O., Christopher, C., Lingah, T., and Moran, M. (2023). 'The Kawa Model: A Self-Reflection Tool for Occupational Therapy Student Development in Practice Placements in Australia' *Occupational Therapy International* 12, 2768898. https://doi.org/10.1155/2023/2768898

Niemi, R., Kumpulainen, K., and Lipponen, L. (2015). 'Pupils As Active Participants: Diamond Ranking As a Tool to Investigate Pupils' Experiences of Classroom Practices' *European Educational Research Journal* 14(2), 138–150.

Nienaber, B., and Kriszan, A. (2023). 'Thinking With the Hands: LEGO® Serious Play® a Game-Based Tool to Empower Young Migrants Integrating' *Migration Letters* 20(3), 443–452. https://doi.org/10.59670/ml.v20i3.2902

Pain, H. (2012). 'A Literature Review to Evaluate the Choice and Use of Visual Methods' *International Journal of Qualitative Methods* 11(4), 303–319.

Pera, R., Quinton, S., and Baima, G. (2021). 'The Use of Embedded Visual Methods in Unveiling Consumers' Values: A Digital Ethnography Perspective' *Psychology & Marketing* 39(2), 309–319.

Price, A., Clarke, M., Staniszewska, S., Chu, L., Tembo, D., Kirkpatrick, M., and Nelken, Y. (2022). 'Patient and Public Involvement in Research: A Journey to Co-production' *Patient Education and Counseling* 105(4), 1041–1047.

Rockett, M., and Percival, S. (2002). *Thinking for Learning*. London, Bloomsbury.

Sharma, L. R. (2022). 'Thematic Analysis of Laxmi Prasad Devkota's Poem "The Lunatic"' *International Research Journal of MMC* 3(3), 98–109. https://doi.org/10.3126/irjmmc.v3i3.48641

Söderlund, P., and von Schoultz, Å. (2024). Trajectories of the Personal Vote Under Open-List Proportional Representation: Evidence from Finland, 1999–2019' *Party Politics* 30(1), 12–23.

Stahl, B. C., Tremblay, M. C., and LeRouge, C. M. (2011). 'Focus Groups and Critical Social IS Research: How the Choice of Method can Promote Emancipation of Respondents and Researchers' *European Journal of Information Systems* 20(4), 378–394.

Staley, K., Cockcroft, E., and Shelly, A. (2019). 'What Can I Do that Will Most Help Researchers?' A Different Approach to Training the Public At the Start of Their Involvement in Research' *Research Involvement and Engagement* 5(1). https://doi.org/10.1186/s40900-019-0144-4

Swain, J. (2018). 'A Hybrid Approach to Thematic Analysis in Qualitative Research: Using a Practical Example' *Sage Research Methods*. https://methods.sagepub.com/case/hybrid-approach-thematic-analysis-qualitative-research-a-practical-example

Tobi, H., and Kampen, J. K. (2018). 'Research Design: The Methodology for Interdisciplinary Research Framework' *Qual Quant* 52, 1209–1225.

Trainor, L. R., and Bundon, A. (2020). 'Developing the Craft: Reflexive Accounts of Doing Reflexive Thematic Analysis' *Qualitative Research in Sport, Exercise and Health* 13, 705–726.

Vindrola-Padros, C., Martins, A., Coyne, I., Bryan, G., and Gibson, F. (2016). 'From Informed Consent to Dissemination: Using Participatory Visual Methods with Young People with Long-term Conditions at Different Stages of Research' *Global Public Health* 11(5–6), 636–650.

Vusio, F., Thompson, A., and Birchwood, M. (2022). 'A Novel Application of the Lego® Serious Play® Methodology in Mental Health Research: Understanding Service Users' Experiences of the 0-19 Mental Health Model in the United Kingdom' *Early Intervention in Psychiatry* 16(8), 845–853. https://doi.org/10.1111/eip.13223

Wall, K., Higgins, S., Hall, E., and Woolner, P. (2013). "That's not Quite the Way We See It': The Epistemological Challenge of Visual Data' *International Journal of Research & Method in Education* 36(1), 3–22. https://doi.org/10.1080/1743727X.2012.730278

Warin, J. (2011). 'Ethical Mindfulness and Reflexivity' *Qualitative Inquiry* 17(9), 805–814.

Wezyk, A., Arden-Close, E., and Turner-Cobb, J. M. (2020). 'Trapped Under a Tonne of Rubble': Using LEGO® to Explore Conceptual Metaphors of Psychological Stress' *QMiP (Qualitative Methods in Psychology) Bulletin* 30. https://doi.org/10.53841/bpsqmip.2020.1.30.40

Wheeler, S., Passmore, J., and Gold, R. (2020). 'All to Play for: LEGO® SERIOUS PLAY® and Its Impact on Team Cohesion, Collaboration and Psychological Safety in Organisational Settings Using a Coaching Approach' *Journal of Work-Applied Management* 12(2), 141–157.

Williams, A., Wood, S., Warner, N., Cummings, A., Hodges, H., El-Banna, A., and Daher, S. (2020). *Unlocking the Facts: Young People Referred to Secure Children's Homes*. Cardiff: CASCADE Retrieved from https://whatworks-csc.org.uk/wp-content/uploads/WWCSC_Unlocking_the_Facts_SCH_technical_report_Dec2020.pdf

Woolner, P. et al. (2012). 'What Is Learning? Views of Ideal and Institutional Learning Held by HE, FE andSchool Teachers Engaged in Practitioner Enquiry' (The European Association for Practitioner Research on Improving Learning (EAPRIL) Conference Paper) 24th-26th November 2010.
Youth Justice Board (2020) *Strategic Plan 2021–2024*. London: YJB.

PART III

Lived experiences of practice

Children and young people's voices within narratives of co-production

12

YOUTH JUSTICE LIVED EXPERIENCE AS CARCERAL CAPITAL IN THE CO-PRODUCTION OF PEER SUPPORT PROGRAMMES IN PRISONS

Sarah Nixon

Introduction

Peer support work has the potential to help overcome experiences of disempowerment or criminal justice system contact that has induced trauma (Johns et al., 2022). Unlike research with adult offenders, peer mentoring (PM) is a relatively new development in youth justice contexts. In this chapter, the terms PM, peer support programmes (PSPs) and peer support workers (PSW) will be used interchangeably.

PSPs allow for reciprocity. Mentees feel supported emotionally and feel understood by mentors and, according to Creaney (2018), they are potentially more motivated to (re)engage with services. In addition, mentors can relate to mentees through shared lived experiences and act as intermediaries to help mentees engage with other services, which assists with addressing systemic harms and inequalities experienced (Johns et al., 2022). Thompson and Spacey (2023) conclude that peer mentoring as a participatory practice promotes individual, relational and broader social outcomes that can be useful within youth justice contexts, promoting desistance for justice-involved children and young people and supporting engagement with those who may otherwise feel disempowered.

Interest has increased in recent years around the role of user engagement and co-production within youth and adult justice contexts, encouraging more voices to be heard with the aim of improving service delivery (Cunningham and Wakeling, 2022). Weaver and McCulloch (2012) define user engagement within the criminal justice system as a participatory and collaborative approach between citizen consumers of services, policymakers and professionals towards the design, delivery and evaluation of criminal

DOI: 10.4324/9781003602996-16

justice policies, services and practices. There are many ways in which user engagement and co-production can be applied within criminal justice settings, ranging from gathering feedback from those with lived experience to involvement in quality assurance and monitoring or evaluation of service provision. Porteous and Goodman's (2023) study adds to existing knowledge of the benefits and challenges of involving children with recent experience of the youth justice system in service delivery and in co-production work with policymakers and service providers.

This chapter builds on previous discussions of co-production within youth justice services by extending debates around co-production and co-delivery of services within adult prisons. Central to this discussion is the concept of carceral capital (Brierley and Best, 2025), which illustrates how knowledge, skills and social networks developed through experiences within the criminal justice system are utilised to navigate criminal justice institutions. Lived experience of prisons or probation can offer legitimacy and credibility within peer mentoring settings and during interactions with criminal justice professionals (Brierley and Best, 2025). Relatable experiences around trauma, Adverse Childhood Experiences (ACEs), substance misuse and mental health, alongside other indicators of marginalisation, demonstrate the potential value of co-production for peer support services in both prison and community contexts.

There are, however, unique risks associated with providing peer support in prison that are not experienced in the community. Penal conditions are progressively worsening due to overcrowding, increasing levels of violence, staff shortages and the availability of drugs, which impact the operationalisation of purposeful regimes (Nixon and Woodward, 2025). Intimidating carceral environments and fraught relationships can affect the ability of peer support workers to navigate high expectations within a context of minimal support structures. While it is beyond the scope of this chapter to explore in depth the differences between all custodial settings, it is important to acknowledge the distinctions between secure children's homes, young offender institutions and adult prisons. For children serving long sentences who may transition from YOIs into adult prisons, peer mentoring roles may assist with adjustment to adult custodial environments.

The focus of this chapter is therefore to explore the benefits and challenges of peer support in adult custodial settings and consider how these experiences may inform youth justice practice. Drawing on empirical insights from peer support work in an adult male prison, the chapter examines how carceral capital and participatory approaches can shape peer support practices and how these insights may be applied within youth justice contexts. Having introduced key concepts around peer support practitioners within prison, this chapter presents three themes that evidence lived experience of peer support work in an adult male prison context. Drawing upon carceral capital as credible lived experience to underpin the importance of co-production in PSPs, parallels with youth justice contexts will be explored.

By the end of this chapter, we will have:

Identified the potential of drawing upon PSWs as 'experts by experience' through application of carceral capital to support desistance in both mentor and mentee.

Explored the benefits and challenges of using justice-involved individuals in co-design, co-delivery and participatory approaches within peer support services, with particular focus on liminality and validation as equals.

Debated the extent to which co-production and co-delivery of peer support services offer a transformative approach to supporting desistance.

While co-delivery of PSPs with criminal justice professionals allows prisoners opportunities to address unequal power balances with uniformed and civilian staff, tensions remain regarding power, status and trust. The next section therefore explores debates surrounding co-production, peer support and desistance within criminal justice contexts.

Co-production, peer support and desistance in criminal justice

Prisons should not allow prisoners to simply mark their time in a pointless fashion but should instead encourage engagement in meaningful and challenging activities (Edgar et al., 2011). Opportunities exist for prisoners to pursue autonomy and contribute positively within institutional environments, even within cultures that may otherwise promote indifference (Crewe and Bennett, 2012). Jaffe (2012) highlighted the emotional burden placed on prison Listeners who support prisoners experiencing distress while simultaneously navigating their own custodial experiences.

Participation within criminal justice contexts is frequently constrained by the ways in which criminalised individuals are positioned within policy and practice. Tomczak and Buck (2019) argue that people who are criminalised are often perceived as passive and problematic recipients of services designed by others who 'know best', with participation extended only as far as consultation. Similarly, Haines and Case (2015) note that participation is often limited, offering little opportunity for meaningful involvement in decision-making processes.

Co-production within criminal justice services can therefore be difficult to achieve within systems characterised by regulation, coercion and control (Garland, 2002). McCulloch (2016) questions whether co-production can truly operate within corrective institutions where those involved in the criminal justice system are frequently positioned as objects upon which justice is enacted. Goddard and Myers (2016) also identify how practices of 'othering' reinforce risk-based approaches that can further marginalise those involved in criminal justice systems.

Nevertheless, peer support has demonstrated benefits for individuals giving and receiving support, for organisations within which peer support is situated and for society more broadly (McCulloch, 2020). Peer support workers can inspire, educate and advise others through sharing lived experiences of system contact (Burns and Creaney, 2023). However, the impact of peer support varies depending upon the level of involvement afforded to peer workers and the nature of interactions with professionals and institutions (Burns and Creaney, 2023).

Arnstein's (1969) ladder of participation illustrates how involvement can range from minimal engagement, such as informing or consultation, through to co-design and co-production based upon reciprocal partnerships and shared decision-making. Within criminal justice settings, however, participatory practices risk becoming tokenistic if they are implemented without genuine shifts in power relations. Johns et al. (2022) caution against 'faux participation', where participatory practices function primarily as symbolic gestures rather than meaningful attempts to redistribute power. At the same time, lived experience can play an important role in shaping criminal justice interventions. Marsh and Maruna (2017) highlight how individuals with direct experience of the justice system can provide valuable insights into how interventions might be improved. Similarly, research with peer mentors demonstrates that individuals who have experienced imprisonment can offer unique understanding of isolation, stigma and the challenges associated with reintegration following release (Lenkens et al., 2020). These insights reflect the significance of carceral capital, where lived experience becomes a resource that can support engagement, credibility and relational understanding within peer support practices.

These debates intersect with research on desistance from crime. Desistance is shaped by opportunities, relationships and supportive interactions with professionals and institutions (Weaver, 2019a; 2019b). Within youth justice contexts, harnessing strengths and providing opportunities for participation aligns with child-first approaches that emphasise agency and positive development (Burns and Creaney, 2023; YJB, 2025). The themes discussed in this section therefore underpin the analysis presented in the following sections of the chapter, which examine peer support practices in adult prisons and consider their relevance for youth justice contexts.

Utilisation of carceral capital as an asset within the co-production/co-delivery of peer support programmes

There is a divergence between experiential knowledge/lived experiences of criminality, desistance, carceral capital, and professional knowledge gained from education/training. In addition, Brierley and Best (2025) argue that street and carceral experiences often lack value within a criminal justice service that is driven predominantly by results. However, Maruna and Mann (2019) argue that narratives as success stories *should be* counted as evidence within criminal justice. Desistance capital and carceral capital *are* assets to be used within the co-production of peer support services to enhance success outcomes for all parties involved in youth/adult contexts. A fundamental theme running through many peer support workers' narratives was a desire to use self as a source of wisdom, internalise an 'expert by experience' identity and a progressive generative desire to 'give something back' (see Maruna, 2001; Nixon, 2019).

DT contextualises how his early experiences of the youth justice system, followed by adult criminal justice experiences motivated him to get involved in mentoring young people. His draws upon his carceral capital as both a catalyst and asset, allowing him to give back and support youths on the cusp of criminalisation or transitioning between institutions:

> My first crime was 7 ...left school at 13...17 I started to sell drugs...I was charged with a section 18...armed robbery and got a life sentence...drugs and alcohol were a big issues for me...I have spent 22 years in prison off and on...it's a real waste of a life...if I could just affect one kid and hopefully point him in a different direction, that would be really good.
>
> *(DT, ACEs mentor)*

Working collaboratively with institutions that had previously proved challenging for DT (police and education), he was recruited from a Category 'D' prison to mentor young people with ACEs (as part of a Midlands UK-based initiative). He was recruited to use his experiences of the criminal justice system to help children understand the harsh realities of a criminal career and lengthy prison sentences:

> I was welcomed by the police on the project...they were really nice to me, which touched me...the project involved going to a pupil referral unit...we did sessions on joint enterprise, drugs, knife crime...we'd let the kids explain their experience of drugs...no teachers were present... we told them 'what is said in here, stay's in here, unless you're gonna hurt somebody or yourself'...I'd tell my life story...drugs, prison and how I'd got clean...we'd get permission from their parents, get a police van, arrest them, lock them in a cell, take them to court...we had a proper judge. Working with the chief inspector of (a police force in the Midlands)- he is all about prevention rather than nicking people.
>
> *(DT, ACES mentor)*

Understanding carceral capital as a facet of lived experience is important when identifying reasons of how and why co-production works. Street capital is defined as mastery of criminal activity and violence within a street culture, which generates rewards, gains, profits, and sanctions (Sandberg, 2008). Carceral capital, according to Brierley and Best (2025), is defined as an extension of street capital through experiential knowledge of successfully navigating prison and beyond. These forms of capital are useful in co-producing and co-delivering services alongside criminal justice professionals, thus bridging the gap through their lived experience, adding depth, weight and authentic credibility within criminal/youth justice contexts.

BW, who left school aged 13/14, started shoplifting at 15 and states he was '...attracted to trouble'. He continued to say that 'a lot of the PMs want to get a job working within criminal /youth justice...being a peer mentor has helped to break down some serious barriers'.

Brierley and Best (2025) identify that reserves of street and carceral capital can be potentially threatening to professionals who lack a natural/organic ability to build trust and legitimacy because of a lack of comprehension *from the other side*. However, in terms of application to youth justice, there needs to be a greater affinity towards utilising adult mentors with carceral and desistance capital, to role model success to youth offenders and to co-design and co-produce peer support programmes. Many peer support workers identify a genuine desire to 'give back', sharing experience, strength and hope through role modelling to young people through the lens of lived experience. Generative desires (see Maruna, 2001) to help others were echoed by many who progressed into PSW programmes:

> I'm 35, my first prison sentence was 16...I have spent 14 years in prison... I've been through a lot...sexual abuse, violence, depression, heroin, crack...it makes me a better PM....a better understanding of the people I work with...I like telling my story because the shit I have been through, if I can't use it to make a difference, what a waste.
>
> *(LW PM)*

LWs' experiences identify the utility of drawing upon carceral capital reserves to help and share lived experience with others who need support and guidance to navigate carceral spaces. The next section will explore staff perspectives around how carceral capital can shape and develop staff to understand both the lived experience of incarceration and the power of peer support collaborations using prisoners as assets; a strengths-based model harnessing potential (see Burnett and Maruna, 2006).

Staff perspectives on co-production and co-delivery of peer support services

This section will present views from criminal justice staff on the value and utility of co-producing, co-designing and co-delivering services with prisoners in relation to peer support work. In addition, institutional challenges faced that might impede progress towards inclusive participatory practices are considered. Carceral capital becomes a vital component in the success of justice-involved individuals working with service professionals – in prison and beyond.

A particular example of co-production in prisons is between the Samaritans; civilians who train prisoners wanting to become Listeners and prisoners selected for their potential to work voluntarily to deliver confidential safer custody peer support services to other prisoners. This approach simultaneously helps a voluntary sector organisation (Samaritans) to utilise the lived experience and carceral capital of prisoners to support safer custody policies and practices, while also helping prisoners to gain capital through providing 24/7 peer support in carceral settings:

> We use existing Listeners in the training because of the contributions they can make.... they are really good at expressing the realities of daily prison life.... I think they really appreciate being regarded as experienced and worthy of being Listeners.
>
> *(J, Samaritans)*

However, there are power dynamics at play around provision of peer support services in prison, particularly with the Listeners:

> ...the staff (prison officers) play mind games when we come out of a call (interaction with a prisoner in crisis). They always say, 'what did he want?' and I say 'if you are interested, ask him yourself...it's confidential'.
>
> *(AB Listener)*

This is an interesting dynamic to explore. While Buck and Tomczak (2019) found that prison officers were often present in 'confidential' meetings between Samaritans and Listeners, a safer custody coordinator (senior prison officer tasked with safer custody responsibility) offered a different perspective:

> *The Listeners have a meeting with the Samaritans every week. They can discuss and talk openly about any issues they have got. It's support for them... if they (Samaritans) have any concerns they speak to me...apart from that it is confidential and separate from prison staff...they organise proceedings to meet their agendas' (DL safer custody coordinator)*
>
> Different peer support services have greater levels of equality and reciprocity within co-production, codesign and co-delivery. Whilst Listeners have greater levels of autonomy than other PSWs in order to perform their work, they are reliant on (mostly prison officers) to facilitate their mobility around the prison. Other PMs, who reside on dedicated substance misuse units/wings are not as reliant on uniformed staff to mobilise

and facilitate their movements, which can allow for a deeper proactive approach towards co-delivery with civilian staff facilitating recovery programmes. CARATS staff (Counselling, Assessment, Referral, Advice and Throughcare) co-design and co deliver substance misuse modules with prisoners, drawing upon their expertise of substance misuse and recovery to contextualise delivery. A CARATS staff member spoke positively about KC's contributions towards co-delivery of a substance misuse programme

'KC as a peer mentor in prison... it brings out the best in him. He is wicked in groups, very deep and insightful... with him here it's like having a prisoner and a half.

(JT, CARATS)

The raw honesty of PSW's lived experiences of substance misuse enhances service provision through working alongside those who are delivering approved training courses to reduce re-offending (but have little experiential knowledge to draw upon):

> In PM...we were helping to deliver 'gateway to change' courses with CARATS...broken down into modules like victim awareness, high risk situations, relationships...drug addiction affects every aspect of your life.... a strength of the PM...it's all very well the CARATS team sitting there and delivering it...but they have not 'walked the walk'. That is no disrespect to them, but an addict is always going to listen to another addict...so, delivering groups with CARATS was a big part...showing the lads it is possible to remain drug free in prison.
>
> *(KC, substance abuse peer mentor)*

Moving on to identify the impact and importance of co-production beyond prison, IM was a young male who served a short sentence in prison and upon release he was recruited to work with probation. He was identified as having the potential to become a peer mentor and received recognition from civilian staff for his proactive conduct in prison through participation on a course to help him improve personal/domestic relationships, while also supporting others with similar charges:

> ...I was doing the BBR (building better relationships) course...when that ended ...and I was released...the tutors spoke to my PO (probation officer) and PM co-ordinator...my PO was getting feedback telling her that I had been offering support to people in my group...I was contributing to every session...they recommended me for peer mentoring...I am street wise as well as intelligent...I was brought up on estates...I was fast-tracked to PM....
>
> *(IM, Probation PM)*

Introduced in 2015 (under the Offender Rehabilitation Act, 2014), RARs (Rehabilitation Activity Requirements) allow providers of probation services greater flexibility to decide on the best ways to rehabilitate individuals (Gov. Uk, 2019). Building on from securing his PM role, in 2015 IM was tasked (alongside another PM) by the director of a Community Rehabilitation Company (CRC) (Midlands) to co-design and co-deliver the 'Transition and Hope' RAR. The director explains:

> We got 2 PMs to design and deliver the RAR session 'Transition and Hope'…this session could be part of someone's journey…the PMs tell their story …. 'this is how I felt when I came in, how my life has changed, and how your life can change too!' …and it is fantastic for us because they (PMs) are really committed…these guys go the extra mile…however, there are obviously going to be some people (within probation) who don't agree with this approach….
>
> *(CP, director of Community Rehabilitation Company, CRC)*

While innovative approaches (like including PMs in the design and delivery of RARs) can lead to new forms of knowledge, values and social relations (Filipe et al, 2017), it also requires senior managers to take a 'leap of faith' and acceptance that it might not prove to be successful. CP demonstrates flexibility, creativity, vision, strategic leadership and trust through recognising the impact that user engagement of PMs would have in the supporting desistance of others who access the RAR as part of their licence conditions. Co-production involves shifts of power, with a hands-off style of leadership to allow probationers to share their experiences in service design and delivery stages (see Weaver, 2019). Effective programmes can be constructed through trust co-created between practitioners and peer mentors, and belief in the power of lived experience from both parties. Johns et al (2022) identify the power of collaboration, reciprocity, power sharing and co-designing of projects that are grounded by lived experience and partnership working. IM explains his experience of working in partnership with senior probation staff:

> …we did research and put together the 'Transition and Hope' RAR…after finalisation…basically it is us telling our story. It hits home to people who have gone through similar…when they listen to our stories, they are more likely to take something in…it makes me feel that I am not worthless anymore…the director of the CRC (CP)…she is very impressed with us…the pilot was done in front of her…she went teary eyed listening to our stories.
>
> *(IM Probation PM)*

The reciprocal benefits for those *delivering* and *receiving* narratives of transition and hope align with a strengths-based approach to co-delivering criminal justice that potentially supports desistance (see McCulloch, 2020). The power of telling one's life story to others is the cornerstone of many mutual aid groups (12 Step groups for example). Maruna's (2001) study on desistance identified that a shift in narrative identity is possible when self-concept is aligned with a coherent desistance narrative. Following on, Maruna (2001) also stated that some offenders do not look back on their life with disdain and do not recall their criminal pasts as shameful, but rather as a necessary prelude to some newfound calling. Wilful cognitive distortions allow offenders to integrate their past into a new biography, which helps them to find meaning, unity and purpose in generative pursuits (Maruna 2001) rather than 'doomed to further deviance'. Working alongside criminal justice professionals is one such mechanism:

> ...the PMs deliver sessions with me...it gives them development and reinforces learning for them...when preparing for sessions, we discuss for example boundaries...I deliver theory, but as soon as the PM start delivering there is more engagement...it's very real...we start the first session with the PMs saying 'I've been where you are sitting'...a lot of PMs would like to work with youths to try and make sure that they don't end up where they are...that aspiration comes up a lot.
>
> *(SH Probation PM Coordinator)*

Carceral capital can help to bridge gaps between service users and criminal justice staff in service provision, while also situating justice-involved individuals providing peer support in 'liminal' territories. This is a contested domain both within youth and adult services around validation of lived experiences between current service users and professional staff within criminal justice:

> ...a lot of the time I have to walk through town to go home... I will get introduced as 'this guy works for CJDT (drug services) but he is one of us'...I think bridging the gap between service users that are still using and staff that don't know what to do with them is important... it took me a while to learn, but the staff where I work...they all know my history...if they want to talk to service users about any part of my history, I am happy for that...as long as it has some benefit for the service user, not just 'let me tell you a story about (name)...with no bearing or relevance... Being kicked out of Poundland's doorway (sleeping rough) might be useful to a service user who is homeless, so saying that I used to be homeless...I would encourage that. It has more credibility if you have been there yourself.
>
> *(LM, Substance misuse coordinator)*

Co-production and co-delivery of services within organisational structures of criminal justice agencies were not always met positively. For example, log-in access to sensitive data was mediated around risk.

LG had served multiple sentences as a youth and adult for drug- and theft-related offences. Using his carceral capital to serve his community through peer support and transitioning to paid employment, he expresses personal challenges towards his reintegration:

> I get the feeling that some people (in probation) are still hostile towards you 'cos they think 'hold on you have lived this life of crime, you have used drugs and now you are employed working here at the same level as me...... we shouldn't be having people in recovery working in this environment, with confidential information. What if they relapse?' I wouldn't feel good enough...just my sensitivity......if I picked up on something and I could see that this person didn't enjoy working with me, I took a back step......made me feel shit about myself...that is life though I guess.
>
> *(LG, HT)*

Aligning with LG's narrative, professionals who had worked with peer mentors as previous users of youth services had prejudices around investment in the PM system and also capacity to change (Busso *et al*, 2024). In addition, Johns *et al* (2022) consider how criminal justice bureaucracy constrains human relationships and creativity through, for example, overreliance on risk-management priorities. However, Johns *et al* (2022) identify the potential for co-production to enable active citizenship of justice-involved individuals through participation, transformation of human relationships damaged by criminal 'othering' and stigma, and the potential to facilitate power-sharing, thus allowing new non-criminal identities to emerge. These issues occur within youth justice alongside adults within the criminal justice system. It is imperative therefore that further training is required for criminal justice professionals to fully accept and validate the important contributions that are made from justice-involved individuals who engage in peer support work. Of equal importance is that practitioners treat them as equals by valuing their lived experiences (Creaney and Burns, 2023). The final section of this chapter explores the desistance potential of co-production and participatory approaches for justice-involved individuals.

Co-production/co-delivery as a transformative approach to support desistance

The final section will explore the potential for peer support work to support desistance, which has been theorised in both youth and adult contexts within criminal justice. Maruna (2001) states that offenders who find ways to make contributions to society, through mentoring, assisting and enhancing the life of other people appear to be more successful at giving up crime, particularly if they are recognised by significant others. Significant others are those who work with (and believe in) young people/adults, thus involving them in key aspects of decision making, service design and delivery-/co-production. Alongside supporting criminal justice staff, people who display 'helper orientations' have a higher level of self-esteem, display greater satisfaction with their life and develop negative attitudes towards continued criminality, thus role modelling desistance. The act of helping others is beneficial for both *helper* and the person *being helped* (Lebel, 2007):

> *...there is nothing more therapeutic than one addict helping another... I've noticed when delivering groups... paid members of staff have said something and it's like 'yeah, whatever'. I make it apparent that I have been a druggie, and the group listens...I may say exactly the same thing, but from them it may sound patronising. But from me, it sounds empathetic... PM was a huge step forward...it gave me the basic foundations to bridge the gap between service user and service provider. I used to moan like fuck 'why can't we have this; why aren't we allowed to do that?' ...then I did the training, and it gave me so much insight... I am an 'expert by experience' ...we only keep what we have by giving it away.*
>
> *(JG, PM)*

Maruna and McNeill (2007) identified the importance of agency and generativity in the desistance process and postulate that at the heart of effective practice with young people who are justice-involved should be the development, encouragement and facilitation of generativity rather than the current preoccupation with risk and needs. Involving PSWs in the design and delivery aspects of providing support services recognises them as assets from a strengths-based perspective (Burnett and Maruna. 2006); which is a key principle of co-production. Wigzell and Patterson-Young (2024, in HM Inspectorate of Probation Academic Insights 2025/05) shed light on progressive desistance practices in youth justice, drawing upon key themes of context-dependent approaches and the importance of relationships to support policy and practice within youth justice. Focus provided by Wigzell and Patterson-Young (2024) suggests that a wider lens of desistance rather than a narrow focus on reducing offending is productive. This will help young people to build non-stigmatising socio-structural support to facilitate pathways from offending. Therefore, the importance of using justice-involved individuals in services like peer support work (as both mentor, to convey their own lived experience and carceral capital) and progression for mentee to become mentor, with integrative support from criminal justice professionals – highlights the importance of adopting a co-productive/participatory approach – doing things 'with' and not 'on' them.

Conclusion

This chapter has brought attention to the importance of using carceral capital as a key asset in the co-production and co-delivery of services, with a specific focus upon PM /peer support in prisons (and extending beyond). While empirical evidence has focused on adult peer mentors, the relevance for youth justice is transferable, and the same benefits and challenges to co-production and co-delivery of peer support services exist in both domains.

This chapter has outlined staff responses towards co-producing peer support services, highlighting challenges around trust and legitimacy. There need to be clear definitive role descriptors and structures in place, to avoid role ambiguity, role confusion and exploitation of peer support workers; in other words, getting them to do the work of paid staff (see Nixon, 2020) – evident within the domain of youth justice alongside adult institutions. Barriers towards co-production/co-delivery occur when criminal justice staff perceive and interpret new modes of knowledge production as conflicting with (and potentially threatening) their own positionality in an organisation. Within prison, PSWs are given opportunities that are built into the prison regime and their inclusion in co-delivery is instrumental towards the collation of purposeful activity data, supporting positive outcomes. Edgar *et al* (2011) identified that while the evidence is positive in reinforcing the importance of co-production and engagement for people with lived experience, contributions from justice-involved individuals rely upon effective leadership, communication and clear structures that help to establish legitimacy without taking advantage of lived experience, for example, *collaboration* rather than *exploitation* – and a clear message of how reciprocity can work when promoting agendas for change. Buck *et al* (2020) identify that co-production needs to be more than just 'tokenism'; a tick-box exercise to demonstrate inclusivity. The authors also identify the need to be sensitive and responsive to the impact that sharing personal lived experiences can have in terms of

re-traumatisation for peer support workers, relevant to discussions about peer support in both youth justice and adult justice contexts. In addition, consideration needs to be given to the diversity of lived experiences encountered within criminal justice-involved individuals and a greater synergy is needed between criminal justice staff to validate the importance and presence of peer support workers.

To conclude, providing prisoners (youth and adult) with opportunities to shape, change, direct and improve outcomes… has the capacity to promote civic reintegration, build trust, respect and community inclusion (Cunningham and Wakeling, 2022) and working 'with' and not *'against'* or 'on' those who provide peer support – can shape future successes in the co-production and co-delivery of services to support desistance and reduce recidivism.

Carceral capital is an asset to be utilised from a strengths/asset-based perspective. This applies to both youth and adult offenders. The key points of this chapter were to identify the mechanisms of how carceral capital is utilised in the co-production of PSPs in prison (and beyond), to explore staff perspectives on participatory approaches, and the challenges of liminality when using justice-involved individuals to bridge gaps between service users and staff.

What does this mean for youth justice? The transmission of lived experience – carceral capital and desistance capital – are essential to help understand and navigate youth justice services for all parties involved. Adults desisters with lived experience of youth justice services can give back and help others – transmitting capital that comes from experiencing youth justice services. Buck (2016) identifies the concept of mimesis; Nixon (2019) identifies hierarchy of influence – essentially frameworks to understand transmission of positive values to help desist away from further offending. While this context is provided by Buck and Nixon around peer support/mentoring, can it be wider than this? Johns *et al* (2022) ask the question 'who makes the 'co' in 'co-production?' While youth and criminal justice systems constrain co-production efforts through exaggerated power relations or perceptions of unequal power and status, the values of carceral capital in supporting professional staff to understand crime, punishment and prison are integral to develop further knowledge exchanges; co-production can disrupt (but also rebuild) power inequalities and create space and meaning for lived experience to shape future developments within youth/adult justice contexts.

References

Arnstein, S. R. (1969). A ladder of citizen participation. *Journal of the American Institute of Planners*, 35(4), 216–224.

Bovaird, T. & Loeffler, E. (2013). "We're all in this together: Harnessing user and community co-production of public outcomes". In C. Staite (Ed), *Making Sense of the Future: Do We Need a New Model of Public Services?* Birmingham: INLOGOV.

Brierley, A. & Best, D. (2025). Desistance habitus: Strategically Using experience in practice. *Incarceration*, 6. https://journals.sagepub.com/doi/10.1177/26326663241310603

Buck, G. (2016). I wanted to feel the way they did: Mimesis as a situational dynamic of peer mentoring by ex-offenders. *Deviant Behavior*, 38(9), 1027–1041.

Buck, G., Harriott, P., Ryan, K., Ryan, N., & Tomczak, P. (2020). All our justice: People with convictions and 'participatory' criminal justice. In H. McLaughlin, P. Beresford, C. Cameron, H. Casey, & J. Duffy (Eds.), *The Routledge Handbook of Service User Involvement in Human Services Research and Education* (pp. 285–295). Routledge.

Burnett, R., & Maruna, S. (2006). The kindness of prisoners: Strength-based resettlement in theory and in action. *Criminology and Criminal Justice*, 6, 83–106.

Burns, S., & Creaney, S. (2023). Embracing children 's voices: Transforming youth justice practice through co-production and child first participation. In S. Case & N. Hazel (Eds.), *Child First: Developing a New Youth Justice System*. London: Palgrave Macmillan. https://doi.org/10.1007/978-3-031-19272-2_12

Bussu, A., Creaney, S., Price, J., Burns, S., & Myles, K. (2024). "It's a six sense…I see you, you see me, and we've been there" Benefits and challenges of developing a peer mentoring scheme with young people in youth justice services. *British Journal of Community Justice*, 19(2), 4–19.

Creaney, S. (2018). Children's voices – are we listening? Progressing peer mentoring in the youth justice system. *Child Care in Practice*. Advance online publication. https://doi.org/10.1080/13575279.2018.1521381

Creaney, S., Bussau, A., Price, J., & Burns, S. (2023). Peer Mentoring in a youth justice context: Benefits and challenges. *British Society of Criminology Conference, Preston, United Kingdom*, 28/06/23–30/06/23.

Crewe, B., & Bennett, J. (Eds.) (2012). *The Prisoner*. London: Routledge

Cuningham, N., & Wakeling, H. (2022). Engagement and co-production with people with lived experience of prison and probation: A synthesis of the evidence base. *Prison Service Journal*, 262, 3–11

Edgar, K., Jacobson, J., & Biggar, K. (2011). Time well spent: A practical guide to active citizenship and volunteering in prison. London: *Prison Reform Trust.*

Filipe, A., Renedo, A., & Marston, C. (2017). The co-production of what? Knowledge, values, and social relations in health care. *PLOS Biology*, 15(5), e2001403.

Fledderus, J. (2018). The effects of co-production on trust. In T. Brandsen, B. Vershuere & T. Steen (Eds.), *Co-Production and Co-Creation* (pp. 258–265). Routledge.

Garland, D. (2002). *The Culture of Control: Crime and Social Order in Contemporary Society*. Oxford University Press.

Goddard, T., & Myers, R. R. (2016). Against evidence-based oppression: Marginalized youth and the politics of risk-based assessment and intervention. *Theoretical Criminology*, 21(2), 151–167.

Gov.UK (2019). RAR guidance. Available at: www.gov.uk/government/publications/the-rehabilitation-activity-requirement-in-probation/rar-guidance

Haines, K., & Case, S. (2015). *Positive Youth Justice: Children First, Offenders Second*. Policy Press.

Jaffe, M. (2012). *Peer support and seeking help in prison: a study of the Listener scheme in four prisons in England* (Doctoral dissertation, Keele University, UK).

Johns, D., Flynn, C., Hall, M., Spivakovsky, C., & Turner, S. (2022). *Co-production and Criminal Justice (1st ed.)*. Routledge.

Lebel, T. P. (2007). An examination of the impact of formerly incarcerated persons helping others. *Journal of Offender Rehabilitation*, 46(1–2), 1–24.

Lenkens, M, Nagelhout, G. E., Schenk, L., Sentse, M., Severiens, S., Engbersen, G., … van Lenthe, F. J. (2021). 'I (really) know what you mean'. Mechanisms of experiential peer support for young people with criminal behavior: A qualitative study. *Journal of Crime and Justice*, 44(5), 535–552.

Marsh, B., & Maruna, S. (2017). 'Desistance and restorative justice: Learning from success stories of Northern Ireland's Youth Justice Agency. *Restorative Justice*, 4(3), 369–387.

Maruna, S. (2001). *Making Good: How Ex-Convicts Reform and Rebuild Their Lives*. American Psychological Association.

Maruna, S., & Mann, R. (2019). *Reconciling 'Desistance' and 'What Works.' HM Inspectorate of Probation Academic Insights 2019/1*. London: HMI Probation

McCulloch, T. (2016). Co-producing justice sanctions? Citizen perspectives. *Criminology & Criminal Justice*, 16(4), 431–451.

McCulloch, T. (2020). Co-producing desistance: The role of peer support. In E. Loeffler & T. Bovaird (Eds.), *Palgrave Handbook on Co-production of Public Services and Outcomes* (pp. 409–426). Palgrave Macmillan.

McNeill, F., & Maruna, S. (2007). Giving up and giving back: Desistance, generativity and social work with offenders. In G McIvor & P Raynor (Eds.), *Developments in Social Work with Offenders. Research Highlights in Social work* (pp. 224–339), no. 48. Jessica Kingsley Publisher.

Nixon, S. (2019). "I just want to give something back" peer work and desistance Unpublished thesis De Montfort University England.

Nixon, S. (2020). The emotional labour of prison listeners. In J. Phillips, J. Waters, C. Westaby, & A. Fowler (Eds.), *Emotional Labour in Criminal Justice and Criminology (1st ed.)*. Routledge.

Nixon, S., & Woodward, D. (2025). *Role Exit in Prison Officers: 'Returning to Civvy Street'* (1st ed.). Routledge.

Porteous, D., & Goodman, A. (2023). "If I had had a me": The benefits and challenges of involving children with lived experience in youth justice services. *Safer Communities*, 22(3), 172–185.

Sandberg, S. (2008). Street capital: Ethnicity and violence on the streets of Oslo. *Theoretical Criminology*, 12(2), 153–171.

Thompson, N., & Spacey, M. (2023). "I would want to see young people working in here, that's what I want to see…" How peer support opportunities in youth offending services can support a Child First, trauma-informed, and reparative model of practice for Youth Justice. *Safer Communities*, 22(3), 200–216.

Tomczak, P., & Buck, G. (2019). The criminal justice voluntary sector: Concepts and an agenda for an emerging field. *The Howard Journal of Crime and Justice*, 58, 276–297.

Weaver, B. (2019a). Understanding desistance: A critical review of theories of desistance. *Psychology, Crime & Law*, 25(6), 641–658.

Weaver, B. (2019b). Co-production, governance and practice: The dynamics and effects of User Voice Prison Councils. *Social Policy & Administration*, 53(2), 249–264.

Weaver, B., & McCulloch, P. (2012). Co-producing criminal justice. *Scottish Centre for Crime and Justice Research*. Available at: www.sccjr.ac.uk/wpcontent/uploads/2012/11/Co-producing_Criminal_Justice.pdf

Wigzell, A. & Patterson-Young, C. (2024). *Progressive desistance in youth justice practice*. https://cloud-platform-e218f50a4812967ba1215eaecede923f.s3.amazonaws.com/uploads/sites/32/2025/05/Academic-Insights-Wigzell-and-Paterson-Young.pdf accessed on 30/06/2025.

Youth Justice Board (2025). Applying the child-first framework in youth justice services. London: Crest Advisory.

13

'I WOULD WANT TO SEE YOUNG PEOPLE WORKING IN HERE, THAT'S WHAT I WANT TO SEE…'

How peer support opportunities in youth justice services can support a Child First, trauma-informed, and reparative model of practice for youth justice[1]

Naomi Thompson and Morgan Spacey

Introduction

This chapter draws on data collected as part of a research study in a youth justice service (YJS) in London. The research focused on exploring the effectiveness of the YJS model of practice, which combined a trauma-informed approach with restorative justice and awareness of bias and discrimination. We focus on the overall themes and findings from this research in another paper (Spacey and Thompson, 2021). In this chapter, we extrapolate in detail one qualitative theme that emerged from our research, this being young people's desire for peer support opportunities in the YJS. We explore how implementing peer support into practice combines trauma-informed, Child First and reparative approaches to youth justice. Our research suggests that while the provision of peer support opportunities is a key principle of the trauma-informed approach (SAMHSA, 2014) it has arguably not been implemented and formalised to the extent that young people are asking for. Deficit and risk-based framings of young people as well as procedural barriers have contributed to this (Burns and Creaney, 2023). For example, young people under 18 and those with convictions face restrictions to undertaking volunteering roles in youth justice settings (Ministry of Justice, 2018). We use our research data on peer support to demonstrate how overcoming these barriers to fully embed such opportunities might offer a reconceptualising of restorative practice that is Child First and trauma-informed, co-produced by young people with lived experience of YJSs.

DOI: 10.4324/9781003602996-17

The examples in our study of young people's deep-felt empathy for their peers and their keen desire to offer support and even develop careers working with young people present a challenge to research that suggests young people who have been involved in criminal activity struggle to empathise (see, for example, Edwards, Adler and Gray, 2016; Trivedi-Bateman, 2015). Instead, we argue that typical restorative interventions have been misdirected and need to be reframed to be more child-centred, connecting with young people's empathic associations.

A reparative approach that focuses on young people's empathy for their peers, and desire to 'give back' to the communities they are part of supports a form of practice that centres the young person. Rethinking dominant victim-centred approaches to restorative justice to move towards a focus on immediate peers (a group that young people often more easily relate to) is more compatible with the Child First and trauma-informed practices. Strang (2017) recognises that definitional challenges in restorative justice have led to some practices being labelled as such incorrectly, arguing particularly that interventions that do not involve the direct victims of crime do not fit the definition of restorative justice. She also recognises the credible use of wider community members in restorative justice, alongside the role of the victim. As such, we argue the peer support approach explored in this paper draws on some of the principles of restorative *approaches* or *practices* but cannot be defined specifically as restorative *justice*. In order to acknowledge the definitional tensions, we primarily refer to the peer support approach as *reparative* rather than *restorative* practice. While we recognise that incorporating work with peers sits within the broad spectrum of restorative practices, we focus on it being a *reparative* approach that reconceptualises and draws on some principles of *restorative* practices because it would not fit with strict definitions of restorative approaches. This is due to the fact we are suggesting it as an *alternative* to involving the victim. We also recognise that through a Child First and trauma-informed lens, justice-involved children and young people need to be seen in the context of harm they have endured and not simplistically as perpetrators of harm. In this sense, they might be seen as the victims at the centre of a reconceptualised approach to reparative practice. As such, this reframing involves developing a mutual process of reparation where victim-offender binaries are rejected.

Essential to this is ensuring new approaches are co-produced by young people themselves. This means involving them as equal partners in the co-design and co-delivery of new approaches (SCIE, 2022).

By the end of this chapter, you will:

- Understand young people's empathic associations for their peers and the potential to more fully incorporate this into reparative practice.

- Recognise young people's desire to 'give back' as part of their post-offending journeys.
- Consider how peer support opportunities might contribute to a form of co-produced reparative practice.

The Child First approach

Youth justice interventions in England have traditionally been framed by a 'law and order' discourse that focuses on the crime and its penal consequences rather than the vulnerabilities of the perpetrator – and this approach has been widely criticised (Darke, 2011; Hughes, 2011). Internationally, approaches that centre the young person and their needs and recognise the links between maltreatment and offending have been found to be more effective (Arthur, 2010; Baglivio et al, 2015; Hughes, 2011).

In the United Kingdom, alternative models for youth justice have emerged. Case and Haines (2015) developed the 'Children First, Offenders Second' approach to youth justice work, arguing that young people who offend should be recognised first as children and not treated as 'mini adults'. They refer to the ongoing tendency in youth justice, to adultify children and young people, as the 'neoliberal responsibilisation' of them. The 'children first' approach accepts that young people are vulnerable, rather than simply criminal, and focuses on support over punishment. More recently branded as 'Child First', the approach is underpinned by principles of inclusion, participation, a focus on the welfare of the child, and holistic support tailored to the individual's needs that enables them to reach their full potential (Day, 2022).

The Child First model has been adopted by statutory YJSs across the UK in recent years and is now recognised and promoted by the Youth Justice Board for England and Wales (YJB, 2021). However, Day (2022) argues that the approach has yet to be adopted consistently at the local level. She identifies varying reasons for this including resistance from practitioners and services as well as contradictory messages from different areas of government about approaches to youth justice practice. Day identifies that a persistence of risk- and deficit-focused approaches to the monitoring of YJSs presents a significant barrier. As such, tensions emerge between what is promoted *in principle* by a Child First policy framing and what is possible *in practice* within procedures, regulations and outcomes frameworks.

Trauma-informed practice

Justice-involved children are significantly more likely than other children to have a history of exposure to traumatic adversity (Liddle et al, 2016). HM Inspectorate of Probation (2017) conducted a review of YJSs and, in examining 115 case files for young people who had committed a serious offence, found 81% had reported trauma. A key recommendation following this review was national incorporation of trauma-informed approaches in YJSs.

There is evidence to suggest that interrupting the influence of trauma and enabling young people to access recovery and healthy coping methods can lead to greater levels of engagement with interventions and a reduction in re-offending (Levenson & Willis, 2019; Loughran and Reid, 2018: Skuse and Matthew, 2015). It is also recognised that a trauma-informed approach is needed in other social, community and health services, before and alongside young people's engagement with the justice system (McCartan, 2020).

A working definition of the trauma-informed approach was developed by the USA's Substance Abuse and Mental Health Services Administration (SAMHSA, 2014). This definition provides a set of key practice approaches and principles. The fundamental approaches to trauma-informed practice are to *realise* the impact of trauma; *recognise* and *respond to* generalised and individual presentations of trauma; and *resist* (re)traumatisation, with the goal of supporting service-users to access potential avenues of *recovery*. The key principles underpinning the trauma-informed model are: Safety; Trustworthiness and Transparency; Peer Support; Collaboration and Mutuality; Empowerment, Voice and Choice; recognising Cultural, Historical and Gender Issues. SAMHSA suggest the trauma-informed approach works best when these principles are embedded in policies, practices, values, and environments of a service.

In this chapter, we are particularly interested in the 'peer support' principle of trauma-informed practice and how this can be better utilised in YJSs. This principle is a crucial element of trauma-informed practice because peer support opportunities 'are key vehicles for establishing safety and hope, building trust, enhancing collaboration, and utilising stories and lived experience to promote recovery and healing' (SAMHSA, 2014: 11).

Restorative practices

Restorative justice has become popular in UK youth justice over recent decades. Victims are invited to contribute to youth justice panels, and reparation can be a requirement of a young person's referral order (Ministry of Justice, 2018). Research has suggested that drawing on young people's empathy for others may be an effective alternative to focusing on punitive measures (Walklate, 1998). However, more recently, dominant restorative justice approaches have been critiqued by Child First advocates for placing the needs of the victim rather than those of the child at the centre of the intervention (Case and Haines, 2015).

Young people's connection to their peer communities has arguably been under-considered as an alternative form of reparative practice to the dominant focus on reparation with victims. Community participation has been widely emphasised in restorative justice with peers, close friends and family of the justice-involved young person suggested as key participants (Rossner and Bruce, 2016). However, this practice of community involvement has been researched and implemented only as an *addition* to victim involvement, rather than an *alternative* form of reparative practice centred on the young person and their immediate networks. The current research, while focused on community involvement alongside victim involvement, does offer some indication of the benefits of such an alternative approach. Rossner (2008) outlines the benefits of collective emotion in restorative justice and how the involvement of the justice-involved person's community can facilitate *reintegrative* shaming that differs from the *stigmatic* shaming of the court process and supports reintegration into the community. Arguably, however, any process described as 'shaming' would not be appropriate within a Child First and trauma-informed framing for restorative justice.

Research suggests young people who have committed offences can struggle to develop empathy for their victims (Edwards, Adler & Gray, 2016; Trivedi-Bateman, 2015). This may be particularly so where they cannot relate to them and are disconnected from their lives and experiences (Spacey & Thompson, 2021). In a large-scale study on empathy in young people with criminal convictions, Trivedi-Bateman (2015) found that those convicted of violent offences have less empathy for their victims than others – and that lower levels of empathy correlate with lower levels of shame and guilt for their violent offences. This led her to conclude that lower levels of empathy, shame and guilt make someone more likely to engage with crime, and particularly violent crime. However, while the guilt, shame and empathy scales used in Trivedi-Bateman's (2015) research did make some wider reference to others beyond the victim, such as family and friends, the emphasis of these measures was on the person who had offended being merely observed by these people in their lives or of them being aware of their wrongdoing, rather than there being a focus on understanding any negative impacts of their behaviour for their families and communities. Her interviews with young people who had offended focused primarily on the victim and then on how they would feel if parents or others found out – but, again, not on the consequences of their offending on their families and communities. Trivedi-Bateman's overall focus was on *empathy for victims* rather than others in the young people's lives. This suggests there is a gap in the research as to who young people might feel empathy for, beyond their victim.

Many of the benefits of restorative justice outlined by research focus on positive impacts for the victim (Rossner, 2008; Strang, 2017). While this is an important part of restorative justice, it compromises a Child First approach because it centres the victim rather than the child (Case and Haines, 2015).

Arguably, a narrow focus on 'victim-perpetrator' binaries does not recognise that the child may also be a victim of harm. Additionally, young people may be better able to relate to their immediate peers and communities than to victims and a focus on this in considering Child First, trauma-informed and restorative interventions could offer a reconceptualisation that brings the principles of these approaches together.

To present our suggested approach as restorative would require a significant reconceptualising of restorative practice away from centring victims. However, when viewed through a trauma-informed and Child First lens, children and young people who have offended must be seen as *harmed* and not simply as *harmers*. As identified by HMIP (2017), the vast majority are victims of trauma themselves. Further, a number of scholars have identified that justice-involved young people face a range of social adversities and vulnerabilities – and have argued that interventions should approach them as vulnerable rather than criminal (Case & Haines, 2015; McAra and McVie, 2016; Thompson, 2019). These studies recognise the blurred line between victim and offender and the role of exploitation in young people's criminal involvement (Thompson, 2019). In this sense, the *young people themselves* are the *victims* at the centre of Child First and trauma-informed interventions. This means restorative interventions within this frame need to move beyond 'victim-offender' binaries and incorporate complexities such as reparation of harm to, and not just by, the child and involve people in their lives they can attempt to relate to in a mutually empathic process.

Co-production

An essential route to ensuring any reframing of reparative practices is more mutual, relevant and meaningful for young people is to ensure they are co-producers in the design and delivery of new interventions. There is an increasing body of scholarship that advocates for young people's co-production in youth justice, not least the book that this chapter is located within.

Co-production is loosely defined as 'partnership working between people who draw on care and support, carers and citizens to improve public services' by SCIE (2022). They identify that this means services engage with these partners in 'co-design', 'co-decision making', 'co-delivery' and 'co-evaluation'. The principles of co-production as defined by SCIE (2022) are:

1 'Equality' through shifting power towards those using services and drawing on the assets they bring.
2 'Diversity' through ensuring that the most marginalised groups are represented.

3 'Accessibility' through providing the appropriate environments, resources and information to ensure all can participate on an equal basis.
4 'Reciprocity' through ensuring those who take part in co-production activities benefit from their participation.

When these principles are fully embedded in a service, co-production can be 'transformative' rather than simply 'descriptive' (where participants are involved in delivery but not able to meaningfully change or challenge the service) or 'intermediate' (where there is more mutuality and participants may help train practitioners, for example, but again meaningful change is not fully realised) (SCIE, 2022). Arguably, the risk focus and barriers in youth justice practice (identified by Day, 2022) prevent the implementation of transformative co-production. One of the key features of successful co-production is when services draw on 'peer and personal networks alongside professional networks' (SCIE, 2022). Overall, this suggests a more embedded structure of peer support in youth justice could transform services.

Recent research has identified the benefits of involving peers in co-produced youth justice work. Brierley (2023) argues the involvement of experiential peers in youth justice creates a participatory culture that supports desistance. He identifies, however, that more research is needed to develop the key characteristics of such experiential peer work including whether these peers can be supported to develop professional careers in youth justice. Porteous and Goodman (2023) found that the involvement of children with lived experience as peer navigators, offering support for other young people in a YJS helped build trust, higher levels of engagement as well as increasing self-worth and positive outcomes for the children and young people involved. In this case, the project was led by a charity that was free from the restrictions of the YJS and were able to employ young people with recent lived experience as volunteers and even paid employees. This meant that young people in the YJS could take on such roles as they graduated from the service and benefit from long-term support from the charity including support into relevant degree-level training and employment. Porteous and Goodman recognise this level of child-first engagement is challenging for statutory services to implement due to the restrictions and barriers they must comply with. In an academic report for HMIP, Buck (2021) recognises the growing emphasis on peer mentoring in youth justice as well as the current challenges including lack of funding and skilled management of mentors as well as the contradictions of delivering supportive mentoring in punitive environments. She argues substantial investment is needed as well as development of structures for training, supervision and support of mentors with recognition of the safety and ethics if such work is to be developed as an effective and long-term practice in youth justice.

Methodology

Our research took place in a YJS in a diverse London borough. We conducted observational research in the YJS over a four-month period and conducted surveys and interviews with young people and parents/caregivers. The survey contained a mix of closed and open questions about young people's experiences of the YJS and its impact on their lives. The survey was disseminated to potential respondents via YJS staff. Interviewees were recruited via a question in the survey and via YJS staff who put potential interviewees in touch with the research team. Recruitment to interviews was disrupted by the Covid-19 lockdown and a shift to a reliance on remote contact, meaning that earlier interviews took place in person and later ones predominantly by telephone.

A total of 63 surveys were completed by 44 young people and 19 parents. Nine interviews took place with six young people and three parents/caregivers. 81% of participants were from Black and other racially minoritised backgrounds. 63% of survey participants were male, 35% were female, and 2% stated 'other' or 'prefer not to say'. Of the young people who took part in the survey, ten were aged 13–15 years and 34 were aged 16 or over. The six young people who took part in interviews all identified as Black, two of them identified as female and four as male. One of these young people had finished their time with the YJS but returned regularly to visit, one had almost finished their time with the YJS, three were in the latter half of their time and one had recently commenced their time. The three parents/caregivers who took part in interviews all identified as Black women.

The data were subject to thematic analysis, where themes and sub-themes were identified through manual coding of the data (Braun and Clarke, 2006). The YJS were working to a model of practice that focused on three elements, these being trauma-informed practice, restorative justice and awareness of unconscious bias. As such, the surveys and interviews were designed, and the research data we gathered were analysed, primarily in relation to these three elements. These became broad deductive themes within which a range of inductive sub-themes emerged. Young people's desire for peer support opportunities within the YJS was one such inductive theme.

We were reflexive as to our positionality as white researchers, particularly in the interviews with black young people and parents/caregivers. We were aware that we might be associated with the authority of the YJS and we took care to emphasise and re-confirm consent before all interviews. We were also aware of how this positionality might have impacted on what data emerged in interviews. The peer support theme in itself, and the expressed desire to have more young people present in the YJS might reflect how the service (and possibly also us, if seen as an extension of them in that moment) was not seen as fully representative and relatable to minoritised young people and their families. The way this was expressed to us may reflect a call for a greater diversity of representation more broadly (SCIE, 2022). The sense of responsibility young people felt to support their peers might also reflect the adultification that is projected on young people who offend and most sharply on young people from racially minoritised backgrounds (Davis, 2022).

The peer support theme was most present in the interviews, where it emerged in all six of the young people's narratives. For the young people who had completed or almost completed their time with the YJS, it emerged most explicitly as a desire to take on roles as peer representatives in the YJS and even to develop long-term careers in work with young people. For those who had been with the YJS less time, it emerged more explicitly as a desire to see young people represented in the YJS, with a sense that they would have the skills and understanding to contribute, but this was articulated less boldly than by those who had been engaged for longer. In the young people's surveys, which were primarily completed by those who had been with the YJS for less than six months, reference to peer influence primarily emerged as a growing recognition of the negative impact of previous peer groups and the need to disassociate from these and form new connections, as well as some less prevalent comments about the desire to see young people represented in the YJS. For parents/caregivers in the surveys and interviews, there was caution expressed about the influence of peers even where the young people seemed to be moving on with their lives. This chapter focuses specifically on the data from interviews with young people relating to the peer support theme and analyses it in relation to how it connects with Child First, trauma-informed and reparative practices.

The need for peer support opportunities in youth justice

The young people in our study viewed peer support as something that would help to counter the feelings of judgement that exist for young people when they access the YJS and feel that they are under the 'adult gaze'. In this way, it arguably offers a form of resistance to the 'neoliberal responsibilisation' identified and critiqued by Case and Haines (2015). Young people suggested peer support opportunities would make the YJS feel safe for other young people. This supports avoiding (re)traumatisation and contributes to a trauma-sensitive environment. Additionally, young people saw peer support as a way of 'giving back', a form of reparative and restorative practice. This suggests it might support a co-produced approach to reparative practice that centres young people and embeds principles of power-sharing and reciprocity (SCIE, 2022).

Peer support enhances a trauma-informed approach

Peer support is a key principle of the trauma-informed approach (SAMHSA, 2014). The young people in our study articulated that access to peer role models would make services feel safer and less intimidating.

> Some young people don't trust adults in general. So, they're coming to a place like this and having to express their feelings to an adult, they're bound to find it hard. That's when they feel more closed up, don't say nothing… [There should be] young people because when you see young people in this type of environment doing something good, it changes other young people's minds.
>
> *(Young person 1)*

This and other examples (see those quoted in the next section) demonstrate that our participants understood how young people experience the 'adult gaze'. The same young person went on to recognise that their first impressions had not been correct, stating 'Even though they know what you've done, they don't really look at you like how other people look at you' (Young person 1). However, it demonstrates how having peer role models present at first access might support young people to experience YJSs as less threatening. This builds on Porteous and Goodman's (2023) findings in their paper titled 'If I had had a me' that peer support builds trust and engagement. Our participants understood that a 'trust gap' exists between young people and adults in authority, particularly for justice-involved young people who experience the 'adult gaze' most sharply.

The example above supports SAMHSA's (2014) proposition that peer support can enable someone to remain connected with and progress with their trauma recovery process through connection to a role model they can relate to and that they observe also making progress. The young person also articulated a key outcome of peer support, *changing minds*, highlighting how negative and often internalised narratives of young people can be challenged by the presence of other young people in positive roles. For young people in YJSs, challenging these narratives arguably plays a significant role in the formation of self-identity and esteem, a substantial element of the trauma recovery process (Skuse & Matthew, 2015).

Incorporating peer support develops a co-produced and Child First approach

The young people who had been engaged over a substantial period of time or had finished their time with the YJS expressed an interest in working at the YJS. They explained it would benefit service-users, both at first access and in their ongoing support.

> I would want to see young people working in here, that's what I want to see… because once you have young people … helping other young people, that's when the ratings go more up in my eyes… Even volunteering, that would still be good because they will still be making a change to young

> people... Just like a small little conversation you can have with a young person, you can change their whole aspect completely.
>
> *(Young person 4)*

This was something that the young people were offering to be involved in co-producing and that they keenly felt they could contribute to because of their own experiences.

> Because I found that because of my experiences, I'll be able to understand some of the young people, why they do the stuff that they do, what they're going through because I've gone through similar stuff. So, experience... Because someone could tell you something and you would understand them – like why they would have done something like that and what they're going through at the time, how – what effects it has on them.
>
> *(Young person 2)*

This reflects Brierley's (2023) assertion that involving experiential peers builds a participatory culture in youth justice. Implementing this co-produced model would support a Child First approach where young people influence service delivery and are supported to build their own skills and self-esteem.

The desire to work in the YJS came particularly from those who were reaching the end of their time with the YJS or who had already moved on. As such, it would offer a way for them to remain connected to support while also getting involved in a positive opportunity that supports their ongoing development and recovery. This presents an opportunity and a challenge. It offers the potential to develop a long-term form of reparative practice through the long-term involvement of young people in supporting their peers, beyond the time period of their own orders. However, it would require additional resources to support young people who have completed their orders to undertake such roles with the appropriate supervision and critical reflection (Harris, 2019; Buck, 2021). There is a need for further research, co-produced with young people, to further define how this long-term peer support model could be designed and developed in a meaningful and appropriate way that enhances support for young people in YJSs and contributes to ongoing recovery and career development for those 'giving back' (SCIE, 2022).

Having young people who have been through the service on youth justice referral order panels, as well as in the service itself, could support an approach that remains Child First. However, at present, people under the age of 18 and those with particular or recent convictions are barred from voluntary roles on these panels, while victims are encouraged to take part (Ministry of Justice, 2018). This involvement of victims but not young people shifts the process away from being child-centred (Case and Haines, 2015). The development of a new role for youth members on panels would support co-produced and Child First practice to be more clearly centred in the referral order process. This could bring new relevance to referral order panels which have been argued to be disconnected from Child First principles and in need of reform (Allen-Fellows, 2024).

Peer support opportunities as a form of co-produced reparative practice

When victim-centred restorative justice does not work, it is often concluded that the young people lack capacity for the empathic understanding required for such reparative work (Trivedi-Bateman, 2015). However, young people in our research felt a strong sense of empathy, directed at their peers (as already shown in the examples above). The young person quoted below articulated this empathic understanding for their peers particularly clearly.

> My upbringing was all over the place, but because of it I understand – I've gone through things people my age couldn't cope with. My dad, he never got to watch me grow up because he passed early, so that just set in my mind, I just want to do him proud and that… I don't know what instilled it into me, I think it was just the way I saw my dad and that, but even if I see someone on the road, just getting bullied or something, I wouldn't just stand there and watch it, I would – like me in my heart, like my heart will tell me that, 'You have to get involved.' I don't know why, but even today I came out of school and I saw a boy in a younger year crying, and I asked him what was wrong. He said he got strangled and threw down the stairs. I was like – 'Why did he do that to you? Did you say something?' He said, 'No I just laughed when I was walking past him.' But he said it was because he was on the phone and the boy just came out of nowhere. I got involved. I took the boy to one of the teachers that was talking to him and that and I think it got sorted out.
>
> *(Young person 6)*

The young people who expressed a strong desire to work in the YJS viewed this as a way to 'give back' to their peers and communities. Supporting such opportunities could allow reparative practice to be co-produced by young people, centred on their needs and choices, building mutual support, and not shifting focus from child to victim. However, there is a need to ensure that the burden of responsibility to support peers does not emerge from projected adultification and that young people are able to identify and engage with their own personal development through such a process. This means ensuring the principle of reciprocity is embedded to allow for transformative rather than tokenistic co-production (SCIE, 2022).

The young people identified how working at the YJS would benefit them (and fulfil their personal and professional development ambitions) as the young people offering the support, rather than just benefiting those receiving it. They also recognised there were procedural barriers to fulfilling these ambitions.

> I think you've got to have a certain qualification. You've got to be over 18, as I know. Yeah, so I just need to get the qualifications and then hopefully I can probably. I tried a couple of months ago, quite a long time ago, I tried to ask them if they could sort out apprenticeships there because that would be good for young people that wanted to look into working with young people. But I don't know if they managed to sort that out but that's what I would want to do here to be honest, that would be good.
>
> *(Young person 5)*

Such opportunities were seen as something that would build on skills they had developed or become more aware of in themselves through their own engagement with the YJS. The same young person drew on the leadership skills they felt they would bring to such a role.

> To me, from my perspective, to be honest, a good leader to me is someone that could face up to anything and everything, no matter what the circumstances is... And to be honest that's me. Anything that comes my way I'm willing to take it, hard or not.
>
> *(Young person 5)*

Other young people reflected on the insights and advocacy skills they would bring from their own experiences, recognising that their developing awareness of their insights and skills had been supported by their time with the YJS.

> Insight, it's given me insight about certain stuff. And understanding as well... Insight to myself and people in general, like why some people act the way they do. It depends on how they grew up and that... I – yeah, it will help me because say because of when I come here and work here, it's like the fact that I can judge someone's personality by hearing how they talk or how they act. It's like it will be helpful because I'm obviously going to want a job here.
>
> *(Young person 2)*

> I would bring a lot to the table because I've seen a lot, been through a lot, heard a lot, I could show them a lot I guess. Because a lot of young people need like an advocate as well as an adult that has experienced things that

> they're going through. So, they can have that person that relates to things that they're feeling, so it makes it better when they're communicating.
>
> *(Young person 1)*

These examples of how young people felt they would benefit from working in the YJS and draw on their own skills and insights illustrate potential for a Child First model of reparative practice for the young people providing the support as well as those they are supporting. These young people saw themselves as relatable role models where mutual empathy can be developed.

The young people's reflections above suggest their time with the YJS encouraged them to feel confident in their abilities to help support, guide and empower their peers, drawing on their own empathy and lived experiences. It appears from our study that there was still work to do to fully explore and embed the co-produced peer support opportunities the young people identified as helpful, and one challenge to this is clearly that young people may only be ready to take such a role when they have completed (or almost completed) their time with the service. The data suggests young people were asking for these opportunities but that they had not yet materialised to the extent they were asking for, particularly in the form of training, apprenticeships and long-term opportunities for career development. This reflects Burns and Creaney's (2023) argument that risk-based approaches and a resistance to relinquishing adult control are restraining forces to participatory practice in youth justice. It also mirrors Porteous and Goodman's (2023) recognition that statutory services are limited in their capacity to embed long-term peer support practice facilitated by young people with recent experience of the youth justice system. Legalities and structural barriers are an issue here – for example, the rules about who can be on the referral order panel or work more long-term with young people in the justice system. Dominant risk and deficit narratives of young people feed such legality issues around how easily a young person with criminal convictions can develop a long-term career in the sector. Young people in our research were aware of and frustrated by these limitations.

Conclusion

The analysis above demonstrates how peer support might contribute to a Child First, trauma-informed and reparative approach to youth justice. Peer support could enable continuing personal growth and recovery for young people who have previously attended and who no longer have direct access to service supervision and care. For young people accessing services, access to peer role models could support a child-centred and trauma-sensitive experience.

Our research also demonstrates how peer support might address the tensions inherent in restorative practices that focus on the victim rather than the child, by drawing on young people's empathy for their peers. It presents a challenge to the notion that young people who have been involved in crime cannot empathise with others, with multiple examples from our study demonstrating young people's deep sense of empathy for peers. Rather than young people lacking empathy, some of the typical interventions designed to draw on their empathy for others may have been misdirected. A reframing of reparative practices to centre the child and focus on reparation with their immediate peers could be a possible alternative. While allowing young people to play a role in referral order panels, the currently dominant mechanism for incorporating restorative justice in young people's justice process would be a start. This is a limited mechanism, focused on defining the content of young people's referral orders. More meaningful, long-term, creative and co-produced models are arguably needed. At the policy level, work is needed to remove legal and structural barriers to young people's meaningful involvement in YJSs, supporting them with training and long-term career development where they have a desire to work in the sector.

Within any reframing of reparative practices, there is a need to recognise that young people in the justice system have experienced harm and trauma themselves, rather than them being simplistically framed as the enactors of harm in restorative and reparative practices. This means rejecting victim-offender binaries and developing new reparative approaches that allow for mutual processes of empathy and reconciliation. The Child First and trauma-informed approaches to youth justice reinforce the need for reparative approaches that centre 'harm done to (and not just by) young people, including by the professionals and institutions and that should protect them' (Spacey and Thompson, 2021: 33). A key way to mitigate harm and (re)traumatisation by YJSs could be through co-produced peer involvement in the design and delivery of services. Within the research presented in this chapter, it is clear justice-involved young people have something unique and insightful to offer in developing new forms of practice that draw on young people's empathy for each other to deliver more representative support and to provide opportunities for further development beyond their time as service users. They expressed ambitions to develop long-term careers supporting young people. Young people with lived experience of the justice system need to be co-producers in the research and piloting to inform the design and delivery of such new peer support interventions to ensure they are fully transformative for both the young people offering and receiving the support.

Note

1 This chapter is based on an article previously published in *Safer Communities* journal (Thompson and Spacey, 2023).

Bibliography

Allen-Fellows, J. (2024). Jewel in the crown: Why referral orders fail to shine in a Child First world. *CrimRxiv*. https://doi.org/10.21428/cb6ab371.43dafa3e.

Arthur, R. (2010). Protecting the best interests of the child: A comparative analysis of the youth justice systems in Ireland, England and Scotland. *International Journal of Children's Rights,* 18, pp. 217–231.

Baglivio, M. T., Wolff, K. T., Piquero, A. R. & Epps, N. (2015). The relationship between Adverse Childhood Experiences (ACE) and juvenile offending trajectories in a juvenile offender sample. *Journal of Criminal Justice,* 43(3), pp. 229–241.

Braun, V. & Clarke, V. (2006). Using thematic analysis in psychology. *Qualitative Research in Psychology,* 3, pp. 77–101.

Brierley, A. (2023). Experiential peers cultivate a participation culture in youth justice. *Safer Communities*, 22(2), pp. 78–90. https://doi.org/10.1108/SC-07-2022-0024.

Buck, G. (2021). *Mentoring and Peer Mentoring.* Manchester: HMIP.

Burns, S. & Creaney, S. (2023). Embracing children 's voices: Transforming youth justice practice through co-production and child first participation. In Case, S., Hazel, N. (Eds.) *Child First: Developing a New Youth Justice System.* London: Palgrave Macmillan.

Case, S. & Haines, K. (2015). *Positive Youth Justice.* Bristol: Policy Press.

Darke, S. (2011). The enforcement approach to crime prevention. *Critical Social Policy,* 31(3), pp. 410–430.

Davis, J. (2022). *Adultification Bias Within Child Protection and Safeguarding.* Manchester: HMIP.

Day, A.-M. (2022). 'It's a hard balance to find': The perspectives of youth justice practitioners in England on the place of 'risk' in an emerging 'Child-First' world. *Youth Justice.* https://doi.org/10.1177/14732254221075205.

Edwards, S. K., Adler, J. R. & Gray, J. M. (2016). *Empathy, Mentalisation and Violent Behaviour: Interim Report.* London: Middlesex University.

Harris, P. (2019) 'Down with the kids?' Examining the male youth worker as role model and mentor to young men involved in youth violence. *Youth & Policy.* www.youthandpolicy.org/articles/down-with-the-kids/.

HM Inspectorate of Probation. (2017). *The Work of Youth Offending Teams to Protect the Public.* London: Crown copyright.

Hughes, N. (2011). Young people 'as risk' or young people 'at risk': Comparing discourses of anti-social behaviour in England and Victoria. *Critical Social Policy,* 31(3), pp. 388–409.

Levenson, J. S. & Willis, G. M. (2019). Implementing trauma-informed care in correctional treatment and supervision. *Journal of Aggression, Maltreatment and Trauma,* 28(4), pp. 481–501.

Liddle, M., Boswell, G., Wright, S., Francis, V. & Perry,R. (2016). *Trauma and Young Offenders, A Review of the Research and Practice Literature: A Research Summary.* London: Beyond Youth Custody.

Loughran, T. A. & Reid, J. (2018). *A Longitudinal Investigation of Trauma Exposure, Retraumatization, and Post-Traumatic Stress of Justice-Involved Adolescents.* Washington DC, US: US Department of Justice.

McAra, L. & McVie, S. (2016) Understanding youth violence: The mediating effects of gender, poverty and vulnerability. *Journal of Criminal Justice*, 45, pp. 71–77.

McCartan, K. (2020). Trauma-informed practice. Manchester: Her Majesty's Inspectorate of Probation. Available at: www.justiceinspectorates.gov.uk/hmiprobation/wp-content/uploads/sites/5/2020/07/Academic-Insights-McCartan.pdf.

Ministry of Justice. (2018). *Referral Order Guidance*. London: Crown copyright. Available at: https://assets.publishing.service.gov.uk/government/uploads/system/uploads/attachment_data/file/746365/referral-order-guidance-9-october-2018.pdf.

Porteous, D. & Goodman, A. (2023). "If I had had a me": The benefits and challenges of involving children with lived experience in youth justice services. *Safer Communities*, 22(3), pp. 172–185. https://doi.org/10.1108/SC-10-2022-0043.

Rossner, M. (2008). Healing victims and offenders and reducing crime: A critical assessment of restorative justice practice and theory. *Sociology Compass*, 2(6), pp. 1734–1749. https://doi.org/10.1111/j.1751-9020.2008.00170.x.

Rossner, M. & Bruce, J. (2016). Community participation in restorative justice: Rituals, reintegration, and quasi-professionalization. *Victims & Offenders*, 11(1), pp. 107–125. https://doi.org/10.1080/15564886.2015.1125980.

SAMHSA's Trauma and Justice Strategic Initiative. (2014). *SAMHSA's Concept of Trauma and Guidance for a Trauma-Informed Approach*. Rockville, MD, US: Substance Abuse and Mental Health Services Administration.

SCIE. (2022). Co-production: What it is and how to do it. Available at: www.scie.org.uk/co-production/what-how/.

Skuse, D. T. & Matthew, J. (2015). The trauma recovery model: Sequencing youth justice interventions for young people with complex needs. *Prison Service Journal*, 1(220), pp. 16–25.

Spacey, M. & Thompson, N. (2021). Beyond individual trauma: Towards a multi-faceted trauma-informed restorative approach to youth justice that connects individual trauma with family reparation and recognition of bias and discrimination. *British Journal of Community Justice*, 18(1), pp. 18–35.

Strang, H. (2017). Experiments in restorative justice. In Drahos, P. (Ed.) *Regulatory Theory* (pp. 483–498). Canberra, Australia: ANU Press.

Thompson, N. (2019). "It's a no-win scenario, either the police or the gang will get you!" Young people and organised crime – vulnerable or criminal? *Youth Justice*, 19(20), pp.102–119.

Thompson, N. & Spacey, M. (2023). "I would want to see young people working in here, that's what I want to see..." how peer support opportunities in youth offending services can support a Child First, trauma-informed, and reparative model of practice for youth justice. *Safer Communities*, 22(3), pp. 200–216.

Trivedi-Bateman, N. (2015). *The Roles of Empathy, Shame, and Guilt in Violence Decision-Making*. Doctoral Thesis. Cambridge, UK: University of Cambridge. https://doi.org/10.17863/CAM.16553.

Walklate, S. (1998). 'No more excuses!': Young people, victims and making amends. *Policy Studies*, 19(3-4), pp. 213–222.

Youth Justice Board. (2021). *Strategic Plan 2021-2024*. London: Youth Justice Board for England and Wales.

14

DRAWING ON LIVED EXPERIENCE IN A YOUTH JUSTICE CONTEXT

David Porteous and Anthony Goodman

Introduction

The partnership project discussed in this chapter aims to enhance justice-involved children's opportunities in education, training and employment by enabling them to draw on and share their lived experience of youth justice in work with peers, youth justice service (YJS) professionals and other stakeholders in the criminal justice system. Bussu et al. (2024) characterise this as using experiential knowledge from firsthand or lived experiences gained by young people to provide 'unique insights' to children currently in the youth justice system. Mentors and peer mentors have important contributions to make within the criminal justice system, with the former being the most common practice. Mentors give their time to support and encourage others, and peer mentors often have life experiences similar to those they seek to help. This raises the potential for 'inspirational' role modelling, through reassurance and showing that change is possible (Buck, 2021).

The project has distinctive characteristics, which make it an interesting model of co-production in a youth justice setting. The term co-production can have different meanings and be a somewhat 'elastic' concept (McCulloch, 2016). This is because the term can be used to describe the differing levels of involvement between the professionals, the mentors, and the 'clients'. In this instance the main consideration was the relationship between those with lived experience and those currently on supervision. At the end of the supervisory period, the youth justice team ceased to have contact with those they were mandated to supervise. The mentors did not see this as a termination of their

DOI: 10.4324/9781003602996-18

support, which they were interested to continue. This leads to a number of dualisms:

- The relationship between the youth justice team and the children under supervision
- The relationship between the mentors and the children under supervision
- The relationship between the youth justice team and the mentors

One indicator of this is that the findings presented here come from a small-scale qualitative study commissioned by the Youth Justice Board for England and Wales (YJB) as one of six 'Child First diversion' pathfinder projects. The project had in effect already been singled out as novel, and promising and so the task for researchers was to assess whether and why this acclaim was merited. In the words of the YJB: 'The project will evaluate the use of lived experience as a tool to help prevent reoffending. The learning from this will be … shared across the sector to promote good practice in relation to diversionary activity' (YJB, 2021: 24). This chapter can be seen as one attempt to contribute to the second of these two aims.

The project focused mainly on the co-production between the peer mentors and the children attending the YJS, rather than on how it impacted on the relationship between youth justice practitioners and the children. Practitioners interviewed were positive about the benefits of peer mentoring, but there could be an element of self-selection with those not so positive declining to speak to the evaluators. The peer mentors were independent of the youth justice team and shared knowledge of who they were engaging with and what they were doing with them (the terms children and young people are used interchangeably in the chapter).

Having briefly described the methods used to conduct the research, the chapter will summarise relevant findings with the three key objectives being to:

- describe the project's activities to show how it fosters co-production within a youth justice setting,
- identify the positive impact of the project for various beneficiaries and stakeholders and the reasons for these,
- assess the strengths and weaknesses of the model, highlighting what appear to be its distinguishing features.

The research study

The study took place over a two-year period, between 2021 and 2023. The researchers adopted a primarily qualitative approach, deeming this to be the most effective means of identifying how the project worked in practice and whether it was meeting its objectives as well as of assessing its strengths and limitations. Qualitative research: 'can aim to "give voice" to those whose accounts tend to be marginalised or discounted' (Willig, 2006: 12). In this instance it provided the children with the opportunity to have this voice. This was important to them, for example, in how they articulated how influential they felt when talking to people in authority who wanted to learn from them. They felt important and empowered. This aligned with a 'strengths' approach where they saw themselves as 'community assets' and not 'liabilities to be supervised' (Burnett and Maruna, 2006: 4), in Buck (2021).

The principal form of data collection was via semi-structured interviews, the majority conducted online via Zoom. Of seventeen interviews overall, four were held with project staff, two with former participants, six with YJS staff, three with YJS managers and two with representatives of external organisations with which the project has worked. In broad terms, the interviews asked respondents to describe the project and its different activities, providing examples where possible, and to assess its impact, both for individuals involved as well as the YJS and other stakeholders. In addition, the researchers visited the project on a small number of occasions and so were able to observe in a limited way interactions between project staff and children attending the YJS and/or the project as well as to hold informal conversations with them. Finally, project records and reports, YJS data and online media about the project were collated and analysed, and a review was undertaken of other recent research examining the use of lived experience in criminal justice settings.

The study had clear limitations. The sampling strategy was one of convenience (or pragmatism). A list of potential interviewees was supplied by the project manager to the researchers, and our impression was that of those who agreed to be interviewed, many did so because they were favourably disposed towards the project. To be fair, from these interviews emerged examples of, or reference tensions within the partnership and of negative views about it but nevertheless a more representative sample would have added both reliability and validity. In this respect the observation by Hampson et al. (2024: 46) is pertinent, namely that youth justice has been slow to involve children in youth justice research, while it has been used in other disciplines for many years, e.g. education, childhood studies and health.

A second weakness lay with the limitations of project monitoring records and YJS information system data. This allowed for some analysis of levels of participation in and satisfaction with project activities etc. but the gaps and inconsistencies meant only tentative conclusions regarding, for example, levels of reoffending, were possible. Perhaps the most disappointing aspect of the study was the small number of children encountered who had participated in the project. At the outset we did discuss the possibility of involving project staff and participants in the design of the research and/or in focus group discussions led by their peers. However, for several reasons, these attempts at introducing an element of co-production to the research proved unsuccessful. Therefore, while we believe the findings and our interpretation of them to be fair and accurate representation of the project, there is no doubt that giving greater voice and weight to the children it works with would have strengthened and enriched the evaluation. The power dynamics involved in this form of participatory research have the potential to limit how much input can be obtained from the most marginalised child populations (Smithson and Jones, 2021). The research tried to overcome this by interviewing children who had completed their formal involvement with the project.

Co-production in practice: project development and activities

Before its establishment in 2016, the charity's CEO and founder had previously been involved in a partnership project between the YJS and 'User Voice', a national organisation working to promote the voice of offenders in prison and community settings (see Barry et al., 2016 for an evaluation of User Voice's work). The vision underpinning this project was to embed this form of co-production within a YJS. The broad aims of the original project were to 'offer young people an opportunity to volunteer, to have a voice, also work alongside youth justice service staff… and most importantly to use their lived experience to support other young people in the criminal justice system' (Project CEO). 'Our Journey', the first 'Personal Social Health Education' (PSHE) Programme delivered, focused on developing self-esteem and confidence through providing the 'opportunity for young people to build relationships with adults and peers developing social and life skills, particularly around communication (public speaking); decision making; negotiation, conflict resolution and learning to work as part of a team' (Project documentation). Of the 22 children who completed the programme, 10 went on to become what were known originally as 'Peer Leaders' who provided mentoring and support to other young people on orders at the YJS.

This model was consolidated the following year (2017-2018), beginning with a consultation exercise which sought to establish the level of support for this kind of provision and to shape and fashion the programme itself. From an initial pool of 125 young people who completed survey questionnaires, 15 went on to participate in focus group discussions and 10 to complete the (newly termed) 'Peer Support Navigator' (PSN) training and so become eligible to support peers in the YJS. Over time then, young people first introduced to the project as service users themselves have graduated to become first volunteers, then paid sessional workers and finally employees on longer-term contracts. Hence, the young people who are being referred to the project today are meeting and being supported by peers with recent lived experience, not only of offending and of the criminal justice system, but of this specific YJS and the project itself. There is a positive effect for the peer supporters. Other studies have found that being a peer supporter enhanced their social capital and gave them the opportunity to form relationships with youth justice and other professionals with an enhanced sense of belonging (see Elisha and Shachaf-Friedman, 2024: 483).

By the time of the Pathfinder Project, the PSN network therefore comprised a core group of PSN staff, now young adults employed by the charity, who led PSN on all its activities and a wider group of more recently trained PSN volunteers who act as peer mentors to current participants. This network collectively engages in a variety of activities, both within the charity's own workspace and with the YJS, its other partners and external organisations. Internally, the project continues to run a programme of PSHE workshops focused both on generic issues of interest for participants (such as emotional wellbeing and mental health) and on enhancing employability skills. More broadly, the workshops were described as a space in which young people could talk about their lives and experiences with others in, or having been in, a similar situation. The project CEO emphasised that the 'expertise' offered by facilitators is informed by but not grounded in training manuals and formal qualifications but rather in their day-to-day experience of similar circumstances. A guiding motif for the mental health-oriented workshops for example is that if you have experienced mental health issues, you are an expert.

In the field of drug addiction, Elisha and Strachan (2024: 480) have observed that peer mentors were positive about helping others, describing this as fulfilling and integral to their changed outlook. Similarly, in the youth justice context, Bussu et al. (2024: 11) comment that '(p)eer mentors can develop a professional identity and in doing so increase levels of self-confidence and experience a sense of achievement'. The innovative element of the project discussed here is that the peer mentors are recruited, trained and supported by a person who has lived experience of serious offending and who is independent of the youth justice team. Relatedly, its 'Just Hear Us' programme involves young people in 'co-production platforms' in which they share their lived experiences and views with service providers and community organisations. Preparatory activities and the development of materials (posters, presentations) in advance of specific sessions on particular topics are organised by PSN staff. Organisations who have consulted children through the project include the Ministry of Justice and Youth Justice Board, local Judges and Magistrates, Crown Prosecution and Police services, local schools, charities and parent groups. Examples of topics on which the children have been consulted include unconscious bias in the youth justice system, knife-related crime, cannabis use and the experience of being in custody or in court.

The project also runs a weekly peer-led conversation hub. This is by design open-ended, based on whatever issues or opportunities the children themselves wish to explore or have support with. Within the hub may take place group conversations about aspects of offending such as county lines or knife carrying or one-to-one support with individuals looking for job opportunities or for advice on caring arrangements in the family. The hub operates primarily as a safe place within the YJS for children to meet with each other and discuss mutual concerns and interests. As such, it can serve as a springboard for engagement with other activities run by the project (as above) or by other YJS partners, both statutory and voluntary. The Lundy model of 'space, voice, audience and influence' discusses the creation of a safe and non-threatening space, where children have 'freedom of thought'. In addition, they have control over setting the agenda and decision making. They must also be free to express their opinions (Price and Creaney, 2025: 17).

From the perspective of YJS practitioners, as significant as these internally run activities, is the one-to-one support provided by the project staff to children in YJS and partner-led interventions. This can take the form of informal conversations (within or outside of the YJS premises), introductions and accompaniment to sporting or artistic organisations, support with finding paid work or with finding and taking up education or training opportunities and referral to or liaison with other statutory providers, primarily in health and education. PSN staff have also supported other projects run within the YJS by practitioners or partner organisations in the local community including a drama group, a boxing club and residential programmes run by youth justice practitioners in holiday periods. In these contexts, the PSN's role is to facilitate participation through building trust and confidence among the children in the value of these activities. This has been recognised by professionals in a youth justice setting: 'peer mentors were more likely to be able to show empathy and connect with the child' (Bussu et al., 2024, 11).

Impact

A consistent claim made by interviewees regarding the value of the project was that it facilitated engagement with the wider service. Former participants spoke positively about meeting the project CEO and staff, saying they found them relatable, that the atmosphere was relaxed and informal and that it was good to be among and discuss with others going (or having gone) through similar problems to themselves. In this regard, Case has commented on the 'neglect of children's voices in youth justice processes', and 'the underlying emphasis on enforcement and compliance' (2022: 291). The dual impact of these two comments is that it is advantageous to children to have someone with similar life experiences to act as a support.

One former participant, recollecting his first encounter with the project, said:

> I think X (a PSN) first introduced me to it and asked me a few questions. At first, I thought who is this guy bugging me, but he was telling me he was doing this workshop … and I thought why not, obviously there was a lot of other young people there and I thought this might be interesting. It was a good place to have a conversation at first then obviously more things came into it. That is how it started really.
>
> *(Former Participant)*

Another contrasted his feelings about the project staff with those about YJS practitioners:

> Yeah, you can relate, that's what I say. I mean the workers, they are just paid to be here. He's been through it, he knows the work, he knows the system, he knows how you think.
>
> *(Former participant)*

Similarly, YJS staff themselves were very open about the fact that the characteristics of project staff, even though they too were paid workers, made them easier for young people to relate to and to trust:

> It's a more accessible practitioner group I think, for some of our young people, because of the peer navigators, because of their lived experience, but because of course, even before you know about their lived experiences, because of their age, their gender, some in some cases their race, which I think is just a more comfortable set of people to be talking to for a young person who's quite anxious about talking to professionals, who they might have had difficult experiences of.
>
> *(YJS Practitioner)*

Interviews with YJS staff suggested that the project was better able to engage children, at least in the first instance, in conversations about their mental health. Mentors might be able to be more empathic on cultural pressures, and find it easier to gain the child's trust:

> The fact that they're able to even talk about their own life experiences. Some of them don't even talk to me about it and haven't talked to me about it. So, you know that in itself, you know, is a great credit to them because they've been able to you know, get that from young people, and work with that, and like the emotional stuff that, a lot of, especially our young men, don't want to share with us.
>
> *(Youth Justice Practitioner)*

Linked to this, some participants were also perceived as having benefited in terms of their relationships with peers:

> So, it gave her sort of the opportunity to sort of like meet with the young people in a safe space. She's quite vulnerable as well, so it was good that it was in a safe space.... And so yeah, they're sort of done that and you know you can really see It's boosted her confidence, and she really enjoys it, and she knows she now wants to sort of help other young people in her life .... So yeah, I think it's helping giving people sort of a shift in their identity, if you like, in terms of a more pro-social identity, and things that they can sort of strive and achieve for.
>
> *(Youth Justice Practitioner)*

This sense of young people undergoing a kind of 'identity shift' resonates with existing research into desistance from offending (Maruna, 2001; Giordano et al., 2007). That being more confident is a significant part of this was particularly evident in one conversation with a former participant who said that we would not believe he was the same person had we met him when he first came to the YJS:

> I was a bit more quieter. I couldn't come out as much as I liked, and I couldn't express myself. When you think I even done counselling. I have just been more self-aware and know what I want.
>
> *(Former Participant)*

This young person referred to the Peer Led Conversation Hub as 'just a healthy way of discussing things, discussing young people's thoughts' but a boost in self-esteem was also evident in this comment about his participation in the Just Hear Us initiative:

> Yeah, well that is very insightful – to see their thoughts and have someone actually listening and appreciate your training what you have been on.
>
> *(Former Participant)*

Alongside improving children's emotional and mental health, developing their PSHE skills and knowledge and providing them with opportunities to engage or re-engage in education, training and employment is a key aim of the project. The fact that the charity trains and employs young people to work as PSNs with their peers is only the most obvious way in which this goal is realised. The project has strong local links, especially with local employers, and this corresponds to the concept of co-production between the private sector and the project (see McCulloch, 2016: 433). Other forms of support range from assisting with CV writing and applications to more direct interventions including approaching prospective employers on the young person's behalf.

Two former participants we spoke to had both been supported into work and stressed how this had been facilitated by their engagement with the project:

> When I first came to YJS I was like crime was the way to get money and then X (Project CEO) like broke it down to me like you are not going to get anywhere if you commit a crime, you are not going to be able to have anything to your name, it is just temporary wins, that's what they call it. They helped me get a job, like keep on a job, keep the mindset and that convinced me to work and not bunk off and go do this and do that instead.
>
> *(Former Participant)*

> So, I started coming to YOT, I met X (Project CEO) and that and then they introduced me to the (PSHE) programme and what that programme was all about. I understood from it at first that if I go through the programme, I was getting more life skills and they help you get a job etc and from there I just carried on working for them and I became part of (the project) as well, I volunteered. I was there for about 2 years and then I got a job next door, X helped me get that … It kind of gave me a different perspective of what I wanted to do because I was young at the time, I was like 16 or 17 and I went on to Uni, I was still doing [the project] and I got another job next door, so I was doing 3 things at once.
>
> *(Former Participant)*

Discussions with one former participant in particular provided an interesting insight into how his involvement with the project and especially being given the opportunity to do paid work had helped him desist from offending. As we have heard already, in the young person's early conversations with the project's CEO, he recalled how the latter had impressed upon him the likely consequences if they continued to offend – 'if you commit a crime, you are not going to be able to have anything to your name, it is just temporary wins, that's what they call it'. As the conversation continued, the young person went on to explain how having a job had gradually transformed his outlook and circumstances:

> (Q) It's a bit of a personal question but has your life changed from your kind of work, sort of like friendship groups and so on.
>
> Yeah 100%. Anything at life, as you progress you are less likely to put what you have so it's at risk. So, if you do something you are likely to lose your job. So, you think about that as well.
>
> (Q) So, carrying on your involvement with the project you changed your friends?

Yeah, I changed everyone I was associated with more or less because now I work a legit lifestyle – you change your friendship groups to more legit people.

Q It is a dramatic change?

Yeah, I think with a 9-5 your whole life kind of revolves around it so you can't really do things. I think those on 9-5, its all they really talk about....

(Q) Has it changed your mindset?

Yeah, that is it, changed my whole mindset about life basically... At the time yeah, I still, when I first started... I was still caught up in that criminal world but then... lots of stuff, I was still caught up but then you realise you aren't really part of it no more if that makes sense

(Q) Like an outsider looking in?

Yeah, I think that is the best way to kind of look at it.

(Former Participant)

Research into desistance has emphasised that the process is rarely linear and often involves bumps in the road (Maruna, 2001). Space does not permit a detailed discussion on this important area. The importance of context is central when considering children and desistance; also, the importance of care in relationships (Wigzell and Paterson-Young (2025). Indeed, concern has been expressed on children's desistance that: 'the alignment of childhood law-breaking to the framework of 'desistance' risks stifling advancements in our understanding of children's development in all its richness and complexity'. Little, R. and Haines, K. (2024, online) Children may be unable to break free from obsessive police surveillance.

In this young person's case, one challenge was that the police, to whom he was well known, initially continued to stop and search him, including on one occasion, when he was making his way to work in the early morning. He reported this to the project who in turn spoke to the police and explained that he was now in employment and no longer offending, at which point their interest in him subsided. This is a clear example of the ways in which the project goes 'over and above' in the support it provides. More generally, a distinctive element of its approach is that such support is not time bound and can extend well beyond the length of a sentence. This commitment to participants' longer-term welfare derives from lived experience and the knowledge that desistance takes time and is not a smooth process. Sustainable co-production is desirable but not always achievable. If there are frequent changes in personnel, it may be damaging in terms of trust and social capital (McMullin, 2024). In this instance, for the participants we interviewed, it was both positive and sustained.

As a final testament to the impact such commitment can have, here is a quotation from another former participant the research team spoke to:

> I think without [the project] I would not be working now, I would be in a jail somewhere, that is the reality of it literally. I opened the door; I made my way through and I am doing what I am doing.
>
> *(Former Participant)*

What is striking here is that while acknowledging the project's role, the young person retains a clear sense of agency. The project may have led him to the door, but it was he who chose to open and go through it. To this extent, the work of the project is co-productive in being centred around the needs and wants of the child in an egalitarian manner, ensuring they have a voice in and are able to make choices about their future. As desistance theory suggests, offending patterns and attitudes will be easier to change where and when an individual feels that they are masters of their own destiny (see Maruna, 2025: 19, where he wished that he had used his informants in his original research on desistance more actively in the 'design, data collection and analysis').

Tisdall (2017) considers three concerns related to children's participation: *vulnerability*, which can limit the right of the child to participate in matters that affect them; *social accountability*, where professionals need to act in a transparent manner and ensure that children from marginalised groups (with the least power) are assisted to develop the skills needed to engage; and *co-production*, where in this case, the peer supporter's knowledge and experience are recognised by practitioners. Respect and recognition are integral to the success of the project if the work of the peer supporters is to work. Otherwise, as Tisdall warns, co-production is used as a form of control to make peer supporters merely secondary to the work of the professionals.

Unsurprisingly perhaps, the evidence regarding these transformations in thinking and behaviour was most compelling in the case of the now young adults who had been trained in the early days of the project and had subsequently been employed by the charity to support the CEO and to lead its various activities. They had taken the opportunity to 'grow', using the safe space provided by the project and the journeys they described echoed those of the former participants as above but were more profound still:

> I was on an order at the Youth [Justice] Service, and I joined the PSN network, and I joined the hub and through that I have gone through training, gone through different roles and been able to basically change my whole prospects on life around. I would say to then give back to my community and my people, which for me is great.
>
> *(Project staff member)*

These comments echo Nixon's (2020) analysis of peer mentoring in a probation setting in which she stresses that the opportunity to give back is personally rewarding and sustains their commitment. Citing Buck's (2016) findings, Nixon describes peer mentors in this context as ' "civic experts", with a unique and privileged experiential knowledge, and … a level of credibility that others without an offending past lack' (2020: 50). The peer mentoring role is accordingly empowering, providing a sense of self-worth. This comes from both working with project participants and from the opportunity to speak with, alongside their younger mentees, external organisations with an interest in their experiences, as illustrated here:

> I went through the whole [programme] then I got my order cut…which was a bonus for me and then because of the people I was working with and the things I was experiencing I would never have gone to Central London properly and sat in buildings with people in suits and so for me it was like wow, actually there is a way in for me to making a change. So, for me it made so much sense to drop what I was doing and continue on with this and I have just continued progressing and elevating literally.
>
> *(Project staff)*

For the YJS, just as higher levels of engagement/participation in the YJS represent positive outcomes for programme participants and PSNs, their translation into greater levels of compliance with statutory orders and lower reoffending rates was seen to complement the objectives of the service. Co-production is improved when the child feels safe, is well, and not under threat. Gaining life skills and having support are also important to build on their social capital (McCulloch, 2016). This is the essence of what the project offers.

One manager noted the positive outcomes they believed accrued to the organisation:

> Okay for the YJS greater compliance for our young people at all levels of their intervention, whether it's court orders or pre-court orders. Quicker compliance as well, you know, it's all very well, children coming into the YJS but if they're not saying anything, it's not, so, quicker engagement…
>
> … you know often if we're unable to get our work done during the scheduled length of an order, we might extend it, whereas I think we do that less now because we get quicker engagement. Certainly, our breach levels are really low, because, you know, most young people do actually cooperate with us, because that facilitation process works so well.
>
> *(YJS Manager)*

More broadly, there was widespread agreement among YJS staff interviewed that the impact on both their service as well as other local providers had been positive. The following comments capture well the pride with which many spoke about the project achievements and those of young people with whom it has worked:

> They've been into communities where they're able to you know put their views forward. They've been in meetings where they're able to challenge professionals. You don't get that anywhere, I mean, very rarely do you get that, you know. So those things for me have been incredible, and I think it's been a credit to us as well in a sense that we have the service here.
>
> *(YJS Practitioner)*

> Overall, it's a fantastic resource. I'm delighted to have it, like you know, one of my proudest experiences … was them running a workshop at the YJB convention in 2019 and seeing how well they did that, and the fact it was the last, they got the graveyard slot you know, the last workshop before the closing speeches, you know, the fact they engaged with lots of professionals from all over the country, was, you know, really impressive, and you know they speak really well to judges and magistrates as well. So not only am I proud of what they do with the us, but I think they're fantastic ambassadors for us as well.
>
> *(YJS Manager)*

The involvement of project staff in YJS management meetings, or in meetings with the local mayor or community groups, or in policy making forums with civil servants and policy makers was said to have contributed to policy and practice discussions and developments at local and national levels. One representative of an external organisation commented as follows:

> So, I mean I, I, I love my work with them. I really enjoy it. I learn a lot from them. quite honestly. They teach me a lot. … you know I take huge pleasure in being able to feed back to them, you know, when things do make a difference, and when change is impacted, and, you know, ensuring that they're aware of that and the fundamental difference they make. There's not very many people in their lives who can say that they've, you know, made a difference to youth justice.
>
> *(Representative of External Organisation)*

This illustrates how the project has become a community as well as a YJS resource. As we have described, over time it has worked with a wide range of people and organisations, from school pupils to local judges to national policy makers. What they gain is access to children and young adults with recent experience of offending and of interventions to tackle offending who are prepared and able to speak about these experiences. The outcome is higher levels of awareness of what these young people think about youth crime and youth justice, providing a voice that otherwise struggles to be heard, given the relative powerlessness of young people who offend. Co-production means that young people can feel empowered and indeed in this example, their opinions and experiences are respected when they speak to authority figures who they only encounter when being sentenced.

Strengths and weaknesses

At the core of the project is the simple idea that young people with recent, lived experience of the youth justice system are well placed because of that experience to offer support and advice to young people currently going through the same system, as well as to those who work with them and wider stakeholders in youth justice. The 'lived experience' element makes the PSNs better able, especially in the early stages, to talk to and have talk to them, young people referred to the YJS. Being roughly the same age, knowing the same places, speaking the same language are all important aspects of this but above all the sense that they know of what they speak. Interviewees from external organisations spoke of the PSNs authenticity and of the audience's appreciation of their openness and honesty. For Antojado and McPhee (2024: 5), both formerly incarcerated individuals, lived experience fulfils a multiplicity of functions, while enriching scholarship. These include giving a platform to the marginalised, 'fostering reflexivity' and providing more understanding of the complex interplay between 'crime, victimisation and social control'.

Some of the ways in which the project draws on lived experience mirror existing practice, adding an element of external validity to our findings. The charities User Voice and the St Giles Youth Project, for example, have both been recruiting people with convictions to work with current prisoners and probationers for several years. In a Youth Justice context, organisations like Peer Power similarly draw on young people with experience of 'injustice and inequality' to find 'ways to improve social care, justice and health services by voicing issues for and with other young people' (Peer Power / Youth Justice Board (2021: 5). Our findings also echo those from recent research into peer mentoring schemes in youth justice settings. Creaney (2020), for example, notes that the children he spoke with found their mentors to be relatable, authentic and credible and that they could offer practical guidance on what to expect in places like court. Their experience of similarly difficult life circumstances was said to make them easier to talk to and well placed to empathise with children in trouble. They were able to develop trusting and collaborative relationships, which increased the likelihood of engagement in other activities and programmes.

In accordance with the good practice from the 'Beyond Youth Custody' programme (Liddle et al., 2016) and other youth justice research (Barry et al., 2010) and theory (Brierley, 2021), the project prioritises and specialises in building positive and trusting relationships with young people as a first step towards engagement. Again, in line with existing co-production theory and research (Peer Power, 2021; Case et al., 2020; Burns and Creaney, 2023), project participants are active contributors to activities initially developed by peers who have lived through very similar experiences to their own. In the spirit of the YJB's 'Child First' ethos and the research that has informed its development (Haines and Case, 2015; Case and Browning, 2021a), there is a relentless emphasis on and commitment to providing young people with the support they need to realise their potential, through giving them access to the information, advice and support they require to make positive choices about their future lives.

The nature of the partnership with the YJS is significant. Unusually, the charity, its offices and workspace, is based inside the YJS building and embedded in other ways, represented for example in YJS management meetings and frequently involved in activities led by YJS professionals or by other partner organisations. Co-location facilitates cooperation and understanding between staff in the two organisations, easing referrals and leading to collaborative casework with individual children. For the charity, the core funding it receives from the YJS is more or less existential, leaving the charity with the ability to create its own meaning for its work. Most importantly, the partnership provides a physical space, access to administrative support, a pool of potential clients, a spotlight on its work and numerous contacts with YJS partners and with governmental bodies. For the YJS, the charity provides tailored education, training and work activities and support to children delivered, critically, by staff and volunteers who share their experience of youth justice. Aside from the charity's founder and CEO, all of the project's staff and volunteers have themselves been YJS clients in the near past.

These institutional arrangements provide a particularly advantageous context for co-productive working. This is important because co-production in youth justice is typically thought of in terms of activities jointly undertaken by people rather than by organisations. In this instance, however, the close relationship between the two partner organisations seemed to play an important role over and above the project activities and the individuals involved, literally creating a shared space, facilitating joint access to information and administrative systems as well as a role in managerial processes. In partnering with the charity, the YJS demonstrates its commitment to co-production, to 'working together in equal partnership and for equal benefit' (Johns et al., 2023: 3) with an organisation whose raison d'être is to empower justice-involved children and young people. In this respect, the funding provided enabled the evidence base to grow through the evaluation of the project.

Conclusion

The charity's independent status provides a freedom to act compared with its statutory partner, which has mutual advantages. Co-production, a 'fuzzy' term, can signify many different types of 'service relations', it can be control, management and compliance; it may be innovative and experimental. Pragmatism and the potential to lead to a better service culture can produce better solutions to the problems faced in this case by children (see Evers and Ewert, 2021).

The project emphasises that its support for young people is not limited to the time they are serving an order and does not finish when they reach their eighteenth birthday. This enables the organisation to work with young people, albeit perhaps less frequently, over a much longer period than is the case for the YJS as a statutory body, providing a source of stability. They offer an exit strategy for those coming to an end of their orders, which can be particularly helpful if a case manager still feels that support is needed. Those in transition from custody to the community were felt to be particularly vulnerable, and the PSNs can continue working with them after the YJS has formally closed a case. Vulnerability did not end when orders came to a close, and the project was able to continue providing support beyond this point. In an evidence review Buckland (2025) provides details that young adults (children in the youth justice context) need support to withstand peer pressure and build resistance, as well as reconnect with education or enter into employment.

The project weaknesses are not unusual and mostly relate to the precarious nature of the project. The project's success has been reliant in significant part on the CEO's personal investment of time, commitment and resources, but this also means that the organisation is heavily identified with and in many ways reliant upon one highly talented, charismatic and dedicated individual. Sustaining the organisation and so the project is a constant struggle, given the reliance on time-limited grant funding and the time and effort securing this involves. The fact that the YJS has been able to commit core funding to the project has been critical but is by no means guaranteed over the longer-term term. To develop the model elsewhere would require the same level of financial commitment from other statutory services. Moreover, the project is a victim of its own success in that there is growing demand for its work but a relatively fixed pool of resources. Managing the various commitments to a range of partners in this stretched context is therefore a significant challenge.

PSN staff are potential leaders for future projects having obtained the appropriate experience, knowledge and skills. One YJS manager interviewed observed that there is no obvious pathway forward for these individuals, at least not akin to those available for YJS practitioners. The challenge now is to be able to offer the same level and range of opportunities to trained PSN volunteers as those who have transitioned into becoming PSN staff. What is needed is for youth justice to recognise, nurture and encourage greater involvement from former service users for co-production to add to existing statutory support. This requires direction from the YJB, and their pathfinder shows promising potential.

References

Antojado, D. and McPhee, T. (2024) 'Move over and make space for lived experience criminology: Why we do "lived experience" ', *Journal of Criminology*, Vol 58, No 3, pp. 485–501.

Barry, M., Hester, R., Taylor, W. and Earle, R. (2010) 'Promoting desistance among young people', in Taylor, W., Earle, R. and Hester, R. (Eds) *Youth justice handbook: Theory, policy and practice*, pp. 158–167. Cullompton: Willan.

Barry, M., Weaver, B., Liddle, M. and Schmidt, B. (2016) *Evaluation of the User Voice Prison and Community Councils*. London: User Voice.

Brierley, A. (2021) *Connecting with young people in trouble: Risk, relationships and lived experience*. Hook, UK: Waterside Press.

Buck, G. (2016) 'I wanted to feel the way that they did: Mimesis as a situational dynamic of peer mentoring by ex-offenders', *Deviant Behavior*, Vol 3, No 9, pp. 1027–1041.

Buck, G. (2021) *Mentoring and peer mentoring*. HM Inspectorate of Probation, Academic Insights, 2021/04.

Buckland, G. (2025) *Working with young adults in contact with the criminal justice system. A review of the evidence*. Suffolk: Clinks.

Burnett, R. and Maruna, S. (2006) 'The Kindness of Prisoners: Strengths-based Resettlement in Theory and in Action' *Criminology and Criminal Justice* 6(1), 83–106.

Burns, S. and Creaney, S. (2023) 'Embracing children's voices: Transforming youth justice practice through co-production and child first participation', in Case, S. and Hazel, N. (Eds) *Child First: Developing a new youth justice system*. London: Palgrave Macmillan Cham.

Bussu, A., Creaney, S., Price, J., Burns, S. and Myles, K. (2024) 'It's a sixth sense…I sse you, you see me, and we've been there': Benefits and challenges of developing a peer mentoring scheme with young people in youth justice services', *British Journal of Community Justice*, Vol 19, No 2, pp. 9–19.

Case, S. (2022) *Youth Justice. A Critical Introduction*, 2nd Edition. London: Routledge.

Case, S. and Browning, A. (2021a) *Child first justice: The research evidence-base [Full report]*. Loughborough: Loughborough University.

Case, S., Creaney, S., Coleman, N., Haines, K., Little, R. and Worrall, V. (2020) 'Trusting children to enhance youth justice policy: The importance and value of children's voices', *Youth Voice Journal*. ISBN:978-1-911634-23-2

Creaney, S. (2020) 'Children's voices—Are we listening? Progressing peer mentoring in the youth justice system', *Child Care in Practice*, Vol 26, No 1, pp. 22–37.

Elisha, E. and Shachaf-Friedman, E. (2024) '"For the first time in my life, my past is an advantage": The perceived effects of professional peer work on wounded healers in the field of drug addiction', *Addiction Research and Theory*, Vol 32, No 6, pp. 477–486.

Evers, A. and Ewert, B. (2021) 'Understanding co-production as a social innovation', in Loeffler, E. and Bovaird, A.G (Eds) *The palgrave handbook of co-production of public services and outcomes*. London: Palgrave.

Giordano, P. C., Schroeder, R. D. and Cernkovich, S. A. (2007) 'Emotions and crime over the life course: A neo-meadian perspective on criminal continuity and change', *The American Journal of Sociology*, Vol 112, No 6, pp. 1603–1661.

Haines, K. R. and Case, S. P. (2015) *Positive youth justice: Children first, offenders second*. Bristol: Policy Press.

Hampson, K., Nisbet, A. and Case, S. (2024) 'Child first participatory research – The challenges of involving children in youth justice decision-making', *British Journal of Community Justice*, Vol 19, No 2, pp. 45–65.

Johns, D., Flynn, C., Hall, M., Spivakovsky, C. and Turner, S. (2023) *Co-production and criminal justice*. London: Routledge.

Liddle, M., Boswell, G., Wright, S. and Francis, V. (2016) *Trauma and young offenders: A review of the research and practice literature*. London: Beyond Youth Custody.

Little, R. and Haines, K. (2024) 'Should desistance thinking be applied to children in the criminal justice system?' in Wigzell, A., Paterson-Young, C. and Bateman, T. (Eds) *Desistance and children*. Bristol: Bristol University Press.

Maruna, S. (2001) *Making good: How ex-convicts reform and rebuild their lives*. Washington, DC: American Psychological Association.

Maruna, S (2025) 'Redeeming desistence: From individual journeys to a social movement', *Criminology*, Vol 63, pp. 5–25. Presidential Address.

McCulloch, T. with members of Positive Prison? Positive Futures (2016) 'Co-producing justice sanctions? Citizen perspectives', *Criminology and Criminal Justice*, Vol 16, No 4, pp. 431–451.

McMullin, C. (2024) 'Expectations versus reality: The sustainability of co-production approaches over time. *Public Management Review*, Vol 26, No 12, pp. 3409–3428.

Nixon, S. (2020) '"Giving back and getting on with my life": Peer mentoring, desistance and recovery of ex-offenders', *Probation Journal*, Vol 67, No 1, pp. 47–64.

Peer Power / Youth Justice Board (2021) *Co-creation and participation in practice project*. Peer Power/ YJB. London.

Price, J. and Creaney, S. (2025) 'Enablers and barriers to the development of knowledge and skills in partnerships in youth justice', in Price, J. and Creaney, S. (Eds) *Knowledge and skills partnerships in youth justice*. Abingdon: Routledge.

Smithson, H. and Jones, A. (2021) 'Co-creating youth justice practice with young people: Tackling power dynamics and enabling transformative action', *Children and Society*, Vol 35, pp. 348–362.

Social Care Institute for Excellence (2022) *Co-production: What it is and how to do it*. www.scie.org.uk/co-production/what-how/

Tisdall, E. K. (2017) 'Conceptualising children and young people's participation', *The International Journal of Human Rights*, Vol 21, No 1, pp. 59–75.

Wigzell, A. and Paterson-Young, C. (2025) *Progressive desistance practice in youth justice*. HM Inspectorate of Probation, Academic Insights. London: MOJ.

Willig, C. (2006) *Introducing qualitative research in psychology*. Maidenhead: Open University Press.

15

'YOU LEARN TO REBEL BY BEING LOCKED UP'

Children's experience of restriction, control and agency in the secure estate

Romana Farooq, Katie Burgess, and Hannah Smith

Introduction

The Children and Young People's Secure Estate (CYPSE) provides a restrictive environment where both internal and external doors are locked and may only be unlocked by staff. Children can be accommodated within the CYPSE by the Youth Custody Service (YCS) following custodial sentencing by the criminal courts. This applies to children on remand awaiting trial, sentenced to Detention and Training Orders (DTOs) or guilty of committing a crime chargeable under Section 53(2) of the Children and Young Persons Act 1933. Alternatively, under Section 25 of the Children Act 1989, children can also be sent to the CYPSE by their local authority in a welfare capacity. The Children Act specifies that children may be accommodated within the CYPSE if they have a history of absconding, are likely to abscond, and are perceived to cause significant harm to themselves or others in less secure accommodation. The placement of children in the CYPSE on welfare orders is supposed to be used as a last resort and follows multiple attempts to safeguard and protect children in the community. There are currently 14 secure children's homes within the CYPSE in England and Wales. In 2020, there were 184 children accommodated within these settings, with 48% on welfare orders and the remainder through criminal orders (Department for Education, 2020). Data demonstrates that girls are more likely to be accommodated in a welfare capacity, and boys accommodated in a youth justice capacity. For the years 2017 to 2020, 56% of welfare placements were young girls compared with 4% of youth justice placements (Khan et al., 2021).

At present, only a handful of researchers have explored the provision offered by the CYPSE in England and Wales (O'Neill, 2001; Goldson, 2002; Ellis,

DOI: 10.4324/9781003602996-19

2016; Ellis, 2018). Initial focus has been on the practical implications of secure accommodation for children (Goldson, 2002) and whether secure care is an effective intervention (O'Neill, 2001). Ellis (2016, 2018) explored the feelings and daily experiences of young females accommodated within the CYPSE and found that young girls viewed themselves as 'bad kids', despite being placed in a welfare capacity. In New Zealand, The Office of the Children's Commissioner interviewed children within secure residences to gain insight into their experience. These interviews revealed that children found living in a secure setting hard; they felt that their placement did not always work for them and that their cultural needs are important for staff to consider (Office of the Children's Commissioner, 2019). Further international literature on children subject to detention has highlighted the impact detention and restriction has on the social and emotional development of the child as well as leaves them feeling helpless and criminalised (Kronick et al., 2015). Additionally, a loss of autonomy and privacy was a key theme in research that explored children's experience of a maximum-security detention facility in Australia (Ashkar & Kenny, 2008).

Research exploring children's experience of the CYPSE in the United Kingdom would help to highlight key areas for systemic change and improvement. This will ensure that children receive appropriate care and ensure the CYPSE meets its obligations under the agreements of the United Nations Convention on the Rights of the Child. Exploring children's experience by drawing on creative participatory research methodologies would also enable service providers to better understand what co-production and participation could look like in practice in these settings. Although there are contested and varying definitions of what co-production is and how it is enacted in services, as discussed in previous chapters. Creaney and Burns (2024) state that co-production is 'a relationship where professionals and citizens share power to plan and deliver support together, recognising that both have vital contributions to make in order to improve quality of life for people and communities'. In light of the fact that secure settings have been described as restrictive, it feels important to consider the role of co-production and how the sharing of power could be enacted. This chapter proceeds to discuss theoretical interpretations of children's experiences in the CYPSE, then presents findings from a participatory project with children in a secure children's home, unpacking the concepts of restriction, control and agency as experiences by children.

Theorising children's experiences in the CYPSE

Foucault's panoptic mechanism

Foucault's (1975) theory of power illustrates how institutions are designed to give power and control to the few over others, consequently creating a disciplinary society. Using prison as an exemplary institution for power and control, the Panopticon was designed by Bentham (1791) whereby one prison guard could observe all prisoners, but the prisoners themselves would be unable to view the guard or one another. According to the theory of the Panopticon, an institution is designed to elicit the perception of constant surveillance of those within it (e.g. prison inmates, patients within mental health hospitals or school children) even if those being observed do not know the identity or purpose of the observer. Through this system of surveillance, there is the likelihood that individuals will adapt their behaviour, or 'self-govern' (Foucault, 1975). Order is established and maintained through three key processes: *hierarchical surveillance* to develop continued knowledge of individuals; *normalising judgement* or evaluating behaviour and applying sanctions or privileges; and *examination* (Foucault, 1977). Foucault argues that the effect of the Panopticon is 'to arrange things that the surveillance is permanent in its effects, even if it is discontinuous in its action' (Foucault, 1975, p. 201).

The CYPSE as an institution operates through constant surveillance, judgement and evaluation and therefore it is suggested that it could be viewed as a Panoptic mechanism (Poole, 2015). These ideas have been used to explore and understand the way schools, prisons and secure establishments function and provide a helpful framework to understand the CYPSE (Gallagher, 2010) as well as what effects this is likely to have on the possibility of co-production when there is a need for power to be shared.

Goffman and the total institution

Goffman's (1961) work 'Asylums' investigates the effects of institutionalisation and presents a theory of the 'total institution'. Total institutions are 'a place of residence and work, where many like-situated individuals, cut off from wider society for an appreciable period of time, together lead an enclosed, formally administered…life' (Goffman, 1961: 8). Within total institutions, all aspects of life are conducted under the same single authority, daily activities are tightly scheduled and prearranged, and the sequences of activities are imposed from a system of explicit and formal rules (Goffman, 1961). When individuals enter a total institution, they experience institutional transformation. This is achieved through admission procedures whereby individuals are stripped of their usual appearance (Goffman, 1961). Additionally, individuals are expected to behave in a certain manner and among other things are told how to speak, stand, eat, work and sleep. Goffman (1961) states that the reason these institutions enforce strict rules is because of the belief that those who reside within them have a history of being uncooperative.

Goffman (1959: 28) claims that some individuals within total institutions engage in a 'cynical performance' of compliance. This is due to individuals within total institutions being forced to present as different to their true identity; the activities and manner expected of them may be incompatible with their view of themselves. Additionally, for those residents who feel their placement is unnecessary, showing obedience to an authority that they do not believe is appropriate may cause them to experience degradation (Goffman, 1961). In these cases, individuals may present as reformed, rather than truly reforming. Although ideas around the Total Institution have been used to understand mental health hospitals (Weinstein, 1994), these ideas could be as valuable to the CYPSE, where similar processes and systems are in operation. The CYPSE offers a home, school and recreational environment for children and could therefore be viewed as a total institution. It also feels important to understand how living in a total institution may influence children's participation in the design and delivery of the service they are receiving.

The study

Nine children (five girls and four boys) aged between 13 and 17, voluntarily participated in this study. All were residing at Arrendale Unit (pseudonym), a 15-bedded Secure Children's Home (SCH) in England. The Unit accommodates children in a welfare capacity only, under Section 25 of the Children's Act 1989. Referrals are accepted nationally and include children subject to sexual exploitation, gang violence and modern-day slavery. Further information about the participants who chose to take part can be found in Table 15.1.

All children residing at Arrendale Unit were provided with the opportunity to participate regardless of their background, history or current risk assessment. Ethical principles of informed consent, anonymity, confidentiality and right to withdraw were followed, and it was emphasised to children their decision not to participate would have no impact on their care or detention. Each child's Local Authority was informed of their participation, in place of parental consent given all children were on Full Care Orders. Additionally, as the interviews centralised the experience and perspective of children and positioned them as competent actors, it was important that they had the final say about their participation (Punch 2002; Ellis, 2012). The study was registered and approved as a Service Evaluation with the NHS Trust Research and Development Department.

All interviews were semi-structured, using a topic guide that was co-developed with children in the Secure Estate. The interviews were led by the children, allowing them to focus on only the experiences they felt comfortable discussing. Each interview focussed on a separate theme and covered the three key timepoints for children in the Secure Children's Home, such as 'My Journey into Secure', which included the option of children creating a timeline of their life so far, 'Life in Secure' which included experiences of daily living at Arrendale Unit and 'Leaving Secure' which included reflecting on their experience as they came to the end of their detention.

TABLE 15.1 Demographics of the children

Pseudo-Name:	*Danny*	*Archie*	*Kate*	*Alisha*	*Debbie*	*Hope*	*Maya*	*Brandon*	*Owen*
Gender	Male	Male	Female	Female	Female	Female	Female	Male	Male
Age	17	14	16	15	16	16	13	16	14
Ethnicity	White British	Black Caribbean	White British	Mixed Race	White British	White British	Black Caribbean	White British	White British
Religion	None	Christian	None	Muslim	None	Christian	None	Christian	None
Reason for Admission	Danger to self, Violence	Absconding, Gang Involvement, County Lines	Danger to self	Absconding, Risk of Child Sexual Exploitation	Absconding, Substance Misuse	Absconding, Danger to self	Danger to others	Absconding, Risk of Criminal Exploitation	Danger to others
Home Region	Wales	London	West Midlands	Midlands	North East	West Midlands	London	North East	North East
Miles from Home	332	290	206	162	10	215	290	11	18

The evaluation was informed by narrative enquiry, allowing the experiences and perspectives of children to be centralised. Narrative interviews involve the collection of people's stories about their experiences (Anderson & Kirkpatrick, 2016). The role of the interviewer is to encourage and stimulate the reconstruction of events from the point of view of the interviewee (Hollway & Jefferson, 1997). Therefore, using this methodology highlighted the notion that children are competent social actors and are responsible for shaping their own experiences (James & James 2004).

Findings

The purpose of this evaluation was to understand how children experience living within the CYPSE, the emerging themes are presented in Figure 15.1. For the purposes of this study, key themes are defined as shown in Table 15.2.

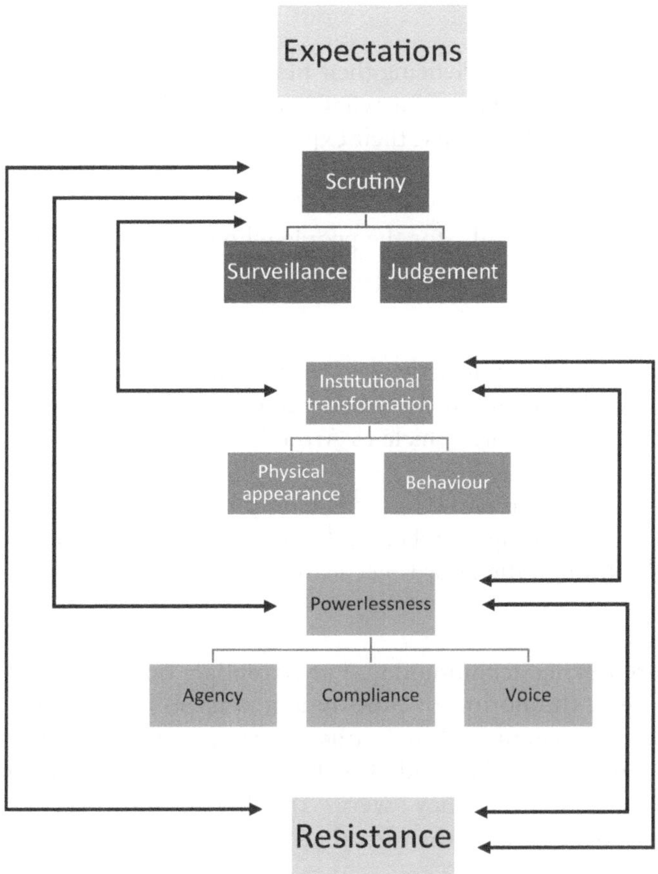

FIGURE 15.1 Thematic map.

TABLE 15.2 Definition of themes

Theme	*Definition*
Scrutiny	critical observation or examination
Surveillance	close observation
Judgement	examining, comparing and forming an opinion
Institutional Transformation	the process of change that happens to a person within an institution
Physical Appearance	the way a person looks
Behavioural	the way a person behaves
Powerlessness	lack of ability, influence or power
Agency	a person's capacity to act independently and make their own choices
Voice	a person's ability to be heard
Resistance	refusing to accept or comply with something

Expectations

Many of the children were experiencing their first admission. Children knew very little about what the SCH was or what it would be like prior to being accommodated. Children shared that their expectations of the SCH were like a prison:

> I thought it was a bit like jail…for the people who do wrong, criminals… like a young prison.
>
> *(Danny)*

The process by which children arrived at Arrendale Unit reinforced this prison environment. The children described being picked up by uniformed men and transported in a secure vehicle to Arrendale:

> The way you turn up, you know I got picked up by the police… I arrived here in hand cuffs… getting searched and that, like the first thing they do when you walk through the door is get searched.
>
> *(Brandon)*

Despite all children being accommodated at Arrendale on welfare orders, for their own safety, the notion of punishment was present within their narratives. This is consistent with previous research by Ellis (2016), who found placement in the CYPSE tended to be perceived as a punishment. Children spoke about how they were 'threatened with secure' by professionals, which reinforced the idea that their detention at Arrendale was punitive.

> Basically I was always threatened with secure as like if you misbehave... you go to secure, secure is for a long period of time, you don't get to see anyone, it's far away, it's like prison basically but for children, so that's how I was told what secure was
>
> *(Kate)*

Scrutiny

Surveillance

Children described their experience of living at Arrendale Unit in the context of a hierarchical system of overt and covert monitoring. The children shared continuous monitoring and surveillance took place through the use of cameras, which were present in all areas of the Unit apart from their bedrooms. While the presence of cameras elicited the perception of constant surveillance, the identity of the observer was not always clear to the children:

> I thought my local authority had all the cameras at first... I honestly thought at first I was being watched by people like, by people that knew me to try and see what I was like in secure... thought I was being spied on...I sometimes feel like the police are watching us... like they can see these cameras in here.
>
> *(Kate)*

Despite the absence of cameras in the children's bedrooms, they shared that surveillance continued through regular and frequent checks from staff. Children shared their experience of these checks as intrusive and disturbing:

> I was surprised they check on you every five minutes... open the hatch, close the hatch, open the hatch, close the hatch, like how the hell do you expect me to sleep.
>
> *(Kate)*

It is within these narratives that the view of the CYPSE as a Panoptic mechanism begins to emerge, with the children describing a system of constant surveillance. The children shared that risk assessments at Arrendale Unit are continuous and staff are assessing their risk even when they are not aware. Participation in seemingly everyday tasks such as completing laundry, engaging in education and meal sittings may be observed by staff to inform the risk that children present to themselves and others:

> It's all about risk assessment and that...and how you respond. So if I respond well, you get moved forward, d'ya get what I mean...And they

> just test you without you even knowing...You go into the kitchen and that's them testing you in the kitchen, d'ya know what I mean?
>
> *(Danny)*

Drawing upon Foucault's (1975) theory, the likelihood of children self-governing their behaviour is increased with the notion of constant surveillance and the purpose of surveillance being unclear.

Judgement

Upon being accommodated at Arrendale, children described a series of assessments, which were experienced as 'long' (Hope) and 'boring' (Maya). Archie described the assessment period as 'the worst time of you being in here'. They struggled to understand the reasoning behind the high level of restriction on daily living activities on arrival, such as having to use plastic cutlery. Restrictions such as these are experienced by the children as frustrating while staff establish their risk.

> like you don't need to be tested with plastic like I'm pretty sure nearly being 17 I can use my cutlery, like you know what I mean...Like carrying a tennis racket round site, no the staff have to hold the tennis racket in case we end up smashing a window or hitting another young person. Just, ah it's pathetic.
>
> *(Hope)*

Following the initial assessment period, children described that their behaviour remained subject to scrutiny from staff and consequently, either privileges or sanctions were put in place. Often, they described staff inappropriately judging their behaviour as 'risky' or being overly strict with sanctions:

> They just like separate you from the group for like arguing with a staff member. I'm not being funny but cos you've argued with a staff member that doesn't mean you're a risk to the other young people.
>
> *(Hope)*

> I didn't say please for something, I was taken to my room just for not saying please and then after that they took three [privilege] points off me for not saying please, and then after that they talked about keeping me away from the group for not saying please, like all I did was not say please.
>
> *(Archie)*

Each young person within Arrendale is able to gain privilege points through a unique personal success and privilege programme that consists of positive behaviours and actions they can perform. These behaviours and actions are converted to points that determine the privileges children can access. In their narratives, we begin to see the emergence of the second key process within Foucault's (1975) Panoptic mechanism; normalising judgement. As the children are assumed by staff to present with risk, all aspects of their daily living within the SCH are subject to scrutiny and judgement. This process becomes normalised, and a disciplinary society consequently occurs.

Institutional transformation

Physical appearance

Upon entering Arrendale, children described having to make alterations to their physical appearance, which compromised their sense of identity:

> I was in like this like lounge for a long time because obviously like I wear hair extensions and obviously they had metal clips in them and they wanted them and I said I'm not giving them ya cause obviously that's part of my personal identity, that's how I feel comfortable.
>
> *(Hope)*

> you're not allowed metal tongue bars... I've got a metal tongue bar and I've got to have a plastic one and it's horrible.
>
> *(Debbie)*

Once they were residing on the unit, further restrictions of their physical appearance emerged:

> you're not allowed rips above the knee, you're not allowed shorts, you're not allowed vests, you're not allowed anything that doesn't cover your shoulders or your chest, you're not allowed erm, dresses, skirts, shorts, tank tops, you're not allowed a lot of clothes, you know like crop tops either, like you've got to be covered everywhere... you're not allowed tassles in your pants, you're not allowed belts... you're not allowed coats on inside, you're not allowed hats, you're not allowed your hood up.
>
> *(Debbie)*

The restrictions on physical appearance that children describe are consistent with the process of institutional transformation (Goffman, 1961). It is important to highlight here that young girls experienced greater institutional transformation than the young boys within the study. For example, one young girl explained that while numerous restrictions exist regarding the clothing girls can wear, 'the boys are allowed to wear shorts... the boys can wear vests' (Debbie).

Behaviour

Children described their life at Arrendale existing within the context of a 'privilege programme' whereby they are required to behave in a certain manner to achieve points and access subsequent privileges. Children are required to have appropriate table manners, engage in activities, not swear, tidy their bedroom, communicate appropriately, follow staff instruction, and go to bed on time to achieve points and privileges from staff:

> ...Band 1 you can do more things like you can go play badminton in the gym, go off unit, just stuff like that really. Band 2 you get your speaker, you can have your makeup in your room and you stay up till 10 to 10... And then band 3 you can have your makeup in your room all the time, your speaker and your ipod in your room all the times, you can have a PS4 in your room with a tv overnight.
>
> *(Alisha)*

This programme described by the children is further compatible with the process of institutional transformation (Goffman, 1961), whereby individuals are told how to speak, stand, eat, work and sleep. Additionally, the final key process of a panoptic mechanism emerges; 'examination', as processes which allow for differentiation and comparison between individuals are present (Foucault, 1977) Many of the children shared that the behaviour and conduct expected of them at Arrendale prevents them from being their true selves:

> I don't feel you can be yourself in secure...because if you get annoyed like it's seen a lot worse than it actually is, everything just escalates too quickly in secure. Like, you just can't show your emotions, and I think that's one hard like for me being in secure.
>
> *(Kate)*

Children also shared a difference between how they would react to situations 'on the outside' compared to how they must react at Arrendale, for fear of their behaviour being misinterpreted or having negative consequences:

> I'm normally really gobby like on the outside, like, if someone annoys me or I get pushed into in like say a queue or something, like it does annoy me and I will say something, but like here say if one of the kids like walked into you and stuff you couldn't kick off because then you're classed as being aggressive and you get taken away from the group so it's just, you have to ignore it.
>
> *(Hope)*

Children tended to interpret attempts from staff to adapt their behaviour, for example by providing consequences for negative behaviour, as staff trying to control them and stop them from acting authentically, rather than supporting them to use more helpful coping or communication strategies.

Powerlessness

Agency

Life at Arrendale was described by children as following a tightly scheduled and prearranged routine. The imposed schedule provides children with little choice or opportunity to decide how to spend their time:

> So…you get up at eight…you start school about nine fifteen…some people have breakfast some people don't, get a drink, take your box through, do you morning job and then there's like Good Morning Britain on the tele and then you watch that till like nine fifteen… And then you go down to education…and then you have two lessons, then you've got break…after education…you have half an hour then it's first sitting…when it comes to meal times…And then it's free time which you have like thirty minutes to do what you want. And then you have to do activities for the rest of the night and I feel it's a bit much. I feel it shouldn't be like education, meals, education, tea, activities like all the way til nine o'clock. I feel like if you don't want to do it you should be given the choice, d'ya know what I mean like, you shouldn't lose points for not wanting to participate in it.
>
> *(Kate)*

The children's description of a tight schedule that is pre-arranged and imposed upon them further supports the idea that the CYPSE can be viewed as a total institution (Goffman, 1961).

Additionally, the rules enforced at Arrendale further limit the decisions children can make. For example, they described dietary restrictions at Arrendale:

> You're allowed three sachets of ketchup, you're allowed two sugars in your tea. Just stupid shit like that. Like you're only allowed one biscuit in your tea. Like if I'm at home mate I'm eating the whole, like the whole thing…The whole packet of biscuits, they're gone mate, you ain't telling me I'm eating one biscuit, you know what I'm saying like, I'm not fat or anything but like obviously, I like food…we're not in here because we need to manage our weight, we're in here because things have happened in our past… my social worker won't give a flying fuck if I eat two packets of biscuits, you know what I mean, she just cares that I'm safe…It makes me feel like special, like proper special needed, like you can't do anything yourself.
>
> *(Hope)*

Goffman (1961) explains that individuals who feel their placement within the total institution is unnecessary may experience degradation in showing obedience to an authority that they do not believe is appropriate.

Compliance

Children shared that living at Arrendale involved complying with various rules. They shared that life at Arrendale was 'easier' when they complied and therefore, children often followed staff instruction even when it contradicted with what they wanted to do:

> ...cause you're not allowed metal so obviously I have my belly and my tongue pierced and I had to take them out and they gave me plastic ones and now obviously when I chew my food I'm chewing my tongue bar, I didn't want to do it at first, they were like alright well we'll have to take you away from the group, so the easier you complied with the staff, the easier it was for you, so I just took it out and got a plastic one.
>
> *(Debbie)*

Additionally, they shared experiences of having to supress their thoughts and feelings to remain compliant:

> if...you wanna have like an easy life in secure, you have to bite your tongue, I used to be a proper violent person, I used to kick off because I could, but here if you kick off there will be consequences, so you just have to comply, it's not really a choice, you just do it if you want an easy life, if you get what I mean, you just do it, you get on with it, you just take it on the chin, even though it, it really annoys you, you just have to do it.
>
> *(Hope)*

Furthermore, children described compliance as a strategy to reduce their length of stay at Arrendale. It was apparent in the narratives that children who are compliant progress to achieve privileges quicker and are discharged from Arrendale sooner:

> *it depends how you go about coming in, if you just take it on the chin... then you're fine everything gets done a lot quicker but if you kick off it makes it a long process for you.*
>
> *(Hope)*

While the intention of rules and restrictions within secure settings is to encourage positive behaviour change, the notion of compliance present within the narratives may suggest that children at Arrendale present as 'reformed' as opposed to truly reforming. This claim is consistent with

Goffman's (1961) explanation of 'cynical performance'. It may be that children engage in superficial compliance to avoid becoming stuck within a setting in which they feel they do not belong. Arguably, learning to comply with rules may have benefitted the children, particularly once released into the community, but it seemed clear that they perceived it negatively while in Arrendale.

Voice

Children shared that there were opportunities at Arrendale where they could speak and voice their concerns; however, they felt that the power their voices carried was limited. They described their experience of weekly 'young people's meetings':

> oh they may as well not happen, honestly, because we say stuff every single week that we want and then it never gets done, ever.
>
> *(Debbie)*

> ... like what's the point in having young people's meetings if I can't say what I think?
>
> *(Archie)*

The children described complaint procedures at Arrendale with a similar narrative:

> ...yeah I've put in like 10 complaints about certain staff and nothing's really happened...when I write a complaint that's when I think I'm letting staff know, but they don't really do anything, I feel like you just have to deal with it innit until you leave... I've tried to say but I don't think they care, like I've said, I don't think they care what I think.
>
> *(Archie)*

Article 12 of the United Conventions on the Rights of the Child states that 'children have the right to say what they think should happen when adults are making decisions that affect them and to have their opinions taken into account'. Equality is a core principle of co-production, emphasising that all individuals' voices are equally important, whether they be children or adults, service users or professionals (Social Care Institute for Excellence, 2022). It is therefore important that processes within the CYPSE exist that support the practice of co-production, allowing children's voices to be heard. However, while children's accounts suggest that these children feel they are being listened to, they don't see any action from this, suggesting that co-production in this setting is not upholding principles of power sharing and equal partnerships.

Resistance

Children's narratives are also presented with resistance and a search for agency. Archie spoke about how the process of being detained at Arrendale had internally driven him to resist and protect himself:

> Obviously no one wants to be put in a place where they have no freedom especially at a young age, this is your learning curve, you don't learn by being locked up…You learn to rebel by being locked up.
>
> *(Archie)*

Children also spoke about behaviours that they engaged in as a means of taking a stance against these systems of power, surveillance, and scrutiny. Hope spoke about how she attempted to make a final stand when Secure Escorts arrived to transport her to Arrendale:

Hope:	*I was like I'm not taking any clothes, I'm not going, I was like I'm mortified*
Interviewer:	*so that was like you making a stand, not packing any of your clothes*
Hope:	*(laughs) yeah I was like I'll take my straighteners (laughs) but I aint taking nothing else*

Children often spoke about taking a stand using their personal belongings as a means of resisting the system:

> They were trying to pull us off the van and I was like nah, I'm not getting off this van without my bike…But they were stood there for about good half an hour cos I was arguing they were like errm 'you need to hand your shoes in' I was like 'nah yous aren't getting them I paid for them' so I just stood there for half an hour arguing with them.
>
> *(Owen)*

Children's narratives also consisted of examples of their attempts at resisting power, hierarchy, and the normalisation of judgement within these establishments.

> …they sanctioned me down for giving poor responses apparently, and all I did was explain what was wrong, they asked me what was wrong. So then ever since from that day now I didn't say please for tissue, took me outside, they was shouting at me saying 'you need to have manners' like... If he'd said it nicely like just say please…it wouldn't have been a problem but if he's shouting like that I'm not really going to say please am I? If I shout at you to go get me a blackcurrant you're not going to get it for me

> are you? 'Ah Archie, you can't speak to me like that I'm the staff, you're the child', I hate it when people say stuff like that, like we're both human beings.
>
> *(Archie)*

Resistance may have also been expressed by the children within the context of the interviews. For example, children were provided with an opportunity to develop a timeline of their life experiences prior to secure. This was an opportunity for them to share their own preferred narrative of their life experiences. However, children often chose not to partake in this exercise.

Interviewer: *...I thought we could spend a bit of a time doing like a bit of a timeline...so we've got, if this is you born at the end here and this is you now, I thought we could spend a bit of time talking about things that have happened in between here that are like important to you or that are err significant to you. So I'll give you, I'll give you a pen...*
Kate: *I don't know what to write*
Interviewer: *You can write anything down, so anything you think that's happened that's important to you or that you want to tell me about*
Kate: *Nothin' really*

Throughout various moments in the interviews, children would choose to remain silent or state 'no comment' (Maya) and use emphatic interjections such as 'Mmm' (Brandon) to resist or evade answering questions in the interviews. This could be interpreted as them attempting to resist the pressures placed on them by what they perceived to be part of the system of surveillance and power. This highlights the importance of relational working and relational safety with children in secure settings, where building trust is vital in order for children to feel safe to talk about things that are personal to them and overcome the need for resistance. Rapport built with the participants of this study allowed some children to feel safe enough to provide the insights demonstrated above, while for others the interviews taking place within the secure setting and by a member of staff likely meant they interpreted this as a way to practise resistance.

Discussion

The present study sought to better understand children's experience of residing in an SCH. Specifically, their subjective experience of restriction and management in this setting. Evident in the interviews was that children's experience of restriction was complex and interconnected, as depicted by the thematic map that is proposed in this chapter. Interviews with children in this study suggest that their lived experience consists of residing in a space in which power is exercised through surveillance, scrutiny, order, control, restriction, and discipline. Their narratives also suggest they attempt to resist and take a stance against the way in which power operates and is exercised.

Restrictions and restrictiveness in these establishments are influenced by risk management, resources and the purpose and function of the CYPSE. This is particularly prominent as these settings were traditionally concerned with the management and restriction of children in the criminal justice system. It is suggested that the systems of order within the CYPSE could be better understood from the perspective of power relations, disciplinary regimes, and normalisation (Foucault, 1975). In line with children's narratives, it may also be helpful to rethink ideas around resistance and agency to recognise that 'where there is power, there is resistance' (Foucault, 1978, p. 95). The idea being that if these environments are inherently driven by power and power struggles then resistance is natural, rather than problematic. There is significant evidence to suggest that limited access to resources and feelings of powerlessness can have a detrimental impact on children's wellbeing (Prilleltensky et al., 2001). In addition, other studies have also reported how the restriction on personal belongings and the built environment can leave patients feeling punished and lacking autonomy (To et al., 2015; Tomlin et al., 2020). There is also evidence to suggest that rigid ward rules have been found to lead to power struggles (Urheim et al., 2011) and can leave patients feeling infantilised due to lack of agency and control over their daily routine (To et al., 2015).

Furthermore, children discussed several consequences of restriction, which not only included resistance but attempts to take back control of their life narratives. This is usually presented as children selectively choosing aspects of themselves to share and/or conceal. It is therefore suggested that children's attempts to choose what they share or conceal should perhaps be interpreted with more complexity and that children who are subject to intense scrutiny may engage in selective disclosure as a means of retaining a degree of agency as they navigate authoritative and powerful systems (Chase, 2010; Wilson, 2003). Therefore, there is a need to reflect on the way in which children's voices are understood, conceptualised and produced, the power imbalances that shape them, and the ideological contexts which inform their production, reception and reproduction. These findings also have direct implications for true co-production and participation.

Children spoke about complying with the system or biting their tongue to survive and get through. There are studies in mental health units that have reported that some patients aim to 'play the system' to avoid being stuck in settings they don't think they belong in (Goffman, 1961; McKeown et al., 2014). Similarly to other studies with adults, children in this study described not being listened to or taken seriously (Davies et al., 2006; McKeown et al., 2014) and having their behaviours assessed as problematic (Larkin et al., 2009). It is evident that the experiences of restriction and restrictiveness described by children in this study reflect life in Arrendale as subjectively experienced by them.

Conclusion: what does this mean for the practice of co-production?

The interviews in this study provide a rich account of children's experiences of life in the CYPSE and encourage us to reflect critically on the CYPSE. In particular, with respect to the consequences of restriction in these settings and whether true co-production and participation are possible. The narratives of these children should inform decision-making and commissioning priorities when thinking about creating relationally and psychologically safe environments for children as well as should inform the practice of co-production.

This study highlights that the experience of children within the CYPSE is one of restriction and surveillance. The imbalance of power described by children is at odds with the principles of co-production, which emphasise the importance of meaningful collaboration with children. When children feel their behaviour is constantly being observed and judged, do they have the freedom to truly collaborate? Similarly, when they feel they are being stripped of their identity, can they express their true thoughts, feelings and opinions? If not, they cannot engage meaningfully with co-production, and this therefore means that authentic co-production and participation within custodial settings needs to be critically interrogated.

There is a risk that co-production in these settings becomes tokenistic, with children feeling their opinion is not truly valued or listened to, rather collected to tick a box (Walker, 2023). This may not be the intention of the adults delivering participatory activity, but the power imbalances within the system make it an inevitability. This is exemplified within the theme entitled Voice, which explores examples of children attempting to share their opinions and feeling unheard and dismissed. Archie asks the question 'what's the point in having young people's meetings if I can't say what I think?', highlighting that he does not feel he can authentically participate.

Furthermore, building trust with children is key to co-production (Creaney et al., 2024) and this is evidently more difficult within a system that inherently breeds mistrust. During this study, which was designed to allow children to express themselves, children evidenced their mistrust of the process and the system by not answering certain questions they were asked or stating, 'no comment'. This suggests children may not feel safe to express themselves fully and authentically. There is clearly work to be done to increase children's trust of the system and sense of safety in the custodial environment as prerequisites before they can be expected to engage in co-production.

However, on the other hand, co-production could be used as a tool to increase children's trust in the system, if it is high-quality and delivered in line with Child First principles (Case & Browning, 2021). Carefully delivered co-production could reduce feelings of powerlessness, which have been explored in this study, and increase feelings of agency. This evaluation has demonstrated that children are able to participate in research which asks them to express their thoughts and opinions, despite taking place within a restrictive setting. Therefore, this study provides hope for the possibility of meaningful co-production in secure settings, while being mindful of the significant barriers in place caused by the inherently restrictive nature of secure settings and the risk-focused culture which often comes with this.

Gender differences in the experience of the CYPSE began to emerge in this study, with young girls experiencing greater levels of restriction than young boys. Future research should further explore the different experiences of boys and girls. Future research should also consider exploring the role race, ethnicity and culture play in the experience of the CYPSE. Research in New Zealand found it was important for staff to consider the cultural needs of children (Office of the Children's Commissioner, 2019). The needs and experiences of racially minoritised children within these settings should be explored to accurately depict the lived experience of all children living within the CYPSE. These different identities of children may have an impact on who is able to coproduce, and who is more likely to be excluded within the CYPSE through future co-production initiatives.

Key learning and recommendations

- Co-production and participation within the CYPSE is a complex task influenced by children's experience of scrutiny, surveillance and risk management.
- Listening to the narratives and voices of children's experience of restriction and surveillance and the subsequent impact on their voice and identity can better help to inform the practice of co-production.
- For children to engage with co-production they must be living in an environment that values their personal identity, values and opinions. For true, authentic co-production to take place within the CYPSE, a radical overhaul of practice in these settings is required. Significant work must be undertaken to improve children's experiences of secure care, prioritising psychological safety over restriction and surveillance.

References

Anderson, C., & Kirkpatrick, S. (2016). Narrative interviewing. *International Journal of Clinical Pharmacy*, *38*, 631–634.

Ashkar, P. J., & Kenny, D. T. (2008). Views from the inside: Young offenders' subjective experiences of incarceration. *International Journal of Offender Therapy and Comparative Criminology*, *52:5*, 584–597.

Bentham, J. (1791). *Panopticon or the Inspection House*. Retrieved from: https://books.google.co.uk/books?hl=en&lr=&id=NM4TAAAAQAAJ&oi=fnd&pg=PA1&dq=jeremy+bentham+panopticon&ots=Y2hSxXWOZE&sig=22eLN6d-6purwat2EYijGOJzp7g#v=onepage&q=jeremy%20bentham%20panopticon&f=false

Case, S., & Browning, A. (2021). *Child first justice: The research evidence-base*. Retrieved from: https://repository.lboro.ac.uk/articles/report/Child_First_Justice_the_research_evidence-base_Full_report_/14152040?file=26748341

Chase, E. (2010). Agency and silence: Young people seeking asylum alone in the UK. *British Journal of Social Work*, *40*, 2050–2068.

Creaney, S., & Burns, S. (2024). Freedom from symbolic violence? Facilitators and barriers to participatory practices in youth justice. *Youth Justice*, *24:1*, 31–52.

Creaney, S., Burns, S., Douglas, A-M., Brierly, A., & Falconer, C. (2024). Desistance through participatory practice: involving children in decision-making processes in youth justice. In A. Wigzell, C. Paterson-Young, & T. Bateman (Eds), *Desistance and Children: Critical Reflections from Theory, Research and Practice* (pp. 212–227).

Davies, J. P., Heyman, B., Godin, P. M., Shaw, M. P., & Reynolds, L. (2006). The problems of offenders with mental disorders: A plurality of perspectives within a single mental health care organisation. *Social Science & Medicine*, *63*, 1097–1108.

Department for Education. (2020). *Children accommodated in secure children's homes at 31 March 2018: England and Wales*. Retrieved from: https://explore-education-statistics.service.gov.uk/find-statistics/children-accommodated-in-secure-childrens-homes

Ellis, K. H. (2012). *'There are no good kids here': girls' experiences of secure accommodation* (Doctoral dissertation, University of Sheffield).

Ellis, K. H. (2016). 'He's got some nasty impression of me he has': Listening to children in the secure estate. *The British Journal of Social Work*, *46*, 1553–1567.

Ellis, K. (2018). Contested vulnerability: A case study of girls in secure care. *Children and Youth Services Review*, *88*, 156–163.

Foucault, M. (1975). *Discipline and Punish: The Birth of the Prison*. Harmondsworth: Penguin.

Foucault, M. (1977). *Discipline and Punish*. London: Allen and Lane.

Foucault, M. (1978). *The History of Sexuality Volume 1: An Introduction*. New York: Random House.

Gallagher, M. (2010). Are schools panoptic? *Surveillance & Society*, 7:3, pp. 262–72.

Goffman, E. (1959). *The Presentation of Self in Everyday Life*. Harmondsworth: Penguin.

Goffman, E. (1961). *Asylums: Essays on the Social Situation of Mental Patients and Other Inmates*. New York: Doubleday.

Goldson, B. (2002). *Vulnerable Inside – Children in Secure and Penal Settings*. London: The Children's Society.

Hollway, W., & Jefferson, T. (1997). Eliciting narrative through the in-depth interview. *Qualitative Inquiry*, *3*, 53–70.

James, A., & James, A. (2004). *Constructing Childhood. Theory, Policy and Social Practice*. UK: Palgrave.

Khan, L., Harris, A., & Sinclair, C. (2021). Out of sight: Girls in the children and young people's secure estate. *Centre for Mental Health*. Accessed via: www.centreformentalhealth.org.uk/sites/default/files/publication/download/CentreforMentalHealth_OutOfSight_PDF_4.pdf

Kronick, R., Rousseau, C., & Cleveland, J. (2015). Asylum-seeking children's experiences of detention in Canada: A qualitative study. *The American Journal of Orthopsychiatry, 85*:3, pp. 287–94.

Larkin, M., Clifton, E., & de Visser, R. (2009). Making sense of "consent" in a constrained environment. *International Journal of Law and Psychiatry*, *32*, 176–183.

McKeown, M., Jones, F., Wright, K., Spandler, H., Wright, J., Fletcher, H., ... Turton, W. (2014). It's the talk: A study of involvement initiatives in secure mental health settings. *Health Expectations*, *19*, 570–579.

Office of the Children's Commissioner (2019). *A Hard Place to Be Happy: Voices of Children and Young People in Care and Protection Residences*. Wellington: New Zealand.

O'Neill, T. (2001). *Children in Secure Accommodation: A Gendered Exploration of Locked Institutional Care for Children in Trouble*. London: Jessica Kingsley.

Poole, H. L. (2015). *An examination of the function of education in prisons: Social, political and penal perspectives* (Doctoral Dissertation). UK: University of Birmingham.

Prilleltensky, I., Nelson, G., & Peirson, L. (2001). The role of power and control in children's lives: An ecological analysis of pathways towards wellness, resilience and problems. *Journal of Community & Applied Social Psychology, 11*, pp. 143–158.

Punch, S. (2002). Research with children: The same or different from research with adults?. *Childhood*, *9*, 321–341.

Social Care Institute for Excellence (2022). *Co-production: What it is and how to do it*. Retrieved from: www.scie.org.uk/co-production/what-how/#principles

To, W. T., Vanheule, S., De Smet, S., & Vandevelde, S. (2015). The treatment perspectives of mentally ill offenders in medium and high-secure forensic settings in Flanders. *International Journal of Offender Therapy and Comparative Criminology*, *59*, 1605–1622.

Tomlin, J., Egan, V., Bartlett, P., & Völlm, B. (2020): What do patients find restrictive about forensic mental health services? A qualitative study. *International Journal of Forensic Mental Health*, *19:1*, pp. 44–56.

Urheim, R., Rypdal, K., Palmstierna, T., & Mykletun, A. (2011). Patient autonomy versus risk management: A case study of change in a high security forensic psychiatric ward. *The International Journal of Forensic Mental Health*, *10*, 41–51.

Walker, L. (2023). Tokenism vs meaningful engagement. In H. Sharp, & L. Walker (Eds), *Participation in Children and Young People's Mental Health* (pp. 27–43). New York. Routledge.

Weinstein, R. M. (1994). Goffman's Asylums and the total institution model of mental hospitals. *Psychiatry*, *57*:4, pp. 348–67.

Wilson, D. (2003). 'Keeping quiet' or 'going nuts': Some emerging strategies used by young black people in custody at a time of childhood being re-constructed. *The Howard Journal of Criminal Justice*, *42:5*, pp. 411–425.

16

CO-PRODUCTION AS SOCIAL JUSTICE

A reflection on creative consultations with young adults and young people

Sarah Page, Dana Jundi, Nicky Twemlow, Emma Head, and Zsofia Majer

In the United Kingdom, young people are legally constructed as children until the age of 18 years (Muncie, 2009). The term child and young person is used interchangeably in this chapter to cover this transitionary period. It is a time-period marked with turbulence as the child navigates their emotional, physical, environmental and legal status changes (Muncie, 2009). Historically, children have been 'seen and not heard', with more emphasis today on listening to young people. Participatory research that is 'child-orientated' gives priority to maximising the voice of the child for informing policy and practice (Collins *et al*, 2016). Putting the child first is paramount for participatory research with children and young people to influence service delivery, crime prevention, education, safeguarding and youth justice (Page, 2025). Dupont (2008; 202) asserts that

> unlike traditional researchers, researchers engaged in participatory research are encouraged to take a stand and to be invested in outcomes and policy implementation. They are allied with marginalized individuals and communities with the purpose of improving their well-being and social conditions.

It has been argued that participatory research with children can be successful in gathering evidence for a change objective (Alridge, 2016).

In England and Wales, policy development includes working with young people in participatory ways to prevent and reduce youth offending (Smithson and Jones, 2021; Day, 2022). Therefore, we posit the importance to working with children and young people prior to engagement in offending behaviour, as well as with those within the criminal justice system. International Children's

DOI: 10.4324/9781003602996-20

Rights legislation promotes the need for children to have voice (Muncie, 2009; Creaney and Case, 2021), whether in the community or in a criminal justice context. Practices aligning with treating the child as-a-child-first-and-foremost are welfare minded, ensuring youth justice interventions are done with, rather than done to children (Haines and Case, 2015). Children can become involved in criminal justice for a range of reasons, and noteworthy is that mental health, homelessness, and family circumstances can be contextual to crime (Youth Justice Board England and Wales, 2021;6). There can also be an 'overlap in children and young people between risks of harmful behaviour and victimisation', which may not come to the attention of criminal justice professionals (Rowe and Law, 2024 online). Extra curriculum activity outside of schooling with children can be seen as meeting a diversionary crime prevention agenda and pivotal for safeguarding children. Such activities benefit from being co-produced with children and young people because they will have nuanced insights into what activities would best support them and also fulfil a crime prevention and safeguarding agenda.

Context: young people and austerity in the United Kingdom

Currently, a range of issues seemingly are impacting young people in the United Kingdom. There are growing concerns about children and food insecurity (Padget and Fay, 2023), with a link between children in poverty and increased numbers of children going into looked after care (Bennett *et al*, 2022). Children living in poverty are more likely to experience social isolation and poor physical and mental well-being (Children's Commissioner, 2021). Cummins (2018) notes that austerity measures have drastically reduced services since 2010, disproportionately impacting those in poverty leading to increases in poor mental health corresponding with declines in mental health services. Such austerity measures have negatively impacted youth services (Davies, 2024) which jeopardise child protection measures (Bywaters *et al*, 2018). Many young people find extracurricular youth services a place of safety, with staff perceived as 'extended family' (Hirsch, and Deutsch, 2005). Funding cuts to youth services may have contributed to increases in youth crime, which resulted in some 'gesture funds' from the government to hotspot youth crime areas (Davies, 2024). A further contextual factor is that young people's access to services was compromised through the COVID pandemic with young people's safety and mental health being at risk (Briggs, *et al*, 2021). A social justice issue emerges here pertaining to children not being able to access services, and this failure in service provision may contribute to young people becoming justice involved.

Creaney and Buck (2020) highlight that justice involved young people have 'complex needs', including mental health, and that 'structural oppressions' have created disadvantage. At a population level, there has been public health concern over the increase in mental health support needed for children and young people (Edwards *et al,* 2024). Research shows interconnection between youth homelessness and engagement in offending behaviour and poor mental health (Self *et al*, 2025). Factors contributing to young people becoming homeless include abuse and family relationship breakdown (ibid), with growing numbers of children and young people entering Looked After Care or homeless hostels due to inappropriate and insufficient family support and behaviour (Ofsted, 2024), as well as due to poverty (Bennett *et al*, 2022). Research with children over the age of 16 years who entered a homeless hostel in the North of England reported reasons 'centered around family conflict and family breakdown, with young people reporting that they had been threatened, abused, attacked or asked to leave' (Ellis and Leahy-Laughlin, 2021: 307). Children in looked after care face systematic challenges in the United Kingdom in engaging with education (ibid). Kenny (2023) found that a lack of prosocial adult guidance in the lives of children in care can be a contributing factor to engagement in crime. The reductions to youth services (Bernard, 2019) have also impacted upon accommodation providers being able to offer young people support (Ellis and Leahy-Laughlin, 2021). Children in the United Kingdom are being failed due to a lack of support services available for them to access, and this increases the risk of criminal engagement and/or experiencing crime victimisation and ending up homeless.

Educational engagement can help prevent the onset or continuation of offending behaviour (Machin *et al*, 2011; Kennedy-Turner, 2020). Increases in school exclusion leave thousands of children temporarily excluded from school each year in England, some of whom will be permanently excluded (Wiilliams, 2022; Jay *et al,* 2023). Graham *et al* (2019: 6) note the increased risk of exclusion for children who have special educational needs and disabilities (SEND), mental health needs, a low social-economic household background, low attainment, experiences of trauma, and when a child is from certain ethnic groups. Children and young people with trauma from Adverse Childhood Experiences (ACEs) are more likely to be truant and be expelled from schools (Stewart-Tufescu *et al*, 2022). We posit that this makes any extra-curricular youth activities even more essential. Furthermore, it is important to note that behaviour warranting school exclusion is often the young person communicating an unmet trauma or learning need (Wood and Page, 2026), which is likely to be underpinning offending behaviours within the wider community and as such, punitive terminology and practices can be stigmatising and fail to address root issues.

This backdrop of increased intentions to listen to the voice of children and young people in the United Kingdom and the challenges that children and young people have faced over recent years, due to austerity policy impacts on services and wider socio-economic factors, provides the context for the 'City Level Future Visioning Project', aimed at providing opportunity for young people to have their say on the future of Stoke-on-Trent and the wider Staffordshire area. This chapter will now provide specific context of the City Level Future Visioning Project.

City visioning collaboration

We are cognisant that city-wide decisions have knock-on effects to children and young people and often have limited or no involvement from children and young people themselves. Such city-wide strategic plans often relate to improving infrastructure, commerce, welfare, health, security and education. In the strategic partnerships we have contributed to, we note that organisation leaders are the decision-makers, sometimes with inclusion of adult community members (e.g. Goldstraw and Page, 2023). When adults in the community are consulted with on neighbourhood-level improvement, they report tokenistic consultation, feeling unheard when organisations simply go ahead with their own plans (Page and Griffiths, 2023). Therefore, it is important to genuinely listen to community members and for children to be included in decision-making that has implications for their future. At a national level, young people felt excluded from the important national decision regarding Brexit, despite perceived repercussions for their future (Antonsich *et al*, 2019). However, when communities have their say on city-wide plans, the process and outcomes can combine research and community development activity (Hughes and Knight, 2023). Essentially, this means that developing strategic plans with children can itself be a form of youth work activity that further contributes to crime prevention and safeguarding outcomes.

YMCANS, a charity sector organisation committed to acting on the voices of young people and reducing the barriers that they face to lead fulfilling lives led the consultation, reflected upon here. The consultation was a proactive decision by YMCANS in response to planning for Stoke-on-Trent's centenary year, which felt timely for learning more about what matters to young people in the locality to ensure celebrations and future city-wide plans capture the voice of young people. YMCANS discussed their ideas with Keele University, who then funded the consultation activity, with human resource and creative input from the University of Staffordshire.

Fluidity of co-production

There are two important factors to the language being used in this chapter to describe the 'City Level Future Visioning Project'. Firstly, 'co-production' describes the process undertaken by a small group of young people residing at the YMCANS, and young adults engaged in Higher Education with regard to working together with YMCANS staff and academics to co-create consultation tools to use with a wider group of children and young people. We then use the term 'consultation' to describe collecting insights and ideas from the wider group of children and young people who were not involved in the co-creation stage, so essentially data was being collected from them. We are cognisant in our practice that co-production is fluid, so there may be aspects of a co-produced project that are consultative. The young person co-designing the tools is likely to feel 'done with' as they share their own insights, however, another young person attending an event may well feel 'done to' when asked to respond to questions and activities that they did not directly co-design. Whereas, Dixon, Ward and Blower (2018) describe 'consultation' as a practice of young people being on an advisory board that is consulted upon about project design. Instead, we use the term 'consultation' to reflect the event style of collecting information and ideas from community members, in this instance children and young people.

Peer-consultation-facilitation

The University of Staffordshire criminology undergraduate and postgraduate degree courses include a work placement module, where students undertake 40 hours in a voluntary or public sector organisation addressing a social and/or criminal justice matter. Creaney and Price (2024) place value on criminology students gaining work experience in the field, despite such practices being relatively uncommon (Eason and Bamford, 2018). Students benefit from applying classroom learning into real workplace experience (ibid), commenting on how such placements have employability benefits and reciprocal benefits for both student and placement provider (Bramford and Eason, 2021).

In the 'City Level Future Visioning Project' led by YMCANS, criminology students applied to become peer-consultation-facilitators for their placement. Students were regarded as peers because they were mostly a step ahead of the age bracket of some of the young people who would become consultation participants. Some students had previously engaged in local youth services where participants would be recruited from. The peer-consultation-facilitator role was to engage young people in conversation about their experiences and hopes for the future alongside a team of YMCANS residents, supported by YMCANS staff.

The criminology placement tutor (Sarah Page) organised a collaborative meeting with YMCANS for students to find out more about the organisation and the 'City Level Future Visioning Project'. Despite research methodology training, the language of 'consultation' was unfamiliar to the students, and they were less familiar with creative approaches to collecting data. Traditionally within criminology, quantitative research methods from surveys dominate the field (Kleck *et al*, 2006; Tewksbury *et al*, 2010). While qualitative methods are taught and noted in textbooks (e.g. Wincup, 2017), students may have less experience with directly using them. University of Staffordshire criminology students have opportunities to undertake primary research, but some opt to collect secondary data or survey data and have less experience of conversational data collection. In response to this knowledge gap, the tutor shared information with students on consultations and creative methodologies, and a training session was set up to equip students, YMCANS staff and YMCANS residents to allow the team to co-determine which creative tools to use in the consultation. Dana Jundi (University of Staffordshire) was invited to deliver the creative consultation training session based on her civic engagement experience using creative tools.

Creative methods training

Creative research methods offer an effective and ethical way to engage participants, particularly useful when discussing complex and sensitive issues. Traditional methods of interviews and questionnaires can feel formal or intimidating, relying heavily on verbal and written communication, which can be limiting for some participants (Gratton and Reynolds, 2022). Creative methods can help researchers engage with participants in meaningful ways (Kara, 2015), providing a flexible, interactive approach that captures shared experience and a broader range of perspectives, often leads to unexpected findings.

Creative research methods help tackle ethical concerns and power imbalances that traditional research can reinforce. Traditional approaches can position the researcher as the expert and participants as passive subjects, meaning people feel they are being studied rather than listened to. Kara (2015) notes that participatory and creative methods can redistribute power by valuing participants' knowledge and experiences. We assert that methods like participatory action research (PAR) shift this dynamic by giving young people a role in shaping the study, making the process more inclusive and empowering. Gratton and Beddows (2018) support this notion, indicating that using creating tools helps remove barriers to engagement and encourages 'deliberate dialogue'. However, it is important to note that while creative approaches are popular in participatory practices, for the reasons outlined, Brown (2021) highlights that creative methods do not necessarily make a project participatory. Participatory practice is more about the style and approach for engagement.

To train the consultation team, the creative methods outlined below were incorporated into the delivery of the session, allowing first-hand experience to provide immersive understanding from the perspective of potential participants. These demonstrations enabled reflection on how creative methods could be adapted and applied in the consultation. The creative tools discussed here have been developed over time by the Public Engagement and Research team at the University of Staffordshire and their community partners and are not entirely original creations. Some of the methods were then selected and applied to the consultation.

Creative tool: imagery and illustrations

Peer-consultation-facilitators were asked to pick from a series of illustrations the one that best described their day so far. Each person explained their selection, giving insights that demonstrated the value of using creative tools to encourage dialogue. The group reflected that had they been asked ''how was your day?', they may have given one- or two-word answers, but having the illustrations made it easier to share detail. A variation of this could be to ask participants to draw their own illustration.

Creative tool: washing line activity

This involves string, pegs, and paper cutouts of tops and pants. The tops represent things that are positive ('tip top') and the pants represent negative things (a bit 'pants'!).

Creative tool: modelling

The tactile and sensory nature of creative methods shifts focus away from the pressure of the questions, particularly for sensitive topics. Modelling is an effective approach where participants can use a range of tools – including magnetic tiles, building blocks, Lego, pipe cleaners, modelling clay – to build, mould or create something that represents their response to a question. The creations are often simple, but when explaining their creation, people often give detailed accounts. Participants are encouraged to think metaphorically, so a wall could represent a barrier while a bridge can represent connection. Often people will draw comparisons between their creations and those others have produced, leading to further discussion.

Creative tool: gathering quantitative data

Creative methods can be an engaging way to collect quantitative data. A widely used method is dot voting. PAR research aims to be democratic (Aldridge, 2016), as such, appreciating numerically how many people would want a particular action to occur in the community can be helpful. A mechanism to ascertaining community preferences is dot voting (Turner, 2018). In its simplest form, participants are offered a range of choices and given sticky dots to place on their preferences. It does not need to be sticky dots and paper; it could be sugar cubes in teapots or Lego pieces on a Lego base (Gratton and Reynolds, 2022) – the possibilities are endless.

Reflections on the creative youth consultation

From the YMCANS perspective, what worked well was being able to deliver consultation events in creative ways. The creative methods workshop proved invaluable for supporting the development of data collection tools that engaged children and young people. From the initial idea of a city-wide youth consultation, getting young people involved in the peer-consultation-facilitator roles and at every step of the way was paramount for effective co-production. YMCANS staff and young people who were residents worked closely with university students to develop the questions and activities. The Search Institute Asset-Based Framework of 8 principles were used to develop the questions due to this framework being applied to YMCANS practice more broadly:

1 Support
2 Empowerment
3 Boundaries and Expectations
4 Constructive Use of Time
5 Commitment to Learning
6 Positive Values
7 Social Competencies
8 Positive Identities

YMCANS provided additional training around safeguarding and professional boundaries for the peer-consultation-facilitators and debriefs from events provided an opportunity for sharing any concerns. The creative data collection tools and questions for conversation were tested during a two-week pilot consultation with children and young people and were further adapted for the formal research consultation. On reflection, the washing line 'tops and pants' exercise worked well. The student peer-consultation-facilitators in debrief with the YMCANS manager and university placement tutor, described how older young people were more interested in talking, whereas younger children engaged more with creative activities combined with talking. Students also described how it was helpful to have one consultation facilitator leading the conversation, and another recording the data in writing.

After the pilot phase of the consultation, funds were secured from Quality-Related Participatory Research Funds (QRPR) by Keele University to engage with YMCA North Staff for a more formal research consultation. This phase brought Emma Head from Keele University into collaboration with

Nicky Twemlow (Director of Community and Partnerships, YMCANS). The geographical reach of the project expanded further into Stoke-on-Trent and North Staffordshire, creating spaces for the voices of children and young people to be heard. This broader consultation developed understanding of the emerging needs, risks, and opportunities in the day-to-day lives of children and young people. The aims of this phase of the project included:

- Understanding the diverse lived experiences of children and young people in North Staffordshire and Stoke-on-Trent
- Engaging with local decision-makers and service providers in this area to share the findings of this project
- Impacting service development for children and young people for the YMCA and in the wider locality
- Developing research capacity and understanding within the YMCA

This phase continued with the creative methods outlined earlier and made use of a questionnaire. The questionnaire included a mix of closed and open-ended questions to allow the participants to write as little or as much about their experiences and opinions as they wanted. The questionnaire was a tool that the YMCANS thought would be useful for engaging young people who are happy to write some responses but do not want to chat.

For the formal consultation, participants were 10–24 years old, and a target of 3,000 young people was determined. On reflection, the target was overly ambitious. While the YMCANS are engaged in service delivery across the city at community venues and in schools, there were challenges around engaging with partner and external organisations to recruit children and young people, and it was difficult to find times that mutually suited peer-consultation-facilitators and the hosting organisations. The 3-month time frame of the project was extended. More consultation facilitators were trained to increase capacity and flexibility of when consultations could be delivered. A research assistant was recruited to the project and was in a similar age group to some of the participants; youth workers were also involved in running some of the consultation sessions. The expanded scope of the project and demands of carrying out many consultations and securing access partly explain the move away from peer facilitation to using employees, who nevertheless sometimes shared some similar characteristics to the participants (for example, living in the area and age).

The employed research assistant reflected upon her role:

> As I engaged further with the YMCA, I gained respect for its youth-focused approach. Initially, my role was expected to be that of a standard Research Assistant supporting data collection, input, and analysis alongside Dr. Emma Head, however, it quickly evolved into a coordinator

> role, involving the design of advertising materials and collaboration management. I was responsible for developing guidelines for community groups facilitating their own sessions, training YMCA staff in research practices, and ensuring ethical data handling. I organised staffing and frequently facilitated sessions myself.

As such, young adults were involved in elements of research leadership with support from YMCANS management and academic input from Keele University. The research assistant highlighted that 'discussions with Dr. Emma Head were invaluable in ensuring participants' rights were protected throughout the process'.

Challenge of academic ethical processes

One challenge was the need to gain institutional ethical approval due to bringing together different ways of working to meet the demands of a university ethical review board. YMCANS had not undertaken a consultation of this scale before and wanted to engage in the university ethics process to secure the credibility and robustness of this project. All research documentation, including communications to gatekeepers and information for potential participants (and sometimes their parents/carers) was needed upfront. This deliberate way of working meant that all the project details had to be discussed before the new phase of consultations could begin, introducing a degree of inflexibility into the usual fast-paced speed of working where YMCA staff could usually be more spontaneous and responsive. The role of the academic partner became one of reciprocal learning and support, more in line with participatory research principles. The consultation process, its outcomes and possible impacts had to be prioritised over any possible academic outputs.

YMCANS, as the lead partner, found that engagement in the ethical review process at Keele University was useful, leading to more reflection on communicating with children and young people about what happens to the data they share. The information sheets were formatted in a question-and-answer style to be more accessible to children and young people.

To accompany these, a short video was co-produced, sharing project information. It was recorded by a youth worker and was used at the start of some research consultations, and the website address was included in other research communications to potential participants. In practice, the paperwork required for consent was off-putting to some organisations. On reflection, young people could be hard to engage with when watching the information video and completing consent forms, possibly due to the formality of such ethical requirements despite efforts to make them more youth friendly.

As the project progressed there was a move away from using the longer version of the questionnaire to using some of the questions alongside the creative consultation methods. Some participants found the questionnaire time-consuming to complete, and it was not eliciting the richness of data found with the creative methods. A further issue regarding the questionnaire is captured by the employed research assistant:

> One challenge arose when the ethical approval of the project restricted questionnaire distribution to paper copies for younger participants. This posed financial and environmental challenges, consequently, we adapted by conducting larger-scale qualitative consultations which further enhanced my public speaking and engagement skills.

As the consultation continued, and the team gained experience, consultation facilitators became more confident in their delivery, and this supported engagement.

The YMCANS team felt they learnt a lot through this process, particularly around the value of honing consultation practices with a clear ethical process. Key learning included the value of using a pilot study to test and adapt research methods to get the best engagement from a consultation. The employed research assistant reflected that:

> We influenced each other in meaningful ways: I learned to adapt to a fast-paced, ever-changing environment where decisions often required immediate adjustments .... [I have] built meaningful professional relationships within and beyond the YMCA, and gained a deeper understanding of the city, its young people, and the services that support them. This experience has reinforced my belief in the power of multi-agency cooperation in research and its potential to drive meaningful change.

It is evident that engaging young adults in research can lead to learning and leadership capacity-building beyond what is available in the classroom. The criminology students from the University of Staffordshire undertaking their course placement as consultation facilitators were also able to identify how they had developed skills, knowledge and confidence through being involved in this project.

Planning for influencing change

A key element of participatory practice is a change agenda (Aldridge, 2016), in other words, the findings get used to influence positive reforms. Hampson, Nisbet and Case (2024: 57) highlight a quote from a child who voiced frustration with 1) being consulted with and then nothing happening with the data and 2) being asked to tick boxes but not being allowed the space to articulate answers in more depth. In our project, it was important to ensure that children and young people had a range of ways for articulating issues and suggested improvements, and it was important that findings were disseminated to influence positive reforms. Some themes from the pilot phase of the project remained apparent in the second phase – young people voiced concerns with the environment and climate change; reflections on the impact of poverty on opportunities for young people, and difficulties with the transition through education and into adulthood, including mental health challenges. The results of this consultation combined with a series of recommendations have since been shared with local organisations and decision-makers (from the local authority, health, education and police services, and voluntary sector, along with local councillors and some of the young people involved), the national YMCA network, and used to inform the future direction of service delivery for YMCANS. A largescale event with local stakeholders at a theatre was planned and delivered in conjunction with young people who opted to use creative expressions to articulate the findings (e.g. poetry). At the event, the employed research assistant presented alongside Dr Emma Head from Keele University on the findings and recommendations via power-point presentation. Zsofia explains that she undertook training before the event to support her public speaking delivery 'The YMCA provided significant support for my role. I participated in Loudspeaker training to enhance my public speaking skills and was introduced to tracker systems to streamline project management...'. Importantly, the chief executive officer of the local authority announced at the event that the recommendations from the report would be taken seriously in conjunction with strategic intentions. A further plan for sharing findings is that young people involved in co-facilitation and young people residing in the YMCANS will present to an APPG (All Party Parliamentary Group) in London, which enables local level findings to have national policy influencing potential.

Key takeaways from this reflective chapter

There are three key takeaways from this chapter that we would like to highlight: 1) Austerity policy impacts have impinged upon services supporting and safeguarding young people and have impacted delivery of wider city ambitions that ultimately impact upon young people. 2) Children and young people need to have a say on the future of their communities (and the nation) and creative practices for consultation are useful for engagement; however, asking too many questions, academic language, and ethical requirements can be a hindrance for engaging this demographic. 3) There are challenges to undertaking participatory consultative research with children and young people, and such challenges can be somewhat overcome through shared learning, addressing training needs, collaborative conversations and reflection on practice leading to amendments in practice. In our experience, a significant key challenge for universities in engaging voluntary sector leaders and young people in participatory practice and consultation activity is in navigating ethical paperwork requirements that can be perceived as bureaucratic and long-winded. Paperwork-intense activity can be a barrier to children and young people in engaging with consultation activity where the data will be academically processed and published on. Creative and conversational approaches to capturing data and conveying findings to wider stakeholders seemingly works effectively for all involved to advocate for change. Our project was aimed at engaging a wide range of children and young people, including those who are justice involved, or at greater risk of justice involvement due to life circumstances, and we found that young people wanted a say in city-wide decision making and were keen to get involved. Involvement in the project varied from young people co-designing research tools and being co-researchers at consultation events, through to the children and young people being consulted with and sharing their findings through poems they wrote at a dissemination event. There can be fluctuations with engagement levels, particularly when facilitating a project of this scale. There are limits to how many people can be meaningfully involved with co-production, and as such, consultation may also be happening with a wider group of children and young people simultaneously with co-production practice with a smaller group engaged with leading the project. Partnership working between voluntary sector leaders with a passion for 'Child First' and with established links to wider youth service and education providers enabled a fairly representative sample of children and young people in the locality. However, insights from young people incarcerated at the time of the consultation are not included. Additional bureaucratic layers of ethical permissions and access requests would have been needed and were not viable within the timeframe of the project. Whereas those on the fringes of justice involvement were easier to get access to and engage in co-production and consultation, demonstrating the need for further ethical interrogation of what co-production should and could look like in youth justice contexts.

References

Aldridge, J. (2016) *Participatory Research: Working with Vulnerable Groups in Research and Practice*. Policy Press, Bristol.

Antonsich, M., Sotiropoulou, P., Wilmers, L., Zhaxi, C. and Hyde, S-L. (2019) 'Our nation's future: Discussions of a post-Brexit Britain', In Colombo, C. and Rebughini, P. (eds) *Youth and Politics of the Present: Coping with Complexity and Ambivalence*. Routledge Advances in Sociology, Oxon, pp. 165–180.

Bennett, D.L., Schlüter, D.K., Melis, G., Bywaters, P., Alexiou, A., Barr, B, Wickham, S., Taylor-Robinson, D. (2022) 'Child poverty and children entering care in England, 2015-20: A longitudinal ecological study at the local area level', *Lancet Public Health*, Vol 7(6), pp. e496–e503. https://doi.org/10.1016/S2468-2667(22)00065-2. PMID: 35660211; PMCID: PMC9595441.

Bernard, D. (2019) *Austerity, Youth Policy and the Deconstruction of the Youth Service in England*. Springer Nature, UK.

Bramford, K. and Eason, A.L. (2021) 'Criminology placements: Work-based learning and organisational "buy in"', *Higher Education, Skills and Work-Based Learning*, Vol 11(2), pp. 317–329. https://doi.org/10.1108/HESWBL-10-2019-0133.

Briggs, D., Telford, L., Ellis, A. and Lloyd, A. (2021) 'Closing the door on protection? Exploring the impact of lockdown upon children and young people's services in the UK', In *Critical Youth Voices on the Covid 19 Pandemic: International Perspectives*, Special Issue, *Youth Voice Journal*, Vol 114. www.rj4allpublications.com/product/closing-the-door-on-protection-exploring-the-impact-of-lockdown-upon-children-and-young-peoples-services-in-the-uk/.

Brown, N. (2021) 'Scope and continuum of participatory research' *International Journal of Research & Method in Education*, Vol 45(2), pp. 200–211. https://doi.org/10.1080/1743727X.2021.1902980.

Bywaters, P., Brady, G., Bunting, L., Brigid, D., Featherstone, B., Jones, C., Morris, K., Scourfield, J., Sparks, T. and Webb, C., (2018) 'Inequalities in English child protection practice under austerity: A Universal challenge?' *Child and Family Social Work*, Vol 23(1), pp. 53–61.

Children's Commissioner (2021) *Child Poverty: The Crisis We Can't Keep Ignoring. January 2021*. Children's Commissioner Office, London. Accessed online 01/03/2024 https://assets.childrenscommissioner.gov.uk/wpuploads/2021/01/cco-child-poverty.pdf.

Collings, S., Grace, R. and Llewellyn, G. (2016) 'Negotiating with gatekeepers in research with disadvantaged children: A case study of children of mothers with intellectual disability', *Children & Society*, Vol 30(6), pp. 499–509. https://doi.org/10.1111/chso.12163.

Creaney, S. and Buck, G. (2020) 'Mental health, young people and punishments', In Taylor, P., Morley, S. and Powell, J. (eds), *Mental Health and Punishments Critical Perspectives in Theory and Practice*. Routledge Taylor & Francis Group, pp. 143–158. Abington, Oxfordshire.

Creaney, S. and Case, S. (2021) 'Promoting social inclusion: Participatory rights alternatives to risk discourses in youth justice', In Liamputtong, P. (ed) *Handbook of Social Inclusion Research and Practices in Health and Social Sciences*. Springer, Singapore.

Creaney, S. and Price, J. (2024) 'Criminology placements and work experience opportunities in youth justice', In Price, J. and Creaney, S. (eds) *Knowledge and Skills Partnerships in Youth Justice*. Routledge, London. https://doi.org/10.4324/9781003411192.

Cummins, I. (2018) 'The impact of austerity on mental health service provision: A UK perspective', *International Journal of Environmental Research and Public Health*, Vol 15(6), p. 1145. Available at: https://doi.org/10.3390/ijerph15061145.

Davies, B. (2024) 'The impact of fourteen years of UK Conservative Government policy on open access youth work', *Youth*, Vol 4(2), pp. 492–508. Available at: https://doi.org/10.3390/youth4020034.

Day, A.-M. (2022) "It's a hard balance to find': The perspectives of youth justice practitioners in England on the place of 'risk' in an emerging 'child-first' world', *Youth* Justice, Vol 23(1), pp. 58–75. https://doi.org/10.1177/14732254221075205.

Dixon, J., Ward, J. and Blower, S. (2018) '"They sat and actually listened to what we think about the care system": The use of participation, consultation, peer research and co-production to raise the voices of young people in and leaving care in England', *Child Care in Practice*, Vol 25(1), pp. 6–21. https://doi.org/10.1080/13575279.2018.1521380.

Dupont, I. (2008) 'Beyond doing no harm: A call for participatory action research with marginalized populations in criminological Research', *Critical Criminoloy*, Vol 16(3), pp. 197–207. https://doi.org/10.1007/s10612-008-9055-7.

Eason, A.L. and Bramford, K. (2018) 'The pedagogy of placements in criminology eaching: An interactive parallel model of criminological learning', *Białostockie studia prawnicze (Uniwersytet w Białymstoku)*, Vol 23(3), pp. 85–96. Available at: https://doi.org/10.15290/bsp.2018.23.03.07.

Edwards, D., Carrier, J., Csontos, J., Evans, N., Elliott, M., Gillen, E., Hannigan, B., Lane, R. and Williams, L. (2024) 'Review: Crisis responses for children and young people – A systematic review of effectiveness, experiences and service organisation (CAMH-Crisis)', *Child Adolescent Mental Health*, Vol 29, pp. 70–83. https://doi.org/10.1111/camh.12639.

Ellis, K. and Leahy Laughlin, D. (2021) 'Youth homelessness in austerity Britain: "We can't help you, you need to go back home"', *Child & Youth Services*, Vol 42(3), pp. 302–317. https://doi.org/10.1080/0145935X.2021.1913049.

Goldstraw, K. and Page, S. (2023) Poverty as a public health concern. In Page, S., Coates, M., Tipping, J., Frangos, J. and Goldstraw, K. (eds) *Action on Poverty in the UK*. Springer Nature, Palgrave Macmillan, Switzerland, pp. 73–86.

Graham, B., White, C., Edwards, A., Potter, S. and Street, C. (2019) School exclusion: A literature review on the continued disproportionate exclusion of certain children. https://assets.publishing.service.gov.uk/government/uploads/system/uploads/attachment_data/file/800028/Timpson_review_of_school_exclusion_literature_review.pdf.

Gratton, N. and Beddows, R. (2018) Get talking: Managing to achieve more through creative consultation. In Stout, M. (ed). *From Austerity to Abundance? (Critical Perspectives on International Public Sector Management)*, Vol 6. Emerald Publishing Ltd, Bingley, pp. 141–160. https://doi.org/10.1108/S2045-794420180000006007.

Gratton, N. and Reynolds, J. (2022) 'Participatory evaluation for large-scale arts programmes: Challenges, adaptations and unexpected shifts in culture', *Research for All*, Vol 6(1), pp. 1–14. https://doi.org/10.14324/RFA.06.1.01.

Haines, K. and Case, S. (2015) *Positive Youth Justice: Children First, Offenders Second*. Policy Press, Bristol.

Hampson, K., Nisbet, A. and Case, S. (2024) 'Child first participatory research – The challenges of involving children in youth justice decision-making', *British Journal of Community Justice*, Vol 19(2), pp. 45–65. https://doi.org/10.48411/m8a1-9×83.

Hirsch, B.J. and Deutsch, N. (2005) *'A Second Home', in A Place to Call Home: After-School Programs for Urban Youth*. American Psychological Association, New York, NY, Washington, DC, pp. 41–56. Available at: https://doi.org/10.1037/11087-003.

Hughes, G. and Knight, B. (2023) The hull we want. In Page, S., Coates, M., Tipping, J., Frangos, J., and Goldstraw, K. (eds) *Action on Poverty in the UK*. Palgrave MacMillan, Switzerland, pp. 101–130.

Jay, M.A, McGrath-Lone, L., De Stavola, B. and Gilbert, R. (2023) 'Risk of school exclusion among adolescents receiving social care or special educational needs services: A whole-population administrative data cohort study', *Child Abuse & Neglect*, Vol 144, 106325, ISSN 0145-2134, https://doi.org/10.1016/j.chiabu.2023.106325.

Kara, H. (2015) *Creative Research Methods: A Practical Guide*. SAGE, London.

Kennedy-Turner, K., Serbin, L.A., Stack, D.M., Dickson, D.J, Ledingham, J.E. and Schwartzman, A.E. (2020) 'Prevention of criminal offending: The intervening and protective effects of education for aggressive youth', *The British Journal of Criminology*, Vol 60(3), pp. 537–558. https://doi.org/10.1093/bjc/azz053.

Kenny, K. (2023) 'The educational experiences of children in care across five decades: A new perspective on the education of looked after children in the UK', *Adoption & Fostering*, Vol 47(1), pp. 22–39. https://doi.org/10.1177/03085759231157415.

Kleck, G., Tark, J. and Bellows, J.J. (2006) 'What methods are most frequently used in research in criminology and criminal justice?', *Journal of Criminal Justice*, Vol 34(2), pp. 147–152, ISSN 0047-2352, https://doi.org/10.1016/j.jcrimjus.2006.01.007.

Machin, S., Marie, O. and Vujić, S. (2011) 'The crime reducing effect of education', *The Economic Journal (London)*, Vol 121(552), pp. 463–484. https://doi.org/10.1111/j.14680297.2011.02430.x.

Muncie, J. (2009) *Youth & Crime*. 3rd Ed. SAGE, London.

Ofsted (2024) 'Accredited official statistics main findings: children's social care in England 2024', Published July 2024. Accessed online 10/01/2025 www.gov.uk/government/statistics/childrens-social-care-in-england-2024/a926fc5f-3e0d-4eaf-995d-80a2e5ad54d6.

Padget, E. and Fay, E. (2023) 'Addressing children's food poverty in shropshire: Five years of learning from rural food poverty alliance', In Page, S., Coates, M., Tipping, J., Frangos, J. and Goldstraw, K. (eds) *Action on Poverty in the UK*. Palgrave MacMillan, Switzerland, pp. 211–234.

Page, S. (2023) 'Reflective participatory crime prevention education and solution finding through World Café and Forum Theatre with young people and young adults', *Safer Communities*, Vol 22(3), pp. 156–171. https://doi.org/10.1108/SC-08-2022-0034.

Page, S. (2025) Using the participatory approach of World Café with adaptions to capture crime experiences and crime prevention solutions in the UK. In Martin, G., and Pearce, E. (eds) *Research Handbook on Youth Criminology*. Cheltenham, UK: Edward Elgar Publishing. https://doi.org/10.4337/9781035300754.fm3 pp94-110

Rowe, S. and Law, N. (2024) 'Children and young people and the criminal justice system', Accessed online 14/05/2025 via https://post.parliament.uk/children-and-young-people-and-the-criminal-justice-system/#_edn9.

Self, T., Miles, H. and Harding, B. (2025) 'The relationships between youth homelessness and offending: A systematic review of the UK literature', *Children and Youth Services Review*, Vol 168, pp. 1–11, ISSN 0190-7409, https://doi.org/10.1016/j.childyouth.2024.108032.

Smithson, H. and Jones, A. (2021) 'Co-creating youth justice practice with young people: Tackling power dynamics and enabling transformative action', *Children and Society*, Vol 35(3), pp. 348–362. https://doi.org/10.1111/chso.12441.

Stewart-Tufescu, A., Struck, S., Taillieu, T., Salmon, S., Fortier, J., Brownell, M., Chartier, M., Yakubovich, A.R. and Afifi, T.O. (2022) 'Adverse childhood experiences and education outcomes among adolescents: Linking survey and administrative data', *International Journal of Environmental Research and Public Health*, Vol 19(18), p. 11564. https://doi.org/10.3390/ijerph191811564.

Tewksbury, R., Dabney, D.A. and Copes, H. (2010) 'The prominence of qualitative research in criminology and criminal justice scholarship', *Journal of Criminal Justice Education*, Vol 21(4), pp. 391–411. https://doi.org/10.1080/10511253.2010.516557.

Turner, R. (2018) 'How to perfect the facilitation tool "sticky dot voting"', *Michigan State University Extension*. November 3, 2018. Accessed online July 2019 www.canr.msu.edu/news/how_to_perfect_the_facilitation_tool_sticky_dot_voting.

Williams, T. (2022) An exploration of school leaders' decision-making to exclude a student from school: What can we learn from their experiences? Other thesis, University of Essex & Tavistock and Portman NHS Foundation Trust. https://repository.essex.ac.uk/32897/.

Wincup, E. (2017) *Criminological Research: Understanding Qualitative Methods*. 3rd Ed. SAGE, Los Angeles.

Wood, L. and Page, S. (2026) 'A UK based case study on relational and restorative practice impacts upon school communities, young people and key stakeholders in Staffordshire', In Hobson, J. (ed) *Restorative Justice*. Policy Press, Bristol.

Youth Justice Board for England and Wales (2021) Strategic Plan 2021-2024. Accessed online 23/08/2022 https://assets.publishing.service.gov.uk/government/uploads/system/uploads/attachment_data/file/966200/YJB_Strategic_Plan_2021_-_2024.pdf.

CONCLUSION

Co-production as the vehicle? The journey to transform justice with children and young people

Samantha Burns and Sean Creaney

Introduction

This book grew from a growing network of youth justice academics and professionals engaging in critical reflections around the concepts of co-production and participation across youth justice systems and processes, attempting to shift and evolve ways of viewing and responding to children in a range of public service settings. As co-production in criminal justice gained traction in the criminological sphere (Weaver et al., 2019; Johns et al., 2023), one key aim of this book was to ensure we centred children and young people within the wider debates and developments around co-production across criminal justice. Furthermore, our interest as editors of this book was to understand how co-production has been theorised, interpreted, and applied across a range of youth justice settings and what that means for future learning, as well as to consider how these practical examples can inform public service reform. By this, we mean ways of challenging and transforming current youth justice systems and processes to invoke a more child-centred approach to justice underlined by co-production principles.

In a way, the book has evolved to consider whether co-production can be a vehicle for social justice due to its ability to connect with equality and power sharing and offer the value of transformative outcomes through public service delivery with children in society that come into conflict with the law. From this, we summarised the objectives of the book, considering the extent to which co-production can be drawn upon as an organising principle to guide and shape regulatory responses that enable substantive participation and address power dynamics while also thinking about the relationship between children's international rights frameworks and co-production,

DOI: 10.4324/9781003602996-21

acknowledging the potential harms of co-production within a criminal justice context. Alongside this, there was an interest in the types of co-production processes being developed and practised, which focused on children feeling safe and achieving personal growth, surrounding ideas of desistance (Wigzell et al., 2024), and with an interest in creative participatory methodologies and the value of lived experience in practice. Overall, these multiple and interconnected interests were intended to unpack the meaning(s), value, and presence of co-production across youth justice systems, asking questions which highlight tensions of power and regulation, lived experience, partnership approaches, and reciprocity with principles of risk management and punishment discourses, and to understand to what extent different forms of co-production can be meaningful and effective for children and young people involved in youth justice systems, as well as promote wider systems transformation.

The chapter contributions in this book demonstrate the growing and continued interest in co-production as an analytical lens to explore the tensions and opportunities of children and young people's participation and to consider how practices can be less trauma-inducing, less punitive, and more child-centred (Burrell, 2013; Malvaso et al., 2024). Through a total of 16 chapters, this book is a body of rich and varied insights on co-production, with an overview of how principles can be developed and implemented within youth justice settings, what this can look like in practice, and whether the concept can become a catalyst for systemic and cultural transformation across youth justice policy and practice. This book has been structured into three parts; (1) contextualising the unique challenges of co-production in youth justice, (2) co-production approaches and evidence-informed policymaking, and (3) children and young people's voices within narratives of co-production. The collection includes contributions from both academics and youth justice sector experts at the forefront of critical research and scholarship into the efficacy of co-production principles and practice. This has included case studies and critical accounts of how co-production as a lens has assisted the design, facilitation, and delivery of services, strengthening efforts in foregrounding the voice of the child throughout system contact and their influence in various examples of decision-making processes (for example, see Chapters 7 and 8).

As such, the book provides valuable insight into the contested theoretical framings and messy realities of co-production in practice despite rhetorical policy shifts of participatory rights-based, child-centred, and strengths-based approaches that recognise the value of meaningfully and safely involving young people with lived experience in the design, delivery, and evaluation of youth justice processes and services (Burns, 2023; Creaney et al., 2023a, 2023b; Hampson et al., 2024). This book has revealed both clarity and further contestation of co-production, with divergence of applicability and implementation depending on a range of factors such as gender, race, perceived vulnerabilities, restricted agency and the role of the arts and creative methods. While many of the chapters provide evidence through a national lens, these discussions have international relevance. Crucially, we acknowledge that there is a need for future edited collections to incorporate a greater diversity of knowledge on the relationship between co-production, children, and their journeys through criminal justice systems. Therefore, this book is also an invitation for further debate and discussion about the role of co-production with justice-involved children. The remainder of this chapter reflects on some of the key themes which emerged throughout the book, comprising these themes into a framework for a reflexive and critical approach to co-production in youth justice.

Defining co-production: from origins to practice in youth justice

Co-production has been acknowledged as an umbrella term, covering many different types and levels of involvement. Within a youth justice context, it is important to allow children opportunities to co-design aspects of policy and practice, and in doing so, treating them as capable of contributing to decisions about their lives and how wider systems operate to meet their needs (SCIE, 2022). This book has described the importance of ensuring relationships between children and professionals are non-hierarchical and that systems and processes embrace children's voices (Burns and Creaney, 2023). However, a pressing issue has been the lack of conceptual clarity regarding definitions of co-production due to other similar terms being used interchangeably across countries, disciplines, policy, and fields of practice (see, for example, Bandola-Gill et al. 2023; Curtin and McMullin, 2025). This book began unravelling the conceptual ambiguity of co-production, documenting the origins and evolution of co-production for public service transformation and considerations of how practices of co-production could connect to wider social justice aims. This is evidenced through practice reflections (Chapter 16) which captured young people's views and aspirations on the future of the city of Stoke-on-Trent and the wider Staffordshire area. Co-production occurred between young people, university students, a voluntary sector organisation, and academic experts with the aims of addressing the impact of austerity measures and crime prevention, ultimately reducing children's involvement in youth justice. This demonstrates that from conceptual origins to practice, there could be possibilities of transformation by consulting with children on the fringes of the youth justice system. Co-production, therefore, has wider community value beyond the scope of public service reform.

Moreover, in the English context, the advancement of a Child First approach has inevitably raised challenging questions about the political preoccupation with re-offending and perhaps the appropriateness of a justice system for supporting children's positive outcomes (Wigzell et al., 2024). Chapter 7 illuminated the early process of implementing a Child First approach within West Yorkshire, considering the barriers encountered and, significantly, the steps taken to overcome them. The chapter also explores the enablers to effective co-production, lessons learned, and key takeaways for collaborative working with children. As the author asserts, while co-production can be a time and resource intensive process, it can be used to help empower children to increase their agency. It can also provide contextualised narratives of wider support needed beyond youth justice responses and transform how professionals view children as key for transformative outcomes. This was also exemplified in the Irish youth justice context, explaining the value of co-production and participatory approaches within research in youth justice to advance children's rights and recommendations for transforming legislative frameworks and policymaking (Chapter 6). The relationship between co-production research and practice is important for reflexive approaches to children's participation rights and the role of children as either advisors and/or participants in co-production research that can overcome the challenges of children being 'hard to reach'. This can ultimately support the enhancement of public service design and delivery alongside debates about the development of children's rights-based law, policy, and practice, which can challenge the narrow focus on offending behaviour which can be often seen within youth justice systems.

Punishment, protection, and participation across different settings

Co-production as an analytical lens also invites us to reconsider who holds knowledge, who gets to decide, and how youth justice systems can be made more participatory and responsive to children's lived realities. Yet, the chapters, to varying extents, illustrate how youth justice is historically grounded in surveillance, responsibilisation, and control, demonstrating tensions that are not easily resolved or reconciled through principles of co-production. Indeed, there is somewhat of a paradox of implementing principles of co-production and initiating child-centred practices within punishment-oriented settings (McKenna and Anderson, 2025; Bateman, 2023). Moreover, the persistence of deficit-based narratives and risk labels continues to shape how children are viewed and treated, often in ways that are antithetical to co-production ideals. This position necessarily neglects to focus sufficiently upon the deprivation and disadvantage that is strongly correlated with criminalisation (Yates, 2010; McAra and McVie, 2016), as behaviour tends to be seen 'as a matter of opportunity and rational choice, with young people being responsible for their actions' (Rogowski, 2014: 8).

With this view in mind, the book has identified challenges and potential inconsistencies in implementing a Child First framework within the youth justice system across England through children being constructed as 'unchildlike' when engaged in harmful behaviours (Chapter 3) and when a multi-agency response is required. These become 'high-risk' environments which tend to prohibit co-production (see Chapter 4). Co-production sits uneasy with the use of sanctions and punishments, which magnify children's perceived weaknesses or lack of capabilities to participate in some justice settings. As alluded to in Chapter 4, there is a case provided for enhancing co-production when working with children assessed as 'high risk'. This approach is potentially more inclusive than existing methods which tend to exclude or marginalise their voices. The chapter focuses on the tensions that can exist between the requirement to identify and manage 'risk of harm' (to prioritise victim and/or community safety) alongside expectations to embed rights-based discourses and children's voices into practice. Many of the chapters in this collection address the interconnected notions of risk and protection through youth justice processes and the need to acknowledge wider multi-agency arrangements that interact with criminal justice institutions. As such, youth justice is not a siloed response to children in conflict with the law. This consideration alone alludes to the realisation that any debates regarding co-production in youth justice will be a messy affair due to the complexities around multi-agency partnership arrangements and the power dynamics that are also inherent throughout.

Key features of co-production include safe environments and equality in terms of roles adopted (MacLachlan et al., 2024). However, there are challenges turning this rhetoric into practice, especially in light of concerns around limits on their ability to express agency and shape or influence the content and format of interventions and approaches within youth justice settings. Although they may have limited opportunity to exercise agency, children and young people can apply resistance to unfamiliar, distressing, or uncomfortable situations or circumstances (Creaney, 2020). For instance, in response to increased levels of surveillance, children 'rebelled' within a secure children's home (see Chapter 15). This response is likened to an act of resistance and illustrates how children attempt to gain a sense of power and/or safety in the most punitive environments. The authors of Chapter 15 note the importance of carefully delivered co-production to reduce feelings of powerlessness and increase feelings of safety and protection. Co-production, therefore, can contribute to discussions on the ethics of punishing children, since participation can contribute to greater protection, but questions remain regarding the extent it is leveraging the reduction of punishment and/or regulation.

Elsewhere, it has been argued that there is a need to promote well-being within criminal justice (Buck and Creaney, 2020). However, imprisonment has been identified as having 'a significant negative impact on mental health', not least due to cases of violence and abuse within young offender institutions (Hodgson 2024). The contribution of co-production for trauma-informed practice offers potential for addressing wider health and well-being concerns in children's lives (Chapter 8). There is also a need for further research into perceptions of safety and equality to ensure co-production is effective in carceral settings. Such studies can continue investigating the use of professional authority in the most restrictive and regulated youth justice settings to assess the extent that co-production mechanisms mitigate power inequalities and nurture a culture of open and transparent decision-making.

The (im)possibilities of sharing power?

Despite the inherent broadness associated with the concept of co-production, it does contain and retain a core feature in the quest to create equal partnerships that potentially benefit children, professionals, and other relevant actors in various shapes and forms (Johns et al., 2023). This fundamental consideration of power sharing can help to cement the notion that all stakeholders have a role in contributing to the process and influencing transformative outcomes. However, co-production can be challenging to implement within a youth justice context, as power imbalances are most acute (Chapter 2). Many chapters in this collection have asserted that children's involvement tends to be compulsory and involving adult-centric risk management and community protection agendas, which remain a feature of policy and practice (Burns and Creaney, 2023; Turner, 2019). Reflecting on this, professionals need to work with children as partners, be critically reflexive of their role, and co-create environments that are conducive to countering adult views being dominant, but chapters in this collection have shown that power sharing and the formation of partnerships is challenging in the varied justice contexts.

Subsequently, this book has explored the extent to which justice-involved children and young people can be genuine decision-makers and equal partners with youth justice professionals explicitly holding power over them (Turner, 2019). Co-production is argued to be a transformative process that can upend traditional power structures when striving for the power-sharing ideal while simultaneously acknowledging the genuine power disparities that are inherent to adult–child relationships, especially within forensic or statutory practice contexts, which are acute within youth justice and remain a critical challenge (Chapters 2, 3, and 4; Turner, 2019). Peer mentoring has been argued to disrupt some of the power hierarchies, with the notion of carceral capital used to frame thinking around the value of lived experience and how that can address power inequalities, particularly within prisons, where power sharing is most limited (Chapter 12). Those children also transition between youth and adult services (Price, 2020, 2021a, b; Price and

Turner, 2021), and adults with previous childhood experiences can be drawn upon as valuable knowledge. Furthermore, as Michel and Billingham (2024) assert, relationships must be viewed through a contextualised lens, including wider power structures and relations between different professionals and organisations, both within and outside the criminal justice system. The possibilities of sharing power must be relational and contextual to understand the conducive conditions for co-production to be a valuable approach.

Creativity and the arts: child-centred approaches

A contribution of this collection is the chapters sharing experiences and providing solutions to issues of power and punishment through a repertoire of creative and arts-based methods in both research and practice that can be utilised to engage both children and professionals in co-production research and practice (see Chapters 6, 9, 10, and 11). Throughout the book, various authors reflect on the importance of involving and empowering both professionals and children in processes of co-production, demonstrating the importance of creative methodologies which can invoke feelings of safety. Therefore, a theme has arisen between the use of creative approaches through co-production that can invoke safety and protection. Reflecting on this, it appears that this approach can support the ethical nature of co-production with justice-involved children, both in ethical considerations for research, as well as safeguarding and trauma-informed practice. However, empirical evidence presented in this book suggests that children become resistant to participation when punishment and behaviour management are prioritised (see Chapter 15); therefore, ethical and methodological tensions are still evident in co-production in youth justice.

Nonetheless, the increasing evidence base is demonstrating how embedding arts-based interventions into youth justice policy and practice could transform services to co-create more engaging, rehabilitative, and empowering experiences for young people in the justice system (see Chapter 9). The examples in this book also illustrate the power of young people's voices through nurturing creativity and artistic expression as a strength-based approach to optimise learning and skills development when working with children in conflict with the law. Moreover, contributions in this book have alluded to sport and creative arts through peer-mentoring which may be non-exploitative, and creative methods to evoke effective co-production within youth justice practice (Chapters 5, 13, and 14). The importance of children's needs being recognised and responded to with careful consideration, while ensuring the environment is inclusive so children do not feel disempowered during the process has been suggested. Co-production encompasses a relational practice, whereby trusting relationships need to be developed, and children need to be given the right information so they understand the purpose of their legitimate involvement. This is also considered as a form of procedural justice (Chapter 2). Importantly, it has been argued that children need to believe they are equals within the relationship and trusted to share their unique perspectives. Professionals need to believe this too while also navigating the paradoxes of being responsible for children's best interests through a rights-based approach.

Children's experiences of (in)justice and adversity

Co-production in youth justice has a relationship with children's experiences of injustice and adversity. When listening to children's lived experiences and involving them in decision-making processes for transformative outcomes at the individual, interpersonal, and institutional levels, there has been a thread throughout this book in regard to the extent co-production may be able to contribute to social justice and systems transformation. Justice-involved children are a vulnerable cohort with complex needs who have already experienced restricted agency through socioeconomic and political inequalities, as well as interpersonal trauma and adversities. Co-production needs to redress that in some way through collective responsibility and not just be seen simply as a mode of public management or public sector reform. In addition, contact with the criminal justice system can be a traumatic experience for children who tend to have experienced social harms such as, but not limited to, domestic and peer violence (Firmin, 2020; Levell, 2022), adverse life circumstances (Gray et al., 2023), criminal exploitation (Marshall, 2023; Wroe, 2021), and structural inequalities (Gray and Smith, 2024; Lloyd et al., 2023). Co-production in youth justice might be a harmful practice if not approached with critical reflexivity.

This book has contributed original insights into the importance of listening to and understanding children and young people's experiences of contact with the criminal justice system to identify and address issues of adversity, trauma, and structural discrimination (Chapters 8, 12, 13, and 14). For instance, it has been argued that when co-creating with Black and mixed heritage boys, there needs to be an acknowledgement of the pervasiveness of whiteness, of exclusion and marginalisation on micro, meso, and macro levels, as well as the inherent racial disproportionality of justice responses to ensure co-production approaches can challenge and not reproduce this. Essentially the co-creative process implicitly offers a space whereby alternative space-making can be enacted, and that this ought to be the goal of progressive change (Chapter 10). Research exploring how children are diverted away from the criminal justice system recognises racial disparity throughout the system (Brodie et al., 2025). Co-production as a lens through prioritising a child's capacity to exercise agency, may contribute to challenging processes of discrimination, criminalisation, and injustice. Opportunities for co-production should apply to all children and young people irrespective of their circumstances, characteristics, or character (Creaney and Smith, 2023; Smith, 2010). Children experience inadequate educational provision, poverty, violence, poor health, and lack of care. This alone highlights the importance for those involved in the organisation and delivery of youth justice to proactively address social harms which children experience (Gray and Smith 2024). What emerges clearly is that co-production, while still a contested and evolving concept, holds greater potential to reshape the contours of youth justice, prompting a rethink concerning the efficacy of criminal justice responses to social harms. If the principles of co-production are enacted with transformation in mind, there is further work needed to consider the extent to which co-production supports radical paradigm shifts in how justice is experienced for children and young people.

Towards a framework for youth justice co-production

The chapters within this collection have explored, dissected, and critically reflected upon co-production in youth justice from a range of theoretical, practical, and methodological perspectives. A particularly important thread woven through this collection is the importance of context. The promise and limits of co-production are shaped by policy environments, organisational cultures, and broader societal understandings of childhood, crime, and justice. Examples presented in this book demonstrate that even within restrictive settings, such as the secure estate or high-risk case panels, co-production may be possible. However, its effectiveness is contingent on a variety of factors at the individual, institutional, and systems levels. As such, if there are instances when children must encounter the youth justice system, a focus on co-production has the potential to enhance a sense of procedural justice for children in conflict with the law, ensuring they feel heard, respected, and able to influence decisions. This can only be achieved if all levels are fundamentally addressed (not just acknowledged). Subsequently, based on the themes that have arose out of the book chapters, we have identified seven interrelated dimensions which could be considered as a basis for a framework which may enhance the thinking and application of co-production as a vehicle for transformation across youth justice settings.

Table C.1 consolidates key themes and ideas throughout this book and provides the basis of potential development for a framework to support co-production across youth justice systems. It highlights that co-production is not a single practice or tool but a dynamic and multi-faceted commitment to power-sharing and ethical practice that must be embedded across structures, cultures, and relationships which embody perspectives of childhood and crime and must be challenged for co-production to be effective. Overall, this evolving framework attempts to contribute to the

TABLE C.1 Transformative co-production in youth justice

Dimension of Co-production	*Considerations for Transformation*
Youth Justice Processes	Co-production can occur at all stages of the system: prevention, diversion, court processes, community supervision, custody, and resettlement. Each stage presents distinct opportunities and challenges; where is co-production happening and where is it needed?
Mode of Co-production	What type of co-production is being adopted and in which stage of the youth justice process? • *Co-commissioning*: setting priorities and shaping resources. • *Co-design*: shaping interventions, policies, and tools. • *Co-delivery*: contributing to programmes, peer support, or training. • *Co-evaluation*: leading or co-leading assessments, audits, and research. • Are children only involved at the implementation stage, or has thought been put into how children will be involved at strategic levels, if appropriate?
Depth of Influence	• Drawing on a range continuum(s) and participation models. How were children involved? • How has children's input influenced decision?
Power-Sharing Mechanisms	• Genuine co-production requires institutionalised structures willing to share power; to what extent can power be shared? • What are the conditions that are promoting or inhibiting power sharing in relationships? • How is power sharing understood when there are multiple adult partners involved in the process?
Safeguarding and Ethics	• How has co-production navigated tensions between protection, punishment, and participation? • Has there been a reflexive focus on ethical practice? • Has there been trauma-aware approaches and safeguarding processes that enable rather than silence children's voices?

(Continued)

TABLE C.1 (Continued)

Dimension of Co-production	*Considerations for Transformation*
Conducive Conditions	• Has consideration been given to how co-production affects organisational culture and the wider professional workforce? • What resources are needed for an inclusive and sustained commitment to co-production?
Outcomes for Transformation	• *Child-level*: voice, agency, confidence, well-being, identity transformation. • *Adult-level: Transforming role as facilitator and co-constructor of knowledge. Relational practice.* • *System/practice*: improved service quality, legitimacy, and engagement. • *Rights and social justice:* fairness, non-discrimination, and alignment with international frameworks

awareness that there is both ambiguity of co-production while striving for clarity and transformation, and it is open for critique and further development as we continue our learning on the paradoxical nature of co-production in youth justice.

While co-production might be viewed as an optional add-on to youth justice practice, we view co-production as a necessary foundation for promoting child protection and advocating for reducing and removing the need for punishment, and youth justice system involvement altogether. This framework could help to strengthen the legitimacy of decision-making processes for children and young people, as a precursor for catalysing systemic and cultural transformation across wider youth policy and practice, ensuring the most marginalised voices are involved in developments of public sector reform.

Final thoughts

This book has been an invitation to view co-production as an opportunity for transforming justice with children and young people. While this book advocates for children's participation in youth justice settings and their involvement in co-produced processes, it is important to note that, where possible, reducing youth justice system contact should be the primary aim. Though when children do encounter the youth justice system, the chapter contributions within this collection contain important and original work and offer great potential for reimagining and redesigning youth justice systems and processes, with children and young people at the centre. However, there is still further work to do. Some final questions to invoke further thinking:

- How can co-production be sustained beyond individual projects?
- What structural changes are required to embed it meaningfully across systems?
- How do we ensure that the most marginalised and stigmatised children are not excluded from participatory processes?
- To what extent can co-production contribute as a vehicle for paradigm shifts in how justice is experienced for children and young people?

This book has not attempted to provide a single prescriptive model of co-production. Instead, it has presented rich and diverse set of insights into the meaning, value, and presence of co-production in different youth justice contexts. We urge readers to think critically and ambitiously about what co-production can look like and how it can serve as a tool not just for service improvement but for service innovation and justice transformation that improves the lives and experiences of children and young people. Ultimately, co-production in youth justice is about possibility. It is about (re)imagining and enacting a system where children are not passive recipients of interventions but co-constructors of their own stories and of the systems that support them. As the field of youth justice continues to evolve, this collection offers a foundation and an invitation to build a more just, inclusive, and child-centred youth justice landscape through modes of co-production.

References

Bandola-Gill, J., Arthur, M. and Ivor Leng, R. (2023) 'What is co-production? Conceptualising and understanding co-production of knowledge and policy across different theoretical perspectives', *Evidence & Policy*, 19(2), pp. 275–298.

Bateman, T. (2023) Challenging punitive youth justice. In Case, S., and Hazel, N. (eds) *Child First*. London: Palgrave Macmillan.

Buck, G. and Creaney, S. (2020) Mental health, young people and punishments. In Taylor, P. Morley, S., and Powell, J. (eds) *Mental Health and Punishments: Critical Perspectives in Theory and Practice*. Abingdon: Routledge.

Burns, S. (2023) Exploring partnerships with justice-involved children in Hong Kong: The role of social workers and barriers towards transformation. *Safer Communities*, 22(2): 133–148, https://doi.org/10.1108/SC-09-2022-0042.

Burns, S. and Creaney, S. (2023) Embracing children's voices: Transforming youth justice practice through co-production and child first participation. In Case, S., and Hazel, N. (eds) *Child First: Developing a New Youth Justice System*. London: Palgrave Macmillan.

Brodie, I., Day, A.-M., Kiff, J., Osidipe, T., Pitts, J., and Bateman, T. (2025) *Exploring Racial Disparity in Diversion from the Youth Justice System*. Luton: University of Bedfordshire.

Burrell, S. (2013) *Trauma and the Environment of Care in Juvenile Institutions*. Los Angeles, Durham: National Center for Child Traumatic Stress.

Creaney, S. (2020) "Game playing" and "docility": Youth justice in question. *Safer Communities*, 19(3): 103–118, https://doi.org/10.1108/SC-01-2020-0002.

Creaney, S. and Burns, S. (2023) Freedom from symbolic violence? Facilitators and barriers to participatory practices in youth justice. *Youth Justice*, 24(1): 31–52. https://doi.org/10.1177/14732254231156844 (Original work published 2024).

Creaney, S., Burns, S., and Day, A.-M. (2023a) Guest editorial. *Safer Communities*, 22(2): 73–77, Available from: https://doi.org/10.1108/SC-04-2023-053.

Creaney, S., Burns, S., and Day, A.-M. (2023b) Guest editorial. *Safer Communities*, 22(3): 149–155, Available from: https://doi.org/10.1108/SC-07-2023-054.

Creaney, S. and Smith, R. (2023) Social work and youth justice. In Parker, J. (ed) *Introducing Social Work* (2nd ed.) London: Sage.

Curtin, M. and McMullin, C. (2025) The co-production spectrum: conceptual blurs in theory and practice. *Perspectives on Public Management and Governance*, 8(3): 144–157.

Firmin, C. (2020) *Contextual Safeguarding and Child Protection: Rewriting the Rules* (1st ed.). London: Routledge.

Gray, P., Jump, D., and Smithson, H. (2023) *Adverse Childhood Experiences and Serious Youth Violence* (online edn, Scholarship Online, 18 Jan. 2024). Bristol: Policy Press https://doi.org/10.1332/policypress/9781529225938.001.0001, (Accessed 7 May 2025).

Gray, P. and Smith, R. (2024) Youth justice and social harm: Towards a 'theory of the good'. *Criminology & Criminal Justice*, 0(0). https://journals.sagepub.com/doi/10.1177/17488958241254446

Hampson, K., Creaney S., and Burns, S. (2024) Transforming the balance of power? Child first collaboration: A conceptual analysis. *Societies*, 14(8): 138. www.mdpi.com/2075-4698/14/8/138

Hodgson, J. (2024) Institutionalised violence and child imprisonment in England and Wales: A case for abolition. *Justice, Power and Resistance*, 7(1): 21–38.

Johns, D., Flynn, C., Hall, M., Spivakovsky, C., and Turner, S. (2023) *Co-Production & Criminal Justice*. Abingdon: Routledge.

Levell, J. (2022) *Boys, Childhood Domestic Abuse and Gang Involvement: Violence at Home. Violence On-Road*. Bristol: Bristol University Press.

Lloyd, J., Manister, M., and Wroe, L. (2023) Social care responses to children who experience criminal exploitation and violence: The conditions for a welfare response. *The British Journal of Social Work*, 53(8): 3725–3743.

Lundy, L. (2007) 'Voice' is not enough: Conceptualising Article 12 of the United Nation's Convention on the Rights of the Child. *British Educational Journal*, 33(6): 927–942.

MacLachlan, A., Pemmasani, P., Jamieson-Mackenzie, I., McMellon, C., Cunningham, E., Lewis, R., and Tisdall, E. K. M. (2024) Applying co-production principles in research: Reflections from young people and academics. *Childhood*, 31(3): 309–328. https://doi.org/10.1177/09075682241269692 (Original work published 2024).

Malvaso, C. G., Day, A., and Boyd, C. M. (2024 Apr 22) The outcomes of trauma-informed practice in Youth Justice: An umbrella review. *Journal of Child & Adolescent Trauma*, 17(3): 939–955. https://doi.org/10.1007/s40653-024-00634-5.

Marshall, H. (2023) Victims first? Examining the place of 'child criminal exploitation' within 'child first' youth justice. *Children & Society,* 37(4): 1156–1170.

McAra, L. and McVie, S. (2016) Understanding youth violence: The mediating effects of gender, poverty and vulnerability. *Journal of Criminal Justice*, 45, 71–77. https://doi.org/10.1016/j.jcrimjus.2016.02.011

McKenna, N. C. and Anderson, V. R. (2025) Paradox and punishment: Implementing trauma-informed care in juvenile detention facilities. *Feminist Criminology*, Online First, 10 January 2025. https://doi.org/10.1177/15570851251313786

Michel, C. and Billingham, L. (2024) Creating conducive conditions for resonance and collaboration: Re-thinking relational practice in youth safeguarding systems. Available at: www.resonantcollaboration.co.uk/creating-conducive-conditions-full-article

Peer Power Youth (2021) *Co-Creation and Participation in Practice Project.* London: Peer Power/YJB.

Price, J. (2020) The experience of young people transitioning between youth offending services to probation services. *Probation Journal*, 67(3): 246–263. https://doi.org/10.1177/0264550520939166

Price, J. (2021a). The impacts of the drop in staffing provision in the transition between the youth custody estate and young adult/adult estate. *Prison Service Journal*, 256: 23–29.

Price, J. (2021b) Violence, control and restraint: The harms to young adults particularly upon transition. *The Howard Journal of Crime and Justice*, 60(4): 511–528. https://doi.org/10.1111/hojo.12418

Price, J. and Turner, J. (2021) (Custodial) spaces to grow? Adolescent development during custodial transitions. *Journal of Youth Studies*. 25(2): 225–241, www.tandfonline.com/doi/full/10.1080/13676261.2020.1865525

Rogowski, S. (2014) Radical/critical social work with young offenders: Challenges and possibilities. *Journal of Social Work Practice*, 28(1): 7–21. https://doi.org/10.1080/02650533.2013.828280

Smith, R. (2010) Children's rights and youth justice: 20 Years of no progress. *Child Care in Practice,* 16(1): 3–17.

Social Care Institute for Excellence (SCIE) (2022) *Co-production: what it is and how to do it.* [online] Available at: www.scie.org.uk/co-production/what-how/ (Accessed on 28 February 2025).

Tisdall, E. K. M. (2017) Conceptualising children and young people's participation: Examining vulnerability, social accountability and co-production. *The International Journal of Human Rights,* 21(1): 59–75.

Turner, S. (2019) A critical reflection on 'giving voice' to justice-involved young people. Available at: https://research.monash.edu/en/publications/a-critical-reflection-on-giving-voice-to-justice-involved-young-p/

Weaver, B., Lightowler, C., and Moodie, K. (2019) *Inclusive Justice: Coproducing Change; a Practical Guide to Service User Involvement in Community Justice.* Glasgow: University of Strathclyde, Available from: https://pureportal.strath.ac.uk/en/publications/inclusive-justice-co-producing-change-a-practical-guide-to-servic/

Wigzell, A., Paterson-Young, C., and Bateman, T. (eds) (2024) *Desistance and Children: Critical Reflections from Theory, Research and Practice*. Bristol: Policy Press.

Wroe, L. E. (2021) Young people and 'county lines': A contextual and social account. *Journal of Children's Services*, 16(1): 39–55.

Yates, J. (2010) Structural disadvantage, youth, class, crime and poverty. In Taylor, W, Earle, R., and Hester, R. (eds) *Youth Justice Handbook: Theory, Policy and Practice* (pp. 5–23). Cullompton, United Kingdom: Willan.

Youth Justice Board for England and Wales (2024) *Youth Justice Board Strategic Plan 2024–2027*. Available at: https://assets.publishing.service.gov.uk/media/6603e2ecc34a860011be7607/2024_03_26_-_6.8802_YJB_Strategic_Plan_2024_FINAL_v07_WEB.pdf (Accessed 17 January 2025).

INDEX

Note: Endnotes are indicated by the page number followed by "n" and the note number e.g., 111n5 refers to note 5 on page 111.

active citizenship 18, 20–1; children's rights and 22; of justice-involved individuals 225
adult-centric institutions 25
adult-centric risk management 309
adult–child relations 3, 46, 309
'adult crime, adult time' laws (State of Queensland) 40
adult criminal justice, impact of the arts in 151
adult detention facilities 40
adult-dominated society, children's relative powerlessness in 27
adult gaze 23, 239–40
adultification, process of 169
adult-imposed interventions 24
'adult knows best' mentality, problem of 27
adult-like behaviours, children and young people involved in 56
adults' expertise, in public service professional roles 27
adults in the making 23, 25
adults, transformation of 25
adults working, with young people 44
Adverse Childhood Experiences (ACEs) 55, 216, 289
African diaspora 176–7
African heritage 174; positives of being of 176; qualities of being of 174
Africanness: celebration of 173; philosophy of 173; sense of 175, 177
African successes, culture, knowledge and history of 175
aged care in Australia, 'consumer-directed care' approach to 39
Agile Geoscience 194
Alliance of Sport in Criminal Justice, The 88
All Party Parliamentary Group (APPG) 298
'America First' movement 168
American community policing, co-production in 17
anger 135, 174, 176
anti-racism 177
anxiety 73, 135, 155, 197
arts-based interventions 151, 162; benefits of 163
arts programmes, impact on criminal justice system 157
AssetPlus framework 72
austerity, in the United Kingdom 288–90
Australian youth justice system 136
authentic co-creation 176

becoming, process of 23
being-becoming dichotomy 23
belonging, sense of 88, 155, 252
'Beyond Youth Custody' programme 262
Black Africans 53, 58
Black and Mixed heritage children 8; academic potential and ability 169;

adultification of 169; co-creation 172; creative coproduction with 172; democratic co-participation 174; discriminatory representations and exclusions of 168; disproportionality for 168–9; exclusion and marginalisation of 177; exclusion from education 169–70; experiences in micro-, meso- and macro-structures 168; family trauma 171; institutional (mis)management of 169; institutional responses in criminal justice system 166, 170; issue of everyday racism 167–8; peoples of African heritage 173; philosophy, sociology and politics of Black space making 172–8; practice of strip searching of 170; process of school exclusion 170; psychosocial space in the minds of 176; pupil referral units 170–2; as victim of a violent crime 169; Whiteness, colonialism and the dehumanising of 172
Black Communities of England and Wales 176
Black economy, idea of 173, 176–7
Black education system 177
Black judiciary 177
Black Lives Matter (BLM) movement 166
Blackness of being from Africa, philosophy of 175
Black revolution, idea of 172
Black space making 166, 172–4, 176–8
boundary judgements 46
Brabin, Tracy 120
Brexit 290
British Society of Criminology 188
building better relationships (BBR) course 222

Canadian child welfare systems 70
Canadian GeoConvention 194
capitalism, political economy of 173
carceral capital: as an asset within the coproduction/co-delivery of peer support programmes 218–20; notion of 309; significance of 218
career development, opportunities for 244
care homes 142, 153
case management 140
case management services 138
Case, S. 233
child and adolescent biological development 42
child as-a-child-first-and-foremost policy 288
childcare system 184
child-centred approaches, to overcome exploitation 85–9; creative arts 89–91; peer mentoring 86–8; sport 88–9
child criminal exploitation (CCE) 6, 51, 52; children and young people involved in 56; to commit criminal acts 57; responding to the unchildlike child 56–9; victims of 59
'Child First diversion' pathfinder projects 249
'Child First' policy 6, 8, 16, 30, 40, 51, 74, 119, 152, 284, 299, 308; challenges to 60; collaborating with children 125–6; core principles of 119; deficit-based practice across England 76; developing links to 125–6; to promote a justice system which sees children as children 60; prosocial features of 69; of reparative practice for the young people 244; shift in youth justice policy towards 57; sports-based activities 89; tenets of 72, 119, 121; ten steps for successful engagement 124; and trauma-informed practices 232; in youth justice 69–70, 102, 233
child-friendly justice, concept of 102
child-friendly practices, risk towards 73
childhood: concept of 171; construction of 24; definition of 58; innocence and dependency 54; in Western culture 59
child justice system 82
child 'offenders', social conditions of 54
children: assessed as 'high risk' 71; in conflict with the law 100, 103, 110; emotional and mental health 255; experience of the CYPSE 267; experiences of (in)justice and adversity 311–12; experiences of maltreatment and household challenges 135; exposure to traumatic adversity 233; high-risk management processes 77; impact of stigma on 126; implications for children assessed as 'high risk' 71–4; living in poverty 288; from low-income households 84; mental health and wellbeing 142, 288;

natural curiosity to learn through play and adventure 86; overcoming barriers to effective co-production with 126–7; participation in public services 22; personal empowerment 24; physical appearance 276; police surveillance on 257; prevalence of violence in the lives of 120; risk-averse attitudes 71; safety and prioritisation of risk-reduction strategies 73; security/protection concerns 73; social isolation of 288; social network 88; voice and agency in welfare and criminal justice settings 23; ways to empower in co-producing knowledge 206; wellbeing of 147
Children Act 1989 (the '1989 Act') 184; section 25 of 266, 269
Children and Young People's Secure Estate (CYPSE) 10, 266; children's experience of 267–9; children's resistance and a search for agency 280; definition of themes 272; in England and Wales 266; expectations of children 272–3; findings of study on children residing at Arrendale Unit 271; institutional transformation 275–7; key learning and recommendations 284; placement of children in 266; powerlessness of children 277–9; purpose and function of 282; relational working and relational safety with children 281; scrutiny of children 273–5; study on children residing at Arrendale Unit 269–71; thematic map 271
Children and Young Persons Act (1933): section 53(2) of 266
'*children first and offenders second*' policy 57
'Children First, Offenders Second' approach, to youth justice work 233
children in conflict with the law, trauma-informed principles of 83
Children's General Comment No. 24 (2019), on children's rights 82
children's lived experiences: connectivity through space and time 28; social and biological development in 23
Children's Research Advisory Group (CRAGs) 115n3
children's rights: to be heard 23; in conflict with the law 100; and co-production 99–101; human rights 23–4, 83, 91; within the Irish youth justice system 105; legal rights 82; to participate in youth justice systems under international human rights law 101–4; to participation under Article 12 of UNCRC 100; participatory rights within the youth justice 72, 101, 136; participatory studies with young people 101; under the UNCRC 105; youth justice research in Ireland 104
children's rights-based youth justice research in Ireland, reflections on 104–6; for children in conflict with the law 110; insights from young people 110–12; participation and representation of young people 108–10; Youth Advisory Groups (YAGs) 106–8
Children's Social Care 62, 68, 189
children's views, systemic neglect of 85
children's voices, organisation of 123–5
citizen-driven services, governance notion of 17
citizen rights movements 37
citizenship rights 25
City Level Future Visioning Project 10, 289–91, 290
city visioning collaboration 290
co-constructors of knowledge 25, 26–7, 31
co-creation 3, 8, 15–17, 19, 29, 78, 152–3, 159, 172–3, 175–6, 185–7, 192, 196, 207, 291
co-delivery 100, 137, 217–18, 220–2, 225, 227, 232, 236
co-design 10, 15, 19, 29, 41, 62, 68, 100, 163, 217–18, 220, 222–3, 236, 291, 306
co-evaluation 100, 137, 236
co-innovation 19
co-learning 24
collaborative music-making 155
communities of colour 168
community-based supervision 137
community-based trauma 137
Community Champions 174
community development 1, 37, 290
community organisations 45, 252
community protection agendas 309
community protection model 69, 71–2, 78

community sector organisations 41
community self-determination 137
community sports schemes 88
Community Youth Justice (CYJ) 138
conflict resolution 251
consumer choice 39–40
consumer rights movements 37
conversation style, of young person 42
co-production 62, 309, 315; in American community policing 17; arts-based approaches to 153; associated with the children's rights 2; with Black and Mixed heritage children 8; with children and young people 22–3; co-existence with regulation 21; concept of 1–2, 15, 17, 24, 77, 255; conceptual ambiguity of 18–20; considered transformative with children and young people 24–6; counteraction with social injustice 27–8; in criminal justice systems 29, 38; definition of 136, 236–7; as a democratic and empowering process 20; dependency to interdependency 26; duality of 20; effectiveness and legitimacy of 28; equitable decision-making process 15; ethical nature of 310; ethos of 43; evolution of 5; fluidity of 290–1; focused on individual outcomes 21; impact on children's participation rights 2; key features of 73; as a key part of a trauma-informed response to service delivery 136–8; origins of 16–18; from origins to practice in youth justice 306–7; overcoming intergenerational hierarchies of knowledge 27; for peer support services in both prison and community contexts 216; principles of 59, 236–7; process of 152; project development and activities 251–3; within public management 25; reciprocal professional–child dynamic 27; and regulation relationship 21–2; regulation via 20–1; relational and social transformation through 27; role of adults in 26; theory and practice of 3; as a transformative approach to support desistance 225–6; utilisation of carceral capital as an asset within 218–20; in youth justice 2–5
cost–benefit analysis 40
Counselling, Assessment, Referral, Advice and Throughcare (CARATS) 222
COVID-19 pandemic 154, 156, 238, 288
creative arts: approaches to co-production in youth justice 153; challenges in implementing arts-based approaches 162; child-centred approach to 89–91, 310–11; creativity and 310–11; and engagement and compliance with justice services 156–7; flexibility and adaptation through creative and statutory programmes 161–2; and identity development in youth justice settings 156; impact on children in contact with the YJSs 154; importance of co-production in 158–60; interventions based on 157; music-making activities 154; principles for co-creating and implementing in youth justice 158–60; role in rehabilitation and desistance from crime 157; role in three youth justice settings in England 153–4; staff training and engagement 162; and youth justice 152–3, 155, 158–60
creative methods training 292–3
creative service 153–4, 158–61
creative tool: gathering quantitative data 293–4; imagery and illustrations 293; modelling 293; washing line activity 293
creative youth consultation, reflections on 294–8; challenge of academic ethical processes 296–7; planning for influencing change 297–8
crime victimisation 261, 289
criminal identity 41
criminality, risk of 71
criminal justice agencies 136, 225
criminal justice system 4, 16, 21, 40, 105, 160, 169, 176–7, 215, 248, 287, 310; Arnstein's ladder of participation in 218; co-production in 29, 38, 217–18; impact of arts programmes in 157; institutional responses to Black and Mixed heritage boys in 166; management and restriction of children in 282; peer support and desistance in 217–18; power inequalities in 147

criminal legal systems 39
critical thinking skills 192
cynical performance 268, 279

data-sharing restrictions 158
decision-making processes 3, 23, 42, 56, 70, 121, 160, 218, 251, 283, 290, 299; adults' 23; child participation in 71, 100, 103, 125; children's participatory rights and 136; co-decision making 236; co-production in 15; experiences of children's involvement in 75; organisational 194; risk assessment and 71
democratic governance 18, 28
Department for Child Protection (DCP) 142
depression 135, 220
Detention and Training Orders (DTOs) 266
Diamond9 (thinking skills tool) 196–205, 206; benefits of using 197
distrust, sense of 3
'drill' music genre 61
drug addiction 222, 252

educational engagement 152, 289
effective participation, concept of 101–2, 105
emotional development, music as a tool for 155–6
emotional regulation 152, 155–6
England Peer Power 29
enhanced co-production, notion of 22, 25
equal partnerships, principle of 22, 279
equal power-sharing relationship 87
European Court of Human Rights (ECHR) 102
evidence-based practice skills 44
'expert by experience' identity 219
'extra-curricular' arts programmes 161
extra-curricular youth activities 289
extracurricular youth services 288

First Nations children 136, 139
Floyd, George 166
Foucault, Michel 274; panoptic mechanism 267–8; theory of power 267

gang violence 269
Garner, Eric 166
genuine partnerships, ambiguity of 20
gesture funds 288
Goffman, E. 268–9
'good' worker, personal qualities of 140

Haines, K. 233
harm reduction: hybrid culture of 70; welfare/justice binary 70
Head, Emma 298
'high-risk' children 71; implications for 71–4
high-risk management panels, in youth justice 70–1; balance of power 71–2; experiences of children's involvement in decision-making within 75; management of the risk of harm due to children being viewed as a danger to society 74; opportunities for co-producing 74–6; risk assessment and professional decision making 71; on risk towards child-friendly practices 73
HM Inspectorate of Probation (HMIP) 233, 236–7
human capital 92

illegal drug distribution 56
informed consent, principles of 269
Institute of Race Relations (IRR) 170
institutional culture, transformation of 25
interdependent relationships, between police and the community 17
intergenerational inequalities 27
intergenerational power imbalance 23
International Children's Rights legislation 287–8
Irish youth justice system 7, 101, 104–5, 109
Iwama, Michael 195

'Just Hear Us' programme 252, 255
justice-involved children 42, 47–8, 54–5, 138, 232–3; ethical nature of co-production with 310; processes of arts-based methods in youth justice on 155
justice-involved individuals 40–1, 52, 232

Kawa Model 185, 195–6
Keele University 294, 296
knowledge: adult professionals' 'expert' knowledge 27; co-constructors of 26–7, 31; overcoming intergenerational hierarchies of 27

knowledge production 227
knowledge sharing, between professionals 124
Kriszan, A. 192

LEGO Serious Play (LSP) 185, 192–4, 207
liberal democracy 17
life events, impact on the developmental needs and behaviour of children 136
lived experience 237, 257, 282; contribution to better realisation of children's rights 101; in criminal justice practice 42; of 'Peer Support Navigator' (PSN) training 261; of prisons 216; to support positive change with children 87; as a tool to help prevent reoffending 249; value of 309; of young people 157, 231; of youth justice system 261
Lived Experienced Consultant 138
Lundy model, of child participation 7, 101, 104–5, 121, 253; space, voice, audience, and influence 121–2
lyric writing 85, 91, 151–2, 154, 156–7, 159, 163

macro-aggressions 167
managerialism, principles of 39–40, 47
mental health and disability practice 41
mental health practitioners 189
mental health services 53, 288
mental health support, needed for children and young people 289
meso-aggressions 167
methodological interdisciplinary research (MIR) framework 185–6; creative and arts-based approaches to 192; data analysis 205–6; Diamond9 (thinking skills tool) 196–205; ethical considerations in 188; Kawa Model 195–6; learning from research practice 206–7; LEGO Serious Play (LSP) 192–4; measurement plan 190–1; photo elicitation 196; 'scheduled unsessions' with professionals 188–90; solution sketchpad 194–5; use of scheduled (un)sessions 190–1; visual methods 192
microaggressions 167
mimesis, concept of 228
mini adults 86, 233
multi-agency cooperation, in research 297
multi-agency working group for children 122
music genres, cultural relevance of 156
music making 152, 154–6
music production 89, 151, 159
mutuality, principle of 17
mutual trust, between the child and practitioner 74

National Closing the Gap reform (Australia) 137
National Criminal Justice Arts Alliance (NCJAA) 157
National Youth Participation Strategy (Ireland) 105
neoliberal responsibilisation, notion of 233
Nienebar, B. 192
non-hierarchical relationships 87, 92
non-probability snowball sampling 189
NVivo 205

Oberstown Children Detention Campus 105
occupational therapy 195
'offenderisation' of children 57
Offender Rehabilitation Act (2014) 223
oral language competency 44
organisational decision-making 194
organised crime groups 58
'Our Journey' project 251

participation–protection paradox 23–4
participatory action research (PAR) 292–3
participatory power 37
participatory practice, ethos of 42, 59, 72, 102, 108, 112, 137, 157, 215, 218, 221, 244, 292, 297, 299
'Participatory Youth Practice' framework 30
partnerships, idea of 17
Pathfinder Project 249, 252
peer-consultation-facilitation 291–2
peer-consultation-facilitators 291, 293–4
'Peer Leaders' 251
Peer Led Conversation Hub 253, 255
peer mentoring (PM), in youth justice 86–8, 215, 259, 261, 309; barriers and limitations to 87
Peer Power Youth 29, 74–5, 77–8, 127

'Peer Support Navigator' (PSN) training 251, 258, 263; lived experience of 261; strengths and weaknesses of 261–3
peer support practitioners (PSPs) 215–16, 228
peer support services 215; co-production/co-delivery as a transformative approach to support desistance 225–6; as form of co-produced reparative practice 242–4; opportunities in youth justice 239–44; staff perspectives on co-production and co-delivery of 220–5; of trauma-informed practice 234, 239–40; utilisation of carceral capital as an asset within 218–20; value of co-production for 216; young people's desire for 231
personal learning 113
'Personal Social Health Education' (PSHE) Programme 251, 255–6
photo elicitation 196
physical appearance, of children 275
police surveillance, on children 257
political economy, of capitalism 173
political governance 173
posttraumatic stress 135
poverty, children living in 288
power disparities, between adults and children 40; social and political dimensions of 56
power hierarchies 280, 309
power inequalities 28, 309; in criminal justice system 147, 228; in youth justice 4
powerlessness of children: agency 277–8; compliance 278–9; voice 279
power-sharing 15, 28, 37, 147; ambiguity of 20; between government officials and citizens 17; with justice-involved children and young people 43; possibilities of 309–10; principle of 22, 239, 279; private and safe physical and psychological spaces 44; promotion of 43; reciprocity, principle of 41; space and time for co-production 44–6; and youth justice practice 41
practising reflexivity, notion of 46
prisons: co-production of PSPs in 228; as institution for power and control 267–8; lived experience of 216–17
privilege programme 274, 276
procedural justice, principles of 43, 312
professional identity, development of 252
prosocial adult guidance, in the lives of children in care 289
pro-social identities 7, 152, 157
pro-social identity 7, 57, 86, 88, 119, 129, 152, 185, 255; development of 91, 125
pseudo-scientific racism 167
psychological safety 134, 141, 193, 284
psycho-social space 176
public administration: adult-dominated 23; and service reform 17
public and personal decision making, democratisation of 17
public management, co-production within 25
public service delivery 17; children's participation in 22; democratic engagement in 15; duality of co-production and regulation in 20
public service organisations 22
public service reform 2, 4, 15, 20, 28, 30, 304, 306
purposeful engagement, idea of 141

qualitative data analysis 53
qualitative research 250
quality of care 146
quality of life 267
Quality-Related Participatory Research Funds (QRPR) 294
quasi-co-creation, methodological framework of 186–8

racism, intergenerational trauma of 173
racist belief systems 168
'raise the (English/British) Flag' movement 168
rational choice theory 40
reciprocity, principle of 17, 20, 41
reflexive critical pragmatism 46–8
regulation: co-existence with co-production 21; duality of 20; via co-production 20–1
Rehabilitation Activity Requirements (RARs) 223
re-offending, risk of 136, 222, 234, 306
reparative practice, Child First model of 244
residential care homes 142

responsibilisation, strategies of 60
restorative justice 231, 234–6, 238; benefits of collective emotion in 235; Child First approach 235; definition of 232; victim-centred 242
risk assessments 136, 273; and professional decision making 71
risk-averse practice, development of 74
risk-based practices 71
risk-based rationalities 20
risk-focused interventions 92
risk management 29–31, 68–73, 77, 136, 225, 282, 284, 305, 309

Safer Communities journal 3
Sandwell Youth Offending Service (YOS) 89
'scheduled unsession' framework, notion of 188–90
scrutiny of children, living at Arrendale Unit: judgement 274–5; surveillance 273–4
Search Institute Asset-Based Framework of 8 principles 294
Secure Accommodation Network 189
secure care: adult stakeholders of 207; providers of 185
secure care homes (SCHs) 184, 189, 192, 206; design of 185; experiences of children's lives in 187
Secure Stairs Framework for Integrated Care 10
self and procedural justice principles, use of 43–4
self-determination, right to 137
self-esteem 88, 152, 156, 226, 241, 251, 255
self-fulfilling prophesy 43
self-harming behaviours 70, 72
self-identity, formation of 240
serious youth violence (SYV) 51–2, 54; and childhood 'innocence' 57; leading to responsibilisation and adultification of children 57; vulnerability of young people who commit 57; young people engaged in 55–6, 59
service development, in youth justice services 146
service implementation, process of 18
service relations 263
service users: empowerment of 37; personal agency of 37
sexual exploitation, of children 55
shaming, notion of 235
shoplifting 220
social accountability 258
social capital 92, 252, 257, 259
social care 53
Social Care Institute for Excellence (SCIE) 16, 18
social communication 63
social construction, of children and young people 23; and adult-centric role of 'provider' 56; contribution towards ideas of the 'unchildlike child' 52; experiences of harm and victimisation 55; factors effecting 54; on how children engaged in SYV 52; influence of socio-cultural norms on 54; masculine norms associated with 56; moral and social issues 54; victimisation and perpetration of extreme violence 55; welfare-based interventions 54
social control 54, 147, 261
social development, music as a tool for 155–6
social harm 57, 76–7, 311–12
social identities 7, 42, 57, 86, 88, 91, 119, 125, 129, 152
social inclusion 18, 162
social injustice 28; co-production counteraction with 27–8
social interactions 21
social justice 10, 22, 28–9, 31, 288, 304
social policies, austerity-driven 28
social services 37
social transformation 16, 25, 27
sociological paradigm 23
solution sketchpad 194–5
South Australian Office of the Guardian for Children and Young People 143
special educational needs and disabilities (SEND) 289
sport, children's participation in 88–9
Sport for Development Coalition 88
'sports plus' programme 89
statutory youth justice 46
St Giles Youth Project 261
'stop the boats' movement 168
street capital 219–20
Street Games 88
street illiteracy 61
structural inequalities 25, 69, 137, 311
structural inequality 137

Substance Abuse and Mental Health Services Administration (SAMHSA), USA 234, 240
surveillance techniques, to monitor children under the supervision of youth justice services 76
sustainable co-production 257
symbolic violence 21, 85
symptoms, of traumatic childhood experience 135
systemic and cultural transformation 2, 4, 305, 314

Thematic Analysis framework, for the analysis of qualitative data 205
third-sector organisations 17, 52–3, 58, 189
TikTok 57
Training Centre Visitor Scheme 143
trans-Atlantic slavery 172; intergenerational trauma of 174
transformative knowledge, generation of 192, 194
'Transition and Hope' RAR 223
trauma-informed co-production 88, 90
trauma-informed practice (TIP) 238, 310; child-centred orientation 147; for children in conflict with the law 83; co-production as a key part of 136–8; current and future directions of 148; definition of 234; fundamental approaches to 234; importance of 83; key principles of 83, 134, 234; 'peer support' principle 234, 239–40; power-sharing arrangements 147; risk assessment and risk management model of 136; service development in youth justice services 146; staff training and programme development 147; staff training, recruitment and selection 146; to youth justice case management 135, 233–4
trauma-informed services 3
trauma, prevalence of 155
trauma treatment services 136
T. v. the United Kingdom 102
Twemlow, Nicky 295

unchildlike child: approach to working with 58; childhood experiences 52; children involved in or affected by SYV and CCE 53–6; contribution of social constructions of childhood towards ideas of 52; need to capture the authentic voices of 63–4; responding to 56–9; youth participation and capturing the authentic voice of 59–63
unconscious bias, notion of 238, 252
unfairness, perceptions of 43
United Nations (UN): Committee on the Rights of the Child (2009) 99, 102; Riyadh Guidelines 147
United Nations Convention of the Rights of the Child (UNCRC, 1989) 22–3, 82, 121, 267; Article 12 of 47, 82, 99, 100–2, 114, 279; Article 40(2) of 101; pillars of 99; right of children under 105; States Parties to 100
University of Staffordshire 291–2
User Voice 251, 261

'victim-offender' binaries 236
'victim-perpetrator' binaries 236
Violence Reduction Partnership (VRP) 7, 119, 122, 129
Violence Reduction Units (VRUs) 119–20
Voice, Space, Audience, and Influence, key principles of 106
voice without power 19
vulnerable children, in need of protection 59
V. v. the United Kingdom 102

welfare placement 184, 266
wellbeing, of children and young people 147, 282; music as a tool for 155–6
West Yorkshire Child First Framework 120–3; developing links to 125–6; development of 120–3; future directions 127–9; organising of children's voices 123–5; overcoming barriers to effective co-production with children 126–7; reflections and lessons learned 129
West Yorkshire Violence Reduction Partnership 7, 119, 130

YMCA network 298
YMCANS (charity sector organisation) 290–2, 294–8
young people: adults working with 44; assessment of risk of recidivism 45; and austerity in the United Kingdom 288–90; connection to their peer

communities 234; cultivation of trust and mutual respect 59; defiance to law enforcement 43; desire for peer support opportunities in the YJS 231; erosion of trust 60; experiences of arts-based approaches 106; lived experiences of 157, 231; marginalisation of 61; mistrust of police 43; perceptions of the legitimacy of their authority 43; presented as hyper-masculine 61; processes of arts-based methods in youth justice on 155; reality of Blackness 173; risk of involvement in SYV 59; self-image and identity 61; social adversities and vulnerabilities faced by 236; strategies of responsibilisation 60; transition into adulthood 59; wellbeing of 147
young-person-identified priorities 142
Youth Advisory Groups (YAGs) 106–8, 115n3; composition of 106; establishment of 106
Youth Commissions 24
youth crime, aetiology of 60
Youth Custody Service (YCS) 266
youth detention centres 45
Youth Justice Board (YJB) 16, 29–30, 52, 233, 249; case management guidance 72; 'Child First' ethos 262; guiding principle for youth justice in England and Wales 57, 69, 82
youth justice co-production, framework for 312–14
youth justice interventions 102, 233, 288
youth justice music programmes 155
youth justice policy, development of 105
Youth Justice Sport Fund (YJSF) 88
Youth Justice Strategy 2021–2027 105
Youth Justice (YJ) supervision 138; children under 136–7; conceptualising of safety 141; identification of support needs 141–2; prioritising young people's participation in service development 142–3; qualities of 140–1; sense of psychological safety in 141; understanding of case management 140
youth justice systems (YJS) 1–3, 37, 51, 120, 137, 143, 151, 216, 248, 304; adult-centric 57, 85; adult professionals working within 111; aims of 39; 'care and control' function in 38–9; care and ethical considerations 84–5; challenges of transformative co-production within 28; child-centred approaches to overcome exploitation 85–9, 102, 315; 'Child First' principles 57, 69–70, 102, 233, 237; collaborating with children 82; creative arts and 152–3; effectiveness of 231; environment matters for co-production in 91–2; ethical practice for 47; ethics of reciprocal approaches in 41; evidence-based 47; focus on both the 'needs and deeds' of the child and young person 39; functions of 3; high-quality support and guidance 73; 'high- risk' management panels 68; high-risk management panels in 70–1; individual approaches to coproduction in 38; individual forms of co-production in 39; in Ireland 7, 104–6; labelling, lived experience, and identity 41–3; lived experience of 261; managerialism, childism, and 'consumers' of 39–40; marginalisation of young people by 61; methodology for conducting observational research in 238–9; need for peer support opportunities in 239–44; neglect of children's voices in 253; operation of 100; participation and co-creation for 16; person-centred support to 38; power inequalities and systemic barriers in 4; power-sharing and 41; principles for co-creating and implementing creative arts in 158–60; reasons for co-production in 28–31, 38; rehabilitative ideal of 46; research literature about co-production in 38–9; responding to the unchildlike child 56–9; service development in 146; supervision of 8; support for young people in 241; surveillance techniques to monitor the whereabouts of children 76; tokenistic practices in 20; transformative co-production in 313–14; trauma-informed practice 233–4; welfare and justice model 39; young people's desire for peer support opportunities in 231